Bathroom Battlegrounds

The publisher and the University of California Press Foundation gratefully acknowledge the generous support of the Barbara S. Isgur Endowment Fund in Public Affairs.

Bathroom Battlegrounds

HOW PUBLIC RESTROOMS SHAPE
THE GENDER ORDER

Alexander K. Davis

UNIVERSITY OF CALIFORNIA PRESS

University of California Press, one of the most distinguished university presses in the United States, enriches lives around the world by advancing scholarship in the humanities, social sciences, and natural sciences. Its activities are supported by the UC Press Foundation and by philanthropic contributions from individuals and institutions. For more information, visit www.ucpress.edu.

University of California Press
Oakland, California

Library of Congress Cataloging-in-Publication Data

Names: Davis, Alexander K., 1988– author.
Title: Bathroom battlegrounds : how public restrooms shape the gender order / Alexander K. Davis.
Description: Oakland, California : University of California Press, [2020] | Includes bibliographical references and index.
Identifiers: LCCN 2019038566 (print) | LCCN 2019038567 (ebook) | ISBN 9780520300149 (cloth) | ISBN 9780520300156 (paperback) | ISBN 9780520971660 (ebook)
Subjects: LCSH: Sex role—United States. | Restrooms—Social aspects—United States. | Public toilets—Social aspects—United States.
Classification: LCC HQ1075 .D385 2020 (print) | LCC HQ1075 (ebook) | DDC 363.72/940973—dc23
LC record available at https://lccn.loc.gov/2019038566
LC ebook record available at https://lccn.loc.gov/2019038567

Manufactured in the United States of America

28 27 26 25 24 23 22 21 20
10 9 8 7 6 5 4 3 2 1

For my mom

Contents

Illustrations

Acknowledgments

For the last five years, I have used our first day of class to teach the students in my writing seminars three foundational principles for academic inquiry: first, that the starting point for a truly great research project is asking a question that manages to be exhilarating, focused, and worthwhile in equal measure; second, that the only way to achieve that difficult three-way balance is to revise your question (and the thinking behind it) over and over again; and third, that effective revision demands opening yourself up to feedback from your colleagues—because engaging with other curious, incisive, and generous minds is the surest pathway to improving your own work. While I certainly believed in the value of such exhortations well before I started my solo college teaching career, the process of writing and revising and workshopping all the parts of this book have cemented just how accurate they really are. And so, since I have been working to improve this book's question (and the thinking behind it) for over ten years, I have a considerable number of curious, incisive, and generous minds to thank for making this project what it is today.

My first outlay of gratitude goes to my intellectual home for the last five years, the Princeton Writing Program. There, I have been phenomenally lucky to work alongside a vibrant and interdisciplinary group of colleagues who have supported my writing, my teaching, and my passion for blending the two in countless ways. In particular, enormous thanks go to Amanda Irwin Wilkins, whose expert leadership of our program has given me space to develop my approach to undergraduate teaching and my voice as an academic writer in concert with one another, and to Erin Raffety, whose friendship and feedback at our weekly working lunches has been a consistent font of inspiration for all my writing projects.

Because *Bathroom Battlegrounds* was my doctoral dissertation before it was a book, I also owe a tremendous volume of thanks to the five mentors who most encouraged me and supported my work during my time as a graduate student in Princeton University's Department of Sociology. Betsy Armstrong tops that list. Her extraordinary guidance and support over the years—whether in the form of inspiring questions posed as I prepared for my general examinations, astute and attentive comments offered on the umpteenth draft of an article or chapter in progress, or joyful e-mails sent my way to share bathroom-related news clippings—have been paramount to my completion of both my dissertation and the book it has become. Kim Lane Scheppele, Tey Meadow, and Margot Canaday rounded out my incredible dissertation committee; each of them has challenged me to aim for more depth, more ambition, and more imagination throughout the lifespan of this project. And outside of Princeton, Bethany Bryson has been a cherished friend and adviser whose efforts to push me outside of my intellectual comfort zone have left an indelible mark on my scholarship in general and this book in particular.

I am also indebted to the many other individuals and organizations who have contributed to this project over the years. Conversations with and feedback from Wendy Belcher, Mary Anne Case, Bonnie Thornton Dill, Maggie Frye, Judy Gerson, Brian Herrera, Regina Kunzel, Peter Johannessen, Michèle Lamont, Harvey Molotch, Freeden Ouer, Victoria Pitts-Taylor, Gayle Salamon, Kristen Schilt, Keith Shaw, Rachel Sherman, Dara Strolovitch, Judy Swan, Erin Vearncombe, Janet Vertesi, King-to Yeung, and Viviana Zelizer have all enriched my thinking and my writing. Four excellent reviewers enlisted by the University of California Press— Miriam Abelson, Elizabeth A. Armstrong, Cati Connell, and Carla Pfeffer—helped me transform my book proposal into a full-fledged manuscript, and to transform the completed manuscript into a more cohesive final product. Ten semesters of writing-seminar students have read and commented upon a slice of my work in progress as an exercise in furthering their peer-review skills, and in doing so, have pushed me to make my work more analytical and more accessible. Princeton's University Committee on Research in the Humanities and Social Sciences provided me with generous funding for research assistance; Margie Duncan managed all of the behind-the-scenes institutional requirements that came with that funding so I could focus my energy on my students; and Ellie Breitfeld, Y. J. Choi, Mona Clappier, Sanna Lee, and Aidan O'Donnell did an outstanding job of providing that assistance. Special thanks also go to Kamron Soldozy and Madison Werthmann for going above and beyond the call of research-assistant duty by undertaking a careful read of several chapters as I completed my final revisions, as well as to Judy Koo for assembling and polishing my entire bibliography with an enviable level of attention to detail. And, of course, I am so very appreciative that 128 busy professionals made the time to talk with me, back when I was an over-eager young graduate student, about bathrooms.

Additionally, no list of thanks would be complete without voicing my considerable appreciation for Naomi Schneider, whose enthusiasm and support for this book have been constant since we first met. The entire University of California Press team has made the experience of writing this book an undeniably positive one, and I am particularly grateful to Benjy Mailings for his kindness in handling all the questions and anxieties I have thrown his way over the last two years.

But my greatest thanks go to my family. Grams, Pop-Pop, and Uncle Bud have always been there for me in so many ways, and I wish that all three of them had been able to both see me complete my dissertation and transform it into this book. Even still, their pride in my accomplishments has always been—and will always be—a steadfast anchor throughout my life and work. Janet and Charlie have welcomed me into their lives and celebrated my work to such a degree that I find it hard to believe that we were ever not family. I am so incredibly grateful that I lucked into such fantastic in-laws, and I hope this book's density of sociological jargon does not bore them to tears. And Rachel, not only are you my best friend and favorite person, but this book would have never been possible without your unrelenting patience, love, and support. There are no words for how special I feel to have you as my partner each and every day of my life, or for how special I feel to have had you as my partner through each and every step of this book's life.

In the end, though, I dedicate this book to my mom, Dolores. Because I could not convey this sentiment in words beyond those I offered in the acknowledgments to my dissertation, I'll quote myself here: she somehow managed to work a full-time job while cooking dinner from scratch every night; attend every single field trip, marching-band competition, and college football game in which I took part across my entire educational career; and, most remarkably of all, support every choice I've ever made, good and bad alike. In fact, well before I learned the language of feminist and queer theory, she taught me by example what it truly means to be progressive—so much so that, no matter how many years I'll come to spend in the academy, she will always be the smartest woman I know. For all those reasons, and so many more, she is—and will always be—my hero. I miss you every day, Mom, and above all else, I wish I could share this achievement with you.

"Institutions do the classifying" . . .

Mary Douglas, *How Institutions Think*

Introduction

Certainly, the bathroom wars are a bizarrely outsize aspect
of a serious subject.

Ruth Marcus, "Beyond the Bathroom Wars for Transgender
Rights," *Washington Post*, April 2015

steps towards progress

On April 8, 2015, the Obama administration debuted a new, all-gender
restroom in the Eisenhower Executive Office Building—the first of its
kind within the White House complex. The innovative feature offered a
physical counterpart to several other recent updates to policies governing
restroom access in federal workplaces, all of which were intended to make
the White House more inclusive for staff who might be uncomfortable
with more traditional, gender-segregated restroom arrangements. As
White House spokesman Jeff Tiller explained in his comments to the
press that afternoon, the administration had previously undertaken measures to ensure that employees on the White House grounds were allowed
"to use restrooms consistent with their gender identity."[1] The new gender-
neutral space was the next logical step toward inclusivity, as it would offer
an additional option for White House guests and staff to use—an option
that the president's senior advisor Valerie Jarrett described in an op-ed
for the lesbian, gay, bisexual, and transgender–themed magazine *The
Advocate* as an "important step forward" in ensuring that everyone entering the Eisenhower Building would feel "safe and fully respected."[2]

Outside of the federal government, parallel regulatory changes related
to employment, gender identity, and restroom access had been unfolding

motive was that they wanted everyone to feel respected

3

for many years at the local and state levels—and in spheres other than workplaces alone. In 1999, Iowa governor Tom Vilsack issued his own executive order prohibiting discrimination on the basis of gender identity and sexual orientation in state employment, marking the first appearance of the phrase "gender identity" in such a law. Even earlier, in 1993, the Minnesota legislature became the first in the United States to prohibit discrimination in employment, housing, credit, and public accommodations against individuals "having a self-image or identity not traditionally associated with one's biological maleness or femaleness."[3] And with respect to restrooms, landmark amendments to the District of Columbia's 2006 Human Rights Act were among the first in the nation to grant individual citizens "the right to use gender-specific restrooms and other gender-specific facilities . . . consistent with their gender identity or expression" and further mandate that all "single-occupancy restroom facilities" throughout the city would be required to "use gender-neutral signage" moving forward.[4]

But given the Eisenhower Building's location adjacent to the West Wing of the White House, its history of housing the Departments of State, War, and the Navy, and its current function as host to the majority of offices used by White House staff, the new all-gender restroom functioned as an especially meaningful harbinger of support for transgender rights in the United States. As Valerie Jarrett's op-ed further explained, the architectural addition was merely one component of a more comprehensive project on the part of the president to "lead by example" and set the standard for the rest of the nation in expanding "the protections of antidiscrimination to apply to the LGBT community."[5] Indeed, *The Advocate* itself described the entrance of the Obama administration into the "national conversation about trans citizens' access to bathrooms" as one of several "unprecedented" moves that were "affirming of trans citizens," ranging from the appearance of the word *transgender* in the State of the Union address "for the first time ever" to the pioneering work on the part of the Department of Justice to expand federal protections against sex discrimination to include "antitrans discrimination."[6]

In fact, the timing of the Obama administration's announcement of the new all-gender restroom also served a symbolic function, as it coincided with the full activation of Executive Order 13672. Originally signed on

July 21, 2014, the order updated a small handful of presidential directives related to employment discrimination already on the books. First, it added gender identity to the purview of two other executive orders prohibiting discrimination within the federal workforce: those which already protected employees on the basis of race, color, religion, sex, national origin, and sexual orientation. Second, it added both sexual orientation and gender identity to a list of parallel protections against workplace discrimination for the specific benefit of federal government contractors. While the addition of gender identity to the order covering federal workers was put into practice effective immediately, the updates for federal contractors required the Labor Department and the Office of Management and Budget to draft and publish a rule for implementation—a process completed as of the all-gender restroom's debut on April 8.

Yet the tenor of the national conversation about gender and restrooms across the United States in the early 2010s was nowhere near uniformly supportive. Instead, efforts to increase the profile of bathroom-related issues—and transgender rights more broadly—were often met with impassioned opposition. In his remarks to the National Religious Broadcasters Convention in 2015, former Arkansas governor Mike Huckabee infamously criticized recent legal interventions to ensure restroom access for transgender citizens, calling such efforts "inherently wrong," "ridiculous," and a "threat," going so far as to quip that he wished he "would have found [his] feminine side" in high school in order to "shower with the girls."[7] Similarly, in an op-ed following Governor Jerry Brown's approval of a bill in 2013 that would allow each student enrolled in California public schools "to participate in sex-segregated school programs and activities . . . and use facilities consistent with his or her gender identity, irrespective of the gender listed on the pupil's records,"[8] Assemblyman Tim Donnelly accused the new law of facilitating "privacy invasion" and "public humiliation" alike, arguing that "the same politicians who want to end discrimination have actually discriminated against the majority of people who are uncomfortable" with such provisions.[9]

In some states and municipalities, such apprehensions motivated lawmakers to introduce legislative counterproposals of their own, ones meant to increase the stringency of gendered prerequisites for accessing workplace and public restrooms rather than reduce or eliminate them. For instance, in response to Miami-Dade County's addition of the categories "gender identity" and "gender expression" to their human rights ordinance in 2014, state representative Frank Artiles initiated a bill in the Florida House of Representatives for the sake of "public safety."[10] That bill would categorize "knowingly and willfully" entering a "single-sex public facility designated for or restricted to persons of the other sex" as a second-degree misdemeanor.[11] Several months later, state representative Debbie Riddle introduced a pair of even more distinctive proposals to the Texas House of Representatives. The first proposed criminalizing the act of entering a restroom labeled for a gender "that is not the same gender as the individual's gender," and the second aimed to define gender for the sake of access to public locker rooms, showers, and toilets at an unusually detailed level: as "the gender established at the individual's birth or the gender established by the individual's chromosomes."[12]

In fact, such bathroom battles had become so contentious that some political leaders championing transgender rights and activists working toward similar ends distanced their quest for equality from what one *Washington Post* opinion writer called a "frivolous and overheated" obsession with all things restroom-related.[13] When Councilman Tom Quirk introduced a bill in 2012 proposing the addition of gender identity and sexual orientation to Baltimore County's antidiscrimination statutes, he expressed frustration that opponents of his proposal focused on "everything except for what this bill is about." His goal, he emphatically clarified, was to enact "an anti-discrimination bill," "not a bathroom bill."[14] And as Chad Griffen, president of the lesbian and gay civil rights organization Human Rights Campaign, and Mara Kiesling, executive director of the National Center for Transgender Equality, emphasized in an op-ed of their own in 2015, the continued politicization of restrooms in debates about legal protections related to gender identity was a "real tragedy" that "took time and energy away" from combating more pressing aspects of "ignorance, rejection, and discrimination" directed toward transgender people throughout the United States.[15]

But *are* bathrooms truly a distraction from real social problems? Or might there be something more serious underlying the deluge of public attention they've recently received?

WHY STUDY BATHROOMS?

As it turns out, public restrooms are perennial lightning rods for cultural conflict in the United States—and they have been for nearly two centuries. From the middle of the nineteenth century, when unprecedented population growth prompted bitter partisan battles over the necessity of the very first instances of public plumbing, through the first two decades of the twenty-first century, when debates like those I trace above took place, bathrooms have often been a nexus of political crossfire. Such a reality may seem odd at first blush. After all, bathrooms are spaces in which we routinely negotiate one of the basest, most persistently taboo aspects of the human experience: dealing with the effluvia produced at the margins of the body. But as anthropologist Mary Douglas argues in *Purity and Danger*, efforts to distance ourselves from that which is considered "unclean" are not an ingrained, universal human response to the presence of a hygienic breach. Instead, our beliefs about "dirty" things like excretion and "dirty" spaces like bathrooms do important cultural work: work aimed at bringing cohesion and clarity to a world—and a social system—that is, as Douglas puts it, "inherently untidy."[16]

Consequently, when political disagreements erupt over public restrooms, what is ultimately at stake are beliefs about the moral order: what we, as a society, collectively value, collectively believe we owe one another, and collectively agree counts as upstanding social behavior. Bathrooms, in this sense, do much more than mediate what literally counts as clean and what literally counts as dirty. They an important means through which individual citizens and social groups alike accomplish what cultural sociologists call *boundary work:* the separation of people, objects, spaces, and even actions into distinctive categories based on their perceived similarities and differences. Far from being taboo social spaces or an inconsequential dimension of our everyday lives, then, public restrooms serve several symbolic functions. Their availability implicitly suggests which bodies, identities, and communities are expected to be present in the public spaces in which they are installed. Obstacles to their entrances likewise signal which bodies, identities, and communities are not expected or welcome. And where they are separated into multiple spaces, each physically cordoned from one or more others, they communicate which bodies, identities, and communities should not intermingle behind closed doors.

Restrooms are thus crucial sites through which categorical inequalities—that is, those based on group differences like race, disability, or social class—have long been maintained and magnified in the United States. Historians Patricia Cooper and Ruth Oldenziel, for instance, have documented how women of color entering American workplaces during World War II were not segregated from their white counterparts on shop floors. Rather, workplace bathrooms were the sites where such "cherished classifications" were continually enforced and affirmed.[17] More recently, in his reflections on doing ethnographic research in New York City around the turn of the twenty-first century, sociologist Mitch Duneier recounted his surprise at realizing that he—"an upper-middle-class white male"—was able to access restrooms in fast food establishments in Greenwich Village while his "poor and black" research subjects were systematically excluded from such spaces.[18] Even today, the National Council on Disability reports that laws like the Americans with Disabilities Act of 1990 have yielded frustratingly "inconsistent" changes to restroom access and availability for people with disabilities—leaving it difficult for many to carry out the simplest of daily activities.[19]

Yet the social division most central to the design and construction of American public restrooms is, unquestionably, gender. As you likely experienced firsthand the last time you used a public toilet, gender differences abound in bathroom spaces. Men's and women's rooms are often located in separate hallways or opposite corners of a building—sometimes, even occupying space on different floors. They feature distinctive signs and symbols on their doors; they contain markedly different fixtures behind those doors. Norms of etiquette vary drastically between those two kinds of spaces, too, with expectations of silence and distance typical in the men's room and norms of sociality more acceptable within the women's. Such distinctions are so commonplace, so taken for granted, that we might be tempted to think of them as a logical response to inherent bodily and behavioral differences between women and men. But, just as Mary Douglas points out that disgust is less a universal human reflex meant to keep our bodies safe from harm and more an elaborate set of cultural constructions intended to protect our moral beliefs, those gender differences are, likewise, more social than biological.

Psychoanalytic theorist Jacques Lacan describes such realities as "the laws of urinary segregation": that is, the cultural means through which the basic human need to eliminate waste becomes a site of constructed gender difference that appears natural and inevitable.[20] And while we might be further tempted to dismiss Lacan's remarks as a poststructuralist intellectual pretension, ample historical evidence reveals that gender separation in American public restrooms has never been universal or final. Many of the very first public toilets installed on urban street corners in the middle of the nineteenth century—built to discourage men from urinating in public and to accommodate women pursuing commerce and employment outside the home—were designed to serve users of all genders. Nearly a century later, before the rise of late-twentieth-century federal laws that marked restrooms as litigable nexuses of gender discrimination, ungendered restrooms were already commonplace in postwar factories and commercial establishments. And today, as the start of this introduction observes, a new wave of ungendered restrooms has emerged—as various municipalities, states, and even the federal government have begun to undo or rescind public policies requiring that only certain kinds of gendered people with certain kinds of gendered bodies be admitted to certain kinds of gendered restroom spaces.[21]

In short, the increased availability of "gender-neutral," "gender-inclusive," and "all-gender" restrooms in today's colleges and universities, transit centers, shopping malls, restaurants, museums, libraries, and government offices like the Eisenhower Executive Office Building is far from evidence of a novel restroom revolution. Rather, the question of whether to segregate public restrooms by gender in the United States has been a surprisingly open one. And that openness has allowed behind-the-scenes organizational deliberations about the design and construction of public toileting spaces to be critical sites for working out what gender is—and what it means—in the first place.

WHY BATTLE BATHROOMS?

Bathroom Battlegrounds takes the most recent batch of those organizational deliberations as one of its departure points, exploring efforts over the last twenty-five years to design and construct ungendered restrooms in a range of municipal, cultural, and educational organizations across the United States. I center the book on those recent transformations not just because of their timeliness but also because of their distinctive *institutionalization*. That is, only in recent years have there been sustained efforts on the part of individual citizens, bureaucratic entities, and social movements to encourage—or require—the addition of gender-neutral restrooms to buildings as a matter of formal policy.

However, before taking up the emergent issue of gender-inclusive restrooms, I first look backward in history to the book's other departure point: tracing the origins of today's dominant paradigm of gender separation. This is for two reasons. First, to make sense of the increasing imbrication of gender-neutral restrooms in present-day organizations, we first need to understand what, exactly, that new paradigm is striving to overcome. Second, by considering the history through which gendered restrooms became so thoroughly institutionalized and the recent institutionalization of ungendered alternatives in the same analysis, I offer a more varied corpus of restroom-related evidence than either a historical or a contemporary approach alone would yield. That variance, in turn, allows me to draw broader conclusions about where, when, how, and why organizational discourses about restroom design and construction concatenate, producing durable consequences for the social organization of gender.

To that end, the historical portion of *Bathroom Battlegrounds* compiles published scholarship, archival documents related to architectural design, and written opinions from the federal courts to trace the institutional history of gender separation in American public restrooms. As I will show, sweeping cultural, scientific, and technological advancements led to the rise of the indoor water closet between the middle of the nineteenth century and the turn of the twentieth, and the installation of the very first public comfort stations for urban citizens soon followed. Yet the most pervasive adoption of such engineering marvels in nondomestic space did not unfold on city streets. Rather, it occurred among middle- and upper-class leisure establishments in major American cities, which themselves reflected the pervasive gender segregation of nineteenth-century social life. As the availability of public restrooms gradually spread to other commercial and civic spaces, that dominant model of separate men's and women's restrooms persisted, making the influence of deep-seated cultural beliefs about gendered bodies only an oblique influence on the initial development of restroom gender segregation.

That indirect influence, however, has not kept gender politics from being a potent influence on restroom design, construction, and regulation across the United States. On the contrary, from the closing years of the nineteenth century through the middle of the twentieth, novel scientific claims about women's bodies and entrenched moral beliefs about sexual propriety led elected officials to enact the first laws mandating the separation of men's and women's restrooms in work, educational, and civic spaces. Then, as public health and architecture professionals sought legitimacy for their early-twentieth-century work to improve public plumbing, they drew upon appeals to scientific authority and social progress to cement gender separation as the public restroom status quo. By the second half of the twentieth century, courts of law added to that ideological infiltration, drawing on cultural assumptions about embodied gender difference, heterosexuality, and privacy to mandate that restrooms ought to be separate *and* equal for men and for women. Thus, through a series of interconnected institutional processes, a particular constellation of cultural ideologies about gender, sexuality, and social status seeped into building codes and design standards; into interlocking layers of local, state, and federal law; and perhaps most durably of all, into the physical composition of buildings.

The contemporary portion of this book then uses in-depth interviews with respondents from a wide range of municipal, cultural, and educational organizations to explore the effects of that history on the increasing popularity of ungendered restrooms in recent years. As I will show, the "bathroom battle" at hand for such organizations has rarely been the kind of polemical culture war between traditional and progressive values seen in the mass media over the last decade, including the journalistic snippets I quote in the preface to this introduction. Instead, the decision makers I interviewed tend to agree that supporting gender and sexual minorities, families with children or aging relatives of all genders, and people with disabilities by providing ungendered restroom spaces is a desirable, even obvious, choice. The problem, then, has not been ideology but inertia—that is, the tenacity of the gender-segregated architectural and legal infrastructure bequeathed to an organization from the past. Thus, while their ideal vision of restroom arrangements might include at least one gender-neutral space, a complex web of institutional and material obstacles often stood between each respondent and their ability to quickly—or comprehensively—overcome absolute gender separation in their present-day restrooms.

To navigate that labyrinth, my respondents discovered that one resource above all others was key to engendering restroom-related change: the power of conversation. Whether they worked in a local public library, a nationally renowned museum, or a flagship state university, they recognized that connecting the reduction (or removal) of gender-separated restrooms to important organizational goals—such as promoting equity, diversity, and inclusion—would allow them to garner support for local restroom renovations and, by extension, to make the boons of gender-inclusive restrooms more widely known. But as my respondents worked to frame even the smallest of infrastructural updates as evidence of their organizations' progressive commitments, they did more than describe such changes as beneficial for the publics they serve. They also positioned ungendered restrooms as a valuable reputational advantage—one that could signal to their upper- and upper-middle-class patrons that their particular organization is sufficiently forward thinking, morally upstanding, and above all, status laden enough to be on the cutting edge of institutional innovation in the twenty-first century. Consequently, even as they ameliorate certain kinds of categorical inequality—by creating more utile public spaces for gender and sexual minorities, individuals with disabilities, postmodern families, and beyond—today's ungendered restrooms have become a surprising means of reinforcing multiple systems of cultural power and privilege.

Across the nearly two-hundred-year history of American public restrooms it documents, then, *Bathroom Battlegrounds* reveals how beliefs about gender difference have rarely been the most salient determinant of how organizations configure their restrooms—at least in isolation. While the organizations I study have negotiated gender ideologies in many ways, shapes, and forms, they have also traversed several other forms of cultural classification as they have done so. These include the physical boundaries built into architectural design and infrastructure, moral boundaries associated with sex and sexuality, and above all, social boundaries related to class and status. In fact, even when the organizations and individuals I study have striven to optimize bureaucratic efficiency, respond to evolving community values, or ensure access for as many users as possible, I find that they have consistently reinforced existing social hierarchies through their seemingly innocuous plumbing choices—making public restrooms neither as marginal nor as unimportant as they might seem.

Readers interested in the intellectual foundations of that overarching argument should continue reading through the next two sections of this introduction. They situate my research within a broader set of theoretical frameworks within the sociology of gender and the sociology of organizations. Readers who would prefer to dive right into the history of gender separation in restrooms or the recent rise of ungendered alternatives, however, should fast-forward to the final section of this introduction, "A Promise and a Plan," for guidance on how to proceed through the chapters that follow.

A POST-GENDER SOCIETY?

In many respects, the early years of the twenty-first century might seem like a puzzling time for a sociological project like this to focus on gender. After all, popular accounts and social-scientific research alike suggest that the United States is rapidly evolving into a "post-gender" society—and in ways that go far beyond the wonderful world of washrooms. Over the course of the twentieth century, record numbers of women in the United States joined the full-time, paid American workforce; women's wages from that paid work increased at a faster rate than did men's wages; and young women came to outpace young men on a wide range of measures related to educational achievement—from reading skills in childhood to the level of rigor of high school coursework to their collective receipt of bachelor's and master's degrees.[22] Alongside such dramatic shifts, gender segregation in a variety of academic, institutional, and physical spheres has likewise eroded. In colleges and universities, for instance, coeducation grew into the dominant model of higher education, and in the paid workforce, gender integration has increased at all levels of employment.[23] Such trends have also continued into the early years of the twenty-first century. The Department of Defense began integrating women into combat positions and removed gender restrictions from all military positions in the mid-2010s, and today, government agencies like the United States Agency for International Development now incorporate "gender analysis" into their strategic planning to identify when and how institutionalized gender segregation affects their outreach work around the globe.[24]

Yet sociologists of gender tend to emphasize the resilience of gender-related inequalities amid such progress toward a more egalitarian future. In the world of work, women remain unequally distributed across occupational categories and positions; female workers are penalized more harshly than their male counterparts when they take time away from work to care for children or other family members; and "care work"—that is, paid positions typically filled by women that involve teaching, counseling, health services, supervising children, or other forms of emotional labor—pays less than work in other fields, even when accounting for educational attainment and employment experience.[25] In education, men still dominate the sciences, technology, engineering, and mathematics; in fact, even where women have made substantial inroads in STEM, they have done so in areas such as the biological and chemical sciences rather than fields perceived to be more lucrative or math-intensive, such as computer science and physics.[26] And beyond those general trends, the physical separation of women and men persists in many settings, too—often producing novel gender inequalities, such as the awkward moment faced by presidential candidate Hillary Clinton in December 2015 when a lengthy "schlep" to the women's restroom caused a delay in her return to the stage from a break for a televised Democratic debate.[27]

Sociological theory most often attributes such immobility to *gender ideologies:* that is, morally charged beliefs about what it means to be a man or a woman, what makes men and women different from one another, and what the consequences of those differences are—or ought to be. In fact, since feminist social science coalesced into a distinctive intellectual project in the late 1960s and early 1970s, one of the field's central projects has been to conceptualize gender as a fundamentally cultural force. Pushing against the then-conventional understanding that gender differences were a simple consequence of embodied biological difference, scholars like anthropologist Gayle Rubin argued for the analytic separation of *sex* from *gender,* defining the former as "biological raw material" and the latter as "a set of" decidedly cultural "arrangements by which" that bodily foundation "is shaped by human, social intervention."[28] In the nascent sociology of gender, that paradigm shift manifested as research on the allocation of men and women to different social roles. Roles, such thinking went, carry with them expectations about how we should behave, what we should value, who we should aspire to become, and how we should experience our innermost thoughts and emotions.[29] Such insights thus laid critical intellectual groundwork for recognizing men's and women's different experiences—and differential levels of social status—within schools, labor markets, and the family as culturally constructed differences rather than biologically mandated ones.

In the years that followed, the cultural foundations of the gender order occupied an even brighter spotlight as sociologists began to theorize gender as, in the words of Candace West and Don Zimmerman, wholly "the product of social doings of some sort."[30] Rather than describing gender as a coercive set of roles foisted upon unsuspecting individuals, gender scholars in the 1980s and 1990s began to advance an understanding of gender as an agentic, interactionally achieved process.[31] In other words, to return to West and Zimmerman's language, gender became something that we "do" rather than something that we "are." On the one hand, that approach marked a tremendous revolution in the sociology of gender: it launched a new understanding of gendered behavior as connected to local context, contingent on the active participation of individual social actors, and always subject to change. On the other hand, however, gender's surprisingly fluid and flexible character did not make it infinitely open-ended. Whether sociologists emphasized the interactional risks of deviating from gendered expectations, the intersectional influence of race and class on gendered life outcomes, or the ubiquitous cultural valuation of masculinity over femininity, they consistently observed that gendered actions and interactions tended to reinforce the status quo of gender inequality—often in ways subtler (and therefore more insidious) than overt discrimination alone would produce.[32] Truly understanding gender, therefore, required equal attention to its everyday dimensions and its structural character alike.

By the turn of the twenty-first century, sociologists had thus firmly established *that* gender is a multilayered cultural phenomenon. They subsequently moved toward identifying *when* and *how* gender ideologies act on people—and, conversely, how people might be able to change those ideologies and the institutions they sustained. For leading feminist theorists in the first decade of the twenty-first century, including Patricia Yancey Martin and Barbara Risman, this meant exhorting social scientists to attend more fully to the interplay among multiple layers of sociological analysis. The former wrote about gender's "multiple features—ideology, practices, constraints, conflicts, [and] power" in order to "affirm its complexities and multifacetedness"; the latter issued reminders that gender is "deeply embedded as a basis for stratification not just in our personalities, our cultural rules, or institutions but in all these, and in complicated ways."[33] Such calls have been met with a renaissance of "middle-range"[34] empirical research projects in recent years, which have sought to capture the unique nuances of gendered practices in a specific geographic locale or institutional setting while simultaneously offering a generalizable account of how gender works across such spatial or structural differences.[35] All in all, then, five decades of intellectual development have paved the way to an understanding of gender as never fixed, sometimes contradictory, and always evolving.

But as complex and multifaceted as that framework has become, sociological research on gender often remains limited by a much less complex and multifaceted framework for describing the meso level of analysis— that is, the level of *organizations*. Often, theorists framing gender as an "institution" or as a "structure" collapse social forces as diverse as media messaging, legal regulations, and organizational policies into one equivalent package—despite the reality that those forces are themselves mutually influential and sometimes beholden to one another in multiple respects.[36] Similarly, although middle-range empirical studies have come a long way from role theory's presumption that workplaces and family structures are endlessly coercive, today's gender scholars often treat gendered organizations as much less vibrant than the rainbow of gendered individuals and gendered interactions that unfold within them.[37] Now, of course, effective theory construction in the social sciences does, by definition, require the elision of enough nuance to reach a generally applicable abstraction.[38] And certainly, giving empirical primacy to on-the-ground gendered practice is a powerful analytic choice—because thick, attentive description of everyday social action can, in and of itself, reveal how diverse and dynamic gender truly is.[39] Yet, without a full-fledged account of how formal organizations operate amid and among those practices, sociological theories of gender cannot fully explain when and how gender ideologies reinforce—and, at times, transform—the gender order.

TOWARD A RELATIONAL THEORY OF GENDERED ORGANIZATIONS

Of course, the simple observation that organizations matter is not a novel contribution to the sociology of gender. In fact, organizations have been a recurring motif in the fabric of the social-scientific study of gender for over forty years, especially for scholars seeking to understand the gendered organization of work. As far back as Rosabeth Moss Kanter's pathbreaking *Men and Women of the Corporation,* originally published in 1977, sociologists have studied how the structure of an organization itself can beget certain forms of gendered behavior—so much so that bureaucratic policy and procedure can supersede psychological traits or socialized learning in determining how men and women act in the workplace.[40] That basic principle made an even more profound intellectual splash in 1990 with Joan Acker's pioneering article "Hierarchies, Jobs, Bodies: A Theory of Gendered Organizations." Challenging the notion that organizations themselves are gender-neutral entities, Acker argued that gendered assumptions—such as the implicit expectation that workers have no demands on their attention at home, that they think in ways that are unfailingly rational and calculating, and that they value the organization before all else—permeate contemporary bureaucracy.[41] And while the specifics of that "gendering" process vary across institutional fields and geographic boundaries, ample sociological evidence since then has exposed the continued imbrication of gender distinctions in routinized—and often unnoticed or invisible—aspects of everyday organizational functioning.[42]

Today, studies of the gendered organization continue to extend Kanter's and Acker's foundational work in a dazzling array of new directions. Some sociologists take an intersectional approach to the gendered organization, finding that the "ideal worker" imagined by organizational policies and procedures is not only male but also white, middle-to-upper class, and heterosexual.[43] Others seek out the conditions necessary to engender meaningful institutional change, highlighting how, for instance, the mere presence of women in positions of managerial authority can help ameliorate gender-related inequalities throughout an organization.[44] And yet others have moved away from the most commonly studied type of formal organization in sociology, the workplace, and toward studying the processes through which gender and bureaucratic structures entwine to shape gendered identities and gendered practices beyond labor markets alone.[45] But whether they focus on work, medicine, law, or another social sphere altogether, such efforts almost always shine an analytic spotlight on the policies and practices that create (and re-create) the gender order *within* an organization. As such, the myriad cultural and social forces that operate *across* such bureaucratic entities—and the broader institutional fields of which they are a part—remain far less frequently accounted for within sociological takes on the gendered organization.

In contrast, for organizational theorists working outside the realm of gender, no organization is an island. Although Max Weber canonically theorized bureaucracy in the early twentieth century as a rational enterprise through which organizations independently strive to optimize their own efficiency,[46] multiple sociological developments since then have revealed the fundamental interdependence of organizations.[47] One such development, organizational ecology, contends that organizations influence one another in much the same way that a population of organisms within a shared ecosystem would. Variation in organizational form and behavior emerges (both by chance and by design), struggle ensues between those different organizational strategies, and certain strategies survive while others become extinct.[48] Another major thread, neo-institutional theory, attributes organizational behavior less to conflict over scarce resources and more to the construction of shared meaning within an organization's broader environment. For scholars leveraging that more cultural framework, shared meanings can emerge from common legal constraints, from common professional personnel, and from common uncertainties about how best to act—all of which induce comparable organizations to act and to structure themselves in ways that are extraordinarily homogeneous.[49] But whether organizational theorists emphasize competition or culture, their intellectual legacy has been a *relational* approach to the sociological study of bureaucracy: that is, an understanding that any one organization's ability to survive and achieve success is contingent on its responsiveness to the actions, policies, and procedures pursued within other, similar organizations.

That relational emphasis brings us full circle to this chapter's opening discussion of boundary processes. Why? Because if an organization is to act in accordance with other, similar organizations, it must first determine which of those others are, in fact, similar enough to merit their attention.[50] And those categorization processes have profound consequences. On the positive side, the categories to which an organization belongs, whether imposed externally or established internally, comprise an important part of that organization's identity.[51] That identity, in turn, affects if, when, and how a particular organization will adopt innovative policies or practices.[52] On the negative side, organizations whose behavior defies categorical expectations can quickly find themselves in peril. For example, as manufacturing taxonomies in the nineteenth-century United States became increasingly rigid, businesses spanning multiple industry categories received lower credit ratings than their single-category counterparts—regardless of their actual performance.[53] Such classificatory consequences also accrue to the products an organization produces or the policies it adopts. Films spanning multiple genres, for instance, hold less appeal for both critics and moviegoing audiences, but if an organization with sought-after category memberships endorses such ambiguous goods, an undesirable taboo can readily become an applauded necessity.[54] In short, the same cognitive impulse that induces each of us to group together similar people, objects, and spaces into shared social categories also induces us to group similar organizations together and, moreover, to use those categories as a powerful lens for evaluating organizational behavior.

But just as sociologists of gender have moved from arguing *that* to asking *when* and *how* over the last two decades, so, too, have sociologists of organizations. After all, as Tim Hallett and Marc Ventresca write, "Institutions are not inert containers of meaning; rather they are 'inhabited' by people and their doings."[55] Thus, by analyzing how "people" within organizations generate shared meanings, cooperate and collide over courses of action, and respond to the ever-changing demands of their wider cultural environments, sociologists have revealed how boundary work shapes every part of their bureaucratic "doings": the emotion and embodiment felt by individual workers, the conversation and rhetoric exchanged in the course of everyday administrative work, the pressures of evaluation and reputation that impinge on firms from the outside, and more.[56] In many respects, that turn toward the human underpinnings of the institutional order resonates with canonical insights from feminist sociology. The notion that organizations are "inhabited" evokes Dorothy Smith's classic work on institutional analysis, wherein she suggests that "talking with people" is an important avenue through which social scientists can uncover "how things work" within a particular setting or context.[57] Furthermore, for many decades, sociologists of gender have rightfully asserted that "the gender order"—that is, R.W. Connell's term for the structure of gender relations in a particular society at a particular moment in history—is maintained as much through unassuming, everyday human activity, including cultural processes of classification and categorization, as through political structures, the gendered division of labor, and other macrosociological structures.[58]

The problem, however, is that such existing paradigms rarely, if ever, theorize the complexity of intra- and interorganizational dynamics with the level of sensitivity they allot to the complexity of gender's social construction. And, to be fair, the problem is mutual: sociologists who take a relational approach to studying organizations rarely, if ever, conceptualize gender's complex character with the dynamism they so often ascribe to bureaucratic behavior. But unless sociologists meld together the best of gender theory with the best of organizational theory—by adopting a truly *processual* approach to both—we cannot fully account for one of the most important realities of social life: that embodied cultural distinctions like gender and meso-level social groupings like formal organizations are constantly *co-constructing* one another.

A PROMISE AND A PLAN

Consequently, *Bathroom Battlegrounds* analyzes historical and contemporary discourse about gender and public restrooms in the United States not only as an end in and of itself but also as a conduit for building a new and more meaningful dialogue between sociological theories of gender and sociological theories of organizations. As I show in the six chapters that follow, decision makers within formal organizations draw upon, grapple with, reinforce, and transform many localized and idiosyncratic social forces as they work to shape their restrooms, especially gender ideologies. But cutting across that multiplicity is a constant undertow of interorganizational dynamics, especially those tied up with emotion, conversation, and reputation. In particular, my analysis reveals that the ongoing efforts of affluent organizations (and the affluent individuals associated with them) to distinguish themselves as morally superior to other social groups have had a profound impact on the gendering of American public restrooms for their nearly two-hundred-year history. That impact has been so pronounced that public restrooms—and the gender ideologies they represent—have functioned as a surprisingly potent form of moral currency for cultural elites and the organizations they inhabit. In other words, even the most well-intentioned and progressive efforts to rethink the gender order, have, counterintuitively, allowed certain individuals and certain organizations to consistently claim and justify their membership among more privileged social strata.

To make sense of that recurring theme in my textual and interview data, *Bathroom Battlegrounds* offers sociologists a new theory of gender—a theory that foregrounds the intersecting, three-way influence of ideology, institutions, and inequality on the gender order. As existing scholarship teaches us, gender is a cultural phenomenon subject to perpetual negotiation, actively shaped and reshaped through tasks as mundane as planning or updating restroom infrastructure. But gender never acts alone. Rather, gender's plasticity makes it fundamentally constrained and enabled by a wide range of other cultural pressures, institutional relationships, and material structures, especially those that directly impinge on organizational policies, procedures, and actions. Thus, when organizations and the individuals acting within them go about designing, building, and imagining public restrooms, they also design, build, and imagine what gender itself is—and ought to be.

Borrowing from West and Zimmerman's classic formulation of gender as an interactional "accomplishment," and the many feminist theorists who have spotlighted gender's "institutional" character in recent years, I refer to this relational process as the *institutional accomplishment of gender*: a dynamic social undertaking through which individual social actors work actively to solve pressing organizational problems; draw from existing gender ideologies—or produce new ones—in order to creatively and effectively navigate those issues; respond to and reproduce the status hierarchies predominant in their local institutional field as a part of that navigation; concretize the results of all that cultural and interactional labor into organizational procedures, regulatory structures, and physical spaces (including, but certainly not limited to, restrooms); and grapple anew with the history of those concretized choices as new and pressing organizational problems emerge.

The rest of this book delivers on that overarching promise, as each chapter that follows incrementally fleshes out the findings of my restroom research alongside the various subcomponents of that novel theoretical framework. Chapter 1 does so by extending the intellectual groundwork laid in this introduction; chapters 2 and 3 use historical evidence to explain how gender-segregated public restrooms became institutionalized in the United States; chapters 4, 5, and 6 use interview data to explore contemporary efforts to challenge or amend that status quo with ungendered restrooms; and the conclusion offers a final rejoinder to the questions and themes featured in this introduction—both theoretical, for academic readers, and practical, for a wider audience. I also include a supplementary appendix, "Data and Methodology," for readers interested in the epistemological and practical considerations underlying my research design and analytic choices.

Specifically, chapter 1 sets up the book's five empirical chapters with a condensed, synthetic overview of "potty politics" in the United States from the last two centuries. Drawing from published historical, sociological, and gender studies scholarship, it follows the evolution of public restrooms from their multiple precursors, including public baths and the first domestic indoor water closets, all the way up through the late-twentieth-century adoption of "potty parity" laws designed to ensure the equivalence of men's and women's public restroom facilities. That overview of American restroom architecture and restroom-related public policy builds on the framing work of this chapter with a brief review of the existing social-scientific literature on public restrooms. But it also uses that synthesis to justify the book's sustained focus on certain kinds of formal organizations and certain kinds of restroom spaces within them. In doing so, it starts to document how the social organization of everyday life in the United

States, technological shifts in restroom infrastructure, the work of professional associations and political institutions, and changing moral values related to gender and sexuality have all intertwined to shape the gendering of restroom spaces. Moreover, because those social realities and symbolic ideals have been quite literally built into the physical and legal architecture of public restrooms, the chapter also serves as a necessary backdrop to the organizational discourses and decision-making processes analyzed in subsequent chapters.

Chapters 2 through 6, whose contents I preview in detail at appropriate moments in chapter 1, then offer a behind-the-scenes tour of restroom decision-making in five different institutional contexts. For readers interested in a particular type of organization, restroom-related issue, theoretical emphasis, or nonlinear reading experience, I structure all of those data-driven chapters as standalone entities. Each opens with a short, journalistic window into public discourse about restrooms from the chapter's historical epoch; those opening gambits then feed into a preview of the chapter's aims and argument. Next, every chapter segues into a detailed analysis of my textual or interview evidence, moving iteratively between my empirical findings and existing theoretical concepts in the sociological study of gender, culture, and/or organizations. That dialogic approach allows me to effectively build novel sociological concepts of my own in each chapter, which I then recapitulate and build upon in each chapter's local conclusion. All that said, however, the book is sequenced largely in chronological order and, therefore, is best read in the traditional front-to-back fashion. That holistic approach would be especially beneficial for readers interested in the book's core project of theorizing the institutional accomplishment of gender, as each chapter's local conclusion also ties the details of my evidence and analysis to that overarching intellectual aim.

Finally, the conclusion draws together the various empirical threads comprising the heart of my analysis and discusses their implications for sociological theories of gender; for the complex intersections of culture, organizations, and inequality that emerge consistently throughout my qualitative data; and for the possibility of social transformation—for restrooms, for gender, and for other systems of power—more broadly.

1 Politicizing the Potty

An eminent sanitarian has said that "the relations between sociology and hygiene are extremely intimate"—a fact which seems not sufficiently appreciated by the students of either subject.

Marion Talbot, "Sanitation and Sociology," *American Journal of Sociology*, July 1896

In the spring of 1970, Harvard University and Radcliffe College embarked on a bold experiment: an exchange in which 150 Radcliffe students and 150 Harvard students would swap housing arrangements, live in coeducational dormitories, and share residential bathrooms for a single semester. Following "unanimous approval of the faculty," the two institutions became the most recent schools in the United States to adopt a mixed-gender living scheme that one *Wall Street Journal* article described as "the biggest thing in college dormitories since the hotplate."[1] In part, Harvard faculty and administrators approved coeducational housing as a response to similar, increasingly unavoidable pressures from other institutions. Elsewhere in the Ivy League, more and more previously all-male institutions were admitting their first-ever pool of female applicants, and Harvard and Radcliffe were themselves enmeshed in negotiations about when and how to merge into a single coeducational university in the coming years. The success or failure of coeducational housing was thus understood "to have a significant bearing on plans for a full, permanent merger."[2]

But the national trend toward coeducation was not the only rationale motivating the Harvard faculty's approval of a mixed-gender housing

program. Much more mundane considerations, such as enabling undergraduate men and women to mingle with one another serendipitously—but
without amorous trappings—also precipitated administrative interest in the
new venture. As the head of one of Harvard's merger committees reported,
the new housing exchange would allow "Harvard men who would just like to
talk to a Radcliffe woman in a common room or [while] taking a walk along
the Charles" to do so without having to use "the only apparatus" currently
available to him: asking her out on a date. After all, he added, "The date car-
ries with it subtle but clearly palpable expectations as to how one should
behave," and those expectations would undoubtedly "interfere with the originally quite simple expectation"[3] of cultivating a friendship across gendered
lines.

Harvard and Radcliffe students also welcomed shared dormitory arrangements for equally platonic reasons, though clear gender differences abounded
in the details of each group's appreciation for their newly shared spaces.
Harvard's male students were particularly taken with the many improvements to their residence life that women offered, praising the "improved
housekeeping" in their halls and their newfound proximity to "excellent
sources of classroom notes at all hours." Radcliffe's female students, on the
other hand, welcomed the opportunity to convince the Harvard men to
rethink such tired gender stereotypes and to see them as worthy colleagues
rather than "supermachines."[4] For them, coeducational dormitories represented an opportunity to overcome a long-standing impediment to their
learning and academic growth: the physical isolation of the Radcliffe dorms.
No longer restricted by such "socially undesirable" circumstances, female
students now found themselves able to tap into "the intellectual advantages
of the Harvard house system"[5]—and thus into the possibility of achieving
true educational equity with their male counterparts.

Those differences aside, Harvard men and Radcliffe women were
united in finding the new dorms to be much more "natural," "normal," and
"like home" than conventional gender-segregated housing arrangements.
And they were not alone. Outside of Cambridge, students at the many
other institutions of higher education throughout the United States
experimenting with coeducational spaces in the early 1970s described
their new housemates in similarly familial terms. One female student at
Wilmington College found that her foray into coed living was analogous to

living with "a whole bunch of brothers," and a male student likewise noted that mixed-gender living helped him with "perpetuating relationships" with women—"not sexually," he carefully added, "but as friends, brothers and sisters." Although many parents worried that such appeals to family values were a thin veneer beneath which the "panty-raids and Saturday afternoon open-houses" that they experienced in their own college days were now omnipresent, students and university staff alike stressed that sexual activity was genuinely no more or less rampant than before gender integration. Indeed, as one publicist from Brown University put it in his public rejoinder intended to quell such fears: "There wasn't any more or any less fooling around than there used to be."[6]

Shared bathrooms, however, were met with much less enthusiasm. One critical dimension of ensuring that the faculty would favor the Harvard-Radcliffe housing exchange was an administrative condition that newly co-residing students would continue to have their most private residential spaces separated by gender. For the first round of coeducational housing, female Radcliffe students "could easily be placed anywhere in the three houses" that Harvard offered, because Harvard housing was "arranged in self-contained suites, each with its own bathroom." In contrast, because "such suites" did "not exist at Radcliffe," the Harvard men had to be assigned to living quarters "in separate corridors in the South, North and East houses."[7] At other universities, too, mixed-gender bathrooms remained largely off the table even as coed dorms multiplied dramatically. One staff member at Indiana University's Office of Residence Life determined that "70% of some 315 colleges had some type of coed dorm by 1971, compared to 51% of 376 institutions in 1967," but "shared bathrooms" had only "come to 15% of the campuses." Plus, in that first survey from 1967, researchers "didn't even consider" counting shared bathrooms, because of their rarity.[8] So, while students at Harvard, Radcliffe, and beyond were enjoying the opportunity to challenge some long-standing residential gender boundaries, common bathrooms remained comparatively verboten.

In fact, even when Harvard and Radcliffe incorporated mixed-gender bathrooms into coeducational dorms the very next semester, students bristled at the loss of separation. Although some recounted that managing shared bathroom space was as simple as "holler[ing] before you go into the shower,"[9] many others were nonplussed at the substantial "inconveniences" that resulted. One Harvard student quipped that he could not "leave his razor in the bathroom overnight," because he found it "dulled by female bathroom mates using it to shave their legs." And because shared facilities were largely relabeled without being renovated, Radcliffe women found themselves inventing new roles for the "exotic" plumbing fixtures "built originally for men"—by, for instance, creatively repurposing urinals into racks "for hanging your laundry over" so that their male housemates would cease using them as intended. The net effect, according to one dean, was that once the novelty of shared space had worn off, students began to have "second thoughts about sharing bathrooms." "It was a cool thing at first to have shared bathrooms as an experiment," she offered, but in looking ahead to the next year, "the students wanted the dorm restructured in separate suites, to allow separate bathrooms." But perhaps most telling of all was the onslaught of complaints about shared restrooms to the college psychiatrist, who candidly quipped to the *Wall Street Journal* reporter covering coed housing: "You know, these kids are not as cool as you think they are."[10]

.   .   .   .   .

Throughout the 1960s and 1970s, a torrent of restroom-related news was surging into the popular press from American colleges—and not just because journalists were in a tizzy over the "intimate revolution"[11] yielding open dormitories and coed bathrooms across the country. Many institutions of higher education found their names featured prominently in the mass media for another reason: their engineering, natural science, and social science faculty were publishing the results of rigorous, peer-reviewed studies about all things toilet. One article in the *Washington Post*, for instance, celebrated the most recent issue of the American Chemical Society's journal *Environmental Science* for thinking beyond the "flush toilet"—because such familiar forms of sanitary technology were "a technological mistake" prone to depleting "the diminishing supply of fresh water."[12] Another piece, in *Life* magazine, labeled the week of May 15, 1966, as a watershed moment for "the U.S. bathroom, that worldwide symbol of cleanliness, luxury, and civilization." As it reported, Cornell architecture professor Alexander Kira had just released a study finding that "hygiene-happy Americans are not as clean as they think they are."

The culprit, according to his team of researchers? Inadequate bathroom fixtures and toileting technologies—which, Kira argued, were surprisingly serious problems in need of equally serious solutions. In fact, while he reported that several of his "distinguished senior colleagues" thought his choice to study bathrooms "was irresponsibly funny," his research participants—and the journalist assigned to write about his forthcoming book, *The Bathroom*—"seemed wonderfully relieved that the whole bathroom question was out in the open at last."[13]

Since then, social-scientific research on restrooms has proliferated. Over the last four decades, demographers and public health scholars have documented the necessity of clean, safe, and accessible public bathrooms for individual and community-wide wellness.[14] Historians of the body and urban historians have frequently addressed public toilets in tandem with their accounts of eighteenth- and nineteenth-century public life in the United States, whether their archival excavations have foregrounded shifting norms of bodily cleanliness or the constant churn of political support for publicly funded urban infrastructure.[15] Microsociologists and social psychologists interested in the dynamics of "backstage" social practices and social interactions—that is, those actions that people undertake when they are largely out of the view of others—have highlighted public restrooms as revelatory sites of inquiry, largely owing to their status as private spaces in the midst of public life.[16] And as I briefly described in this book's introduction, researchers studying inequalities of race, class, ability, and sexuality across disciplinary boundaries have illustrated that public restrooms in the United States are critical sites for the production (and reproduction) of various forms of social and political exclusion. But because the persistent taboo associated with bathrooms has never fully disintegrated, the academic study of all things toilet-related has never fully moved from the margins of intellectual inquiry to the mainstream. Instead, such contributions have unfolded more as disconnected odds and ends of academic fabric rather than as a cohesive intellectual project.

In response, this chapter stitches together many of those social-scientific fat quarters into an interdisciplinary quilt of existing scholarship on American public restrooms. But rather than doing so with the conventional, thematic organization used in most social-scientific literature reviews, I structure this chapter in a way that also crafts a synthetic history of gendered "potty politics" in the United States. This allows me to accomplish two interrelated ends. The first is, as before, to remedy the disconnected character of so much existing restroom-related research by producing a cohesive narrative of how gender has shaped public restrooms over the last two hundred years. But my second aim is to establish the topical motivation for my intellectual work in *Bathroom Battlegrounds*— in complement to the theoretical motivation I outlined in the introduction. Specifically, by documenting what scholars already know about gender and public restrooms and, relatedly, what they do not know, I use this chapter to lay the groundwork for the empirical analysis I pursue in the five chapters that follow—work that will track how various kinds of formal organizations choose to gender their restrooms and, moreover, reveal how bureaucratic talk of toilets diverges, and often notably so, from the more public conversations summarized here.

FROM THE PRIVATE BATH TO THE (QUASI-) PUBLIC TOILET: 1800–1905

Of the many revolutionary changes to American culture that occurred over the course of the nineteenth century, one of the most transformative of everyday life was the rise of personal cleanliness as a normative, everyday aspiration for the majority of the population. Although the body's evacuative processes had been a site of cultural concern since well before the nation's founding, owing largely to the emphasis placed on such matters in European and North American medical thinking, maintaining a properly clean and orderly body became a ubiquitous social practice to an unprecedented degree. In part, such shifts were driven by uniquely American beliefs about the individualistic pursuit of upward mobility. As guidebooks outlining the necessities of respectable living began to celebrate the boons associated with regular washing, bathing and toileting practices understood to enhance personal hygiene began to trickle down from the most affluent social circles in the United States to the growing middle class. Moral reformers extended that diffusion even further as they peddled the myth of meritocracy to less affluent groups. As they collectively argued, regular bathing was an easy way for working-class individuals to find acceptance within middle- and upper-class society and for immigrants to demonstrate that they had fully assimilated to native-born culture. Cleanliness thus became a matter of personal self-development for most Americans—and was especially requisite for any citizen interested in climbing (or maintaining their current position on) the social ladder.[17]

But in part, the new value placed on the clean body was driven by beliefs about what it meant to participate in the collective project of American democracy. Stemming from eighteenth-century beliefs in American exceptionalism, two of the central projects of nineteenth-century American politics were defining the character of the United States as a nation and demonstrating the success of that character over its European counterparts. By the middle of the century, a tight connection between an individual's quest for personal development and the nation's quest for showcasing the unique strengths of American democracy had emerged. Publicly showcasing signals of one's moral stature subsequently came to function as a way for individuals to convey their commitment to themselves and their country in simultaneity, allowing regular bathing and "clean" toileting practices to proliferate in popularity for men and women alike. That popularity, however, followed gendered tropes. For men, hygiene was a symbol of masculinity that was thought to protect the state from the numerous perils associated with a weak or effeminate citizenry, while for women, hygienic knowledge was an important dimension of effectively maintaining the health and moral character of one's household. Hygiene thus served a dual function throughout the first few decades of the nineteenth century: it could not only uplift the masses, offering an opportunity for individuals to shed moral filth alongside physical dirt and pursue the American Dream, but it could also uplift the nation as a whole.[18]

That revolution in American hygiene was given several additional boosts by infrastructural and institutional developments leading up to the Progressive Era. One was a series of technological advancements that enabled public water systems to begin delivering water to private homes. By the middle of the nineteenth century, middle-class Americans had largely adopted the view that cleanliness was of personal and collective value; however, most cities did not have fully functioning municipal water systems until the 1870s and 1880s. The emergence of such systems therefore allowed more Americans than ever before to have technologies like running water and indoor water closets in their homes. In the wake of such emergent technologies, advertising as an institutional field also began to emerge. Manufacturers of soap, bathroom fixtures, and other such wares harnessed the new moral standard of cleanliness in the service of marketing bathing products to consumers interested in appearing as healthy and as respectable as possible: marketing messages upheld "toileting soap" as a distinctive and essential household need (despite having identical ingredients to laundry and other household soaps); plumbing supply houses began producing toilets with the domestic sensibilities of American men and women in mind; and international trade shows sensationalized American preferences for sanitation and hygiene as superior to those more prevalent in other parts of the globe. In short, plumbing and marketing innovations worked together to provide much of the necessary glue to adhere cleanliness, individual morality, and collective American identity together into a tight and compelling cultural package.[19]

Even more crucial, however, was the rise of another institutional field in the late nineteenth century: public health. Once a scattered set of localized moral reform campaigns, the American public health movement had evolved through the midcentury years into a centralized scientific and medical enterprise. Amid mounting scientific evidence that disease arose from microorganisms and not miasmas of bad air, medical professionals became actively involved in political advocacy for a number of transformations to civic law and health education meant to control the spread of contagious disease. By the turn of the twentieth century, such work had turned to cleaning up urban spaces. The combined effects of industrialization, urbanization, and population growth had brought unprecedented levels of filth to city streets in the United States, and a lack of effective water-cleaning technology meant that the increasing popularity of water closets in American homes was also leading to dangerous levels of contamination in urban water supplies. Numerous doctors and representatives from new public health organizations thus approached local and state politicians to address those issues in a range of American cities and towns. However, their requests were met with a divided response. When it came to private domiciles and the cleanliness of the water supply, local politicians and civic organizations were quick to implement design standards that would homogenize plumbing for the modern American home and more effectively filter waste to ensure drinking water was as safe as possible. But rather than investing extensively in public infrastructure (as many European nations were in the closing years of the nineteenth century), public restrooms were often dismissed as too costly or too trivial. Consequently, early progress toward indoor plumbing in the United States was largely restricted to the most American of institutions: private domiciles and the families who resided within them.[20]

The very first public comfort stations, restrooms, and toilets in the United States were thus, in many cases, not particularly public at all. The scant few public restrooms that were genuinely open to the public tended to be financed by private philanthropists who believed that such spaces were essential to improving the lot of urban slum dwellers. Yet financiers were generally more interested in providing the city's underclass with the opportunity to bathe—because of the moral boons still thought to derive from regular washing—rather than in facilitating the broader public's access to a clean toilet. As a result, where the ancestors to contemporary public restrooms were provided, they more often featured fixtures for bathing than for toileting, and they were typically located near tenements rather than in the commercial and industrial areas with the highest levels of pedestrian traffic. Where true public toilets existed in more centralized locations, they were often poorly maintained, not connected to a sewer, open to men and women alike, and in spaces that were within view of hundreds of passersby—which induced urban women to avoid them, local business owners to protest their existence, and city officials to agitate for their removal in the immediate wake of their construction. The consequence, then, was that the overwhelming majority of "public" toilets installed in the United States in the second half of the nineteenth century were located within privately owned middle- or upper-class establishments, such as hotels, railroad stations, and department stores. Such arrangements separated affluent city dwellers from the working class and the urban poor not only in a literal sense but in a symbolic sense as well: by enabling class-privileged citizens alone to maintain a respectable relationship to bodily waste in the public sphere.[21]

But such tendencies toward domesticity and privatization were not (yet) the death knell of the public toilet. Instead, thanks to the Progressive Era's explosion of social activism and political reform, the members of the citizenry least likely to use public conveniences for their own bodily needs—that is, affluent white women—mounted a series of urban crusades against poor hygiene, which included lobbying for the creation and expansion of public comfort stations. Where that lobbying work was most effective, however, was not with civic leaders—at least not directly. Instead, as chapter 2 explores in greater depth, their persuasive efforts found their strongest degree of resonance in the rapidly expanding professional fields of architecture, civil engineering, and urban planning, wherein builders and designers of all stripes were eager to establish themselves as legitimate experts on all things infrastructure. That flurry of concurrent changes in the upper- and upper-middle classes paved the way for the development of numerous public toilets in major American cities around the start of the twentieth century. At the same time, however, it also inaugurated a set of professional trends that would imbricate an affluent preference for gender separation into restroom design and construction for decades to come.

FROM ONE WORKPLACE WATER CLOSET TO TWO: 1880–1920

As the increasing popularity and potency of affluent women's Progressive Era activism suggests, the closing decades of the nineteenth century brought about more than dramatic changes to public plumbing. Those years also radically transformed the social organization of gender across the United States. Around the same time that medical and scientific discourses about sanitation were gaining traction in civic spheres, the accumulation of medical and scientific advances from the eighteenth and nineteenth centuries was also bringing about a profound revolution in defining the sex of bodies. In what historian Alice Dreger refers to as the "Age of Gonads," efforts to definitively categorize gendered bodies began to rely upon physical markers, such as the distinction between ovarian and testicular tissue, as the defining characteristic that differentiated the newly scientific categories of female and male from one another. Abundant efforts to identify the corporeal characteristics of each sex soon followed, and American researchers cataloged an endless array of embodied distinctions between female and male forms. Genitals, patterns of facial and body hair, adipose and muscular tissues, endocrine systems, erotic desires and drives, personality characteristics, and even personal hobbies were transmogrified into evidence of supposedly biological and immutable sexual difference. In short, no longer was gender understood to be an aspect of one's character or moral constitution, as it had for many centuries before; instead, it came to represent an empirically observable quality of the material body—one that professional scientists alone appeared to be equipped to explore.[22]

The power and authority vested in such findings had far-reaching implications for how women and their bodies would be treated in a variety of institutional spheres, but they were unusually resonant in late nineteenth-century labor markets—where two other cultural shifts were also under way. First, lawmakers began to take an interest in the labor movement and in protecting all members of the American workforce from employer abuses; the nascent legislation that grew out of that interest included provisions that would require employers to provide their employees with adequate toilet facilities. Second, scientific management, a new administrative paradigm that harnessed scientific principles in order to evaluate individual workers and workplace procedures alike, was quickly gaining traction as a reigning ideology in the world of work. The provision of showers and toilets, rest periods of a specially calculated length, and shorter workdays became an integral component of enabling business owners to maximize employment efficiency and, thus, their profit margins. With a mounting corpus of empirical research about the unique physical capacities of men and women, gender quickly became integral to both workplace transformations. A number of state legislatures passed laws mandating rest periods and workday lengths that differed for men and women, and scientific management provided a fertile foundation on which such gender-distinct treatment could be justified. As a result, where debates about the politics of gender were all but absent in civic discourse about public toilets—or about the quasi-public restrooms available in leisure spaces—they were omnipresent in discussions of workplace restrooms.[23]

Far from mandating equivalent treatment, however, the guidance of nascent sex-difference science held that female bodies were inherently weaker and more vulnerable than male ones. Indeed, as sanitation came to the forefront of legislative agendas in the early twentieth century, the first discussions requiring the gender separation of restrooms in any sphere revolved around the allegedly unique perils of factory work for women's bodies. When Massachusetts passed the first state law requiring the sex-segregation of public toilets, for instance, the law pertained only to businesses in which "male and female persons" were "employed in the same factory or workshop."[24] Similarly, when New York became the second state to legally require that "the water-closets used by females shall be separate and apart from those used by males" in work settings, the rationale offered for that and other toilet statutes explicitly drew on language about the health and well-being of female workers.[25] And by the turn of the twentieth century, as federal policymakers started to take an interest in workplace safety and sanitation, even Department of Labor studies described workplace restrooms as a haven in which women could rest and recuperate when the onerousness of factory labor depleted them physically. Gender-separated restrooms consequently became a bureaucratic metric for determining whether or not a factory provided acceptable working conditions for its growing female workforce—allowing gender difference *and* gender inequality to be built into new workplace policies and procedures at a breakneck pace.[26]

But in the documents and conversations surrounding such changes, even more important than protecting the health and safety of working women was protecting the health and safety of their imagined future offspring. Because paid labor was perceived as a detriment to women's physical condition for pregnancy, public debates about women at work—and about infrastructural transformations, like the gender separation of workplace restrooms—often revolved around safeguarding women's reproductive potential and ability to fulfill the domestic and maternal duties expected of them. What the architects of protective statutes had in mind, however, was not just a woman and her own family; rather, they imagined that gender-separated workplace bathrooms would protect the entire nation from the spread of rampant deviance and immoral behavior. Such anxieties about the possibility of large-scale social disorder also found a ready companion in legal thought: for instance, in the Supreme Court's landmark decision in *Muller v. Oregon*, which unanimously justified the constitutionality of protective statues in 1908, Justice Brewer wrote, "As

[handwritten: women only matter bc they reproduce]

healthy mothers are essential to vigorous offspring, the physical well-being of woman becomes an object of public interest."[27] In short, a lack of workplace restrooms and toilets for women not only threatened workplace sanitation, violated the new science of gendered bodily difference, and promised an individual's moral degeneration; a lack of available, clean, and well-furnished workplace restrooms was also an omen of community disintegration—and, consequently, seemed to portend the downfall of the United States as a whole.[28]

Those imagined risks to collective morality were so rhetorically persuasive that they also allowed a new cache of more granular restroom regulations to emerge across the country—ones that required the provision of screens, doors, and locks to ensure that individuals using workplace restrooms would not have their most intimate bodily functions observed by onlookers. Once again, the rationales for such policies were unavoidably gendered. Although some elected officials appealed to a need for working men and women alike to preserve their modesty, most described privacy features as beneficial to women in particular—so that they would be able to veil their uncovered bodies from the potentially prying eyes of male coworkers. In other words, lawmakers openly inserted a series of reigning cultural beliefs about gender and sexuality into restroom regulations: beliefs that men could not be trusted to control themselves, beliefs that women could not be trusted to protect their own virtue, and beliefs that all working people could not be trusted to preserve social and sexual hygiene without a deluge of privacy accommodations to encourage them. Consequently, by 1920, such fears of prophesized social problems and desires to protect an imagined future America had pushed nearly every other state in the country to join Massachusetts and New York in enacting laws mandating gender separation in workplace restrooms, with many states opting for multiple privacy regulations on top of that basic fare.[29]

Thus, instead of leveraging the more egalitarian rhetoric that led to feminist successes around women's suffrage rights—such as overt challenges to the presumed distinction between public and private spheres—efforts to enact laws mandating gender-specific workplace restrooms ultimately reinforced cultural messages about men's and women's supposedly intrinsic differences and about unbridled heterosexual desire. Paradoxically, then, new laws governing workplace bathrooms were "equal but separate":

[handwritten: screwed up women's suffrage too]

they required restroom facilities for female workers equivalent to those already in place for male workers, but the organizational and legal logics underlying that push for equivalence tended to distinguish women's bodies as uniquely weak, vulnerable, maternal, and above all, at risk of sexual predation. And that transcription of gender ideologies into the letter of the law would only grow stronger in the decades to come. Starting in the 1960s, restroom-related legislation in the United States gave way to restroom-related litigation, as cases began to arrive on the dockets of the federal courts that questioned just how equal and just how separate gender-specific workplace restrooms had to be. I trace the evolution of that jurisprudence from its postwar emergence through twenty-first-century courtroom conflicts—with particular attention to whether (and why) beliefs about embodied gender difference influence legal decision-making—in chapter 3.

FROM QUASI-PUBLIC RESTROOMS TO PUBLIC CONVENIENCES AND BACK AGAIN: 1905–1970

The cultural connection between femininity and domesticity may have reinforced a number of pernicious stereotypes about women's bodies and gendered privacy when it came to twentieth-century workplace restrooms, but it also offered a surprisingly progressive foundation for the expansion of true public restrooms thereafter. Owing to a collective belief that their role as the moral guardians of the home extended into the public sphere, affluent women launched a series of moral reform campaigns across the United States in the early twentieth century to increase the safety, decency, and cleanliness of cities and towns—campaigns that extended for several decades beyond the close of the Progressive Era. Not only could restrooms promote personal hygiene and lessen the spread of disease among urban denizens, as they were so celebrated for doing at the turn of the century, but they would also allow businessmen, travelers, and families in town for only one afternoon to access proper toilets, sinks, and resting areas while they were visiting. That interest in providing for an increasingly mobile citizenry found an additional burst of support in a series of federal works projects in the 1920s and 1930s, which led to the creation of new public comfort stations and public restrooms in parks, roadways, railway stops, and other municipal attractions in the outskirts of many growing American cities. Indeed, until the depths of the Great Depression struck and curtailed public spending on virtually all civic fronts, public restrooms soared in number and popularity throughout the United States in the first three decades of the twentieth century.[30]

Outside of major metropolitan areas and their immediate surroundings, the quantity and quality of public toilets was also increasing—but not entirely as a consequence of targeted political activism or even the indirect effects of changes to federal bureaucracy. Rather, in rural areas and the rapidly expanding American suburbs, public restrooms expanded as a response to a wider cultural and technological shift unfolding in the United States: the rise of the automobile. Existing forms of public transportation, such as locomotives, had previously limited where and when Americans could readily travel, and the high cost of private transportation (typically via horse and buggy) was not financially accessible to most citizens. Cars, however, offered a huge number of Americans a newfound ability to live, work, and play in a greater diversity of places than ever before, and they provided ready-made opportunities for civil servants and small business owners alike to expand public infrastructure. To that end, new organizational forms and attendant restroom spaces erupted over the next few decades on American roadsides. In the 1910s, municipal campgrounds cropped up, allowing travelers to camp overnight with access to running water and outdoor privies; in the 1920s, roadside service stations, eager to outdo one another, began offering products for automotive maintenance and transformed their unisex outdoor privies into indoor, gendersegregated restrooms; and in the 1930s, federal public works projects created an unprecedented number of restrooms in public parks and alongside the growing American interstate system. Thus, true public restrooms were reaching an unprecedented level of accessibility and availability throughout the country.[31] *now they are everywhere*

But at the same time, that golden age of American restrooms was far from an egalitarian new future for public facilities. All too often, newly constructed restrooms reproduced familiar inequalities between social groups. In urban comfort stations, suburban service centers, and railway terminals, the high cost of public restroom maintenance induced many lawmakers and small business owners to charge fees for toilet access, making public facilities virtually inaccessible to would-be poor users and discouraging women from using them—as, in many cases, fees were either heftier for women or only assessed for the use of a toilet stall. In cities where women's groups had lobbied so intensively for the provision of public comfort stations, affluent women tended to favor the toilet options available to them in department stores, hotels, and restaurants. This was for multiple reasons: comfort stations were often less well-maintained than quasi-public restrooms, they sometimes lacked full doors or stalls, and they put upper-class women in close contact with immigrants and lower-class men loitering at the entrance. And as plans to build new comfort stations expanded beyond the Northeast and Midwest and into Southern cities like Atlanta and Baltimore, Jim Crow laws mandating racial segregation spread from schools, workplaces, and public transit centers to new public restroom facilities as well—largely to neutralize the perception of any threats to the safety of affluent white women in public spaces. In effect, the net number of public toilets in the United States was steadily increasing, but access to public facilities remained heavily fractured—or became even more fractured—along gendered, classed, and racial lines.[32]

By the middle of the twentieth century, however, laws related to restroom provision took yet another swing back in the direction of democratization. Following the successes of the civil rights movement in the 1950s and 1960s, architectural traces of racial segregation—such as separate building entrances, duplicate water fountains, and basement toilets—were among the first effects of Jim Crow laws to be relabeled, repurposed, or removed throughout the American South. Around that same time, the congressional passage of the Federal-Aid Highway Act of 1954 and President Eisenhower's commitment to improving America's interstate transit system led to extensive federal funding for highway expansion and maintenance—an investment that created a revenue stream for fixtures such as rest stops and public restrooms in addition to asphalt and signage. Over the course of the 1960s and 1970s, the growing women's liberation movement pushed for women's voices to be heard in the public sphere, and new physical spaces were created to reflect that increasing public presence—all the way down to the modest public toilet. The tyranny of the pay toilet fell, too. Thanks to the combined efforts of that growing feminist movement, an intrepid and insistent group of college students who branded themselves as the "Committee to End Pay Toilets in America," and local lawmakers throughout the country, the ten-cent charge associated with accessing many comfort stations and washrooms became a relic of the past. In short, the future of public restrooms in the United States seemed decidedly optimistic.[33] ↳ all movements pushed to ban the pay

Unfortunately, while laws related to public restroom availability and access were moving in a dramatically more equitable direction, on-the-ground support for public facilities waned just as dramatically. With the revenue that came from dime locks on toilet stalls now unavailable and no new sources of local funding implemented to replace them, public restrooms became more and more dirty, more and more broken, and more and more abandoned by the towns and cities that had installed them in previous decades. Without the presence of paid attendants to supervise them, crime and illicit behavior—both real and imagined—flourished in abandoned comfort stations and public toilets. Not only did police activity and crime reports related to vandalism, drug dealing, and sex work in or around public restrooms skyrocket in many American cities from the 1960s through the 1980s, but anxieties about public sexuality (and especially public homosexuality) from many decades before resurfaced with a vengeance—helped along by scholarly research arguing that homosexuality was a psychological dysfunction and media furor about men having sex with other men in public washrooms. So, with little funding left to support them, and the rise of widespread skepticism about their safety, the overwhelming majority of true public restrooms were shut down at some point in the second half of the twentieth century.[34]

But even as the number of truly public restrooms in the United States headed toward that unfortunate nadir, a flood of new restrooms—ungendered ones—began to emerge in the final two decades of the twentieth century. They simply did so behind the gatekeeping doors of many libraries, museums, restaurants, civic centers, and other such organizations—whose efforts to build gender-neutral restrooms are the central focus of chapters 4 and 5. Specifically, chapter 4 kicks off the contemporary half of the book by investigating the diverse institutional impulses that led civic and municipal organizations to seek out ungendered restrooms around the turn of the twenty-first century—and shows that an even more diverse set of architectural forces thwarted the more widespread adoption of such toileting spaces. Chapter 5 follows up with a parallel excavation of gender-neutral restroom adoption among cultural organizations, but with a more inward approach—by focusing attention on organizational actors themselves and how they use the power of conversation to manage the meaning of their restrooms to their patrons and the broader public.

FROM SEPARATE SPACES TO EQUAL SQUARE FOOTAGE: 1945–1995

Around the same time that beliefs about the value of public conveniences were oscillating tumultuously throughout the United States, equally radical shifts in beliefs about men's and women's roles, too, were afoot. In the wake of World War II, an increased cultural emphasis on domestic roles for women arose and brought about a surge in marriage and childbirth rates; however, by the 1960s, those trends had begun to slow, and the character of American families began to shift dramatically. Beliefs about family formation shifted from an understanding of marriage as a pairing of complementary roles toward a more individualized view of the institution as a vehicle for personal fulfillment. The suggestion that laws regarding separation, divorce, and remarriage should be loosened or altered began to materialize in state legislatures around the country. Perhaps most importantly, an unprecedented number of women pursued opportunities for higher education and entered the market for paid work—and slowly but surely began to outpace men in their rates of college enrollment and completion. Against this dynamic cultural backdrop, fierce debates about workplace gender equity took center stage at the national level. Working-class women, some of whom had been in the labor force for many years, began to agitate about workplace gender discrimination and pushed politicians at all governmental levels to recognize their concerns. Wealthier women found representation within the National Woman's Party, which sought to repeal much protective legislation from earlier decades and replace those laws with more equitable—and less sexist—

regulations. And for all women, the changing relationship between gender and work in the United States would reverberate through law and politics for years to come.[35]

Such expanding interest in workplace parity got an unexpected bump in the 1960s from the inclusion of the word *sex* in the Civil Rights Act of 1964. Unexpected, because the amendment that added gender to Title VII—that is, the portion of the act governing employment—was a tactic originally designed to diminish congressional interest in passing the bill. The act nonetheless passed in both the House and the Senate by an overwhelming margin and was signed into law by President Lyndon B. Johnson two weeks later. But given the unusual circumstances of the inclusion of a sex-discrimination clause in the final law, the new Equal Employment Opportunity Commission initially hesitated to pursue legal action about gender inequality. Unlike their implementation of the race-oriented portions of the act, which they understood to apply as written, the commission attempted to balance the language of the sex discrimination provision with their own understanding of the purportedly unique needs of actual women workers. Most employment laws differentiating workers on the basis of race were thus quickly targeted and repealed, while state protective laws that distinguished men from women often remained intact—often because academics and activists who fully supported codified gender equity in the 1960s believed that removing such distinctions altogether would be harmful.[36] (Or, as Pauli Murray and Mary O. Eastwood wrote in the *George Washington Law Review* in 1965, "Obviously, society has a legitimate interest in the protection of women's maternal and familial functions."[37]) Consequently, in the years that followed, separating justifiable gender differentiation from unjustifiable gender discrimination became a challenge for legislative bodies and federal agencies to untangle.[38]

Workplace restrooms thus became an unusually contentious and politically charged site for delineating when, where, and why men and women could be physically segregated in the second half of the twentieth century. At the federal level, the Equal Employment Opportunity Commission continued to adjust and amend its general employment guidelines, eventually determining in the early 1970s that any laws providing benefits like minimum wage guarantees, premium overtime, or the meal- and rest-period laws from earlier decades to women alone would indeed constitute

tension in the workplace surrounding gender equality → tension in the bathroom

a violation of Title VII. Plus, the creation of the Department of Labor's Occupational Safety and Health Administration in the early 1970s instituted new national requirements for the availability of a prescribed number of sanitary toilets in all permanent workplaces; those requirements further stipulated that, if the number of employees in permanent workplaces exceeded a certain minimum, the toilets in those workplaces also needed to be separated by gender. In an effort to maintain compliance with those new federal guidelines, many states subsequently repealed or amended existing laws related to gender and workplace restrooms. The few statutes that escaped unscathed tended to espouse the more gender-neutral language sanctioned by the Equal Employment Opportunity Commission, requiring employers to arrange for "separate toilets and washrooms for *males and females*" or "separate lavatories or toilet rooms *for each sex*" (emphases mine).[39] The net effect of all such transformations was a shift in the dominant legal framework for restroom regulation from paternalistic protection for women toward equivalent treatment for men and women alike.[40]

But moves toward restroom equity for women were not restricted solely to American workplaces; instead, such legislative efforts extended into educational and public spheres as well. When it came to education, gender took center stage with congressional passage of the Education Amendments of 1972—better known today as Title IX. Although Title IX did not explicitly mention restrooms (instead quietly covering them with the broader umbrella of "facilities"), concern about their separation nonetheless erupted on the Capitol floor itself as the bill was being discussed. Concerned senators, for instance, clashed over how best to legislate equity into college sports programs while also enabling toilets, locker rooms, and shower facilities to continue to be gender-segregated. And when it came to public spaces, professional organizations and restroom activists alike pushed local and state lawmakers to champion "potty parity" for women in commercial and civic establishments. Twenty-four states and hundreds of municipalities heeded those pleas, passing statutes that acknowledged the unique challenges that women confront in public restrooms—such as complications in feminine dress that make toilet use difficult and the persistent onus of children's bathroom and other care needs—and mandated that newly constructed or renovated buildings were to reserve extra square footage for women's restrooms. Thus, gender separation was once again being written into multiple layers of law governing restrooms at an unprecedented rate.[41]

By the closing years of the century, a new political force further refracted such public conversations about gender and restroom access: the transgender rights movement. At once a part of and apart from the lesbian and gay rights movement that had begun to coalesce in the United States in the mid-1970s, transgender activism exploded in the 1990s as middle-class activists and social movement organizations began to lobby for legal rights, access to medical services, and other institutional changes that spoke specifically to the needs of individuals whose gender identity or expression differed from that which they were assigned at birth. Academic researchers and community activists subsequently worked together to shed light on the high likelihood of interrogation, verbal harassment, and physical assault faced by transgender people, masculine women, and feminine men alike in public restrooms. That attention has allowed support for gender-neutral bathrooms to grow substantially in recent years, with notable inroads being made at colleges and universities, upscale restaurants, shopping centers, and transportation hubs in some parts of the United States. And even more recently, those conversations have extended into municipal, state, and federal lawmaking bodies, which have introduced—and, in many cases, passed—new legislative proposals that mandate the addition of gender-neutral restroom spaces to public, commercial, and educational establishments whenever space allows.[42]

Of those many ongoing changes, one of the most visible and hotly contested has been the increasing popularity of gender-inclusive facilities at American colleges and universities since the turn of the twenty-first century. Specifically, in the last twenty years, over two hundred institutions of higher education in the United States have adopted policies allowing undergraduate students to reside in gender-neutral housing, and dozens more have converted some of their restrooms into ungendered facilities. Both sets of changes have sought to reduce the occurrence of harassment and violence directed toward transgender students, faculty, and staff and to convey a broader message of institutional inclusion for students with diverse gender identities and expressions. Despite those lofty aims, however, the diffusion of support for such students and such spaces has not been a smooth

Colleges have made the biggest efforts

and seamless process. I explore that tension in chapter 6, as I uncover how administrators and staff from colleges and universities across the country accomplish radical institutional transformations when confronted with seemingly insurmountable bureaucratic obstacles. Moreover, in doing so, I also document how an abundance of interactional and institutional work happens behind the scenes to bring restroom renovations in all manner of formal organizations to fruition.

THE HIDDEN PRIVILEGE OF "POTTY POLITICS"

All in all, then, the history of restroom gendering and un-gendering in the United States has been a discontinuous, sometimes turbulent, often repetitive series of fits and starts—through which tradition and progress have operated in simultaneity. In the nineteenth century, as the public-bath movement strove to spread the new science of cleanliness in many North American cities, it helped usher in strong local support for investments in indoor plumbing. Yet movement activists also advocated that recent immigrants adopt modes of bodily care that would highlight their commitment to the gender-bifurcated and class-inflected ideals of masculine citizenship or feminine domesticity. Around the turn of the twentieth century, as elected officials argued in favor of the first-ever laws mandating gender separation in workplace restrooms, they sought to enact some of the first-ever legal protections for white-collar workers to ensure their health and safety. But they also drew from the highly politicized science of sex differences and beliefs in scientific management to argue for those ends. And in the second half of the twentieth century, as activists and politicians rode the coattails of the women's movement and the civil rights movement to push for legal mandates for restroom equity, they successfully engendered the expansion of true public restrooms throughout the United States. Unfortunately, however, those interventions also laid the groundwork for restroom facilities to retreat back into private establishments—creating new inequalities of access through de facto means rather than de jure ones.

In part, my telling of that discontinuous and turbulent history makes an intellectual contribution in its own right, because it reveals how the

↗ history repeats itself

restroom debates of the present often repeat the restroom debates of the past. In larger part, moreover, that history starts to establish three central themes for *Bathroom Battlegrounds*—themes that have recurred across the overlapping restroom eras I document in this chapter, and themes that will recur over the rest of this book.

First, and most related to my introduction's theoretical overview, the history of public restrooms and the history of gender in the United States are inextricable from one another. Sweeping changes to cultural beliefs about sexed bodies, political rights for women, and everyday expectations about gendered interactions have all been important motivating factors for a wide range of historical debates about public restrooms: where they are needed, who ought to be responsible for their construction and maintenance, when they should be separated by gender, and why they ultimately take the physical form that they do. But conversely, because of their tight connections to the physical body and to our most personal sense of privacy, restrooms have also been critical prisms through which individuals and organizations alike have sought to define gender—because they have been inextricably intertwined with public conversations about what constitutes femaleness and maleness in the first place. This is perhaps most palpable in the contentious restroom politics of the Progressive Era, wherein gendered toilets worked as a guise for debating the physical potential of childbearing bodies, but it has been no less relevant a hundred years later, as today's colleges and universities grapple with the reach and consequences of gender equity laws like Title IX.

Gender, however, has never been the sole input or output of such restroom debates. Instead, whether public agitators for a restroom revolution were nineteenth-century public bath reformers, twentieth-century activists lobbying for protective legislation, or twenty-first-century proponents of restroom ungendering, another set of cultural distinctions has accompanied gender through every one of those historical epochs: status boundaries. Second, then, the shifting shape of American public restrooms has tended to reflect—or even amplify—cultural and material hierarchies associated with social class. For instance, the discursive appeals to cleanliness, children, and contagion that first motivated the gender separation of public restrooms in the nineteenth and twentieth centuries were as much about ensuring the ascendancy of affluent Americans as about reflecting deep-seated beliefs in gender difference. And although there have been passing moments across those same centuries in which true public restrooms have flourished in cities and towns across the United States, owing most notably to the lobbying efforts of affluent women's groups invested in public hygiene around the turn of the twentieth century, most of those restrooms have quite literally disintegrated as the political interests of the privileged classes have moved on to different priorities. In fact, even where legal regulations or professional building codes were put into place to ensure the gender separation of so-called "public" restrooms, those regulations have tended to be narrowly focused on one type of formal organization, such as hotels, restaurants, or performance spaces.

As a result, the third theme of this book—and the most important takeaway from this chapter—is this: patterns of class stratification have consistently shaped the definition of what a "public" restroom in the United States is, and that definition has almost always been more restricted than truly public. In other words, the history of American public restrooms has largely been a history of *quasi*-public restrooms: that is, those housed within the confines of restaurants, libraries, workplaces, and so forth. Individual organizations have therefore enjoyed a tremendous amount of discretion in shaping not only the physical realities of their restrooms, but the conversation about all restrooms across the United States. Indeed, for gender-segregated leisure spaces in the nineteenth century, such as barbershops and ladies' reading rooms, business owners set out to provide a convenience for their patrons, not to start the ball rolling on a multicentury process of imbricating beliefs about gendered propriety into the built environment. Likewise, for lawmakers in the second half of the twentieth century, progressive impulses fueled attempts to legally ensure gender equity in workplace restrooms and public establishments alike, but those efforts required "public" restrooms to be available only in those establishments frequented by the consumer class. Even today, state statutes requiring single-occupancy restrooms to be relabeled gender-neutral, like the one signed into law in California in late 2016, apply only to buildings in which a single-user restroom is already available—which puts the onus on property owners and managers to create such a space in the first place.

Thus, while many social scientists studying restrooms over the last forty years have found that "dirty" discourses—about bodily waste, about elimination behaviors, and about toilets themselves—are often deliberately invoked to subjugate already marginalized social groups,[43] I end this short historical tour by suggesting a corollary: that social inequalities produced in and through restroom infrastructure are just as much a side effect of mundane organizational processes as they are a deliberate act of discrimination. As Chuck Tilly argues in *Durable Inequality,* when organizational actors deploy cultural categories to solve their everyday problems—which, for better or for worse, they must do to weather the incessant crush of decisions that must be made within bureaucracies of all kinds—the result is often the unintentional manufacturing of inequality.[44] And while those incidental, sometimes even accidental, forms of social stratification may seem less insidious than more overt acts of bias or exclusion, the reality is often the opposite. Because such acts do not fit the conventional American paradigm for what inequality looks like—that is, intentional acts of prejudice carried out by ill-meaning social actors—they are much more challenging to see, let alone eradicate. This, I would argue, is even more profoundly true of organizational decision-making related to taboo social topics like toilets and restrooms, because such topics so often veer toward the unmentionable. In other words, because "potty politics" seem so marginal, so unimportant, so impolite, they are an especially potent means of producing and reproducing multiple social hierarchies.

Across what remains of this book, then, I take those mundane organizational processes seriously. By doing so, I will first show how gender is not simply an independent variable that has exerted—and continues to exert—an influence on the shape and separation of American public restrooms at any given moment in time. Although the organizations I study do draw on hegemonic gender ideologies to inform their restroom-related choices, those choices and, indeed, the very meaning of gender itself are also shaped by a wide range of other cultural phenomena: the quest for legitimacy among new professions, emotional responses to bodily exposure, the clever invocation of law to overcome the material limits of buildings, the ease with which one comports oneself in conversation, and the interpersonal interactions that enable support for once-unthink-able kinds of institutional innovation to blossom.

Then, once I have shown how those varied social forces collude to shape public restrooms and the meaning of gender in simultaneity, I can turn to my ultimate hope for *Bathroom Battlegrounds:* that, in revealing the complex interplay among ideology, institutions, and inequality at the heart of the gender order, my work will accelerate the dissolution of the interlocking social hierarchies that "potty politics" so often uphold. To both those projects, I now turn.

2 Professionalizing Plumbing

> While the accommodating and progressive business men of
> our city are making preparations for erecting a free lodg-
> ing-house and feed stable for the convenience of customers
> from a distance, would it not be well to consider the fitting
> up of a toilet-room for the wives and daughters of farmers
> who come to our city for a day's shopping?
>
> An anonymous reader, "Current Comment in Mississippi,"
> *Times-Picayune*, October 1899

In April of 1907, the city engineer of Hartford, Connecticut, Frederick L. Ford, mailed a report to Eugene Levering, the president of Baltimore's Free Bath Commission, "advocating the establishment of public comfort stations in Baltimore." Before sending his correspondence, Ford had spent some time in Baltimore surveying the city's neighborhoods and development, both for his own edification and in the spirit of helping members of the commission determine where best to install public conveniences. Although the city council had recently approved an ordinance allocating $20,000—which, accounting for inflation, would total nearly half a million dollars today—"for the establishment of one or two stations," the council needed to pass another bill to finalize the location of the facilities' construction. With Ford's guidance in mind, the commission proposed that the new attraction occupy the corner of Lombard Street and Centre Market Place, an "especially desirable" location, in Ford's words, "because it will serve the three monumental public markets which the city is now erecting" as well as "a large section of the city to the north and east."[1]

Elsewhere in Baltimore, residents were abuzz with the possibility that a similar structure might make its way to their neighborhood. Some imagined that new public toilets and washrooms could help offer "a great comfort and convenience" to the most "densely populated" sections of the city. Citizens living and working along South Broadway, for instance, believed that a comfort station installed nearby would quite literally clean up the streets—particularly in light of the unsavory habits of certain "seafaring men" who "board near the wharves at the foot of Broadway."[2] Others hoped that public plumbing could substitute in for other forms of city development and, by extension, help quash other social ills across the city. As one prominent member of the South Baltimore Business Men's Association reported to a *Baltimore Sun* reporter, a comfort station on the lot adjacent to the State Tobacco Warehouse would be a vast improvement over the "iron-covered shed" the city council originally planned to put into place, because that structure, while useful for storing tobacco barrels, would undoubtedly become "a loafing place for negroes and tramps."[3]

Most of all, many local business owners expected that the establishment or expansion of such facilities would lead to palpable economic gains. One druggist owning a small pharmacy near Canton Avenue was "enthusiastic" for multiple reasons over the interest his fellow merchants had shown toward the possibility of a South Broadway station. In addition to serving the "large number of sailors who come ashore at the foot of Broadway from sailboats that lay in the flats," a comfort station would be a tremendous benefit, he contended, to the enormous influx of customers and retailers who exchanged goods in his neighborhood once a week. "Every market day thousands of persons from all over East Baltimore, Highlandtown, and Canton go to the market," he observed, and "[f]armers from Baltimore county go to the market to sell their wares" as well. That "densely populated section around the market" was, in his view, "sufficient proof of the great need" for civic investment in public conveniences. Thus, he concluded, "[a] public comfort station should be built on South Broadway at once."[4]

Not every resident and business owner saw rising interest in public comfort stations as a positive trend, however. One cigar store owner worried that the city would "have a great deal of difficulty" in keeping a comfort station near Pratt Street from being flooded because of its alarmingly close "proximity to the harbor." A hide dealer expressed apprehensions that passersby would find the Pratt station "positively objectionable," so much so that they would cease "us[ing] the thoroughfare" and eventually drive down his sales.⁵ And foreshadowing Baltimore's twenty-first-century ranking as one of the twenty most congested metropolitan areas in America,⁶ one "close observer" with "wide knowledge of the needs of the municipality" pointed out that both sides of Pratt Street faced "a constant stream of vehicles all day long." As a result, even if the comfort station were installed underground, "the approaches would have to be above the ground," meaning that "traffic could be handled with less freedom." In short, he groused, "Where else in the city is traffic so congested?"⁷

But as that denunciation suggested, it was not the *idea* of comfort stations that posed a problem for most opponents. Rather, they reasoned, the *details* of their installation simply needed reconsideration. According to one group of merchants threatening "to protest against the proposed action" of installing a comfort station in Hopkins Place, the mayor and Public Bath Commission both erred egregiously in approving funds to put such a "nuisance" in a spot "hallowed by historical significance that clings to none other in the city"—one the merchants believed to be deserving of a monument to the Continental Congress, which "held a number of important meetings" there, or even to the street's namesake, Johns Hopkins. They recommended moving the installation to the Baltimore-Washington railway terminal, "up nearer to the shopping district," where it would also "be of greater service to the ladies for whom the building is chiefly provided." For another group of objectors, the problem was more aesthetic than historical. Some worried about the "harmonious appearance" of nearby buildings; others conceded that a "conspicuous" comfort station "would be useful," but "the less pretentious, the better it would be." Otherwise, one gentleman worried, "it might become an eyesore."⁸

To ameliorate those concerns, city planners and builders in Baltimore opted for a strategy common in other American cities investing in public conveniences in the same era: making the South Broadway station more ostentatious than subdued. Just as one of New York City's most popular comfort stations featured "ornate entrances" with "three ornamental lamps" between the separate men's and women's doors, the comfort station endorsed in Frederick L. Ford's correspondence with Eugene Levering came to be a "prettily constructed one story affair, with two rooms, one for women and the other for men."⁹ Moreover, as the city council planned the development of "several more stations" throughout "the central part of the city," they found that city residents were quite agreeable to their construction—if they planned them "along lines that will have regard not alone for growth, but also for beauty."[10] Public conveniences, therefore, did not just need to be "built in a sanitary manner and kept scrupulously clean," as president Levering averred, but also erected in a fashion "no different from the best toilet facilities in the best hotels and apartment houses in the city."[11]

.   .   .   .   .

At the dawn of the twentieth century, nearly every corner of American society was changing, and rapidly so. Technological advances like the development of the modern electrical grid took hold in American industry, allowing production and profits to reach unprecedented new heights. Economic growth fueled the creation of more and larger industrial factories, which drew citizens into urban areas from the countryside for work; there, they settled and established families, causing the population of cities like Chicago, New York, and Philadelphia to increase seven- to tenfold between the mid-1800s and early 1900s. Plus, new scientific advances, especially the germ theory of disease and the development of vaccinations for contagious threats like typhoid fever and cholera, allowed an average adult's life expectancy to steadily ascend. Yet those incredible gains were not without drawbacks. As the United States started to become a paragon of industrial growth, it also started to become a paragon of wealth inequality, with waves of new immigrants and the urban working class unable to achieve the same gains from factory expansion as their middle- and upper-class employers. Industrialization and urbanization brought about increasingly crowded and unsanitary living conditions, making the spread of disease accelerate even as medical advances able to thwart that diffusion were accumulating. Thus, as historian Peter Baldwin observes, increasing inequality and urban density conspired to make "the sight and smell of bodily waste obtrusive facts of life."[12]

Because of that "obtrusive" reality, indoor plumbing was a critical nexus of scientific and technological development in that same era. As early as the 1840s, frustrations with the troublesome and odorous character of outdoor privies led architects to bring plumbing indoors, both in private domiciles and in businesses such as hotels and department stores. The invention of the indoor water closet soon followed, with porcelain bowls quickly supplanting metal ones, siphonic flushing mechanisms replacing the prone-to-contamination hopper, and dedicated toilet rooms becoming a necessary design feature in all manner of new buildings. It was not until the closing decades of the century, however, that those transformations drew attention in more-public spheres. Owing to a parallel renovation in municipal government, local politicians began to stop branding themselves as responsive only to the needs of their most affluent citizens and well-off business owners. Instead, they adopted a more liberal ethos of community service provision, investing in public education, public health services, and public infrastructure. But politicians were not alone in directing their attention to toilets. The emerging professional class—filled with medical experts eager to establish their competence at protecting public health, as well as architects and engineers looking to build the most up-to-date public structures possible—was just as integral to cultivating support for the expansion of late-nineteenth-century public plumbing.[13]

This chapter explores those two institutional fields, the health professions and the building professions, with the help of 186 articles published in academic and trade periodicals about toilet-related infrastructure between 1872 and 1926—an archival proxy for how specialists and experts would have talked aloud about public plumbing in those years. Specifically, I compare and contrast the language and logics deployed in articles published in health and medical periodicals with those published in architectural, engineering, and planning periodicals. As that multi-institutional and comparative approach allows me to show, new scientific findings about the nature of gendered bodies were a site of robust intellectual debate for public health professionals in the late nineteenth century. Yet when it came to the prospect of public water closets, medical experts distanced themselves from the vagaries of nineteenth-century gender politics. Instead, they drew on new studies of disease and hygiene to establish themselves as credible experts in the management of the public's health and, by extension, of public plumbing. Specifically, their logic went, they collectively owed the public the benefit of their knowledge and expertise, and that necessitated their involvement in turn-of-the-twentieth-century "potty politics."

no interest in gender, interest in everyone's health and sanitation

But for builders and engineers, the science of sanitation opened a very different set of political possibilities. Although they, too, leveraged scientific vocabulary to mark their training and expertise as specialized and thus inimitable by outsiders, only medical experts extolled the virtues of science for the public good. Architectural professionals, on the other hand, took a more privatized approach—by celebrating the marketability of scientific principles and the aura of modernity those principles enabled. For comfort stations and public restrooms in particular, the efficacy of that aura further hinged on the visible alignment of such spaces with the private toileting facilities already available to affluent citizens in the business establishments they frequented—which, around the turn of the twentieth century, were increasingly gender segregated by design. That process of quietly absorbing middle- and upper-class expectations about gendered privacy and sexual propriety into professional guidelines for planning public space, which I refer to as *occupational osmosis*, was an important pathway through which gender separation grew from an elite affectation into a defining feature of American public restrooms. Moreover, that osmosis would do more than divide turn-of-the-century comfort stations into distinctive men's and women's compartments. It would also bring a tenacious form of institutional and material inertia to the fore—one that would overdetermine the shape of restroom regulations and plumbing infrastructure in the United States for decades to come.

elite class played a large role at this time

"THE PROPER PROVISION OF PUBLIC-COMFORT STATIONS IS AXIOMATIC"

Nineteenth-century gender relations in the United States are often described with the metaphor of "separate spheres." Women, such thinking goes, were relegated to the private domain to care for their homes and raise their families, while men freely worked in public industry and civic affairs. And many dimensions of American social life two centuries ago did embody what historian Barbara Welter calls "the cult of True Womanhood"—by preserving the visage of women's piety, purity, and domesticity through spatial gender segregation.[14] Men and women generally engaged in different leisure pursuits, and they participated in different civic associations with different goals for neighborhood improvement. Even where gender mixing did occur in public spaces, businesses often reinforced spatial gender distinctions by offering separate parlors and waiting rooms for men and for women. But those social boundaries, historians now acknowledge, were much more permeable than permanent. For instance, as Theda Skocpol found in her research on social policy provision in the late nineteenth century, local women's clubs formed coalitions across the country to lobby elected officials to increase welfare spending, expand labor regulations, and pursue health education—decades before they had obtained the right to vote. The Progressive Era, therefore, was not exclusively dominated by regressive gender politics, nor was it wholly a brave new world for public-minded women. Rather, it was a historical period—like so many others—in which beliefs about gender roles were actively contested, reworked, and transformed.[15] *Many progressive women came before men*

Unsurprisingly, then, debates about the place of American women appeared in many pages of professional periodicals in the late nineteenth century. Particularly in the field of health and medicine, experts battled about the necessity of separate physical spaces for men and women, often arguing about the science of embodied gender difference as they did so. Proponents of separate schools for girls and boys, for instance, drew on arguments about "external and anatomical" differences to scaffold their claims. As one health publication asked, "It is asserted that woman in her natural state is the physical equal of man, and the primitive or savage woman is constantly pointed to as an example of this supposed axiom. Do those who make these assertions know how well the savage is aware of the weakness of woman and of her susceptibilities at certain periods of her life, and with what care he protects her from harm at these periods so that health may be retained?" After all, the author went on to reason, "[t]he life of woman does not run smoothly like that of a man. It is characterized by marked periodicity, by ebbs and floods, by great life-waves, which are dominant in the sphere of her especial functions"—with those functions being defined by "the supremacy of the reproductive function."[16] On the flip side, however, proponents of coeducation charged that such arguments were little more than "assertions and opinions." For instance, as another author wrote, the problem with opposition to coeducation was that it lacked adequate grounding in "any facts or statistics." In fact, if one looked at reliable

[handwritten annotation: Women are better at being Educated than Men]

data, one would find that "co-educated and scientifically-educated women generally *improve* in health during the college course; not only this, but their average health is better than that of the men who pursue the same course of studies and make equal proficiency."[17]

Yet when it came to another hot-button issue in the Progressive Era—public toilets—beliefs about gendered bodies and gendered geography were more an amuse-bouche than a main course. A subtle sense that men dominated the city streets was palpable in such texts, especially given the assessments proffered by numerous health and medical experts about the myriad ills attributed to a lack of public conveniences—ranging from literal ailments, like a "hypertrophied prostate," to social ones, like being forced into a saloon should one wish to empty one's bladder. One writer for a medical periodical described that dilemma for New Yorkers as follows: "As New York now stands it is either, burst your bladder or go to a grog-shop, where courtesy as well as custom demands that you buy a drink in exchange for the privilege granted you—of leaving one!" Moreover, should one give in to the urge to eliminate on the city's streets, one might end up like "a lowly and doubtless very ill-bred and indelicate citizen" who recently headlined local newspapers for "the act of urinating against the spokes of his truck wheels." He was, perhaps unsurprisingly, arrested "*in flagrante delictu* [*sic*], toted to court, and fined five dollars."[18] But several medical writers of the same era did consider the plight of urban women, often in ways that were surprisingly egalitarian. "The female population have not even the saloon as a resort, and can relieve themselves only when in the vicinity of department stores," bemoaned one health expert, calling for American politicians to follow the lead of "several European models of public relief stations" and invest in public infrastructure. Doing so would thus allow men and women alike to achieve "intestinal relief" when out and about in the city.[19]

In other words, rather than invoking the "deceptive distinctions"[20] so plentiful in nineteenth-century debates about coeducation, as Cynthia Fuchs Epstein terms social gender differences portrayed as innate or inherent, medical periodicals discussing public plumbing eschewed overt talk of gender. Instead, to the extent that they reinforced pernicious social distinctions and stereotypes, they tended to focus on ethnic and class divisions. As the proponent of "intestinal relief" went on to argue, the cleanliness of the body enabled by the expansion of public toilets would fruitfully carry over into cleaner morality: "A child will derive far more good from a ready access to bath-tub and water-closet than from a life-long attendance at Sunday-school and church, with the temple of the human soul permanently unclean." And while such hygienic ideals were important for all citizens, the author maintained it was especially so for those in need of "growth and refinement," such as "Italian or Greek street vendor[s]" or "low-class Polish Jew[s]."[21] Likewise, another author worried about the tendency for "text-books on hygiene" to inform readers "all about the water supply and waste disposal for large cities"—not just because "the greater part of our popula-tion" lived in rural areas, but also because of the backwardness of social and cultural development in those same regions: "In the disposal of excreta the country population has made no advancement since the days of our prehis-toric ancestors, who likely left their excrement on the surface of the ground." But, he added, a well-trained health officer would be well equipped to save the day. By disseminating "the advances made in the preservation of health and the prevention of disease and discomfort," including the care of public privies, that officer's "education of the people" would unquestion-ably "belt their wheels to the shaft of progress."[22]

The notion that "hygiene and health go hand in hand"[23] thus pushed medical professionals to involve themselves in the political quest for sani-tary improvements. In large part, such exhortations were about limiting the spread of contagious disease—an obvious target for practitioners in the health professions. In New York, health authorities joined forces with pub-lic volunteers to create a sanitary protective league meant to educate city residents about "keep[ing] their health," and to lobby for "wise sanitary reforms," which "would have a vastly greater influence in saving money and promoting happiness and morality in the nation."[24] At the annual meeting of the New York Medical Association, one doctor also dramatically argued that, because "[t]he influence of these [contagious] diseases upon the his-tory of our race has always been disastrous," the expedient adoption of an international "system of sanitary administration" was essential.[25] But authors also linked their professional obligations to more mundane mat-ters, including public toilets. Members of the state board of health in California, for instance, convened a panel of doctors and professors to pro-mote "proper sanitary methods" and euphemistically called for special attention to those places that most "[concern] the masses"—that is, wash-rooms and toilets in "public buildings and thoroughfares."[26] An East Coast author was more blunt. "The proper provision of public-comfort stations is axiomatic, and the lack of these conveniences is a disgrace to American cit-ies and towns, and New York in particular," he wrote, concluding that the "Mayor's Committee" needed to "emerge from their cloistered seclusion with a few practical suggestions" to remedy the situation.[27]

Whether they focused on cholera or commodes, however, such dis-courses insinuated that medical and health professionals had a unique ability to protect the American citizenry through their mastery of science. At times, such assertions were subtle, as experts carefully leveraged scien-tific jargon, reported original experimental data, and employed practices of academic citation to substantiate their expertise. In response to his con-cern that lackluster plumbing would increase "the liability to disease, both by the spreading of bacteria and by otherwise producing bad sanitary sur-roundings," one author collected "sixteen specimens of gaseous-smelling earth" from ditches in New York City and assessed them "with strict pre-cautions," including all records being "duplicated for control," for the pres-ence of "disease-germs."[28] At other times, medical articles relied upon melodramatic appeals to the field's scientific superiority—and pulled no punches when doing so. As one periodical contended, "The evils which the social and gregarious instincts of men create, by inducing the modern crowding into cities, must be socially remedied; and the most effective force which society can exert to this end is the influence of the highly trained medical officer. Every physician should be a medical philanthro-pist and missionary, zealous to disseminate knowledge of public hygiene."[29] Most often, though, they occupied a nuanced middle ground, gently meld-ing science with social good to assert the relevance of their expertise for public infrastructure. For instance, one writer worried "whether entirely satisfactory results" when fitting railway "stations, cars, shops, etc." with water closets and other sanitary devices "could be obtained by entrusting this matter to individual systems to carry out according to their own ideas." Instead, he proposed, medical professionals "should have some rec-ognized standard as to what is effectual" and, moreover, lead the establish-ment of "an efficient corps of inspectors . . . to see that measures adopted are put into place."[30]

In short, a small handful of articles in late-nineteenth-century health periodicals about the gendering of public space did roar with gender-related moral panic—that is, an outsized, "fundamentally inappropriate"[31] explosion of fear and concern by key social actors in response to a relatively minor event or cultural shift. But most authors took the opposite approach, opting instead for evidence-driven, science-centered, surprisingly neutral professionalism. Whether they focused on the possibility of expanding coeducation in public schools, delivering more (or better) sanitary instruction to their colleagues and patients, or lobbying local politicians to funnel more funding into plumbing and sewer infrastructure, medical and health professionals writing for their colleagues shared a belief that their profession's strongest asset was a robust foundation of empiricism. Ironically, however, the more scientifically oriented such rhetorical appeals to expand or improve public plumbing became, the more political they also became. For many authors, public plumbing could—and indeed should—be engineered to enhance the health and well-being of the public whenever and wherever possible. Yet achieving the most cutting-edge sanitary outcomes, they also reasoned, would require political involvement on the part of their fellow health and medical experts. In advocating that an expert hand help to shape new plumbing marvels, then, they cemented an understanding that their field alone held the scientific knowledge necessary to fully serve the public good, thereby shoring up their professional legitimacy through the promise of civic improvements.

"THE MEDICAL MAN, THE ARCHITECT, THE PLUMBER, ALL RECOGNIZE THAT PLUMBING IS A SCIENCE"

Yet the medical community was merely one among several loosely-bound occupational associations starting to coalesce into institutionalized groupings at the dawn of the Progressive Era. Such evolutionary processes did not escape the attention of nineteenth-century academic sociologists, who strove to document the unique trajectory of those boundary-drawing efforts as they unfolded in each individual sphere of expertise. In doing so, they would inaugurate a multidecade tradition in the social sciences of studying professionalization—that is, the transformation of isolated, individual practitioners of a given job or occupation into a discrete, firmly-bound, widely recognized group of qualified authorities. By the middle of the twentieth century, that collective intellectual project evolved into attempts to theorize professionalization as a linear, routine, and predictable sequence across multiple occupational settings (rather than within a single one). While different schools of thought begat different understandings of that order of operations, sociologists generally agreed—and still agree today—that the establishment of a shared, centralized body of professional knowledge is an essential ingredient in such developments. In part, such thinking goes, a field's specialized knowledge could gain legitimacy among practitioners and the public alike through structural modifications: the creation of licensure procedures, requirements for formal training, and so forth. But achieving legitimacy requires cultural transformations, too, including rhetorical shifts in professional discourses toward, as Andrew Abbott writes, increased alignment with "the values of rationality, efficiency," and above all, "science."[32]

In keeping with that canonical prediction, architectural, building, and engineering periodicals followed much the same pathway of rhetorical evolution as medical and health periodicals did. This is not to say the two fields did not have their differences. In fact, the early framing of restroom-related issues in early periodicals from the two fields could not have been more different. Where medical discourses favored bombastic claims about public morality, architectural periodicals were more, well, *dry*. "Millions of dollars have been spent in the investigation of new plans and apparently successful systems" for improving upon the ability of "the ordinary water-closet" to handle human waste, one article began theatrically, before devolving into a litany of details about the "construction and material" of water-closet design among cutting-edge plumbing manufacture firms:

> Putty and cement are entirely excluded, as these agents first absorb the noxious odors and vapors which necessarily arise, and then return them to the atmosphere, so as to constantly maintain a dangerous and unpleasant odor. One most important feature is that the basins are larger than those generally used, and retain a larger surface of water than the opening in the seat. Moreover, the water is discharged directly from the centre of the bottom of the bowl the moment the pull is raised, and rushes out with great force, so that at every discharge it clears perfectly the trap. This prevents the trap

from being clogged up with dirt, and avoids the accumulation of foul water, which is certain to give rise to bad smells. The employment of a valve instead of a pan to retain the water, avoids the necessity for the large receiver which is used in other closets; the novel construction of the overflow is also a feature that should recommend them to all that require a perfectly inodorous water closet.[33]

Another, similar article in another periodical began with a poetic ode to the "art of plumbing": "Closets have been invented as numerous and various in style as the leaves of autumn," it opined, before segueing into the sundry details of "protection against emanations from human excreta." After a brief discussion of biological research about "bacteria, bacilli, micrococci, and their vast progeny," it pivoted into a tiresome laundry list of innovations in toileting technology. "The first I notice is the 'Hilliard Hopper,'" which was "one of the simplest in construction, having a bowl attached to a four-inch soil pipe with a three-quarter S trap"; next was "the 'Zane Sanitary Closet,'" which was "much more complicated, and, in some respects, a better closet," owing to its "double protection in the form of two water seals—one in the pipe and one in the bowl"; "[v]ery similar in construction" was "the Demorest," with "many excellent qualities," including a "generally satisfactory" series of "flushing chambers"; and finally, "the invention of H. C. Lowrie, C.E., of Denver," which "form[ed] a perfect seal" and thus "[did] away with all vent pipes."[34]

But by the turn of the twentieth century, articles in architectural and building periodicals started to shift away from a myopic focus on fixture-related innovations and, like medical periodicals, toward taking ownership of sanitation. Some averred that it was their hallowed charge to "arouse the public to the need of discrimination in selecting their plumbers," exhorting their fellow engineers and architects to "no longer remain silent, but speak out and give them the benefit of knowledge acquired in the very best of schools—practical observation, planning and experiment."[35] And while several publications did continue to dispense practical guidance, such as putting a "thin flooring" in place around toilet fixtures to prevent "open joisting and rough plaster"[36] from accumulating dirt or waste, many more began to openly proselytize about the necessity of hiring well-educated plumbers and planners. As one such article observed, "One of the first questions which confronts the modern home-builder is, whether he prefers to pay the doctor's or the plumber's bill. If the plumber does his work conscientiously and well, it will act as a preventive against disease; if he does it carelessly or inefficiently, the services of the physician will certainly be required in the home." In turn, that meant expertise in "[p]roper sanitation" fell squarely "upon the shoulders of the plumber" himself, which required

> an adequate supply of water to flush the various fixtures; enameled iron or porcelain fixtures, in well-lighted and well-ventilated rooms; waste pipes large enough to carry of[f] all waste material but not too large to be self-cleaning; a system of ventilation so arranged that it will ventilate every portion of the drainage system properly; a quality of piping for soil-pipes and drains that will not corrode, or be affected by sudden changes in temperature; and a thorough system of testing and inspection by practical men not only when the work is finished, but during the installment of all the piping.

In other words, the article concluded, "[t]he plumber is the man who can save the doctor's bills, and keep away many diseases from the home, through his skill and knowledge of what good plumbing really means."[37]

And sure enough, those explicit calls for education soon gave way to explicit calls for a more scientific approach to plumbing. Some authors of articles in architectural periodicals compiled bibliographies of worthwhile readings for their fellow architects to consult and consider before designing new public spaces, with titles like "Public Baths and Lavatories" or "Public Comfort Stations and Public Baths."[38] Others celebrated a sea change in the profession's understanding of a scientific approach to their work: "Had anyone, a decade or two ago, intimated that science and plumbing were practically interchangeable terms, he would have been laughed at by most men. To-day, the man who would assert to the contrary, would find there were very few who would not laugh at him." Indeed, the author went on, that change was not just within the field but also applied to the field's broader professional reputation: "The medical man, the architect, the plumber, all recognize that plumbing is a science, and at the conventions which these hold from time to time in various parts of the world, papers dealing scientifically with plumbing are regularly read and commented upon." And that scientific foundation was even more important for "the plumber" than "the medical man": "The careless and

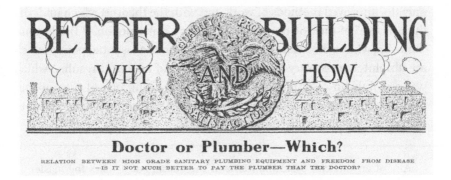

Figure 1. Article header from "Doctor or Plumber—Which?," *American Carpenter and Builder* (1912).

incompetent physician can only work upon one subject at a time, while the careless or incompetent plumber can work upon a whole household at once."[39] Or, as another article put it much more succinctly, "Although generally looked upon as an ordinary trade, there is no branch of the building business which requires more scientific practice than plumbing."[40]

(A quick aside here: not all turn-of-the-century professions pushing for improvements to public plumbing aligned themselves with scientific logics. Academic sociologists, for instance, presented our nascent field's distance from health, medicine, and other turn-of-the-century variants of "normal science"[41] as a rationale for its relevance to plumbing matters. As one author writing for our flagship journal, the *American Journal of Sociology,* lamented, "Councils, legislatures, and congresses pass measures and then turn over the execution of the social will to the physician," who, "himself primarily a student of pathology and disease, tends to emphasize pills rather than public welfare." Unfortunately, that delegation meant "the real problems of social progress" associated with inadequate sanitation would remain unresolved—at least unless "social theories" were taken more seriously.[42])

Crucially, however, where scientific logics led writers for medical periodicals to turn outward—asserting that no other profession could protect the public as successfully as they could—architectural periodicals tended to turn inward. Given "the altered conditions of the trade" in light of recent developments in sanitary science, one piece contended, "the young progressive craftsman" ought to "[fit] himself by acquaintance, with not only the improved methods of work, but with the theories which underlie the practice" of turn-of-the-century building construction.[43] But beyond "knowing what a first-class system requires and the essential points which are absolutely necessary to secure sanitary and healthful results," which was certainly an essential contribution to the rising tide of turn-of-the-century social progress, builders could also use that knowledge base to distinguish themselves as individual experts:

> Almost anyone can build the frame of the house, but it takes the master mind to know just what to put in to bring the house up to the highest standard, measured by the latest refinements. How can one be sure everything is included? Keep posted on modern buildings. Visit the city once in a while. Get around the buildings under construction. See the plans of the leading architects. There are plenty of ways to keep up. Don't fail to send for catalogs of anything you don't fully understand. After you have imbibed all the knowledge you can hold, look around and see how many buildings are completely equipped according to your new standard. Get busy with the owners and start them to thinking. It won't be long before you will be busy at some of this work.[44]

In other words, discursive appeals to sanitary science construed an individual architect's, builder's, planner's, or plumber's personal knowledge as a signal that he—and he alone—was a legitimate practitioner of his craft. Or, as another author observed, "[t]he rapid advance in medical science" over the "last thirty or forty years" had led to a profound "insistence for personal cleanliness," which, "very soon," allowed "the bathroom as a separate component of the house plan" to come into being. However, it was an expert builder's modern touches—the replacement of "the old 'tin-tub'" with "better looking enameled iron or porcelain," the succession of "ugly lead pipes by polished copper or nickel," and the installation of "[t]ile floors and wainscoting"—which truly "transformed this room into a place of beauty and perfect sanitation."[45]

That entrepreneurial spirit, moreover, did not occur just in articles about domestic plumbing. A similar glide from science to style also appeared in articles about public plumbing. "One of the promising signs of the times has been the gradually increasing importance which is being placed on the arrangement and equipment of the public toilet room,"

Figure 2. Article header from W. K. Glen, "Modern Plumbing," *American Builder* (1925).

observed one builder's treatise on the necessity of professional attention to comfort stations and other restrooms. From his perspective, "the plumbing contractor" did have a critical obligation to the public in the wake of "the development of sanitary plumbing fixtures and specialties": men like him should continue to speak out about sanitation "until the possibilities in this direction are matters of common knowledge and of the education of the rank and file of humanity with regard to the need for sanitation and its direct relation to the prevention of disease." Yet the most important audience for the modern plumber's "valuable opinions and experiences" about the spacing of urinal stalls, the maximum number of fixtures reasonable for a given space, and the prevention of "dirt lodgment" in those stalls and those fixtures was other builders—especially those attempting to master the ins and outs of a modern, "really attractive appearance" for the toilet rooms they were tasked with building. Indeed, he quipped, "These the whole plumbing fraternity would be glad to have."[46]

Thus, in medical and architectural periodicals alike, appeals to scientific authority were an important part of professional discourse—and those appeals to scientific authority, in turn, helped to validate the expertise held by individual professionals at a critical moment in each field's development. But the promises made within such legitimizing discourses were quite different in each professional domain. Where articles in medical periodicals about water closets, comfort stations, and the like were geared toward using new scientific discoveries as the basis for political lobbying and, ultimately, improving the welfare of the public, the linkages constructed between science and sanitation in architectural periodicals were much more focused on encouraging individual architects to accrue the knowledge and skills necessary to produce the most up-to-date plumbing infrastructure possible. Moreover, that state-of-the-art character was not geared toward being on the cutting edge of scientific and technological discovery for its own sake, nor was it aimed predominantly at improving sanitation for the public's benefit. Instead, whether architectural articles sang the praises of porcelain technologies for domestic washrooms or visualized the ideal geometry for toilets and urinals in public restrooms, the expert perspective and technical mastery they celebrated was valuable only insofar as it could allow individual professionals to produce unmistakably modern infrastructure. And modernity was not just a new and desirable professional value for builders and plumbers. Modernity, such discourses also reasoned, was quite marketable.

"GOOD PLUMBING INCREASES THE VALUE OF THE BUILDING"

Even more long-standing than social-scientific interest in the professions is social-scientific interest in the complex interplay between markets and morality. As far back as the eighteenth century, Charles de Montesquieu and Adam Smith imagined that global commerce brought out "gentle" manners as well as "probity and punctuality" in individual merchants; by the nineteenth century, Karl Marx and Thorstein Veblen became well known for excoriating the market structures associated with capitalist production as morally corrosive.[47] But just as the sociology of occupations has moved away from the simplistic, black-or-white frameworks that predominated in the field's earliest years of development, economic sociology, too, has moved toward a more processual understanding over time. Today, as Marion Fourcade and Kieran Healy observe, the dominant understanding in the field is that "markets *are* culture, not just because they are the products of human practice and sense making"—which they also are, of course—"but because markets are explicitly moral projects, saturated with normativity" (emphasis mine).[48] Ample research demonstrates, for instance, that local political activism can prompt the emergence of new markets, thereby accelerating the pace of social change far beyond what individual lobbyists could achieve; that markets for morally charged goods like human organs or gametes respond more to shifts in public opinion than the rational rule of supply and demand; and that our most intimate family relationships are suffused with economic exchanges that mark certain social ties as more valuable than others.[49]

That elision of marketability and morality did not escape the notice of architectural and building experts in the second decade of the twentieth century. They feverishly advocated the expansion of indoor plumbing, the adoption of high-tech water closets, and the creation of spacious public comfort stations—not just to one another, but also to profit-minded civic leaders. Where one health periodical reported, for instance, that New Orleans was undertaking "a colossal case of municipal housecleaning," including a multimillion-dollar sewer installation and attendant public conveniences (which would "render it the peer of any American city, from the hygienic standpoint," and make it a "brilliant example [to] be followed by every city in the Union"),[50] a comparable article in an architectural periodical about Columbus's various and sundry sanitary improvements took a different tack. Like New Orleans, the city faced "a rapidly growing population" within an already crowded city. But rather than emphasizing the needs of local Ohioans, the article went on to highlight "the thousands of visitors and strangers coming here for pleasure or business"—and especially for business:

> With a network of steam and traction roads entering Columbus and with many conventions, State fairs and other attractions, people coming to the city daily are numbered by the train load. Thousands of people come to Columbus every Sunday during the excursion season. Men, women and children pour into Columbus not only on Sundays, but on weekdays as well, to see the sights or to visit the public institutions. The large manufacturing and commercial interests of Columbus bring many business men to the Capital. While here many of the visitors do not stop at hotels, being here only for the day.

Without a sufficient sewerage system and public comfort stations, those businessmen lacked "the common conveniences of life" and were forced "to enter houses of business or saloons to beg accommodations." That sad

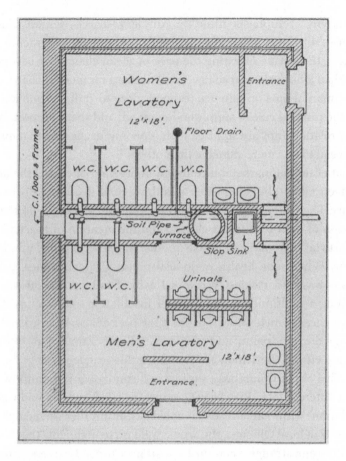

Figure 3. Schematic for Cobb's Hill, New York, public comfort station, originally published in "A Public Comfort Station at Cobb's Hill, N.Y.," *Building Age* (1911).

state of affairs, the author concluded, was "embarrassing to the public and a shame to Columbus."[51]

However, as was the case with the efforts to expand public comfort stations in Baltimore described at the start of this chapter, finding what Roy Suddaby and Royston Greenwood describe as "persuasive language" was critical to making those innovations seem worthwhile and legitimate.[52] Authors therefore positioned the qualities of the most modern, inviting, and beautiful toileting facilities already available in private establishments like hotels and department stores—which were, in that historical era, paragons of spatial gender segregation—as equally desirable for new public facilities.[53] One writer, for instance, celebrated the "ingenuity of the architect" of a station in Cobb's Hill, a suburb of Rochester, New York, who "furnished a design both ornamental and attractive." On the exterior, the "side walls of the building and the sides of the entrance corridors" were composed of "red-pressed brick" with the "portion of the wall which is above the ground . . . finished in plaster." Then, on the interior, users could find "nickel-plated pipe" with "a valve to control the water supply" for flushing and two separate lavatories with top-of-the-line "Acme self-closing coldwater faucets." But most important for morally conscious cities and citizens alike, "[s]tairs" were "provided at different points . . . for entrance to the women's and men's different apartments."[54] Other articles were even more effusive, such as one that valorized a recent comfort station installation in Scranton for locating "[t]he stairways leading to the men's and women's compartments" on "completely different streets." Better yet, to preserve privacy and propriety for all users, both walkways leading up to those stairways were obscured "by shrubbery as not to be over prominent." "An admirable arrangement," the author opined. [55]

That process of cultural absorption, which I call *occupational osmosis*, allows dominant values to infuse the everyday parlance of professional discourse—at once shoring up a professional field's claims to legitimacy while also reinforcing the underlying ideologies in question. Sometimes, that osmosis was quite tangible, as was the case when authors made gender a central feature of their write-ups. After the debut of Newark's new and "centrally located comfort station," for instance, one article celebrated its two architects, not just for "avoid[ing] errors which have been discovered in the design of such buildings in other places," but also for their arrangement of the station "into two parts, with the entrance for men and the entrance for women as widely separated as possible when on the same end of the building."[56] Architects in Seattle likewise channeled bourgeois gender ideologies into their work to respond to "the rapidly developing appreciation on the part of municipal authorities . . . of the unmeasurable convenience of public comfort stations" by locating the "entrances to the men's and women's sections of the station" in areas "as far removed" from one another "as the ends of the canopy" above would allow.[57] But more

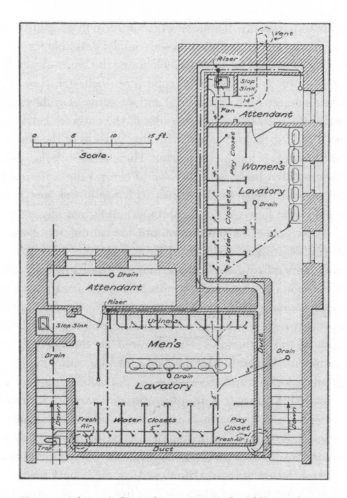

Figure 4. Schematic for Rochester, New York, public comfort station, originally published in "Details of a Public Comfort Station," *Building Age* (1911).

often, the rightfulness and profitableness of gender separation was quietly implied within otherwise mundane technical write-ups. Following the arrival of a new comfort station in Cincinnati, for instance, one author foregrounded the appeal of the station's modern fixtures in detail with a passing nod to the space's provision of separate accommodations for men and women:

The water closets are of the seat action type, with flushing tanks concealed in the space behind the partitions[,] and the specifications suggested fixtures similar to the Douglas Samson combination. The urinals in the men's room, the piping to which is run concealed behind the marble partitions in the rear of them, were specified to be similar to Mott's 6067 R Sanito-Imperial. The lavatories are enameled iron porcelain construction with self-closing faucets. In the women's toilet provision is made for a recessed drinking fountain set in the wall, and in the center of the men's toilet room is to be a drinking fountain similar to the Standard Artisan P 639.[58]

To be clear, architectural discourses never lacked concern for the public altogether, and they did occasionally perpetuate inegalitarian gender ideologies in an unapologetic fashion. However, when it came to concern for the public, wide-ranging pleas to consider the public good were simply less effusive and elaborate than odes to modernity. As one periodical briefly noted before quickly moving on to more pressing matters of park pavilion and church design, "Public comfort stations are needed in cities all over the United States. They are a public necessity, essential to the health and welfare of congested districts everywhere, needed more than ever since the disappearance of saloons which formerly provided some slight facilities."[59] And when it came to gender ideologies, assertions that a woman's place was in the domestic sphere were much more common in lay magazines than professional writing. Such articles positioned women as, in the words of one general-interest publication, "the modern bridge between science and society," with the goal of endorsing "the underlying scientific principles connected with plumbing and instruction in methods conducive to the maintenance of sanitary conditions in the home."[60] The goal in doing so, wrote another article, was for women to "know architecture as well as they know the arts generally classed as domestic," because of "plain need" for women's courses to promote "appreciation in architecture as a means to better human life." Moreover, it was essential for such courses to teach architecture "as a structural science"—that is, "the science of knowing what buildings are for and how they help mankind and womankind." Such instruction could allow women to better "[rule] the home and [rule] it rightly," therefore "making life better and nobler, and getting out of buildings the refinement and influence for good which every work of art should produce."[61]

But as public infrastructure became more and more marketable, architectural and engineering periodicals overwhelmingly anchored their rhetorical appeals in language that would appeal to private investors—and, in so doing, allowed gender distinctions to subtly seep into their words about "the economy of the bathroom."[62] Some asserted that "good plumbing increases the value of the building," promoting the inclusion of "attractive, even luxurious" toilets and urinals in order to appeal to "prospective users" and, in turn, elevate prices for plumbing work.[63] Others touted the boons of "little luxuries and conveniences" in all manner of toileting facilities—domestic, semipublic, and public alike. In houses, for instance, "a modern installation" in the bathroom would drive up the amount "prospective tenants and purchasers" might be willing to pay; in commercial spaces, "business men" were hypothesized to be "almost as interested in the plumbing fixtures of the several buildings under consideration as they are when selecting a house in which to live"; and in public comfort stations, users were becoming savvier and savvier when it came to the "sound design, correct materials, and proper installation" of the fixtures therein, making separate "fittings and fixtures" for men's and women's compartments an important consideration.[64] Yet others envisioned that "modern, sanitary fixture[s] of vitreous china, porcelain or enameled iron, from reliable makers," might soon become another signal of "American superiority" around the globe—one that could be peddled to "older countries" who lagged "far behind" plumbing achievements in the United States.[65] But no matter what, all such discourses reasoned, even if building "the most modern toilet facilities" possible added amply to the total cost of a public space's construction, as it did for Philadelphia's new League Island Park, the cost of "Tennessee marble," "automatic" fixtures, and "complementary" men's and women's spaces was well worth it if the resulting comfort stations were among the "largest and most attractive" in the region and, moreover, "without a duplicate" anywhere in the world.[66]

THE FIRST ELEMENT OF GENDER'S INSTITUTIONAL ACCOMPLISHMENT: INSTITUTIONAL FLUX

Thus, while beliefs about gender were being hotly contested, reworked, and transformed in many spheres of Progressive Era social life, one zone in which they remained immovable was architectural writing about public restrooms. Surprisingly, however, that stasis was not often a direct consequence of cultural beliefs about women's allegedly feeble nature and unique vulnerability in public. Yes, as legal scholar Terry Kogan finds in his historical research on workplace restrooms, a regressive "vision of modesty embraced by late Victorian society"—one that hinged on beliefs "that women are inherently weaker than men in both physical stamina and intellectual ability"—was indeed a potent influence on the rise of legislative mandates that certain kinds of public restrooms be separated by sex.[67] And yes, if we dig deeply enough, the middle- and upper-class vision of privacy and propriety invoked by aspiring plumbing experts was firmly rooted in the presumed helplessness of female bodies and women's nineteenth-century social subordination. But for the expert discourses I study in this chapter, discursive efforts to link the new science of sanitation to a marketable vision of modernity were an equally potent pathway through which gender separation in public restrooms became institutionalized. That process of *occupational osmosis*—that is, the subtle, almost imperceptible, absorption of hegemonic cultural values into the everyday parlance of professional discourse as a legitimizing strategy—ultimately meant that the greatest influence of gender ideologies on American toilet architecture was an oblique one, coming to fruition only through other organizational transformations unfolding around the turn of the twentieth century.

In "Hierarchies, Jobs, Bodies: A Theory of Gendered Organizations," Joan Acker observes that such subtleties of organizational discourse are intimately intertwined with the reproduction of gender inequality. As she explains, although "gender-neutral" organizational logics may suggest an equal playing field between men and women at work, they actually camouflage implicit workplace stratification—because gender neutrality often serves as a guise for the assumption that all organizational actors are male and that they embody cultural markers of masculinity. Put more simply, for Acker, gender is not a cultural force that works apart from the organizational environment that surrounds and shapes gendered behavior; instead, it is a part of—or, perhaps more accurately, a product of—those very same organizational forces. But her article is as much a call to action for scholars who study organizations as it is an effort to overturn gender inequality in those organizations themselves. Where sociologists ignore the tacit ideological assumptions permeating all aspects of bureaucratic function, Acker's argument goes, it is impossible to see cultural classification schemes like gender as the "complex component of processes of control and domination" that they truly are.[68] In other words, to truly understand how gender works, and especially how gender works in and through bureaucratic structures, we must first bring to light the many subtle pathways through which ideologies undergird organizational life.

Given the almost imperceptible ways in which ideological assumptions about gender trickled into them, turn-of-the-century architecture and engineering periodicals certainly confirm a central tenet of Acker's argument—that the ongoing infusion of gender into organizational policy, procedure, and discourse is often more subtle than overt. Were we to look only for conspicuous evidence of gender differences and distinctions, it would be easy to miss the slow and steady absorption of patriarchal presumptions into the plumbing ideals being developed, visualized, and described. In fact, the story of restroom gender separation I tell in this chapter could be expressed more simply (and not inaccurately) were I to focus only on professional processes. That narrative would go something like this: at the dawn of the twentieth century, design practitioners eager to establish their work as a legitimate professional enterprise referenced scientific findings and leveraged scientific vocabulary to mark their training and expertise as specialized—and thus inimitably modern and marketable. Yet Acker's programmatic statement reminds us to seek out the dangers that lurk amid such seemingly neutral language. And here, although architects and engineers may not have set out to intentionally reinforce hegemonic turn-of-the-century beliefs about gender, such beliefs nonetheless crept into their discursive work—and into the professional best practices they promulgated to one another. The veneer of objectivity in their writing thus disguised the infiltration of bourgeois beliefs about gendered bodies, sexual privacy, and appropriate social boundaries into the physical architecture of American cities and communities. In short, as Acker's work on the gendered organization might predict, the apparently value-neutral discourse of architectural professionals camouflaged a decidedly inegalitarian gendered reality.

However, the chemical metaphor of osmosis also allows me to go one step beyond Acker's work, as it foregrounds how changes to other institutional logics are inextricable from the ideological force of the gendered organization. When architectural authors peddled modern infrastructure to civic officials, neighborhood business owners, and would-be toilet users, they slowly assimilated a classed vision of moral propriety into professional discourse, and they did so at two levels. Not only did their discourses draw on a politics of respectability meant to appeal to individual middle- and upper-class readers (whether those readers were professional colleagues or civic officials); their words also sought enhanced occupational status for their professional enterprise as a whole. Now, to be fair, Acker does acknowledge the overlapping influence of class and gender elsewhere in her oeuvre. The very first sentence of "Inequality Regimes: Gender, Class, and Race in Organizations," for instance, reports, "Much of the social and economic inequality in the United States and other industrial countries is created in organizations, in the daily activities of working and organizing the work,"[69] and the article goes on to outline how, exactly, class and race shape our expectations about how gendered individuals (and especially gendered workers) should act in bureaucratic settings. But gender and class shape organizational processes as much as they do outcomes for individual workers, and the ways in which they both shape organizational discourses are thus continually moving and resettling— just as molecules in a solvent would.

By studying those professional processes, I advance the first element of theorizing gender as an institutional accomplishment: a central focus on institutional absorption and adaptation—or, in a word, *flux*. Much like molecules constantly move through and across cell membranes, beliefs about gender constantly move through and across formal organizations. But organizations, like cells, are only selectively permeable. So, if sociologists are to truly understand which gender norms become durably institutionalized (and why and how they do), we must also study the churn of gender-adjacent beliefs—especially those that might allow gender-centered ideologies to seep into official organizational discourse. For instance, it would remain difficult to comprehend why gender separation became a constitutive element of public plumbing at the specific historical moment it did without first noticing the need for civic engineers to establish legitimacy for their professional work. Similarly, if we overlooked the considerable overlap between the floor plans of new public conveniences and those of their department store counterparts, we might miss how class politics quite literally shaped the ancestors of today's public restrooms. If we look for change contiguous to gender, however, we can more easily see where—and how—certain gendered expectations (like tenacious middle- and upper-class beliefs about sexed bodies and sexual privacy) can be quietly absorbed into organizational processes that, at first glance, are not so obviously related to gender (like the crystallization of plumbing-related "best practices" at the close of the nineteenth century). And that, in turn, allows us to see how traditional gender ideologies often persist in light of radical social change—as was the case when gender segregation found its way into public conveniences at a historical moment when more American women than ever before were starting to share space on the shop floor and city streets with American men.

And that particular instantiation of institutional flux would continue to shape the evolution of restroom infrastructure for decades to come, well past the 1930s, when the vast majority of the public comfort stations featured in this chapter had shut down.[70] When the International Conference of Building Officials convened in California in 1927 to draft and approve the first Uniform Building Code, the spatial distinctions predominant in elite businesses and urban comfort stations became written into professional guidelines for the "safe and stable design"[71] of all buildings and structures henceforth constructed. Thus, while women in other parts of the globe had to wage a multidecade campaign to have previously gender-neutral public toilets achieve gender separation,[72] most new restrooms built in the twentieth-century United States would automatically be installed as gender-segregated spaces. And as city health officers began agitating for ensuring the "safety and purity" of domestic and civic plumbing in the 1940s and 1950s, they pushed to have plumbing codes consolidated into centralized guidance that would alleviate "the confusion and lack of uniformity caused by a multiplicity of different codes."[73] But they also advocated that "architects, building contractors, plumbing contractors, journeyman plumbers, consulting engineers,"[74] and the health department be solely at the helm of that consolidation. Thus, while a physician could indeed "only work upon one subject at a time," and a plumber could "work upon a whole household at once,"[75] the collective force of the new professions of architecture and civic engineering would come to work a tremendous influence upon all parts of the future of twentieth-century American plumbing.

3 Regulating Restrooms

In days of yore, when the late, lamented Equal Rights
Amendment was slogging through state legislatures, some
opponent was always around to warn that "if we have an
ERA, we'll have to have unisex toilets."

Ellen Goodman, "Separate for Equal?" *Washington Post*,
February 1998

In August of 1970, over twenty thousand women gathered in the streets of
New York for the Women's Strike for Equality. Timed to occur on the anniversary of the passage of the Nineteenth Amendment—which had
occurred fifty years and two days earlier than the strike, thanks to a narrow
approval by Tennessee, the thirty-sixth state necessary for ratification—
the mass demonstration was what *Time* magazine described as "easily the
largest women's rights rally since the suffrage protests."[1] The founder of
the National Organization for Women, Betty Friedan, had been strategizing for some time about how best to channel increasing interest in the
women's liberation movement into a conspicuous burst of collective
action, and she had originally envisioned a true strike: mothers would
"leave their children in government and business offices to dramatize the
need for a national child care system," secretaries would "stop typing," and
young women untethered to families or jobs would "stop shopping."[2] But
rather than putting working women in the precarious position of walking
out of their jobs, even temporarily, an "enthusiastic rally" marched down
Fifth Avenue at just after five o'clock in the evening—with a turnout
Friedan described as "beyond our wildest dreams."[3]

Also exceeding Friedan's expectations was the popularity of parallel events across the nation. While New York's record-breaking turnout was certainly singular—in fact, the city's best efforts to "confine the women's parade to a single lane" at the height of rush hour could not prevent a "continuing traffic tie-up" that "filled the air with blaring horns"[4] for many hours—other gatherings were remarkable in their own right. In the District of Columbia, well over a thousand women, led by a banner emblazoned "We Demand Equality," stormed down Connecticut Avenue in the early part of the afternoon, while government workers unable to join them led "a teach-in [about women's rights] at the Old Senate Office Building."[5] In Los Angeles, a throng of female protesters managed to distribute flyers to journalists, civic officials, and passing workers while "confined to the sidewalk," successfully bringing attention to their "low pay" and a bigger problem of increasing unemployment. In Berkeley, women took to the streets with "pots and pans strapped to their backs"; in Boston, one woman marched solo, "chained to an oversize paper typewriter." Four rogue Pennsylvanians were even caught "hurling eggs at a Pittsburgh radio station" whose disc jockey dared to mock the women's movement.[6] "All in all," one journalist concluded, "the day won new support and undoubtedly new awareness among both men and women of the case for female rights."[7]

That "new support" and "new awareness" were even more useful for securing another monumental step forward for the women's rights movement that same August: success in finally landing the Equal Rights Amendment to the United States Constitution on the floor of the House of Representatives. The would-be amendment, which simply stated, "Equality of rights under the law shall not be diminished or abridged by the United States or any state on account of sex," originally debuted in Congress for the first time nearly fifty years earlier, and it had been reintroduced for consideration each and every year "for more than 40 years."[8] But thanks to a "massive coalition of women's organizations" working in tandem with well-established federal lobbyists and a diverse array of grassroots activists, support among federal lawmakers to "wipe out the last vestiges of legal inequality for women"[9] coalesced with sufficient density to bring the amendment to a vote in 1970. And just as quickly as "the ERA" had moved from the House Judiciary Committee to the House floor, it passed—overwhelmingly—on October 12, 1971 and moved on to the Senate.[10]

Unfortunately, however, the path to bicameral approval was not without obstacles. Long-standing fractures in the women's movement posed one set of speed bumps, including the division between the affluent, highly educated, mostly white women who supported the ERA wholesale and the working-class women who had actively lobbied against the law for its entire multidecade history. As one union leader from Detroit explained, the highly open-ended character of the ERA threatened protective statutes that "set maximum daily and weekly hours of work for women"—a highly dangerous proposition for those who, "when their day's work on the assembly line or in the laundry or hotel" was done, still had to "go home and cook and clean and take care of children."[11] Other detractors worried that the amendment might "knock out state laws making fathers responsible for supporting their children,"[12] or worse yet, that young women might be subject to the same military draft and combat regulations as young men. Or, as Senate Armed Services Committee chairman John Stennis thunderously put it, "How many senators would like to see the young women of this country, many of them mothers with small children, living in barracks, wearing combat boots?"[13]

But the biggest obstacle of all was an encroaching suspicion that the ERA might obliterate gender difference in the law—and perhaps even society—altogether. Indeed, as the Senate Judiciary Committee considered possible changes to the amendment's language to leave existing family law and military procedures intact, Senator Sam Ervin became infamous in the Senate chambers for his "oratorical flights concerning the 'good Lord's plan' that men and women should be different."[14] (His wife, incidentally, fully supported such verbal voyages. "I suppose you would like me to say I disagree with my husband on this," she remarked to the press. "But I think Sam's exactly right. I think he's trying to help women." But she also admitted that not all women might see it that way: "My daughter is a little unhappy herself."[15]) Central to Ervin's accusations that ERA supporters were "crucifying women on a cross of equality"[16] was one alarm bell above all others: the possibility that the amendment would make "such sex distinctions as separate prisons and separate public toilets" illegal.[17] Moreover, emboldened by accusations among ERA supporters that such claims were "a smokescreen" to stall its forward progress through the Senate, Ervin enlisted two law professors—one from Harvard and the other from the University of Chicago—to affirm that state laws requiring "separate toilet facilities for women and men"[18] would likely be invalidated should the ERA come to pass.

ERA supporters continued to challenge Ervin's reduction of the movement for women's rights to the most banal possible register of "a bathroom joke,"[19] which eventually allowed the amendment to pass through the Senate—again, overwhelmingly—on March 22, 1972. They even found support for ratification thereafter in states like New York, where worries that the ERA would "force men and women to share public toilets" yielded a surprising gender skew in multiple counties, with more men than women favoring the amendment's approval. But pro-ERA activists in many other states were not so lucky. Virginia's state senate, for instance, came one vote short of approval, and that vote might very well have gone the other way had the state senator in question been convinced that states would still be allowed to "pass laws taking physical differences between males and females into account," particularly those related to "privacy with respect to sexual differences."[20] Even Tennessee—which had been the deciding vote for suffrage mere decades before, as well as one of the first ten states to initially approve the ERA—fell prey to the "emotional campaign" of anti-ERA rhetoric, with the specter of "'unisex' toilets" ultimately inducing a reversal of the state's earlier ratifying vote.[21]

.   .   .   .   .

As the trials and tribulations of the Equal Rights Amendment illustrate, the legal landscape for gender in the mid-twentieth-century United States was a dizzying affair—a reality attributable, in many respects, to equally vertiginous changes unfolding in the postwar world of work. To be fair, the mere presence of women in the American workforce was not a midcentury novelty (especially outside of affluent communities), and laws meant to support the unique plight of female employees had existed for many decades (even if those laws were more paternalistic than truly protective). But where involvement in the paid labor market was once a temporary stop for middle-class women en route to their more permanent calling as wives and mothers, a majority of American women began holding full-time positions throughout their adult years—even positions in male-dominated fields such as business, law, and medicine. Where there was once a profound cultural stigma associated with labor force participation for married women and women with children in all income brackets, young women began to expect that their lives would be defined more by their career field than their marital status—and invested accordingly in educational opportunities that would set them up for future professional success. And where statutes restricting women's employment options were once a ubiquitous fixture of state labor regulations, state and federal laws emerged to prevent gender discrimination rather than ensure it—especially Title VII of the Civil Rights Act of 1964, which prohibited employment discrimination based on race, color, religion, national origin, and most importantly for this chapter, sex.[22]

Such nascent legislative frameworks would have many cascading effects on American workplaces in the decades to follow, including the arrival of a new legal horizon for restrooms within those workplaces: the possibility that, should adequate toileting facilities not be provided for men and for women, they might be litigable nexuses of gender discrimination in the federal courts. As I outline in greater depth in chapter 1's synthetic history of restroom-related public policy, state laws requiring equal-but-separate men's and women's restrooms in American workplaces skyrocketed in number as women's labor force participation increased from the 1960s through the 1990s. Toward the turn of the twenty-first century, however, legislative interest in regulating workplace restrooms on gendered grounds reached a saturation point and largely tapered off.[23] In contrast, ever since the first federal cases involving gender and workplace restrooms became an issue occupying space on federal dockets in the late 1960s, the total number of cases heard and ruled upon in each decade has steadily and exponentially increased. While only seventeen cases in which litigants offered arguments about inequalities related to gender and workplace restrooms were heard in the 1970s, that number more than quadrupled over the 1980s and 1990s, totaling over one hundred cases; by the end of the first decade of the twenty-first century, that hundred had been joined by another hundred—with an equally rapid proliferation of cases continuing into the 2010s. *more interest has grown throughout the years*

This chapter considers the textual residue of those legal and cultural transformations by analyzing 256 federal opinions about workplace restrooms written between 1967 and 2013. The federal courts have addressed a surprisingly diverse range of restroom-related complaints in that time frame, considering legal frameworks as distinctive as freedom of speech and tax law, but I restrict my focus to cases in which restrooms were enfolded specifically in charges of gender discrimination—cases that, despite their apparent topical narrowness, have been integral to delineating the broader reach of Title VII. In fact, rather than dismissing complaints over the shape, scope, or separation of workplace restrooms as frivolous, the federal courts have taken restroom-related discrimination more and more seriously with each passing decade. As they have responded to structural changes in the social organization of work and the institutional evolution of legal precedent, they have blended together emergent cultural narratives about gender equality with creative reinterpretations of authoritative discrimination suits already on the books. In so doing, they have not only helped mandate the provision of equally available and equally accessible restrooms for men and for women in workplaces across the United States, but they have also continually expanded the definition of actionable gender discrimination in the eyes of the law.

Alongside that progress toward gender equity, however, has been a pernicious cultural stasis. As my analysis reveals both in its content and through its thematic (rather than strictly chronological) structure, the legal arguments about restroom-related discrimination that resonate most resoundingly with the courts are those that rest on claims of inherent gender difference. In particular, litigants seeking judicial intervention use feelings of isolation, ostracism, humiliation, embarrassment, and more as palpable evidence for their claims of discrimination—and federal judges, too, use that embodied emotional fallout to assess whether or not a legally actionable bathroom violation has indeed occurred. Moreover, while some written opinions invoke the affective experience of being a gendered body—an experience I refer to as *feeling gender*—in equivalent ways for men and women, as well as for cisgender and transgender litigants, most frame cisgender women's bodies as unusually susceptible to harm. Thus, whenever the federal courts assess the legal limits of gender discrimination, they also embed cultural beliefs about gender difference into the letter and spirit of American law; perpetuate ideologies of women's bodies as vulnerable and their privacy as expressly sacred; and most importantly of all, insinuate that we all ought to perceive one of the most personal aspects of the material world, our own bodies, as gendered entities.

"THERE WERE NO BATHROOMS"

As both legal historians and high school seniors studying for their Advanced Placement U.S. Government and Politics examinations know, one of the most defining characteristics of the American federal courts is one borrowed from English common law: *stare decisis*. In response to widespread beliefs in the nineteenth century that the judicial branch was verging too political and lacked legitimate procedures for deciding cases, the Supreme Court adopted a norm of following the precedent established by past decisions—that is, *stare decisis*—to better ensure the fairness and neutrality of the conclusions it reached. Since then, that practice has trickled down to all levels of the federal court system, with precedential logics now further codified through the practice of accompanying legal decisions with written opinions. And today, while political scientists, legal scholars, and sociologists alike debate how much precedent truly shapes judicial behavior—with legal scholars generally arguing, "most of it," and social scientists contending, as is our custom, "not as much as one might like to think"—we all tend to agree that precedent plays a critical role in the content of those written justifications. In fact, recent empirical evidence suggests that older Supreme Court cases are more likely to be cited in newer cases if they are firmly rooted in convincing precedential logics, and new decisions meant to overrule older ones tend to feature a more careful grounding in past precedent than cases that confirm or uphold the legal status quo—whether the author of the opinion is on the conservative or liberal side of the bench.[24]

Given that ongoing need for written consonance with the rulings of the past, several of the earliest federal cases arbitrating workplace conflicts over gender and restrooms revolved around the most familiar language of gender discrimination possible: claims that employers deliberately used bathroom facilities as a ploy to not train, hire, or promote women. In the first case at the federal level to address restrooms as a possible conduit of workplace gender inequality, *Ostapowicz v. Johnson Bronze Co.* (1973), a group of women filed a class-action suit alleging intentional discrimination in the treatment of female machine operators. Training at their plant was "given by observation only," and when the plant's machines were being assembled for use, "women were told to go to the ladies' restroom instead of being permitted to stand and observe the setups."[25] That use of work-place restrooms to confer a direct advantage on male workers that female workers could not access—that is, through the physical corralling of already-employed women away from valuable job experiences or training—established a clear path for other restroom-related gender-discrimination cases to follow. Such cases involved employers who refused to hire women in the first place, such as *Rhoades v. Jim Dandy Co.* (1978) because "there were no bathrooms" for them;[26] women who were denied opportunities for overtime work and wages because there would be no restroom facilities available after hours; and female workers who were fired to spare employers from having to construct a separate, permanent, or clean bathroom for them.

But the federal courts also began to hear a wider range of restroom-related cases in subsequent decades, and those cases helped usher in broader changes to the legal definition of sex discrimination. Often, this required the federal courts to dive into and evaluate the finer details of workplace restrooms, because, many plaintiffs argued, providing a sepa-rate women's restroom was insufficient if that restroom was in an undesir-able location or contained unsatisfactory fixtures. In *Stapp v. Overnite Transportation Co.* (1998), for instance, a terminal supervisor told a female freight trucker that she needed to "use 'the little brown building with a moon on it'" when she asked where to find the women's room, and another supervisor forced her to "wait for long periods of time" to use the undersized and "not well lit" women's restroom.[27] Continuing into the twenty-first century, *Wedow v. City of Kansas City* (2006) featured two fire department battalion chiefs who sued the city because of a variety of problems with restroom facilities in the stations they frequented. These included locating women's restrooms "in the male locker rooms with the male shower room," using them "as storage rooms" for items like "food and water for the station's pet dog," and maintaining them in an especially "unsanitary" condition.[28] Even more recently, in *Spees v. James Marine*,

Inc. (2009), the only female employee in a welding shop "did not have access to running water" in her washroom, and the water closet provided for her use was "a portable toilet instead of a formal restroom."[29] The ruling in each of these cases was that restroom deficiencies constituted far more than "a mere inconvenience"—that is, they more than exceeded the minimum requirement for a finding of actionable discrimination—because the absence of sufficient restrooms "jeopardize[d]" female workers' ability "to perform the core functions" of their jobs.[30] good

In addition to those incremental changes, the scope of Title VII also experienced a huge leap in the wake of *Meritor v. Vinson* (1986), through which the Supreme Court recognized certain forms of sexual harassment as actionable sex discrimination. For restrooms in particular, *Meritor* opened up new pathways for litigants and federal judges alike to justify claims of toilet-related workplace harm. In one such case, *Reed v. Shepard* (1991), the court's opinion goes to great lengths to establish how all employees at Indiana's Vanderburgh County Jail, "male and female" alike, "were treated similarly in compensation and in other respects." The problem, however, was with the less-than-egalitarian behavior of "the deputies and jailers" therein and, more specifically, how they "liked to entertain themselves during slow periods at the jail." As the opinion quotes from the lower court's ruling:

> Plaintiff contends that she was handcuffed to the drunk tank and sally port doors, that she was subjected to suggestive remarks . . . , that conversations often centered around oral sex, that she was physically hit and punched in the kidneys, that her head was grabbed and forcefully placed in members laps, and that she was the subject of lewd jokes and remarks. She testified that she had chairs pulled out from under her, a cattle prod with an electrical shock was placed between her legs, and that they frequently tickled her. She was placed in a laundry basket, handcuffed inside an elevator, handcuffed to the toilet and her face pushed into the water, and maced.[31]

Another restroom-related harassment case from the same decade, *Koschoff v. Runyon* (1999), focused on the plaintiff's experience of "discriminatory acts" at the hands of her new supervisor outside of the restroom rather than within it. The crux of Koschoff's claim involved the limitations that her supervisor had placed on her bathroom usage: "she was not permitted to take bathroom breaks while making deliveries" and "was disciplined for using the bathroom without seeking permission, even though male employees were not disciplined for doing so."[32] This unwritten requirement that she "notify management" whenever she needed to use the restroom continued for several months until the medical consequences of her "work-related stress"[33]—ranging from sleep disturbances to recurring migraine headaches—became so severe that she applied for disability retirement. *That's GOBOLD*

But even with the new precedent established by cases like *Meritor*, comparable sexual harassment cases involving restrooms—even cases unfolding in the same federal court in the same decade—often reached opposite conclusions. In cases like *Johnson v. Atlantic County* (2010), which revolved around an "incident of hazing" not altogether different from Reed's, with results that were "quite humiliating" and "physically threatening" for the plaintiff, and in *Rodriguez v. Flow-Zone* (2011), wherein a male coworker's use of the women's restroom caused the plaintiff to "cry uncontrollably" and suffer "a panic attack," both district judges ruled that the women in question were subject to severe sexual harassment—"effectuated," as the judge in the Johnson case remarked, by male employees "allegedly known for" their "disparate interpersonal treatment of women."[34] But in Reed's and Koschoff's cases, despite the extreme targeting to which they were subjected, each court found in favor of the case's defendant. In Reed's case, her "enthusiastic receptiveness to sexually suggestive jokes and activities" served as evidence that she understood her coworkers' behaviors to be far from "harassing and abusive."[35] And in Koschoff's case, the physical toll that her employer's restroom restrictions exacted on her body was, in the eyes of the court, insufficient to conclude than any sort of "adverse employment action" had taken place. While unpleasant, the opinion contends, actions like a superior's oversight of an employee's bathroom usage "effectuate no real change in the employee's compensation, terms, conditions, or privileges of employment."[36] This made her experience of harassment insufficiently "severe or pervasive," in the language of *Meritor*'s definition of actionable sexual harassment, for her case to be heard or resolved in her favor.

In fact, sexual harassment cases were not alone in "mean[ing] different things in different places,"[37] as Abigail Saguy finds in her comparative

I'm sorry but now is that sexual harass-ment?

analysis of American and French sexual harassment law. Instead, a parallel pattern of bifurcated outcomes also appeared in classic sex discrimination cases closely aligned with existing precedent. Where cases like *Catlett v. Missouri Highway and Transportation Commission* (1983) were resolved in the plaintiff's favor, with the court finding ample evidence of discrimination in the facts "that there were no restroom facilities for women to use while the maintenance crews were on duty, and that the job required long hours and involved dangerous activities in inclement weather,"[38] many other charges of restroom-related gender discrimination were unsuccessful. For instance, in *Mackey v. Shalala* (1999), the plaintiff alleged that one of the directors in a subdivision of the National Institutes of Health "conducted informal meetings in the men's restroom"[39] and thereby restricted her from the opportunities for promotion available to her male colleagues. But the court found that, if such events did occur, they were insufficient to qualify as "intentional discrimination."[40] Similarly, in *Gasperini v. Dominion Energy New England, Inc.* (2012), the plaintiff's male colleagues congregated in the men's locker room during meal breaks, where she could not join them "without the threat of being fired." This may have caused her to be "systemically isolated and excluded from her coworkers," according to the court, but such feelings were "too trivial to constitute adverse employment action."[41]

Despite their diversity, then, federal cases about gender discrimination and workplace restrooms share a common theme: all of them actively configure restrooms as consequential instruments of gender discrimination in employment. While cases like *Mackey* and *Gasperini* did ultimately conclude that the discriminatory acts occurring in or around restrooms were too incidental to qualify for injunctive relief or financial recompense, their very presence on a federal docket suggests that restrooms are not incidental or unimportant parts of the workplace. Instead, restroom facilities, restroom fixtures, and intra-restroom interactions convey who is welcome, who is respected, and who is valued in labor settings—all of which can coalesce into legally recognizable forms of gender discrimination. Moreover, such cases suggest that gender inequality can be reinforced through everyday, taken-for-granted interactional processes as much as they can be through familiar mechanisms like hiring discrimination.[42] But the differences in the outcomes of such cases—

especially cases featuring similar allegations from similar plaintiffs—also pose a puzzle: in the specific circumstance of restroom-related workplace interactions, what distinguishes cases like *Catlett* and *Johnson*, in which the court in question did find convincing evidence of workplace harassment or gender discrimination directed toward the plaintiff, from cases like *Koschoff* or *Gasperini*, in which the court ultimately sided with the defendant?

"THE BODY INVOLVES THE MOST SACRED AND MEANINGFUL OF ALL PRIVACY RIGHTS"

One springboard to an answer to that question can be found in recent sociological scholarship about gender and the law, which traces its intellectual lineage to a paradigm shift in legal scholarship from earlier decades. Toward the end of the twentieth century, feminist legal studies and critical legal studies began framing the American court system as a meaning-making, cultural institution. In other words, although they continued to theorize the judiciary as a regulatory force that operated, to some extent, on "rationally ordained,"[43] autonomous, and self-standing logics, as Max Weber once observed, they also came to view the courts as responsive to other systems of knowledge and power—especially systems that reinforce and reproduce various forms of social marginalization. By the dawn of the twenty-first century, legally oriented social scientists had taken that critical zeitgeist one step further and positioned the law as an origin point for determining what complex social entities such as gender, race, sexuality, and disability are in the first place. That basic impulse—to understand when and how the courts participate in the cultural construction of embodied social categories—has continued to anchor legal research in the contemporary sociology of gender, with recent studies documenting judicial efforts to define the very concepts of "female" and "male," delimit the social relationships between men and women, and specify the consequences of gender-category membership for the litigants in their purview.[44]

For lawsuits about workplace restrooms, claims about the meaning and consequences of gender difference were indeed commonplace. At times, such ideological contentions appeared in the portion of federal opinions devoted to recounting the facts of a given case—thereby capturing what employers or employees allegedly believed about gendered bodies or gendered interactions. *EEOC v. M.D. Pneumatics, Inc.*, (1983) epitomizes this tendency. The opinion notes that two former employees testified to the behind-the-scenes sexist beliefs that their superiors espoused: one hiring manager believed that "if they hired women they would have to build restrooms, that the work was too heavy for women, and that if they hired good looking women in the shop, production would go down," and another indicated aloud that "women would not want to work in the plant" in the first place, "because the work was too heavy and too dirty, and that women would bother the men."[45] But many of those same logics also appeared in the language of the court's justification for its final decision, as was notably the case in *DeClue v. Central Illinois Light Company* (2000). There, the lone female lineman for an electric company charged her employer with creating a hostile work environment—one legally categorized as sexual harassment—owing to a lack of appropriate restroom facilities. Rather than recounting those facts in a neutral way, however, the court intersperses editorial commentary about gender at several points along the way:

> Linemen work where the lines are, and that is often far from any public restroom; nor do the linemen's trucks have bathroom facilities. Male linemen have never felt any inhibitions about urinating in the open, as it were. They do not interrupt their work to go in search of a public restroom. Women are more reticent about urinating in public than men. So while the defendant's male linemen were untroubled by the absence of bathroom facilities at the job site, the plaintiff was very troubled and repeatedly but unsuccessfully sought corrective action, for example the installation of some sort of toilet facilities in the linemen's trucks.[46]

Moreover, the opinion's final conclusion indicates that employers have an obligation to "make accommodations for differences in upper-body strength or other characteristics that differ systematically between the sexes,"[47] including urinary processes. Such themes of physical gender difference as self-evident further recur in the dissenting opinion, even as the opinion itself disagrees with the majority's ruling. As it opines, "The fact is, biology has given men less to do in the restroom and made it much easier for them to do it. If men are less reluctant to urinate outdoors, it is in significant part because they need only unzip and take aim."[48]

But federal cases also considered another key issue as they made sense of gendered biology and other forms of gender difference: bodily privacy. Those considerations were especially palpable in cases stemming from work settings in which the exposure of nude bodies was an unavoidable reality rather than an imagined possibility. In *Backus v. Baptist Medical Center* (1981), for instance, a male nurse charged a hospital with gender discrimination, but the district court sided wholeheartedly with the defendant. As the opinion observes while recounting relevant judicial precedent, "Those courts coming squarely to deal with this issue have determined that the body involves the most sacred and meaningful of all privacy rights,"[49] and so, it adds, "[g]iving respect to [the] deep-seated feeling of personal privacy involving one's own genital area" is a more important consideration for employers than "the employee's competence."[50] More volatile were cases involving carceral settings, in which claims for gender equity in employment might conflict with a prisoner's bodily privacy. On the one hand, several opinions contended that gender equity should be the preeminent deciding factor when gender-based employment conflicts arise in prisons. As *Dothard v. Rawlinson* (1977) states, "To deprive women of job opportunities because of the threatened behavior of convicted criminals is to turn our social priorities upside down."[51] On the other hand, as the opinion for *Women Prisoners of District of Columbia Department of Corrections v. District of Columbia* (1994) notes, inmates are in an unusually vulnerable position because all of their activities, innocuous and intimate alike, are supervised by prison personnel: "The women [inmates] are tightly confined, making their escape from harassment as unlikely as escape from the jail itself. Routine invasions of bodily privacy, such as men peering into women's cells at CTF [i.e., the Correctional Treatment Facility, a series of buildings in the larger prison complex] or the unannounced presence of male guards in female living areas provide a reminder to women prisoners that their exposure to abuse is almost endless."[52]

And as that last quote suggests, such privacy logics systematically intertwined with logics of gender difference—with the opinion in *Forts v. Ward* (1978) being especially illustrative of that reality. With respect to the possibility of prisoners' privacy rights, the case referenced the precedent established in *Wolfish v. Levi* (1977), saying, "Obviously, an individual's normal right of privacy must necessarily be abridged upon incarceration in the interest of security of the institution," and later adding, "Inmates must be kept track of constantly and, on occasion, unexpectedly observed to be sure that plotting is not under way nor is the fashioning of crude but effective weapons, such as pieces of metal sharpened to razor quality to use against either guards or other inmates." At the same time, however, the opinion determined that there should be a limit to the reach of prison surveillance: "Regardless of how limited an inmate's right to privacy is, as viewed by penologists and others, all agree on one thing—that there is such a thing as a right of privacy." Moreover, the right of privacy had an important dimension that had not been properly handled in existing jurisprudence pertaining to employment equity and prison supervision—and that dimension was gender. Thus, the opinion reasoned, the inmates at Bedford Hills had an especially defensible claim about the violation of their privacy: "All agree that it is an invasion of a female inmate's right of privacy for her to be viewed by a male guard while she is using the toilet— even if he is acting in the normal course of his duties."[53]

In fact, the gendered character of bodily privacy was such a deep-seated and powerful force that it could—under the appropriate conditions— override other legal guidelines. The *Forts* decision thus found "no dispute" with claims that correctional duties at Bedford Hills could be "equally well performed by any qualified and trained man or woman"; however, it also concluded that "equal job opportunity must in some measure give way to the right of privacy."[54] Even in a carceral context of ubiquitous surveillance, that meant a female inmate's right to keep her nude body out of the sight line of male guards was inviolable, precisely because of the gendered character of bodily privacy. Citing anthropologist Margaret Mead's *Coming of Age in Samoa*, the court explained its reasoning:

It is perfectly clear that men and women, from the beginning of recorded history, have had an innate need for privacy in certain areas of living. Virtually all societies[,] even those which have little requirement of clothing for adults and none for children[,] have rules for the concealing of female genitals. And while societies such as the Samoan have "ma(d)e use of the beach as a latrine," there being "no privacy and no sense of shame,"[55] the norm in today's western world is to have enclosed toilet facilities in the home and segregated toilet facilities in public places which children are early taught to use. Even small children in the western world are expected to clothe themselves and keep their private parts covered. These societal rules become mandatory as one approaches adult status. The fact that a need for privacy is the product of social conditioning makes it no less embarrassing or occasions no less feeling of shame when the privacy is invaded.[56]

The court consequently charged the prison's administrators to make accommodations to ensure "the preservation of such minimum of human dignity and such remnant of the quality of life as remains possible," including the provision of translucent shower screens and the assignment of job responsibilities that might involve witnessing nudity to female correctional officers alone. Although it found that "maximizing equal job opportunity" was necessary for the prison to maintain compliance with federal law, the court also concluded that "the risk of at least embarrassment or shame or humiliation from actual or potential viewing" that a female inmate might experience at the hands of "males whose duty it is to watch her" far outweighed any concerns of unconditional employment equity in the prison setting.[57]

Moreover, as the foregoing examples also show, such privacy rights were not distributed equally among all gendered groups—with cisgender women emerging victorious much more often than cisgender men or transgender people. Such tendencies were clearest in cases with transgender women as plaintiffs, such as *Kastl v. Maricopa County Community College Dist.* (2004) and *Etsitty v. Utah Transit Authority* (2005). Kastl, who was fired from an adjunct teaching position after she resisted a new institutional restroom policy requiring her to use the men's room, recounts in her deposition that the revised policy caused her to fear "serious bodily harm as a result of usage of the men's restroom" and to worry constantly about "invasion of [her] privacy." Yet the court sided with the defendant, determining that the invasion of privacy concerns raised by *other* users of the women's restroom—which would be resolved upon Kastl's "completion of sex reassignment surgery"—made her termination valid.[58] Confronted with a similar set of circumstances, the majority opinion in *Etsitty* delivered a similar verdict: "Defendant also points out, and the court agrees, that no study is necessary to conclude that many *women* would be upset, embarrassed, and even concerned for their safety if a man used the public restroom designated exclusively for women. Concerns about privacy, safety, and propriety are the reason that gender-specific restrooms are universally accepted in our society" (emphasis mine)."[59] The district court and court of appeals concurred that the bus driver's "male genitalia" and status as a "biological male" would make it impossible to "accommodate her bathroom usage[,] because UTA drivers typically use public restrooms along their routes rather than restrooms at the UTA facility,"[60] and both ruled that her termination should stand unless she, like Kastl, pursued sex reassignment surgery. ➔ *horreove*

In short, federal opinions involving workplace restrooms consistently assume that female and male bodies are incontrovertibly distinctive, and they do so both subtly through the evidence they cite and overtly through the conclusions they articulate. To not have a space "set apart for nudity,"[61] in the words of *Gatena v. County of Orange* (1999), one that keeps different kinds of gendered bodies (or, perhaps more accurately, different kinds of gendered genitals[62]) separate from one another is thus understood across time and across courtrooms to constitute a personal violation of the most serious degree. Indeed, when federal opinions like *DeClue* argue that women have unique physiological needs for elimination, or case law like *Kastl* asserts that transgender women do not have a right to restroom privacy unless they pursue sex reassignment surgery, they "ossify outdated concepts of ideal 'men' and 'women' and of normative masculinity, femininity, and sexuality"[63]—as Tey Meadow astutely observes in her research on judicial debates about the appropriate legal sex category for transgender people. However, the cases in my sample do more than seek alignment between certain kinds of gendered expectations and certain kinds of gendered bodies. Yes, the federal courts appraise physical bodies, and yes, they unquestionably invoke gender norms as a part of that appraisal. But they also consider the psychological states that litigants claim to experience in tandem with perceived gender violations in or around their workplace restrooms. And, in doing so, the courts profess a belief that possessing a gendered body—a body that might be exposed in or around workplace restrooms—is as emotional as it is biological.

[handwritten margin notes: "time to change mark tho"]

"SO UPSET THAT SHE BECAME PHYSICALLY ILL"

The psychological underpinnings of gendered embodiment have been a frequent target of academic inquiry outside the social sciences in recent years, especially within the interdisciplinary field of transgender studies. In part, interest in gendered cognition and emotion derives from the standard cultural narrative that surrounds transgender experience, which "by definition," Jay Prosser writes, requires a person to "feel differently gendered from her or his birth-assigned sex."[64] But it also comes from the field's intellectual grounding in psychoanalysis and phenomenology—philosophical fields fundamentally interested in the interplay between mind and body. As far back as Simone de Beauvoir's well-known assertion that "one is not born, but, rather, becomes woman," feminist scholars have regarded bodies as socially constructed—that is, constantly and unavoidably shaped by cultural forces, both in terms of raw physical makeup and, moreover, in defining what constitutes a body in the first place.[65] But over the last few years, philosophical touchstones like Jacques Lacan's "mirror stage" of development (wherein infants recognize a different version of themselves in a mirror for the first time) and Maurice Merleau-Ponty's excavation of "proprioception" (that is, the process of making sense of one's own bodily movement and spatial orientation)[66] have turned thinking about such cultural processes inward—and, in particular, toward what it means to sense our gender *within* our physical selves. That "felt sense" of the body, as Gayle Salamon refers to it, is simultaneously material, psychological, and social; it intermingles the physical matter of the body; our invisible, internal perceptions of embodiment; and the institutional beliefs about bodies that circulate around us.[67]

And while such philosophical argot was certainly nowhere to be found in restroom-related case law, the visceral experience of bodily feeling certainly was. For instance, much of the testimony in *Waldo v. Consumers Energy Co.* (2011) presented the availability and state of bathroom facilities as core evidence for the plaintiff's claims that she was singled out because of her gender and, by extension, that her workplace could be considered objectively hostile to women. Her supervisor openly "stated that she and other women were not wanted, welcomed, or accepted" and that he "intended to wash her out."[68] Toilet facilities were frequently made unavailable to her, and she was told that "if she needed to use the restroom, she had better urinate 'like the men,' on the bin or steps of the trucks."[69] But emotional issues were the glue that held those claims together. As the case goes on to report, male coworkers would drive their trucks "against the door of the porta-potty to block her escape" and engage in other behaviors that added up to an inescapable backdrop of being "generally ignored or shunned"[70] at work—and those feelings indeed cemented the case in Waldo's favor. *Castro v. New York City Department of Sanitation* (2000) follows a similar trajectory. The absence of women's restrooms, the opinion reasoned, was equivalent to being denied "rest time between assignments," being "questioned and reprimanded without a union representative," or being "given a negative performance evaluation when [a woman's] rating was an overall good one"—all because that absence clearly and definitively communicated that women were "unwelcome" in the workplace.[71]

In other cases, emotional experiences escalated further to the level of "ugly feelings"—psychologist June Price Tangney's term for "global, painful, and devastating experience[s] in which the self, not just behavior, is painfully scrutinized."[72] Such feelings were most often evoked when a colleague of a different gender entered a restroom space that a plaintiff was using. This was the state of affairs in *James v. National Railroad Passenger Corp.* (2005), wherein the plaintiff brought a discrimination suit against Amtrak for the "egregious violations of privacy"[73] that the unisex restrooms at one of their worksites enabled, including the regular occurrence of men walking in on women using the restroom. In other cases, it was not necessary for a coworker or supervisor to physically enter a restroom space to trigger feelings of bodily violation. A tape recorder located in a toilet stall of a police department women's restroom was the source of workplace strife in *Kohler v. City of Wapakoneta* (2005). The male coworker who had planted the device captured only "sounds of water running, doors opening, and other mechanical sounds" and not "voices or 'personal noises'"; however, the knowledge that he had trespassed into the space of the women's room and planted a recording device nonetheless left Kohler feeling "noticeably upset and shaken by the incident."[74] Such reactions often escalated into more tangible forms of illness, too—as in *Cottrill v. MFA, Inc.* (2006), when an employer's construction of a peephole to spy on the plaintiff's restroom use caused her to become "so upset that she became physically ill and had to leave work and retreat to the privacy of her home."[75]

Those emotional experiences were such a powerful form of evidence that the courts virtually never found in a plaintiff's favor when their emotional intensity was low. Judges would acknowledge a litigant's mild to moderate embarrassment or discomfort in many such instances, but they would ultimately consider that sentiment to be insufficient for successfully arguing that legal gender discrimination had occurred. In one, *Munday v. Waste Management of North America, Inc.* (1994), the opinion reports that a supervisor's possession of bathroom keys; comments like, "How bad do you have to go?" when the key was requested; and infrequent restocking of bathroom paper supplies constituted "the sorts of aggravating circumstances which occur in many workplace environments."[76] That aggravation, then, was quite an unpleasant employment experience, but it did not comprise the severe emotional distress required by the court to effectively buttress a sexual harassment suit. In another, *Brown v. Snow* (2004), the court agreed with the plaintiff that it was indeed "uncomfortable" for his female supervisor to require him to report to her when he went to the bathroom, but such discomfort alone could not "rise to the level of actionable sexual harassment."[77] Also "uncomfortable" was managerial oversight of the plaintiff's restroom usage in *Ford-Fugate v. FedEx Freight* (2007); but likewise, that court ruled that the evidence presented could "not amount to a working environment that could be characterized as 'hellish.'"[78] In *Schultze v. White* (2005), too, the plaintiff's case failed because of a complete absence of evidence that her supervisor caused her embarrassment or offense when he was "monitoring her trips to the restroom."[79]

But equally important to a plaintiff's success was a definitively gendered element to those emotional experiences. What the federal courts were evaluating, then, was not just the presence or intensity of mortifying emotions; they were also looking for evidence that each worker was *feeling gender*—that is, viscerally experiencing their embodied emotional response to a given social situation as inextricably linked to their sense of themself as a man, a woman, or another kind of gendered person. Where that evidence was unavailable, as was the situation for a police matron in *Warner v. City of Terre Haute, Indiana* (1998), discrimination was never found to exist. In that case, the plaintiff challenged a workplace policy requiring her "to call the commander whenever she left her station,"[80] and the opinion concedes that it probably was quite "humiliating to have to call a man and ask permission to go to the bathroom." However, because the defendants "demonstrated a business necessity"[81] that applied equally to both men and women, the court found that the policy was legally permissible. Similarly, in *Farmer v. Dixon Electrical Systems and Contracting, Inc.* (2013), a female electrician working in a hospital construction zone sued her employer after being fired "because [she] complained about the urinals so much."[82] The urinals in question were external troughs attached to the standard port-a-potties at the job site, and Farmer found the regular sight of her male coworkers' genitals "humiliating and degrading." "But," the opinion reports, her other female colleagues did not find the urinal setup offensive, and the men using the fixtures "were equally embarrassed by their use."[83] Because that mortification was spread evenly among all the construction employees, it was not gender-specific enough to constitute sex discrimination.

Most importantly of all, though, a litigant's claims about gendered affect had to comport with broader cultural expectations about femaleness and maleness. In *Vroman v. A. Crivelli Buick Pontiac GMC, Inc.* (2010), for instance, a male service technician took issue with his female supervisor occasionally walking through the men's restroom in the building where they worked. Though she did so to access a storage space located in the bathroom, he characterized her conduct as extremely "offensive" and did not think that the apology she issued to him for her restroom entry was "an effective response to the nature and severity of his complaint."[84] In fact, he believed, if he had been a woman and she had been a man, such a restroom intrusion "would have resulted in . . . immediate termination."[85] And his assessment may have been exactly right—because the court did not find evidence of sexual harassment in his case, but other courts often did when the gender roles were reversed. Indeed, in *Adams v. City of New York* (2011), it was neither the absence of convenient restroom facilities for female correctional officers nor the requirement that they announce their restroom-related intentions over the radio to another officer when stepping out that resulted in a decision for the plaintiffs. Rather, the crux of the case was one single event: the sensation of "extreme

discomfort and humiliation" the plaintiffs experienced as a result of a singular comment made by a commanding officer in response to a request for
a restroom break—one asserting that women belonged "at home barefoot
and pregnant."[86]

THE SECOND ELEMENT OF GENDER'S INSTITUTIONAL ACCOMPLISHMENT: EMBODIED AFFECT

All in all, as we might predict from existing sociological scholarship about
the law, federal jurisprudence about gender and workplace restrooms is
firmly grounded in legal precedent and does espouse normative expectations about gender and privacy. But the American courts also seek out a
definitively emotional kind of evidence when attempting to discern
whether or not actionable sex discrimination has occurred in or around a
plaintiff's toileting space at work. Specifically, when it comes to the written opinions I study in this chapter, judicial answers to questions about
restroom inequalities and intrusions revolve around the extent to which,
if at all, litigants are *feeling gender* in response to perceived violations—
that is, sensing themselves as gendered people in ways that are visceral,
affective, and inextricably linked to the physical body. Moreover, as the
federal courts seek those answers, they reinforce several, interrelated
cultural tropes about gendered embodiment: that cisgender men are
insatiable sexual predators, that transgender people are less deserving of
the law's protection than their cisgender counterparts, and above all, that
cisgender women are inherently weak and vulnerable to assault. In other
words, to play on the jurisprudential language of employment discrimination, restroom case law may seem "facially neutral"—that is, based on
rationales that seem to apply equally to all litigants regardless of their
gender category. In reality, however, such case law has a "disparate impact,"
because the emotional underpinnings of written opinions reproduce normative gender expectations—with all of the patriarchal and cissexist
assumptions those expectations entail.

In "Doing Gender," Candace West and Don Zimmerman remind us that
gendered expectations are a cultural creation rather than a biological
imperative. Gender, they write, is "an achieved property of situated con-

duct" that comes to exist only through "a complex of socially guided perceptual, interactional, and micropolitical activities."[87] For them, the frequency and ubiquity of gender-conforming actions in everyday situations are what make the gender system seem "natural, essential, or biological."[88] And while that formulation is perhaps best known and most often cited for its microsociological elements—that is, those local moments of everyday, face-to-face exchange between flesh-and-blood human beings—their theory is every bit as institutional as it is interactional. As they explain by way of reference to their article's title, "doing" gender means managing one's behavior "in light of normative conceptions of attitudes and activities appropriate for one's sex category," and those normative conceptions are very much a product of the "institutional arena in which [social] relationships are enacted."[89] In other words, to "do" gender is not to playfully and agentically perform femaleness, maleness, or something else altogether. Instead, we are all expected to act in accordance with gender norms, and we risk social sanctions should we choose to deviate from those norms. Thus, they conclude, there is a recursive, continuous interplay between the structure of gender-related expectations and the everyday exchanges that fuel those institutional constraints—an interplay that makes some room for human agency but views that agency as rarely able to achieve transformative ends.

In many respects, federal case law about workplace restrooms robustly illustrates West and Zimmerman's basic cycle. On the interactional side, the litigants who seek each court's intercession are very much active and engaged participants in the institutional deliberations that follow. If only because the narratives they recount form the evidentiary foundation from which each court assesses the presence or absence of gender discrimination, plaintiffs and defendants are as much a part of constructing restroom jurisprudence as are the judges who arbitrate their claims. And by surveying restroom case law over a multidecade span, I find ample evidence that institutional structures do respond to the ever-evolving nature of those interactional contributions: sex discrimination precedent has evolved dramatically over time, judicial interpretation does remain fluid and responsive to the details of each case, and the federal courts have consistently used restroom issues to expand the definition of litigable gender discrimination.[90] But on the institutional side, the courts clearly gravitate

consistent

toward conventional understandings of innate gender difference in ways that reinforce gendered hegemony, whether by latching on to a plaintiff's passionate account of a traumatizing workplace experience or by asserting how "most" workers might feel about a certain restroom arrangement. Indeed, only when plaintiffs could convey that their restroom-related troubles fit the court's expectations for how a "reasonable" person would experience bodily exposure to the "opposite" sex would a verdict confirm that gender discrimination had indeed occurred.

Yet equally central to West and Zimmerman's account—though much less frequently cited—are the perceptual activities supplementary to their initial definition. To return to their words again, all members of society learn to participate in "a self-regulating process" through which "they begin to monitor their own and others' conduct with regard to its gender implications."[91] And on the basis of this chapter's evidence, that intrapsychic process ought to be moved from the margins of sociological theories of gender to the mainstream. When the federal courts I study assess allegations of workplace discrimination, their final conclusions revolve less around the raw nature of gender difference or the judicial logics bequeathed by legal precedent—at least in and of themselves—and more around each plaintiff's visceral experience of gendered embodiment at work. Whether they address cases about the complete absence of a sanitary restroom, the inability of employees to conveniently and safely access that restroom, or the failed enforcement of absolute gender separation in toileting spaces, judicial assessments of workplace inequality revolve around whether or not—and how strongly—litigants are *feeling gender* in response to perceived restroom violations. Moreover, whether or not those litigants truly feel the sentiments they report to the courts, the self-referential nature of American jurisprudence means that charges of restroom-related gender discrimination must increasingly align with that pathos-laden precedent if plaintiffs wish to gain a ruling in their favor. That, in turn, fuels a recursive cycle between individual gendered experience and institutional gender expectations, one that continually weaves a narrow, normative vision of what it means to *feel gender* into the very fabric of the law.

The second element of theorizing gender as an institutional accomplishment, therefore, is attention to gender's *affective* dimensions. To be clear here, what I mean is not that sociologists should more assiduously study gendered emotions in and of themselves.[92] Rather, the term *affect* draws our attention to when, where, and how the visceral experience of being a gendered body functions as resinous cultural glue for binding the internal, self-regulatory side of gender to broader cultural expectations about gender—and vice versa.[93] To revisit this chapter's empirical data once more: as emotion has become more and more central to the small subset of gender discrimination case law I study here, the embodied experience of gender and the use of affect as evidence have both become ever more requisite to judicial success. In other words, there is something internal and embodied about the gender order, something every bit as sociological as gender's more observable interactional and institutional components. But as sociologists studying the "microfoundations" of all manner of social phenomena in recent years remind us, such emotional accounts are as scripted by social rules as West and Zimmerman find gender to be.[94] To effectively theorize the affective substrate of gendered sociality, then, is not to try to capture the impulsive, immediate, and unconscious experience of emotion itself. Rather, it is to take seriously the ways in which our innermost feelings—and our interactional accounts of those feelings—intersect with what Arlie Hochschild calls "feeling rules":[95] those emotional expectations that have been institutionalized as sensible for a given social situation, and, I add, as sensible to inhere in certain kinds of gendered bodies.

And when those institutionalized expectations find their way into written federal opinions, they have a reach that extends far beyond future litigation. As Pierre Bourdieu observes, "Law consecrates the established order by consecrating the vision of that order which is held by the State." Moreover, "by proclaiming orthodoxy in the name of and to everyone," it "confers upon" that vision "the practical universality of that which is official."[96] Law, then, is as symbolic as it is regulatory: whenever it presents a set of events or experiences as right or true, it implies that rightness and truthfulness to be universal. When federal opinions describe litigants' felt sense of their bodies in response to the seemingly idiosyncratic problem of workplace restroom violations, those innermost sensations become institutionally recognized more as facts than as feelings—facts that insinuate how each of us ought to experience being a gendered body in the first place. In other words, because legal discourses carry so much social authority, their contents and conclusions appear to us as mere common sense instead of as the contested cultural constructions they truly are. As a result, when courts of law commit an understanding of what gender is and what gender means to words in a published federal opinion, they crystallize a seemingly solid and final vision of gender into future lawmaking efforts, the everyday decision-making work of other organizations, and the architectural environment alike. And that appearance of solidity and finality makes the pursuit of any alternatives or challenges to the gender order remarkably difficult to sustain, including the alternatives and challenges posed by the ungendered restrooms I study in the second half of this book.

. . . but "institutions cannot have minds of their own."

Mary Douglas, *How Institutions Think*

4 Working against the Washroom

Buildings are things you live in. They're not metaphors.

Nicola Fucigna, "Poetry and Architecture," *Construction,*
Summer 2015

In July of 1990, an unexpected detour into a men's restroom caused
Denise Wells, a concertgoer at the Summit, an indoor arena in Houston,
Texas, to be on the receiving end of a police stop and a $200 fine. Having
postponed a trip to the women's room until after the concert began—
expecting that the thirty-woman line beyond the restroom door she found
upon first entering the arena would have dissipated by then—she returned
to discover that the line had instead doubled. Because her need to get into
a restroom "became kind of urgent," and because she had just witnessed "a
guy take his girlfriend" into the men's restroom across the corridor, she
opted to simply follow the couple into the men's room.[1] While that option
"would never" have been her "first choice," as she reported to a Houston-
area journalist in the wake of the incident, she determined that her best
possible course of action was to put her hands over her eyes, proceed past
the urinals, and go into a stall to take care of her bathroom-related business.[2] When she emerged, however, she was greeted by a police officer
who had "received complaints from men" about her excursion into their
facility and slapped with a fine for violating a Houston-area ordinance
prohibiting access to restrooms "designated for the exclusive use of the sex
opposite to such person's sex."[3]

When Wells subsequently chose to fight her fine in court, what started as a run-of-the-mill dispute about a local ordinance quickly escalated into a national brouhaha. One local radio station offered to cover her legal expenses as well as the cost of a ticket to another concert—and to provide a portable toilet for her personal use during the show. The *Chicago Tribune* polled Houston residents about the case and, to the surprise of the editorial board, found that three-quarters of survey takers believed that "the law should look the other way" in the event that "nature calls you to the wrong restroom."[4] And when the case escalated to the point of trial, ten out of thirty potential female jurors reported that they, too, had been driven to use "a public restroom intended for the opposite sex"[5] at some point in their lives. One opined to a *New York Times* writer that Wells "clearly did not mean to cause a disturbance"; another reported that the case was a symptom of a much bigger problem, saying, "I think women's needs have been ignored for too long. It's time we go back to public buildings and provide adequate facilities for women."[6] Wells's lawyer, Valorie Wells Davenport, even received supportive phone calls from women as far away as Canada and Australia who had themselves "sought relief in the men's room" and wished to pay Wells's fine and legal fees.[7] But Davenport turned down every single offer, firing back that the situation had clearly "struck a chord" and thus needed to be pursued to the fullest extent possible. "I don't intend to lose," she explained to the press. "This is too important."[8]

Indeed, although the Wells case resolved itself quite readily, with the jury deliberating for a whopping twenty-three minutes before deciding to acquit her, the national conversation about women and public restrooms that it inspired was not nearly so quick to abate. As one writer for the *Chicago Tribune* observed, Wells may have "provided rich fodder for bathroom puns" across the country, but her plight was far from "amusing" to the countless American women who had found themselves "stranded and fuming in sludge-slow, interminable lines for bathrooms at stadiums, museums, and theaters while enviously eyeing the men's room, where a line rarely, if ever, forms."[9] In response, elected officials took explicit steps to start alleviating the problem. In Wells's home state of Texas, for instance, the state legislature passed one of the first laws in the country to require "a ratio of not less than 2:1 women's-to-men's restrooms" for all "facilities where the public congregates."[10] That effort was so warmly received by Governor Ann Richards that she celebrated the bill's original sponsor, Gonzalo Barrientos, a state senator, as a "hero" when she signed the measure into law, saying, "I thank you, and my two daughters thank you, and my three granddaughters thank you."[11]

But the Summit men's room debacle was not the only impetus for so-called "potty parity" laws in the final years of the twentieth century. Academic research about gender differences in restroom usage was also catalyzing conversations about women's restroom equity—and it did so well before Wells gained national attention. One undergraduate researcher from Cornell found her study of a highway rest stop in Washington State mentioned on the floor of the Florida and Pennsylvania state legislatures, as she had clocked a substantial gender disparity in restroom use time: where men took an average of forty-five seconds to use the toilet, women took seventy-nine.[12] Sandra Rawls, a doctoral candidate at Virginia Tech, likewise inspired elected officials in Virginia to change state laws with her study of gender differences in restroom usage. Across multiple settings—including a highway rest stop, a sports arena, an airport, and a conference center—her team of researchers found an average discrepancy almost three times that of the Cornell study, with women taking an average of ninety-six seconds longer than men to use the bathroom. "And not just because they wash their hands," one journalist was quick to add, nor because of biological issues like menstruation. Instead, she found that women take longer for decidedly cultural reasons: "clothing restrictions, a lack of time-saving equipment (like urinals), and because they often must carry in other items, like purses."[13]

Such quantitative metrics and social analyses offered a useful talking point for engineers, building planners, and architects responsible for designing new public spaces for years to follow. In Baltimore, developers for a new ballpark for the Orioles spoke about research on restroom gender differences as an inspiration for their plan to experiment with a new female urinal. According to the product's designer, Kathie Jones, the new device would use less water per flush, take up fewer square feet than traditional toilet stalls, and above all, "help shorten lines in women's restrooms" because they would "require less undressing and no turning, and there would be no toilet seats to cover with tissue."[14] In Denver, the architect for the Colorado Convention Center took elimination empirics into account when he opted to separate the facility's "men's and women's rooms with a movable wall," one that could produce "women's rooms that are three times bigger than the men's" when needed for, say, an upcoming national convention for the Intravenous Nurses Society.[15] And back in Texas, an equally new convention center in Austin was designed from the outset with a "radical skewing in favor of women's restrooms," allocating 20 percent more toilets to women's rooms than to men's rooms as well as 50 percent more sinks and overall square footage. Plus, like the convention center in Denver, the design readily allowed "center managers to 'reassign' restrooms between the sexes when appropriate."[16]

Yet the biggest coup for proponents of potty parity went beyond the design strategies of individual project managers and into official guidelines for building construction. Inspired by local efforts to quantify restroom usage, the executive director of the American Society of Plumbing Engineers explained to one *Chicago Tribune* reporter that restroom equity for women was "a very big issue." As a result, he was an enthusiastic supporter of the organization's own four-year, $5 million study, meant to determine the ideal ratio of men's to women's restroom facilities across a range of public places.[17] Other professional groups began to recommend permanent changes to building codes and construction standards—such as doubling the number of toilets required for women's rooms in convention halls and performing arts centers across the country—to ensure that "Jane" would have "as many johns as John." (But not in stadiums, reasoning that "female attire for the theater may be more time-consuming in the restroom than leisure or outdoors attire."[18]) And seeking a more universal solution to such gender-related restroom ills, the American Institute of Architects began proposing more inventive alternatives to current bathroom arrangements: "separate lounges where women can smoke, put on makeup and change diapers," communal "hand-washing areas" in between men's and women's restrooms, and most radical of all, massive, multiuser "unisex restrooms."[19]

·   ·   ·   ·   ·

In the penultimate decade of the twentieth century, the American Society of Plumbing Engineers and the American Institute of Architects were two among many professional organizations working toward a more inclusive vision of public space—a shift that owed much of its success to an embrace of demographic difference that began in corporate firms and other workplaces in the 1970s and 1980s. As Frank Dobbin writes in *Inventing Equal Opportunity,* "Before 1960, it wasn't merely difficult for a black man or a white woman to get a job as a manager in most firms, it was impossible. Most American employers wouldn't hire women, blacks, or Latinos for any job a white man would take."[20] By the late 1980s and early 1990s, however, administrative personnel were considerably more diverse than at midcentury, with antibias training, offices of diversity management, and visits from external equality experts all institutionalized as regular business practices. Moreover, such transformations had diffused far beyond the world of work. In grade schools and universities, multiculturalism became an essential educational paradigm, one meant to integrate attention to diversity and difference into a monolithically white and male intellectual canon. Newsrooms and advertisers, too, began to project a more representative array of skin colors and body types on television screens and in print media. Even urban planners considered their city's "appeal to the widest possible groups of citizens,"[21] in the words of historian Lynn Hollen Lees, so that their public spaces might better speak to all residents and visitors—through the landmarks they preserved, the new spaces they built, and the building renovations they approved.[22]

Restroom spaces were an inextricable part of such transformations, especially as new expectations of inclusivity found their way into late-twentieth-century legislative politics. As chapter 1 details at length, "potty parity" laws, including those fueled by the hullabaloo of the Wells case, began to reach beyond large public buildings like airports and stadiums and into smaller spaces like parks and libraries. Mayors and municipal officials resurrected funding streams to install or upgrade true public restrooms in urban neighborhoods, especially those with substantial populations of low-income and homeless citizens. At the federal level, even Congress entered the fray by passing a law that would come to have a tremendous influence on the inclusivity of twenty-first-century restroom infrastructure: the Americans with Disabilities Act of 1990. The ADA inaugurated numerous policies to address discrimination against people with disabilities in both employment and public settings, including

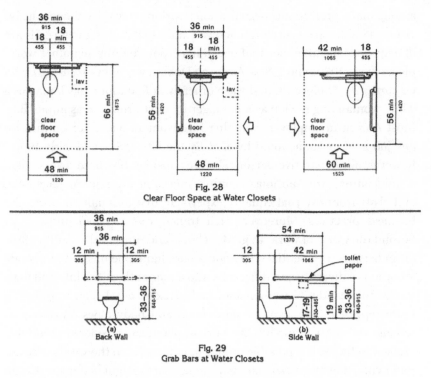

Fig. 28
Clear Floor Space at Water Closets

Fig. 29
Grab Bars at Water Closets

Figure 5. Schematics for "Toilet Stalls," section 4.17 of the *ADA Standards for Accessible Design* (1991).

protocols for workplace hiring, guidelines for accessible public transit, and most pertinently for this book, the Standards for Accessible Design. That 92-page list of construction procedures (later expanded to a 279-page list in the updated 2010 edition) specified, down to the inch, how partitions like stall doors and fixtures like vending machines were to be installed in all new or newly renovated restrooms in "places of public accommodation"[23]—including museums, libraries, restaurants, performance venues, shopping malls, and more.[24]

This chapter takes the public part of the "public accommodation" label seriously, as it delves behind the scenes of three types of municipal organizations—historic sites and landmarks, libraries, and transportation hubs—to understand how laws about "potty parity" and regulations like the ADA Standards for Accessible Design shaped the prevalence of ungendered restroom spaces in such settings over the last three decades. To explore those legal and material intersections, I draw on twenty-four semistructured interviews with organizational directors, facility supervisors, building managers, and other administrative personnel who witnessed and/or helped usher in the arrival of the first ungendered restroom in their respective establishments. In stark contrast to today's contentious public discourse about the promise and perils of ungendered restrooms, my respondents' accounts contained little evidence of dismay, consternation, or outrage about such spaces. Instead, they recalled, cultural shifts toward embracing diversity—like those I described in the foregoing two paragraphs—led them and their colleagues to champion the possibility that their physical plant might become more accessible to all their patrons. Whereas moral resistance was scant, however, the material limits of existing infrastructure and stringent demands of interlocking local, state, and federal law were plentiful, and they made even the most desirable restroom renovations into onerous organizational quagmires.

Yet when I asked respondents to retrace the steps of their most recent restroom renovation in detail, it became apparent that one of those obstacles—the law—was not always an insurmountable obstacle to plumbing upgrades. Instead, if a municipal organization was confronted with inadequate sanitary infrastructure, its personnel could creatively mobilize regulations like the ADA as an impetus for change, particularly if the potential cost of noncompliance with such mandates threatened to exceed the budget necessary for a desired renovation. But even the cleverest maneuvers to cultivate what I call *legal consonance*—that is, the transplantation of obliquely applicable legal frameworks to otherwise intractable organizational problems like the absence of an ungendered restroom—could not overcome the materialized history of gendered plumbing nearly so easily. While my respondents were all able to leverage regulatory requirements in ways that led to the construction of at least one ungendered restroom, only some municipal organizations were geographically and fiscally well-positioned enough to secure renovations that exceeded a bare minimum. Sadly enough, then, their experiences demonstrate how outdated buildings and underfunded civic budgets collude behind the scenes to determine just how inclusive an organization's infrastructure can truly be.

"EXTENSIVE PLUMBING GYMNASTICS"

As the Wells case makes clear, gender—and especially talk of gender difference—is everywhere in contemporary restroom discourse. Whether we look at public conversations about "potty parity" from the final years of the twentieth century or recent rigmarole about "bathroom bills" meant to limit or enhance restroom access for transgender people, vociferous commentary about sexed bodies abounds in conversations about toileting infrastructure. In part, as sociological theories of gender teach us, that intensity derives from our collective attachment to the notion that "female" and "male" are distinctive and oppositional cultural categories. Erving Goffman, for instance, glibly (but accurately) expressed our magnetic draw to categorical gender difference in "The Arrangement between the Sexes" in 1977 by saying, "Gender, not religion, is the opiate of the masses."[25] And countless studies since have found that challenges to gender's allegedly binary character—be they symbolic, like androgynous names, or substantive, like childhood play with the "wrong" type of gender-specific toys—tend to be squelched rather than sustained.[26] But restrooms are a particularly polarizing variant of that general tendency. As Laurel Westbrook and Kristen Schilt find in their analysis of media discourse about transgender people, gender-separated spaces are especially prone to producing "gender panics"—that is, frantic assertions of the stability and innateness of female-male difference that emerge in response to social situations that threaten or disrupt gender's apparent naturalness.[27]

Such gender panic was, occasionally, salient in my interviews with respondents from municipal organizations. "People get kind of squirmy about public toilets, especially when you're talking about a place with as much commuter traffic as we get," observed Charles when I asked him to recall if there was any opposition to his transit center's family restroom. "If you ask me, that's the nature of the beast: so many people come through here each and every day," he added, "and it's not like we have, like, an airport screening setup where the public is barricaded from passengers. So, it seems to a lot of people that anyone could come in and do anything, and the idea that some guy could chase down and assault some woman was a real concern." Margaret, too, reported that being so physically open to the public induced anxieties among her colleagues when their library first began discussions about a gender-neutral restroom option—especially because those conversations emerged "well before it was politically palatable." As she was talking about the various strategies she and her "like-minded colleagues" used to garner a critical mass of staff support, she briefly remarked that "LGBT stuff can still feel really . . . edgy, for lack of a better word, to some of my more conservative colleagues." When I later asked her to follow up on what she meant by "edgy," her response was strikingly similar to Charles's remarks: "Honestly, I think it's less outright homophobia or what have you and more about that there's going to be illicit or lewd behavior. People want to provide for families and youth, but I remember having to issue these reassurances that people wouldn't start coming in and using the bathroom for things you shouldn't be doing in a bathroom."

But as that mention of families and youth portended, most respondents in my sample reported little moral outrage about the prospect of constructing an ungendered restroom. Instead, the overwhelming majority viewed such spaces as productively connected to their organization's mission and values. My conversation with Margaret was, again, illustrative of that trend: she reported to me early in our interview conversation that "inclusive restroom spaces of all types" were "absolutely essential to serving all members" of her urban library's local community. In part, she understood that integral character to be an offshoot of the mission of any public library: "We serve the public," she explained, "and that public comes in all shapes, sizes, and identity categories." But in part, she also felt that her library's "proximity to the gayborhood" gave her building and her staff a particular charge—one that extended into restroom-related decisions:

MARGARET: I've seen lots of teens and young adults come through here over the years to work out gender and sexuality stuff, because they don't feel like they can Google certain things at home. So, the library becomes so much more than a source of information. It's really a safe haven, sometimes the only safe haven they really have.

INTERVIEWER: And you see bathrooms as a part of that?

MARGARET: Exactly. Having a restroom space that's open to all is helpful to a lot of patrons for a lot of reasons, but signals of acceptance as small as a sign on a bathroom door can make a world of difference for a genderqueer or trans-identified kid who's struggling with who they are.

A similar narrative was at the heart of my conversation with Kate, as she recounted how recent changes across the institutional landscape for public libraries had led to an increasing interest among her staff in adding an ungendered restroom to their architectural footprint. As she explained, "One of the big pushes with the ALA [American Library Association] has been toward maximizing library inclusion." For her, that meant suburban libraries had many new responsibilities to the local community: "There are so many online resources now about culturally responsive library programming and effective outreach to community members who might be living in poverty or are underprivileged in some other way, like not having internet access at home," she explained, "and I even came across a pamphlet on the importance of gender-neutral bathrooms in libraries the last time I was looking at diversity programming." She then tied that broader cultural shift to a specific set of local adjustments, saying, "I think librarians get that the choices we make about our space send a message to our patrons, and here at [library name], everyone came on board really quickly with wanting to find a way to create a gender-neutral bathroom."

Yet collective organizational approval was only the tip of the restroom-renovation iceberg. While Kate was not the slightest bit surprised by how quickly her colleagues came together to rally for a gender-neutral restroom, she was astonished to see a new obstacle to its adoption emerge just as quickly: "The problem was that we just weren't prepared for how complicated it would be to find space for it." She paused. "We were really surprised to discover how tricky it would be to find enough square footage for a separate single-stall restroom in a spot that wouldn't require extensive plumbing gymnastics." Charles, too, spoke of material considerations as central to the spatial layout of his transit center's restrooms, though he was not nearly as surprised as Kate was about their relevance to a desired plumbing update. "Any changes to our physical plant are an exercise in creativity amidst constraints," he opined, "because the existing electrical, plumbing, ducts, insulation . . . all that, you want to disturb as little as possible." By way of further explanation, he then segued into a domestic simile: "I think the easiest way to think about it is like new home construction versus a renovation. There are certain places your water supply comes into your lot, which puts a little pressure on the location of your kitchen, your laundry, your bathrooms in a new house, but not much. But once that house is there, doing something like moving your washer and dryer upstairs to be off a master bedroom, or adding a new guest bathroom, is a heck of a lot easier if you can situate them against the wall that already plumbs the master bath."

In other words, for Kate's library and Charles's transit center, present-day renovation possibilities hinged on the architectural choices made for (or placed upon) their organization's physical structure in the past. Occasionally, my respondents described that physical history as a rich treasure trove of plumbing possibilities, as it made unisex restrooms a straightforward adaptation. When I spoke with Erin about her historic site's recent addition of a new ungendered restroom space, for instance, she recounted their construction process with delight: "We really lucked out. New plumbing can be incredibly expensive, especially the labor costs associated with having to hire a city-vetted firm, but we had a janitorial closet with a sink and mop basin sort of attached . . ." She drifted off, making two fists with her hands before placing them knuckle-to-knuckle to visually accompany her next words:

> . . . to the walls in between our men's and women's rooms. What we were able to do was move out the back wall a couple of feet into our back offices, swap out the existing fixtures for regular, handicapped-accessible bathroom ones, and change out the lock so you could actually latch the door from the inside. So yes, to answer your original question, there were definitely things that needed to happen, and those things couldn't happen overnight. But most of what we needed was cosmetic, not skeletal, you know. All things considered, I was pleased with how quickly we got our unisex option in place.

Justin, likewise, described the "unique challenges" of historical architecture that had made "modern plumbing a tall order to add in the first place" as a boon when local elected officials inquired about the possibility of degendering the restrooms in his historic site. "Going gender-neutral was easy for us because we already had single-stall bathrooms," he explained. "So once we made the decision and got township approval, all we had to do was order new signs and track down a screwdriver to replace them."

Much more often, however, the gendered character of existing restroom infrastructure limited more than it enabled. Unlike Justin's report of a quick change of signage, most respondents from municipal organizations

Figure 6. Unisex toilet sign.
(Photo by author)

with older architecture lamented such constraints in our interview conversations. "There's a strange irony in this for us," Kimberly remarked
when I asked if she knew anything about her suburban historic site's
restroom-related history, "in that it was an incredible struggle in the 1980s
to get a separate women's room in the building created in the first place
for our staff." She went on to recount worries that the addition of a wom-
en's restroom would "harm the building's original architecture" and "place
undue stress on a 140-year-old building." But two decades later, she continued, "that women's room that was fought so hard for was the thing in
the way" of adding a much-desired family restroom for the benefit of visitors: "There wasn't really space for the women's room, so when we filled in
the only available corner, that was that. We were totally out of restroom
room." But respondents from buildings with more contemporary histories
also foregrounded similar themes. "I have to start two renovations ago, in
the mid-1990s," David replied when I asked him about the origins of the
family restroom in his urban transit center. He went on: "[The state] had
just passed a law mandating more stalls and fixtures for women's restrooms
in public accommodations, which was fine, because we wanted to expand

things like stall space, walking room around sinks, et cetera. But fast-forward twenty years, that extra space we absorbed into meeting those equity laws made it mighty difficult to find a workable spot for the handicapped unisex bathroom we now had to add."

Thus, for the municipal organizations in my sample, binary gender ideologies were an unquestionable impediment to degendering existing restrooms or adding a new ungendered space, but that ideological hindrance operated much more often through an organization's inherited material environment than through present-day moral outrage. In other words, my respondents and their organizations found themselves confronting what Geoffrey Bowker and Susan Leigh Star call the "inertia" of historical architectural choices and building design standards—that is, the possibilities and limitations embedded in physical infrastructure from cultural and organizational work done in the past.[28] For some respondents, like Erin and Justin, the concretized, physical remnants of gendered laws and gendered history sometimes made the arrival of a new, ungendered restroom readily possible. But more often, that cultural resin functioned as an impasse, especially when a building's original plumbing design had been organized around two equal-but-separate toileting spaces. Indeed, for Kimberly's museum and David's transit hub, plans and policies that represented the cutting edge of restroom equity a mere decade or two ago were already starting to prove obsolete, because they reflected a set of gender mores that was no longer desirable or optimal. Consequently, even though my respondents were committed—and often fervently so—to the hypothetical goal of making their restrooms more inclusive, the existing physical structure of their respective organizations placed a profound limit on their ability to actualize the ungendered spaces they now coveted.

"BORDERLINE-INVENTING THE PRETENSE OF ACCESSIBILITY PROBLEMS"

David's passing remark about state-level restroom requirements, however, foreshadowed the reality that physical structures were not the only obstacle to ungendered restroom creation. In addition, a complex nexus of regulatory structures determines—or, perhaps more accurately, *over*determines—building construction in the contemporary United States. From height maximums on urban skyscrapers to ensure aesthetically pleasing lines of sight to policies mandating heat-resistant construction materials to hinder the spread of a would-be fire, infrastructure is, as many architectural scholars observe, an "incredibly regulated world."[29] Such regulations are especially voluminous when it comes to restrooms. Local ordinances often require certain kinds of signage to be prominently posted outside bathroom doors. State plumbing codes specify the details of the fixtures housed behind those doors, as well as the materials from which those fixtures can legally be engineered. Federal guidelines detail how many toileting spaces must be made available in workplaces, businesses, and municipal spaces, based on how many employees or visitors they serve. Even international building standards feature protocols for optimizing plumbing safety and energy efficiency.[30] Consequently, organizations that share a geographic location or a cultural identity—whether that identity is narrow, like "regional public library," or broad, like this chapter's institutional penumbra of "municipal organization"—tend to share a common approach to plumbing infrastructure. Sociologists of organizations refer to this regularity as "coercive isomorphism"—that is, the tendency of organizations in a shared legal environment to adopt similar practices and policies, most often to avoid the sanctions that might accrue in response to deviating from legally mandated proscriptions.[31]

At times, that coercive influence became relevant to my interview conversations well before I had a chance to ask my respondents about the specifics of their restroom spaces. Genevieve, a decision maker for a suburban public library, apologized for the constraints of local and state building codes early in our interview, saying, "In a lot of ways, it would be fantastic if we had total control over our space—tear a wall down here, create a new nook for our children's collection there. But an awful lot of what would be preferable from our point of view as a staff can't happen without a construction permit from an approved contracting firm, and even then, what we want isn't always building-code compliant." At other times, however, talk of legal codes and requirements arose only when my interviews took a more myopic turn toward the specific conversations and organizational processes that led to the construction of one or more ungendered restrooms in the present day. Amy's recollections about her urban historic site, for instance, took a lighter approach to infrastructure than Genevieve's but ultimately landed on a parallel set of conclusions. "It's funny," she said. "There are so many changes you can't make to registered historic sites in the United States—and for good reason. They're historic!" She paused for a moment before continuing with a bemused expression on her face: "But we have basically the same restroom facilities as the ones you'd see on the side of [interstate name], because a state toilet is a state toilet. The fact that this building is about a hundred and fifty years older than that interstate is irrelevant, because we're all a part of [state name]."

Either way, gender was inextricable from such conversational contributions—as Alan's animated description of his library's ungendered restroom epitomized. Like Genevieve and Amy, he started to tell me the history of all three of their restrooms (one men's room, one women's room, and one family restroom) with quite a bit of emphasis on legal matters. "The trickiest bit for us was that our 'public'"—which he punctuated visually with air quotes made with his pointer and middle fingers—"restrooms are also our employee restrooms. That means . . ." He took a deep breath before rattling off a laundry list of concerns: "We aren't just up against the building, which may or may not have easily rerouted plumbing, and municipal law, which has very specific guidelines about how we allocate building-related expenditures. We *also* have OSHA to contend with, which mandates that workplaces of our size have separate men's and women's restrooms for our employees, *and* state law, which has even more narrow requirements about ensuring those restrooms are a particular kind of comparable" (emphases his). Yet the true nature of the problem, he explained as a coda to his brief monologue, was not just that confusing and contradictory nexus of competing legal dictates about gender. Instead, what made him and his local library system's other supervisors almost "throw up our hands and give up" was that "the firm hired to do the building couldn't give us all of what we wanted and hoped for at the budget we had planned on and gotten approval for." Those complications, in turn, led to a series of "really unusual" plumbing choices—which, when it came time to add "a wheelchair-accessible unisex restroom," foreclosed the option of putting that restroom in "the least historically destructive segment of the building." To make that bathroom finally happen thus required "more time and more reengineering than any of us had imagined possible for such a small bathroom."

Yet the law is far from an omnipotent bully that pushes organizations into one narrow course of action. Instead, as I gently asked my interview respondents to walk me through the history of their ungendered restrooms in as much detail as they could recall, they started to speak of legal mandates as unexpectedly generative—often when the ADA and its attendant Standards for Accessible Design became a topic of conversation. Despite the apparent specificity of some portions of the Standards (like the grab-bar dimensions depicted in figure 5 earlier in this chapter), the ADA is an unusually flexible piece of legislation, and its implementation has changed considerably over time.[32] Just a few sections past the one that provides comprehensive schematics for toilet installation, for instance, the Accessibility Guidelines for Buildings and Facilities advocate the addition of ungendered toilet rooms to an existing floor plan to enhance accessibility:

> Experience has shown that the provision of accessible "unisex" or single-user restrooms is a reasonable way to provide access for wheelchair users and any attendants, especially when attendants are of the opposite sex. Since these facilities have proven so useful, it is often considered advantageous to install a "unisex" toilet room in new facilities in addition to making the multi-stall restrooms accessible, especially in shopping malls, large auditoriums, and convention centers.[33]

Numerous decision makers referenced such sections of the ADA as a critical driving force behind infrastructure-related upgrades, including those from their most recent round of restroom renovations. Harry, for instance, recalled that the Department of Justice's update of the Standards in 2010 gave the managers of his historic site the "nudge" they needed to "order and install new fixtures and stalls to reorganize the space we already had," and that yielded a small, unisex restroom between their two gender-separated ones. Richard, likewise, pointed to the specific single-user clause as his historic site's motivation for building "an entirely new sub-building" with a spacious family restroom—to "head off any possible legal infractions for accessibility violations" that might be assessed to their existing, difficult-to-renovate restrooms.

But part of what made the ADA so generative was a reality familiar to sociologists studying the legal environments of organizations: a human touch is ultimately what translates regulatory guidelines into on-the-ground, organizational practices.[34] For respondents like Judy, an ungendered restroom was thus not a forced, reactive response to federal law; it was the result of her agentic and proactive reconnoitering. Her civic landmark had recently installed not one, but three ungendered restrooms—an arrangement that, she averred, should be more common in all manner of public spaces: "When transgender teens are showing up in *Good Housekeeping* in a positive, family-values kind of way, you know it's time to get with the gender program. It's 2015, for goodness sake. Why is who you pee with still such an issue?" But when I asked how, exactly, they were able to afford multiple single-stall, unisex restrooms on a limited civic budget, gender momentarily vanished from her narrative: "We knew we weren't in lockstep with ADA compliance, and riding the coattails of the grandfather clause clearly wasn't fair to our patrons with accessibility needs. So, a couple of colleagues and I put our heads together and realized we could knock out two birds with one stone: gender-friendliness and wheelchair access." In other words, the ADA offered her bureaucratic ammunition to convince her supervisors to approve a substantial restroom renovation. To that end, they wrote a memo to their director that, in her words, said, "Hey, here are all the legal risks we're taking and how we can fix them. We'll write the grants and call the donors if you agree to let us make this argument." And best of all, she continued with a satisfied smile, "He was obviously happy to sign off."

In other words, Judy was able to strategically deploy the ADA to solve a practical organizational problem and reach desired infrastructural ends—even though the specific piece of federal law she invoked was only obliquely related to the problem at hand. That careful, deliberate cultivation of what I call *legal consonance* was even more necessary for James. Early in our interview about his urban library, he observed, "[Neighborhood] is not a well-off place. Over half of the community we serve has kids on free or reduced lunch, to the point where we organize almost all of our summer programming around food." And even when our conversation moved on to his library's infrastructure, he was quick to jab

Figure 7. All-gender toilet sign.
(Photo by author)

that "corporate donors aren't nearly as willing to give to funding drives here as they are in [name of an affluent, nearby neighborhood]." Forgetting my aim to be a detached, neutral outsider for a moment, I asked, after an empathetic chortle, where they *did* get their money from— as his library had an unusually spacious, state-of-the-art, all-gender restroom. It was at that moment, after double-checking to ensure I would be anonymizing my interview data, that James quietly confessed that he and his staff had "carefully leveraged the ADA guidelines" to prompt restroom renovations—by "borderline-inventing the pretense of accessibility problems" to get an all-gender restroom installed and certain fixtures in their men's and women's restrooms upgraded. He explained further, "Our plumbing hadn't been updated in decades. I mean, I don't know if that's strictly true, but you should have seen the fixtures, the pipes. . . . It was embarrassing." But because such issues "[invited] a lawsuit that'd be shouldered by the county," the ADA posed both a legal threat and an impetus for a renovation that would have been difficult, if not impossible, to achieve otherwise.

Counterintuitively, then, legal obligations that seem constraining—such as federal mandates that require restrooms for workers to be separated by gender *and* wheelchair accessible—could be a surprisingly useful pathway to an ungendered restroom. But my respondents, too, were necessary reagents in such organizational reactions. Only they possessed the creative capacity to transplant a seemingly unrelated (or only tangentially related) legal framework onto a pressing bureaucratic or infrastructural problem to produce *legal consonance,* and only they could pave the way to a renovation that would have otherwise proven challenging or unattainable.[35] As James recalled, funding for his library's expansive all-gender restroom hung just out of reach until his staff began agitating about possible fallout from a costly lawsuit, one that could tear away more of their municipality's already-scarce fiscal resources than the more modest building updates they sought. Or, as Judy's narrative implied, on-the-ground legwork could also allow restroom infrastructure to reflect postmodern gender politics without invoking those politics directly—by, for instance, using the ADA's sidebar about the boons of unisex restrooms to ensure spatial inclusion for visitors marginalized by disability and gender alike. Thus, when my respondents combined their observations about an outdated building with their knowledge of statutory requirements, even the most coercive legal constraints could suddenly transform into a rationale for restroom upgrades and other desired renovations.

"IF WE COULD AFFORD TO RAZE THE BUILDING TO THE GROUND AND START OVER"

Yet as James's quip about "corporate donors" suggested, even the most skillful executions of *legal consonance* did not always yield optimal plumbing outcomes. Instead, the geographic distribution of wealth around a municipal organization exerted quite an influence on the smoothness and scope of restroom renovations—a stratified set of circumstances that dovetail seamlessly with what sociologists know about the spatial contours of social inequality. As far back as the 1920s, when Robert

Park and Ernest Burgess conducted their pathbreaking research on the spatial organization of Chicago, sociologists have explored how the cultural norms and structural organization of physical neighborhoods lead to a wide range of unequal outcomes for their residents—from disparities on classic dependent variables like income, wealth, and educational attainment to modern issues of interest like mental health and internet access.[36] Today, as sociologists continue to study persistent social problems like the gender wage gap, the impact of education on labor market outcomes, and the linkage between race and wealth, geography has once again emerged as an important consideration in conceptual models of inequality.[37] But whether they employ quantitative methods or aspire to a holistic theory of stratification, those many threads of scholarship all point to one overarching conclusion: the "possible means by which a person is able to benefit from things,"[38] as Jesse Ribot and Nancy Lee Peluso write in their classic definition of *access*, is inextricable from matters of geographic inclusion and exclusion.[39]

So, while appeals to the ADA did enable my respondents from less affluent areas to access *a* renovation budget, that budget was often slow to arrive. For Rebecca's suburban library, those budgetary delays meant installing an accessible, unisex restroom in the most perfunctory manner possible: "We took a storage closet, cut a hole in the wall where we knew the plumbing lines were what we needed, and put in a toilet and sink. Problem solved." Worse yet, when renovation budgets did finally materialize, they tended to cover minimal changes, not true solutions. Anne recounted such a situation when discussing her urban transit center, saying, "As our contractors started to trace the existing plumbing through the walls to see what made the most sense, it became more and more apparent that our original budget wasn't going to be enough, or that we were going to have to cut back on how accessible that bathroom could really be." She pointed to the side of the main atrium opposite the one with their ungendered restroom, then continued: "The ideal location would have been behind that wall, because there's a good bit of empty space with enough framing for a big, single-user bathroom." She then moved her hand back to the ungendered restroom's entrance and stopped when her fingers targeted the floor beneath. "But the sewer line was over there, so that's where it ended up. It's fully up to code, of course, because that was the whole point of installing it." She resumed her original posture and looked right at me before concluding: "But you went in there, so you've seen it for yourself. I think you would be hard-pressed to fit a wheelchair or a stroller in there while giving a caretaker enough room to help."

But for municipal organizations located within more affluent areas, such constraints were virtually nonexistent—because financial constraints were, likewise, virtually nonexistent. This was the case for Dan, whose suburban library "made the ADA front and center" in their proposal for a planned renovation in the late 1990s. There, interest in a unisex restroom first emerged in the course of informal conversations about enhancing the library's "wheelchair-friendliness," but the idea became "much more popular" when they started to discuss how to best serve the patrons who most frequently and consistently sought out library resources. As he explained, "With most of our everyday patrons being [either] mothers of preschool-aged children or older, retired adults, we were talking about rearranging our stacks to create reading areas for both groups, which led to rethinking how else we use our space." That led to the "realization that there were multiple reasons that a unisex bathroom made sense" for his library. But it was only because of a "generous capital campaign" that he and his colleagues could fully focus on three crucial questions: "Who are our patrons, what are they using the library for, and are we meeting those needs?" The result was not one but two ungendered restrooms: the first one installed near the library's newspaper section, where "older patrons like to settle in to read the day's news," and a second "smack-dab in the middle of the children's section" with an inviting family restroom sign on the door. Better yet, there was a surplus of funds leftover to enhance inclusion in other ways: ergonomic chairs "adjustable for aging bodies," colorful loveseats "big enough for children and parents to read together," and cutting-edge "screen magnification and screen reading" software for patrons lacking strong visual acuity

A couple of participants whose infrastructural ideals were, like Dan's, able to be actualized openly acknowledged the multiple privileges necessary for that actualization, financial and otherwise. "We're phenomenally lucky to be in such a diverse community in so many ways," Margaret replied when our conversation started to veer toward financial matters, "but one important way is that we have patrons from every income bracket.

Figure 8. Family restroom sign. (Photo by Mark Buckawicki, made available under the Creative Commons CC0 1.0 Universal Public Domain Dedication)

Plus, this is probably the most liberal part of [city name], so there's no shortage of interest in supporting public institutions like us and NPR and whatnot. That's certainly not true everywhere." But more often, such respondents took that capacity for granted. When I asked Richard about the timing of his historic site's addition of an ADA-compliant ungendered restroom, for instance, there was some recognition in his words that ample human and financial capital supported his organization behind the scenes. However, his remarks about the nature of that unflagging public support treated access to that capital as a foregone conclusion:

This is [city name]. We're one of the first cities that comes up in the American Revolution part of US history textbooks, and [organization name] specifically hosts over two hundred field trips a year—first graders all the way through AP government students. Our citizens and our local law-makers really cherish that identity. There's no shortage of interest among the public in ensuring that we preserve that heritage, that tradition, for gen-erations to come.... Whether they're immigrants who came here with nothing and have worked their way up, or Daughters of the American Revolution, [city residents] want to give and keep that tradition alive for their children and grandchildren.

Even Dan, who explicitly mentioned the "generous capital campaign" that financed his library's most recent renovation, downplayed fiscal resources in favor of focusing on his library's organizational mission: "We think of ourselves as a model of community inclusion, and that means being attentive to how the world is changing around us and doing all that we can to respond to what we see. That's all that we strive for—paying attention, being responsive." And going one step further, he punctuated his response with a sweeping final gesture: "That's all that all public libraries should strive for."

In contrast, for respondents from less affluent areas or with less voluminous renovation budgets, that sense of obligation led to a very different conversational tenor. Kevin, for instance, lashed out at multiple moments in our interview about his historical site. "If I'm being honest," he recounted with palpable irritation in his voice, "that handicapped bathroom was a nightmare. Truly a nightmare." He paused for a moment, then issued a caveat: "Now, don't misunderstand me: I absolutely agree with the city and with the state that having sanitary and wheelchair-accessible bathrooms are [*sic*] important, and I would never want one of our visitors with special needs to feel as if they weren't welcome. But," he said, returning to his initial train of thought, "there's a point at which fussing over a single inch of space in a doorway or a wall is frustrating to all of us. I've fielded disgruntled phone calls from my curatorial colleagues all the way down to gift shop staff." He paused again, exhaled with a bit of a chuff, and concluded with a qualification of his previous statement: "It's not about the bathroom, really. But the bathroom becomes the last straw when a dozen other issues associated with constantly changing building code requirements have come up in the last year alone." He furrowed his eyebrows, then concluded that the law was not to blame after all: "It would be one thing if we were regularly operating with a budget surplus. But the coffers for historical landmarks just aren't as full as they used to be, and especially not on this side of [city name]."

Worse yet, for many such respondents, those budgetary limits ultimately begat frustrations and inadequacies that went beyond the ungendered-restroom door. In some cases, the cost of a new, ungendered restroom would leave little funding to update other restroom spaces. As James lamented, "The problem was that the *only* changes we were able to make were whatever got us over the very low bar of compliance" (emphasis his).

When I asked if that explained why their gender-separated restrooms were, by comparison, in poorer condition, he responded in the affirmative: "Right, exactly. We couldn't close them altogether, because the unisex restroom would be uncomfortable for some patrons and because we have to have separate men's and women's rooms for us as staff, but the renovation budget couldn't cover three new bathrooms." Respondents like Jack mourned even more worrisome shortcomings. He expressed discontent at the "undersized" character of his rural library's unisex restroom, which meant there was "no space for a changing table or other useful extras" that would make the space as user-friendly as possible. "But," he quickly added, "that worries me less than the patchy parts of our roof, our terribly slow computers, and, . . ." He trailed off into silence for a moment, then gestured expansively and exasperatedly toward the library stacks while finishing his sentence, saying, ". . . gosh, so much else." A few beats of silence passed. As I scoured my memory for a suitable follow-up question, he quietly filled the space between us: "There are so many things we would do if we could afford to raze the building to the ground and start over, but we're a local public library, and financial support for local public libraries has been steadily declining in the twenty-some-odd years I've been here. Almost everything we do sticks us between a rock and a hard place."

THE THIRD ELEMENT OF GENDER'S INSTITUTIONAL ACCOMPLISHMENT: MATERIAL INERTIA

In short, it was neither pure gender politics nor local and state laws that most shaped a municipal organization's restroom footprint. Certainly, ideology and legality shaped restroom design and construction in the municipal organizations I surveyed, and they did so in complex and powerful ways. But the most intractable obstacle standing between my respondents and their ability to actualize an ungendered restroom was the materialized history of gender their organizations had inherited from the past. And while *legal consonance*—that is, the tactical use of local, state, or federal law to solve organizational problems and reach desired infrastructural ends—could serve as a productive workaround in response to some parts of that history, it could not solve all renovation ills. Indeed, while all the municipal organizations in my sample had, at the time of our interview, at least one ungendered restroom in their purview, the scope and contents of those spaces—as well as the speed with which they could be actualized—cleaved my sample into two unequal groups. One group had to settle for whatever small handful of changes could be made on a liability-induced renovation budget. The other group, however, could avoid infrastructural compromise altogether. Sometimes that avoidance was a happy accident, such as when the pipes and framing hidden behind an organization's walls were surprisingly well-suited to a staff's hopes and dreams for new restrooms. Much more often, though, it was because financial resources were plentiful enough for those organizations to overcome any and all undesirable qualities of existing infrastructure, enabling a kind of true change that remained an unattainable pipedream for less-privileged and less-resourced organizations.

In "Shifting Paradigms and Challenging Categories," Judith Lorber speaks of the possibility of true change related to gender, using the discipline of sociology itself as an example of what would be required to produce a genuine "feminist revolution."[40] The piece begins with an empirical puzzle: on the one hand, she finds that "[m]ainstream sociologists have no problem understanding the social construction of class and racial ethnic differences"—in other words, they understand them to be mutable cultural creations—but they struggle to move beyond biological explanations for gender differences.[41] Worse yet, she finds, that tendency flies in the face of many decades of social-science research on the social construction of gender: "No matter how often and how extensively feminist sociologists show how biology and biological data are socially constructed as well, we are not given the credence in sociology that any study of rats, brain slices, surging hormones, or genetic manipulation gets."[42] To overcome that impulse, she argues, will require all sociologists to adopt research practices that better recognize the "multiplicity of genders, sexes, and sexualities"[43] and thus avoid reproducing the assumption that gender difference is inherent or inevitable. In other words, whether our methodological tool kit for studying the social world relies upon linear regression models or in situ ethnographic observation, the clearest pathway to doing better sociology—and to helping produce a more gender-egalitarian world outside the ivory tower—is to conceptualize gender (and sex and sexuality) without recourse to binary ways of thinking. Or in Lorber's words: "There are radical possibilities inherent in rethinking the categories of gender, sexuality, and physiological sex, especially in moving from binaries to multiplicities."[44]

And while my respondents from municipal organizations occupy a much different social and institutional location than my fellow academic sociologists do, their words demonstrate that rethinking gender is, as Lorber suggests, an important precondition for change. Especially among the organizational representatives who first aspired to ungendered-restroom construction in the 1990s or in the first decade of the twenty-first century, assumptions that "women and men are biologically different"[45] did percolate beneath the surface of restroom-related conversation in ways that slowed or detained such renovations. Plus, the fact that most of my respondents focused on wheelchair accessibility or family-friendliness rather than gendered progress may be implicit evidence that "the supposed natural dichotomies"[46] Lorber describes are still largely alive and well. But to offer a more positive interpretation, the almost total absence of gender-related objections from my interview conversations also means that a recognition of gender's multiplicity has seeped into the everyday work of numerous municipal organizations over the last thirty years. Now, of course, given that each municipal organization in my sample is located within the northeastern United States, I certainly cannot assert that such changes are anywhere near universal. Yet the regular invocation of reference points like the American Library Association's national guidelines and *Good Housekeeping*'s feature on transgender teens suggests that an institutional embrace of what Lorber calls "the strengths of feminism"[47] has very much begun to take hold—and more importantly still, that those reference points have produced a more inclusive vision of civic service among the respondents with whom I spoke.

But because restrooms are fundamentally physical spaces, my findings also reveal that "rethinking" the gender order is far from synonymous with "radical." Even after creatively exploiting building codes and other legal structures to their fullest potential, the most well-intentioned and progressively minded efforts among my respondents to transform their restroom spaces could result in disheartening renovation outcomes. Challenging the gender binary—and the differential allocations of rewards, resources, and advantages it dispenses to men over women and to cisgender individuals over transgender, nonbinary, and other gender-diverse individuals—cannot, therefore, consist only of collective efforts to build more egalitarian social institutions or of symbolic work to advance more acategorical understandings of gender. Those projects matter, of course, and are far from simple. But binary gender ideologies are not just abstract cognitive constructions that can be readily reconceptualized into multiplicities or spectra. They are also constitutive elements of legal frameworks, of organizational histories, and most notably of all, of the built environment. And as my findings in this chapter show, how far organizations are able to "undo" gender is intimately intertwined with their ability to reengineer those elements of gender difference that have been concretized—and literally so—into their physical surroundings. Materiality, therefore, does much more than inform what is possible, or even probable, for organizations to do to their buildings. It also shapes how far a feminist revolution can truly reach.

The third element of gender's institutional accomplishment, then, is the material *inertia* of past cultural ideologies, organizational choices, and institutional requirements that so often constrain gendered possibilities in the present day. In other words, for sociologists to truly grasp how organizations construct gender—and how gender shapes organizations—we must grapple with the ways that the physical environment facilitates and forecloses certain kinds of organizational behavior. This is intuitive, perhaps even obvious, when it comes to spaces that are as explicitly gendered as restrooms are. But gender shapes the built environment in countless other ways: subtle physical cues, for instance, mark certain public libraries and train stations as more welcoming or safe for women, and many long-standing building codes were devised with the presumption that only male bodies would occupy public spaces.[48] Plus, attention to materiality reminds us that organizations are themselves stratified—since an abundance of financial resources can allow problematic material structures to be more quickly or more thoroughly overcome. Certainly, access to infinite renovation resources can make certain physical constraints irrelevant—as it did for the geographically well-positioned organizations featured in this chapter—and changes to local, state, or federal law could, eventually, eliminate gender distinctions in restroom space altogether. (Especially if, unlike the ADA, new legal frameworks did not allow existing construction to remain intact until otherwise renovated.) But in the absence of that infinite resource supply or radical political overhaul, only those municipal organizations in well-off areas will be able to ensure access for patrons with a wide array of bodies, identities, and experiences—gendered and otherwise.

Public spaces are often thought of as integral to American democracy, largely because of their imagined ability to catalyze revolutionary social change. Yet when truly inclusive public spaces are available only to those citizens advantaged by economic privilege, their catalyzing potential will inevitably remain inert—or worse yet, serve to magnify social inequality rather than upend it. In his research about the mainstream gay and lesbian rights movement, Dean Spade observes that the interests of "a small number of elite gay and lesbian professionals"[49] have led to expedient gains for the legalization of same-sex marriage and the popularity of corporate antidiscrimination policies, but those gains have come at the expense of the more holistic vision of social and economic justice on which the quest for queer and transgender rights once depended. So, too, with ungendered restrooms. While affluent communities can afford, financially and figuratively, to have their municipal organizations constructed in ways that support people with disabilities, transgender people, and all others underserved by gender-separated restrooms, less well-off communities remain saddled with the material consequences of yesterday's gender ideologies, fueling a vicious cycle where "the 'haves' come out ahead"[50] over and over again. Thus, while the creation of more ungendered restrooms is far from an unworthy goal for any organization in the twenty-first century, to truly revolutionize restrooms would require moving away from a privatized model of publicity altogether. And that, in turn, would require a very different kind of investment in the public good than the one so often predominant in the United States today.

5 Leveraging the Loo

The water-closet ought to be a luxury.

A. W. Perry and W. H. Mays, editors, *San Francisco Western Lancet*, September 1879

In March of 1991, the Montgomery Mall in Bethesda, Maryland, debuted a one-of-a-kind feature on its upper level: the first-ever family restroom in a shopping center in the United States. Originally conceived of as a means of simplifying the lives of parents with young children at the mall, the new restroom occupied a temporary spotlight in Washington-area newspapers for providing a welcome corrective for "the occasional awkward moment of a dad taking a little daughter into the men's room or a little boy going in there alone while his mom waits in the hallway biting her nails."[1] As the mall's marketing director explained in more detail to one journalist profiling the new space: "If you've got one child, it's hard enough to find a place with enough room to put down your bags," let alone enough space to comfortably "change the baby." But the spacious new facility promised a venue within which fathers and mothers alike could "keep an eye on all the children"[2] while dealing with mundane bathroom-related matters. In fact, the family restroom was so popular with parents that the mall owners quickly amended their plans for their forthcoming new wing, thereby ensuring that a second family restroom would be available for use by the fall season.

But that popularity was not just because the new restroom allowed parents to work around the inherent limitations of conventional, gender-segregated restrooms. It was also because the space offered a number of additional perks for mall-going families, critical in an era of what the *Washington Post* described as "more sharing of parenting responsibilities between men and women." For parents with little ones small enough for strollers—or simply a glut of bags from the day's shopping excursion—the Montgomery renovation included a separate anteroom for worry-free housing of diaper bags, mall purchases big and small, and even that pesky double stroller. For children who were older, but not quite old enough to venture into the multiuser gender-segregated restrooms on their own, the family restroom included two toilet areas: one with a "child-sized toilet and sink" and one with a matched pair of adult-sized fixtures "accessible to the disabled." And for restroom users of all ages, the mall arranged for enthralling drawings from *Alice in Wonderland* to complement the restroom's "buff-colored marble tiles." Plus, a dazzling array of vending machines meant to dispense a range of essential supplies, from fresh diapers (in case of an unexpected shortage) to disposable paper barriers (for lining the oversized changing table), was installed nearby. In short, as one excited father put it, "This is *really* convenient."[3]

Because of the overwhelmingly positive feedback the new family restroom received, the Montgomery Mall's holding company soon followed up on their pilot program in the Washington suburbs by implementing similar family restrooms in several other locales around the country. A few mall executives remained skeptical, such as one regional director who expressed uncertainty about whether "people would like" family restrooms, and a few more simply saw the spaces as a run-of-the-mill customer service issue. The manager of West County Center in St. Louis, for instance, spoke straightforwardly about his mall's new family restroom, saying, "We saw a need, and we answered it."[4] Many more, however, understood the repeated successes of the family restroom to be what one manager for Broward Mall, in the suburbs of Fort Lauderdale, characterized as a "sign of the times"—one that portended an even more family-focused future yet to come for American shopping centers. "Going to the mall has turned into a family event," she observed, and because "more and more families" were "shopping together," family restrooms were first and foremost a change meant to "accommodate those families."[5]

With more and more evidence accruing that family bathrooms in American shopping centers were far from a passing fad or geographically restricted novelty, their popularity continued to swell through the closing years of the twentieth century. One general manager from West Los Angeles even challenged the common belief that the popularity of family bathrooms was a uniquely suburban phenomenon. Instead, he believed that such spaces would soon be making an appearance in his own urban shopping center, because "refocusing on families is the way to go in the '90s."[6] And as a testament to that observation, family-friendly mall transformations often went beyond renovations to restroom spaces alone: at Broward, their family restroom arrived in tandem with "stroller rentals," "nursing couches," and even "child-size public phones"; in nearby Dadeland Mall, "three 'kiddie pits'" offered a place for parents to rest "while the children romp"[7]; and at Topanga Plaza in Canoga Park, California, mall developers even crafted a "'munch bunch' food area with miniature tables and chairs" to boot.[8]

Unsurprisingly, such family-friendly transformations soon began to gain traction in other cultural sites. The architect for Atlanta's new baseball stadium, Turner Field, described mounting pressure among stadium planners in the early 1990s to take "the evolution of baseball parks another step further," noting that a new priority for many team owners was moving away from being "baseball-only facilities" to offering a "total family experience."[9] Family restrooms could, therefore, offer more than safety, space, and convenience: they could be a means of dazzling patrons with a unique customer experience. Back in St. Louis, for instance, where ground was being broken for a new, domed stadium for one of the National Football League's most recently relocated teams, architects and developers tempted investors with a package of "state-of-the-art" features: seats a full "inch wider than the norm," each equipped with its own beverage holder; a variety of food and concession offerings "wider than [those] most major-league stadiums" had ever offered; enormous scoreboards featuring video replay with "resolution like your home TV set" as well as a separate area for up-to-the-minute "game stats, out-of-town scores and other information"; luxury suites with "eight elevators" for visitors unable to comfortably climb stairs; and, as the project executive proudly told journalists covering stadium construction, "the same number of water closets for women as there are urinals for men"—with, of course, plenty of family restrooms on all levels drawn into the stadium's blueprint.[10]

Those offerings, in turn, benefited mall and stadium owners as much as they did their parental patrons. For consumption hubs "struggling mightily to attract Mom, Dad, and the kids," family restrooms could successfully lure back the presence and the discretionary spending of the middle class. According to the same mall manager in West Los Angeles expecting family restrooms to be a forthcoming addition to his food court, any changes to enhance his mall's appeal to families were an obvious choice to make, if only because the "mall did $8 million in children's business last year."[11] Sure enough, as the initial successes of restroom renovations from shopping malls and sports arenas alike continued to garner positive press, one *Newsweek* writer observed that other consumption sites throughout the country were increasingly eager to take advantage of the "marketability" of "this very '90s concept."[12] In fact, as some developers began to realize, family restrooms could be as chic as they were convenient. Indeed, with its "pleasant lighting, the black marble counter/diaper-changing area and the muted mauve tile walls," one new family restroom located in a mall outside of San Jose seemed to one reporter to be "more upscale than the traditional restrooms located on either side of it."[13]

.   .   .   .   .

In the closing decades of the twentieth century, cultural tastes among elites in the United States underwent a monumental shift, concisely summarized in the words of Richard Peterson and Roger Kern as an evolution "from snob to omnivore." Where affluent Americans once espoused a strong preference for "highbrow" genres such as classical music and opera, their musical horizons began to expand into appreciation for historically "lowbrow" genres, including hip-hop and folk music. Where their restaurant patronage was once largely restricted to those high-end restaurants whose sole province was the multicentury tradition of French haute cuisine, they began to value nouvelle cuisine, with its simplicity of preparation and elegance of presentation; to frequent restaurants with a decidedly American culinary perspective; and to laud chefs who drew gastronomic inspiration from beyond Europe and North America. They even ushered in a new age of appreciation for inexpensive, ethnic tastes—provided they offered the most authentic taste possible of *abuela*'s mole or *bubbe*'s latkes. And where the most disinvested segments of major American cities were once assiduously avoided by young, urban professionals, many such areas became popular outlets for their leisure pursuits and considerable volume of discretionary income.[14]

In response to such shifts in taste, cultural organizations, too, have changed. Upscale bars and nightclubs have relocated to formerly working-class neighborhoods, restaurants have crafted farm-to-fork menus drawing from the best of local agriculture, and musical venues housing major American symphony orchestras and opera companies have increasingly scheduled up-and-coming contemporary composers alongside their more traditional fare.[15] By the close of the twentieth century, then, shopping malls and venues for professional sports were not alone in beginning to recognize that seemingly unimportant architectural details, including ungendered restroom spaces, could also be a generative means of appealing to newly omnivorous elites. Such restrooms, of course, had existed in a wide range of consumption outlets, government buildings, and other public areas since the development of indoor water closets over a hundred years earlier. After all, as the historical portion of this book makes clear, gender separation in quasi-public restrooms did become heavily institutionalized over the twentieth century, but it has never been universal or final. However, the ungendered restrooms located within many cultural organizations in the United States evolved from being an unremarkable—and largely uncommented upon—architectural quirk in the 1970s and 1980s to a buzzworthy curiosity in the 1990s and the first two decades of the twenty-first century.

This chapter investigates the causes and consequences of that buzz, using forty semistructured interviews with owners, directors, managers, and other decision makers from four different types of cultural establishments—restaurants, shopping malls, performance venues, and museums—to study how such organizational representatives talk about ungendered restrooms. In contrast to lay and academic accounts of the taboo associated with restroom-related topics, most of the respondents with whom I spoke relished the chance to talk with me in depth about their restrooms.

Although some shied away from bathroom-related banter, many more celebrated the arrival of an ungendered restroom within their infrastructural purview and appreciated my interest in talking with them about that very same restroom. Unlike the decision makers from municipal organizations I profiled in the previous chapter, they frequently described organizational infrastructure as flexible and dynamic, and they often reported that the construction of a new, ungendered restroom was easy to actualize. Moreover, they explained, such transformations did not passively reflect an interest in progressive gender politics, family values, or any other ideological aim. Instead, ungendered restrooms were an active mode of communication—one through which an organization could exercise architectural creativity, extend its mission into every corner of its physical environment, and, of course, convey its responsiveness to the needs and preferences of its core customer base.

Yet ungendered restrooms could not accomplish those communicative ends on their own. As my respondents talked to me, an interested outsider, about their organizations' restrooms, they revealed that a powerful human turbine was behind all such meaning-making achievements. That turbine? Themselves. By energetically describing the smallest of details—such as an elegant, chrome-plated faucet or a toilet's digitized flushing mechanism—as the epitome of style and innovation, the decision makers who spoke on behalf of the cultural organizations in my interview sample were able to skillfully transubstantiate the most mundane of restroom renovations into valuable status signals. Such extraordinarily deftness allowed each respondent to articulate the consonance between their organization's choices and the values presently on trend in their capricious institutional environment—a skill I refer to as the *ease of justification*. But because I also center my firsthand experience in conversation with my interview respondents as a form of social data worth examining in its own right, I also show how, exactly, that ease comes to function as a potent interpersonal resource. Indeed, even when that resource manifests as talk of toilets, it serves as a surprisingly generative way for organizational decision makers to compensate (and then some) for the financial cost of infrastructural updates and, above all, to continually set their organizations apart as fashionable cultural destinations.

the goal of these new restrooms

"YOU MIGHT THINK THAT THEY WOULD BE AN UNIMPORTANT CONSIDERATION"

Restrooms are notoriously taboo subjects, in the real social world and in academic spheres alike. As Erving Goffman observed in his classic theorization of everyday social interaction, *The Presentation of Self in Everyday Life*, restrooms are "backstage" areas not only because they physically shield us from being seen and surveilled by others, allowing us to "step out of character"[16] from our routine public performances of self, but also because of their tight coupling with bodily effluvia. The elimination of bodily waste may indeed be one of the fundamental human needs upon which our higher-order physical and cognitive capabilities depend, but as Goffman goes on to say, the perceptions of contamination associated with urination and defecation are "inconsistent with the cleanliness and purity standards"[17] of public life. That sense of contamination, moreover, does more than induce users to engage in various interpersonal rituals to maintain the decorum of the social order within restroom spaces:[18] it also induces them to avoid talk of restrooms in the countless social settings beyond the bathroom door.[19] In fact, even in the corners of the social sciences devoted to studying socially stigmatized topics, the choice to write about bathrooms at all can seem to be a breach of academic norms and thus all but requires a self-conscious acknowledgment of (if not an outright apology for) the taboo character of one's research subject.

Consequently, even with a goal of studying restrooms at arm's length, by striving to understand organizational decision-making related to restroom spaces rather than surveying restroom behavior itself, that tendency toward taboo caused several of my would-be respondents to balk when asked to participate in my research. One particularly memorable phone call with a potential participant from an urban museum came to an abrupt close shortly after he quipped, "Certainly, you could do more with a Princeton education than ask highly trained professionals about *bathrooms*" (emphasis his). Even among decision makers who agreed to participate in my research, knowing full well that it centered on restroom issues, similar sentiments made their way into our official interview conversations. Mark, for instance, took the very first question on my interview schedule as an opportunity to formalize his befuddlement that I would write an entire dissertation on a topic so base as public restrooms. "First of all," he replied to my query about his urban museum's initial foray into gender-neutral restroom spaces, "let me just say that I never thought I'd be able to say that I participated in an academic research project about restrooms. Art history, yes; the history of [museum name] even, yes. But bathrooms? I guess there really is a corner of the intellectual universe for every little topic." When I tried to brush off his comments with a quick rejoinder about restrooms enjoying an extended moment in the political spotlight, he conceded, "Of course, of course. I just read a piece in *Slate* about abolishing gendered bathrooms in colleges." "But," he continued, "I still can't figure out what you could possibly spend several hundred pages saying!"

While Mark's unabashed editorializing about my research agenda was a singular occurrence, subtle hints of disdain for restroom matters found their way into several of my conversations with other decision makers. My interview with Jerry, for example, started off in an unusually promising direction: the restaurant at which he worked had recently moved into a new building, and he was eager to walk me through all the transformations that had resulted. "Everything is new," he explained, before rattling off an itemized list of everything in sight. "The menu, the bar, the seating, the sign out front, the paint, everything. We've been waiting to do this for such a long time, and it's wonderful to see it all come together." As we continued to chat, he described the minutia of the restaurant's renovation at an ever-increasing level of detail, even spending a few minutes heaping praise on the recent installation of LED light bulbs in the space's recessed light fixtures. When I asked about the gender-neutral restroom at the rear of the building, however, his interest waned considerably:

> JERRY: That wasn't really up to us. With the plumbing and the kitchen, [the city] makes our choices for us.
>
> INTERVIEWER: What does that mean?
>
> JERRY: It means that our contractors look at what the code says, and we make sure that we have the right number of fixtures and spaces for the number of people we have on staff and the number of customers we serve. That's really it.

And from that point forward, all of my questions about the restaurant's gender-neutral bathroom caused Jerry to circle back to that first answer. As I realized that no amount of cajoling was going to convince him that his restaurant's restroom merited more discussion, I switched to asking him a few improvised questions about the menu—which he obliged much more willingly—and I wrapped our conversation up much more hurriedly than I had planned. (I had anticipated that we would talk for forty-five minutes to an hour, but I decided to abandon my interview schedule at just after the fourteen-minute mark—and turned off my recording device after about eighteen total minutes of conversation.)

As my research process unfolded, however, I started to discover that such recalcitrance was more of an outlier than a modal outcome. At first, my interview with Michael seemed like it was going to unfold in parallel to my conversation with Mark or with Jerry, as he was quick to express disappointment that his museum had to work within the confines of legal mandates when they last updated their restrooms. "As much as we attempt to make every single inch of our property part of the [museum] experience," he bemoaned, "we *are* still beholden to the law. We have to choose fixtures that meet building and plumbing code requirements. We still have to have the right number and kind of restroom spaces to keep compliance with state and federal guidelines about size, about number, about wheelchair access" (emphasis his). But as we continued talking, our conversation turned a corner, switching from legal matters to architectural design, and that led Michael to unleash an unexpected deluge of remarks about how much care and consideration went into all aspects of infrastructure for privately funded museums like his:

> It's a common misconception that design matters for some parts of an institution like ours and not for others. I once heard restrooms in art museums described as "functional art," and I find that to be such an apt characterization. Whether you actually commission an artist or an architect to design your restroom space, or they [*sic*] more closely resemble a traditional public restroom, you can be sure that multiple committees were convened to decide where that restroom was going, what should go into it, how it should look, what signs should go outside the door, and so forth.

Shifting gears from such generalizations, he then pivoted to an unexpectedly myopic target—his museum's toilets:

Take the toilets as an example. You might think that they would be an unimportant consideration, or that there wouldn't be much variety to choose from even if you found them important. But it's remarkable how many choices there really are, and how the tiniest details can affect the entire feel of the space. There are decisions to be made about how they flush, whether they fit into the ground or the wall, what the base looks like, what the seat looks like, what the mechanism that flushes the toilet looks like . . . [*pause*] and that doesn't even get into the flooring or walls or stalls around them.

Not only did Michael go on to talk about the gender-neutral restrooms within his organizational purview (and the nuances of the toilets inside them) for much longer than most of my other respondents, but his interview as a whole could not be contained within the hour we had planned to speak—ultimately clocking in at ninety-three minutes, to be exact.

For many such respondents, it was their organization's core identity as a cultural transmitter that seemed to produce easy support for ungendered restrooms—and, more to the point, to produce easy conversation with me about why such restrooms might be worth creating. Rebecca, for instance, defended gender-neutral restrooms as analogous to other straightforward transformations that, she believed, other performance venues should be more willing to take on: "Bigger issues like accessible parking or an elevator can be tricky, but companion seating for wheelchair-bound patrons is another one that requires very little effort. Assistive listening technology should be available at every facility dedicated to live artistic performance. Most of this is not complicated. These are all little changes that make a huge difference." In other words, she went on to say, there was a tangible motivating force for her organization—and, indeed, all cultural organizations—to pursue such accessibility upgrades: the changing needs of their patrons. "We have these patrons who have been coming here for twenty, thirty, even forty years," Rebecca explained, "and it's not acceptable for them to face a literal struggle in attending events here." She paused long enough for me to signal my understanding with a nod, then continued: "We want them to be able to get upstairs; we want them to have an easy time getting down the aisle to their seats; we want them to be able to access a bathroom with enough space for an attendant but enough privacy to do their business. If we're not fully accessible, then we're doing both those patrons and the artists that choose to perform here for those patrons an exceptional disservice."

Such sentiments would turn out to be a recurring theme across organizational types and geographic locations. For Sharon, having at least one ungendered restroom per floor had become critical for her suburban museum several years earlier precisely because of the tight linkage she and her colleagues perceived between architectural features like restrooms and the mission of organizations like hers to "bring the arts to the public." For her, the idea that there might be museums without a wide range of restroom options—including ungendered ones—bordered on unthinkable:

> It surprises me that this is still a hurdle for some museums, because when your stated purpose as an institution is to serve as a bridge between the community and the arts, you do what you need to do to be that bridge. Our programming runs the gamut: we have interactive explorations for moms and tots in the mornings, we have weekly afternoon opportunities for our retired patrons to get involved with the arts, and we do a lot of outreach for adults with developmental disabilities. Unisex restrooms are part of serving all those groups effectively.

And for Taylor, whose target audience was much narrower, that relationship between her organization's mission and the actual flesh-and-blood people who used its space likewise led her urban performance venue to relabel all of its existing single-user restrooms with "gender-inclusive" signage a few months before our interview. As she explained, "We host a lot of programs for underprivileged youth from the local community; and for queer teens especially, dance and music are the spaces in which they can explore their identities in a safe and nonjudgmental space." She paused for a moment, then went on to add, "The all-gender signs are convenient for everyone, for sure, because you don't have to hike down the hall or to the other side of the building when you need to go. But it's about comfort, really. It's hard to tap into your creative energy if you need to pee and there's no safe space for you to do that."

Restrooms, therefore, could function as important evidence for an organizational decision maker's claims about their organization's most cherished values—and for the consonance of those values with those predominant in their organization's wider institutional field. Whether my respondents, like Michael, offered an onslaught of details about toileting fixtures or, like Rebecca, sang the praises of restroom accessibility in general, their accounts framed bathroom spaces as physical manifestations of the identities their organizations claimed and the institutional missions they professed. Furthermore, in doing so, such conversational contributions portrayed restrooms as nexuses of what economic sociologists call "relational work"—that is, a means through which an organization can actively establish, maintain, and reshape a wide range of social ties to its target community of customers and patrons.[20] So, even as spaces like Sharon's suburban museum and Taylor's urban performance venue existed a world apart from one another—both bureaucratically and geographically—there was also a common thread connecting them: the decision makers speaking on their behalf did not treat restrooms as either loci of embarrassment or topics unmentionable in polite conversation. Instead, like so many other elements of their organizations' environments, restrooms were easy, even enjoyable, for many decision makers to discuss. But because not all of my respondents felt that way, a willingness to celebrate restroom renovations aloud with me was not a constant in my interview sample but a variable in need of explanation.

"OUR MANTRA WAS 'DESIGN FIRST'"

As far back as Georg Simmel's observations in his early-twentieth-century essay "The Sociology of Space," the notion that a physical entity like a restroom can mean different things to different people has been axiomatic in the social-scientific study of materiality. But over the last twenty years, an explosion of research on cultural production and cultural reception has led sociologists to become interested in why certain meanings become more salient or sticky at certain times or in certain situations—and that research has shown just how much context matters for everyday efforts to make sense of objects and spaces. For instance, research has shown how a particular medium of delivery can shift the meaning of a nude image from artistic to pornographic, or how a sculpture's physical location alone can change the content and valence of professional evaluations of that piece.

Going one step further, recent empirical studies have emphasized the processual nature of such interpretive practices. In other words, such research observes, discerning the significance of a material object or physical space is not a discrete or one-time-only event, and context does not exert authoritarian control over those meaning-making efforts. Rather, the meaning of material entities derives from an ongoing back-and-forth exchange between the intrinsic characteristics of objects and spaces and the wider-ranging physical and institutional context in which they are embedded.[21]

For my respondents, it seemed that one particular element of context above all others determined whether or not they would maintain a recalcitrant posture toward restroom renovations: financial considerations. Early in my interview with Aaron, a decision maker for an urban restaurant, I asked if he was happy with having a single ungendered restroom in his purview. "Sure," he replied, "but I'm happy with anything that's functional, because the alternative would be obtaining construction permits and hiring contractors to make changes." When I requested that he elaborate more on that alternative's lack of appeal, he explained his perspective by drawing a parallel to his restaurant's kitchen—and bringing in the monetary cost of renovations as central to his decision: "There are things I can't stand about the layout of the kitchen, but I know what we have right now meets all the applicable building codes and safety regulations. Construction isn't cheap or fast in the first place; and in the second place, you have to worry about scheduling the health inspector to double-check everything. And that's if the changes you want will even fit into the city's building code. . . . [pause] So, it's much easier to let the layout be what it is." Luke, too, professed a commitment to financial priorities, albeit with much more colorful language. His biggest priority for his suburban restaurant's most recent renovation was "dealing with that trifling bathroom bullshit with as little work"—and, as he would go on to imply, cost—"as possible." When he and his co-owner hired a contractor in the mid-1990s to have their single-user restroom updated "as quickly and painlessly as possible," his directions to that contractor were therefore simple: "No bells, no whistles. In and out. Done yesterday. And," he added, after a brief pause to punctuate his remarks, "the first guy who didn't try to upsell me on more renovations was the guy we hired."

Complicating matters, however, were the many other decision makers who referenced equally tight budgets but celebrated the fruits of their economic expenditures at length. Throughout my conversation with Ted, a decision maker for a recently opened urban restaurant, we repeatedly circled back to the balance he sought for his space: maximizing his restaurant's visual impact on patrons while also staying within the budget he required as a first-time restaurant owner. "When we were first sketching out our vision of what [the restaurant] would be," he explained, "our mantra was 'design first.' So, for example, we wanted to decide, for us, how many tables we thought would be the right number for how we wanted [the restaurant] to feel and flow, then find a space to rent that would match our plan—rather than the other way around. We wanted to make as few concessions as possible, even with a firm bottom line." At first, then, an ungendered restroom was desirable simply because it would save money. As he explained, "Oddly enough, our original plans called for a pair of bathrooms. You know, one male, one female. But when we checked the codes and realized we could get away with one unisex bathroom, we were stoked. It was a win all around: it was one fewer bathroom to keep clean and maintain, and it gave us a couple more feet to work with in terms of the size of the bar and bar storage." As the renovation unfolded, however, his design team became more and more willing to "customize the space" to better fit their ideal vision—and that meant spending "more and more money" to make that one bathroom "an interesting feature."

As I started to directly compare such accounts, I realized that what differentiated my more frustrated respondents, like Aaron and Luke, from my more animated respondents, like Ted, was more individual than institutional. Specifically, some decision makers from cultural organizations were simply more able—or willing—to assert that their restrooms were an agentic choice, even when they were confronted with constrictive circumstances. For instance, when I asked Jess, a decision maker from a chic, suburban restaurant, to walk me through when and why she had converted both their gender-segregated restrooms into gender-neutral ones, she perfunctorily replied, "We took the whole building down and started over from scratch." Seeing the confusion on my face in response to her nonchalance, she chuckled and followed up with a more detailed explanation:

Not to change the bathrooms, obviously—oh gosh, now that would be funny, right?—but because the building that was on the lot had been built to code in . . . [pause] I want to say 1964. Something like that. So, we had an inspector in to check out all the electrical, all the plumbing, the foundation, the whole deal. And as the list of problems got longer and longer, we started joking that we should just bulldoze the thing and start over. And one day, we sort of all looked at each other and said, "Hey, what would happen if we really did bulldoze the thing and start over?" So, we talked to the architect and priced things out, and decided that we could really do things right if we went for it.

When I asked her to say more about what "doing things right" meant to her, she grabbed a cocktail napkin and asked to borrow my pen. She began drawing lines on the napkin, saying, "One of the big things was relocating the kitchen . . ." Her voice trailed off as she connected those lines to form one large square, then added three smaller squares inside one edge of the first, larger square. She continued: "The previous building had the kitchen and the restrooms back here, in the rear of the building—which is normal, okay, and not a big deal—but if you're building from the ground up . . ." She paused again and drew a second large square, separate from the first. But this time, the three smaller squares were grouped together toward the middle of the larger square. She resumed her train of thought with a gleeful smile:

> You can make choices to use those sort of utility areas to carve up the dining room in an artful way, see? So, the effect is that we now have what feels like three, smaller, more intimate dining areas instead of one big, open room. It makes the dinner experience feel more personal if you can't see how many tables your waiter is really serving. And to get back to your original question: so, even with the bathrooms, we made them oversized for the capacity we seat because of the same principle: a few extra square feet makes everything feel less cramped, which makes everything also feel more upscale.

Other respondents were so excited to provide me with evidence of their organizations' infrastructural agency that our interviews featured walking in addition to talking—because they wanted to take me into an ungendered restroom and narrate its contents firsthand. Especially for the shopping malls I visited, a laundry list of lavish bonuses typically accompanied the installation of an ungendered restroom, and several respondents eagerly offered me a personal tour of those accoutrements. As Keith opined with a chuckle while walking me down a long hallway to his suburban mall's multiple restrooms, "I use the family bathroom just because it's so much more spacious and, on most days, cleaner than the men's room." He then opened the door to reveal a generously sized changing table (complete with cutting-edge restroom technology designed to prevent "accidental infant falls" and "unwanted bacterial transfer," he noted), as well as a scaled-down toilet and sink (designed with the comfort of "preschool bodies" in mind). But malls were not alone in such offerings, and respondents from malls were not my only conversation partners to treat me to a restroom tour. In other interviews at other types of cultural organizations, I walked through restroom-adjacent nursing spaces with oversized, comfortable chairs for mothers with infants; unisex water closets with small televisions installed so that toilet users would not have to miss a minute of the basketball game or boxing match they had come to a bar to watch; and all-gender restrooms with countless kid-friendly factoids about American history, modern art, or dinosaurs painted on the walls—in order to, as Meg, one museum decision maker explained, "entertain an older brother or sister while mom or dad tends to a fussy infant or toddler."

And as some of my most memorable interview conversations revealed, it was not simply that stylish or lavish bathrooms were easier to discuss than staid ones. Even smaller changes could be a conversation piece if honorable organizational intentions were behind them and, in the eyes of my respondents, merited voicing aloud. Chuck, for instance, initially described the spacious ungendered restroom in his suburban museum as "nothing special," because the interior had not been radically overhauled since its construction in the early 1990s. But later in our interview, when we left his office and approached the space on foot, his face lit up. "Actually, *you'll* probably find this interesting" (emphasis his), he reported after he wrapped up his response to one of my previous questions: "that sign over there has changed four times in the last two decades." He then filled me in on the restroom sign's elaborate semiotic history:

> CHUCK: Back in the early nineties, when we substantially reworked all of the parts of the main entrance corridor, we worked with the contracting firm to make sure the sign had a wheelchair on it. We ended up with, I think, a sign that said "restroom." I do

remember that it had three stick figures: one in a dress, one in pants, and one in a wheelchair. That didn't last very long, because we were also changing signs to have more braille. Pretty quickly, they swapped that one [the first sign] out for one with the same stick figures, and it said "accessible restroom and [had] braille letters underneath as well.

INTERVIEWER: But that couldn't have lasted, because this sign is different.

CHUCK: Right. So, I think it was 2003 or 2004, family restrooms were the new big thing that gained notoriety. That one I know, because [names of colleagues and their professional titles] helped me push for a switch over to a "family restroom" sign with four stick figures: one big stick figure in a dress, one small one in a dress, one big one in pants, and another small one in pants. We really liked those stick figures. [*Laughs.*] But they went away a few months ago, when we bought another new sign: this one.

That new sign proudly read "all-gender restroom" and, in the space previously occupied by gendered human outlines, featured a toilet icon. Below was a brief explanation, both in text and in braille: "Anyone may use this restroom, regardless of gender identity or expression." When I asked Chuck what he made of the newest sign, he replied, "You know, I hope we're done buying new signs, because I don't know what you can do to be more inclusive than just have an outline of a toilet."

Thus, much like Viviana Zelizer found in her research on intimate economies, money was not a "single, interchangeable, absolutely impersonal instrument" for my respondents; instead, they "routinely assign[ed] different meanings"[22] to often-expensive plumbing renovations depending on the degree to which they perceived the shape and contents of the resultant restrooms to be an agentic choice. But even more important than their financial perceptions were their verbal remarks. What Jess's artistic improvisation, Keith's hands-on tour, and Chuck's history lesson had in common was a recognition that ungendered restrooms were conversational opportunities for them as much as symbolic opportunities for their respective organizations. All three of them used our dialogues to show me, an interested outsider, how much care, attention, and deliberation went into their organizations' physical infrastructure, all the way down to the nuances of a bathroom sign, and all three of them resorted to improvised visual aids or a restroom excursion to help me see their buildings' design from a more illustrative vantage point. In doing so, their words and actions demonstrated that the many organizational boons of ungendered restrooms require human intervention to actualize. Or, to put it much more simply, respondents like Chuck, Keith, and Jess did not expect their restrooms to speak for themselves. They each understood that it was their mission to give a voice to those values. Indeed, even when it came to two virtually identical restroom spaces in two virtually identical organizations, it was *that* conversational prowess alone—or lack thereof—that could render one an expensive annoyance and the other a valuable investment.

"YOU NEVER KNOW WHAT'LL GET PEOPLE TALKING"

The power of human interaction, however, is itself an organizational resource—and one not evenly distributed across all social groups. In his work on the microsociological foundations of the social class structure, Pierre Bourdieu canonically describes that resource as "cultural capital"—that is, a wealth of knowledge and interactional skills that can be obtained only from growing up in a class-advantaged family. Building on that theoretical foundation in recent decades, sociologists have amassed ample evidence that such knowledge and skills have benefits in all manner of bureaucratic settings—from the schools class-privileged people attend as children to the workplaces they inhabit as adults. Professionals in elite service firms hiring new associates, for instance, assess job seekers on the basis of their perceived "fit" with existing workers, which they impute from the conversational prowess would-be employees exhibit in interview settings. Similarly, middle-class young adults are much more likely than their working-class counterparts to sidestep the stated "rules of the game" and ask universities or employers to accommodate their needs. But as elite culture has moved in the ever more omnivorous direction Peterson and Kern describe, sociologists have found that the effortless exercise of privilege now spawns tremendous advantages in every corner of social life. In fact, as Shamus Khan argues in *Privilege*, one of the most distinguishing characteristics of contemporary status culture is the ability of individual elites to readily navigate all manner of interactional settings with "ease"—which, following from Bourdieu, is the ability of members of the middle and upper classes to appear (and, indeed, be) relaxed and comfortable in any situation.[23]

While I was certainly familiar with such sociological perspectives before embarking on this project, one of the biggest surprises of my entire research process was the extent to which the more talkative respondents in my interview sample embodied those Bourdieusian predictions. Occasionally, such parallels became apparent in the ease with which certain respondents returned to a central narrative each time I asked a new interview question. Julia, a decision maker for a suburban shopping mall, was unapologetic about that strategy as she spoke in detail about the excitement she shared with her colleagues in response to enhancing the "family-friendliness" of their space several years prior. In her recollection of her colleagues' conversations about restroom renovations back in the mid-1990s, she stressed the importance of creating a "*family* restroom—not a wheelchair-accessible unisex restroom" (emphasis hers) as an important component of that more holistic renovation:

> Anyone who's *ever* been a mom with a son or a dad with a daughter has gone through all of the agony of being out in public with your child and not having an easy way to deal with public restrooms. With infants, there's always the question of whether or not you'll be able to find a changing table; and with toddlers, there can be unexpected accidents or they can decide that "today is the day I'd like to crawl out from under the stall." And even with older kids, there's always that worry about sending them behind closed doors with adults you don't know and don't trust in a public place. We've all had those experiences; we've all heard customers come to us with those experiences. So the question wasn't whether we should add a *family*-friendly bathroom space, it was how quickly we could make it happen.

Oddly, however, she not only stressed the word *family* the first two times she said it but also continued to stress it each time she uttered the phrase "family restroom" in our conversation. After the ninth or tenth time she did so, I broke down and asked about her persistently peculiar enunciation. Without skipping a beat, she replied, "Family is something no one can disagree with. It's apolitical. With everything going on in the news about transgender this and bathroom safety that, it's important that we have a consistent message to our customers that every single one of them can get behind and not feel put off by."

More often, my respondents' ease manifested as conversational patience. As I would ask question after question from my prepared interview schedule, several of my respondents would methodically downplay the impact of institutional constraints on their organizations' restrooms and, instead, wait for the right moment to pounce with comments about how interesting or useful their specific ungendered facility was. Keith, for instance, did briefly touch on "the legal regulations" that pushed his mall's management group into a renovation "sooner rather than later," and he also acknowledged that ample "time, energy, and money" went into that very same renovation. But each time I asked him for more details about one or both of those constraints, he demurred and repeated the same, standard answer: "We just wanted to build as family-friendly a restroom as space would allow." When I finally gave an inch and asked him to elaborate on that theme, he took a mile—barreling into a mishmash of customer feedback and his own observations about the restroom's many uses:

> The most common response I get is probably from moms with little kids, because they're really grateful to be able to round up the whole herd in a single space that locks. I've also heard from a few wheelchair-bound customers that the unisex bathroom is more accessible for them than our other restrooms, because the sinks are at multiple heights, and I've seen the bathroom used by customers who have someone with them who has a developmental disability. Oh, and in the height of holiday shopping season, women shopping together will absolutely use it to skip the line for the ladies' room.

After only the briefest of pauses—one just long enough for a self-satisfied grin to appear on his face—he succinctly summarized his monologue: "All-around, it's been a great thing."

Even more revelatory was the ease with which respondents from higher-end cultural establishments overtly manipulated the trajectory of our conversation at every twist and turn, no matter the challenges I posed to their accounts. In my interview with Miles, a decision maker for an urban museum, I struggled to get a word in edgewise after I asked him to explain why building architects had opted to include gender-neutral restrooms in lieu of gender-segregated ones in a handful of galleries. He

responded that those particular choices were "sensible from a design perspective." When I asked a follow-up question about whether he thought
any other considerations entered into his museum's calculus for the
ungendered spaces, even naming the financial cost of optional renovations and state building codes as factors potentially impinging on such
choices, I was met with a cold stare. After a few uncomfortable beats of
silence passed, he finally replied, "As an institution which exists to preserve, protect, and share objects that are the very embodiment of human
creativity and emotion, we take seriously our obligation to provide those
objects with an appropriate backdrop and to provide our visitors with an
all-encompassing aesthetic experience. That vow certainly does not end at
a restroom door." And when I started to interrupt with another follow-up
question, he continued, undeterred: "Think about domestic spaces.
Imagine Mies van der Rohe saying, 'No, I'll design the whole house *except*
the bath.' Never! The great modernists extended the clean lines and
straightforward elegance of the modern home into every single room,
because every single room was integral to the form and function of the
modern home. The same applies here."

In other words, what was so easy for interviewees like Julia, Keith, and
Miles was what I call the *ease of justification:* the ability to readily and
skillfully mobilize a defense of current organizational realities, such as
ungendered restrooms, and persuade others that those realities are an
agentic choice that comports with a reigning set of organizational values.
For instance, when I asked Ted, the restaurant decision maker whose
management team surprised themselves by investing quite a bit of capital
in their solo ungendered restroom, how he had squared those expenditures with what he had previously said about budgeting cautiously, he
replied that "in the age of Yelp and Urbanspoon," well-planned restrooms
could function as "a little bit more of a conversation piece." In fact, even
when such respondents would chase one of my follow-up questions with
an acknowledgment that legal or financial constraints did inform their
restroom-related choices, they unflaggingly reframed such strictures as a
valuable outlay of funds rather than a compulsory hardship. When I challenged Dylan's unusually rosy account of his performance hall's recent
move to add multiple ungendered restrooms, he begrudgingly granted
that "it was an investment, of course. Even the tiniest changes to

infrastructure carry a massive price tag in [city], between getting all of the necessary permits in order and hiring contractors with the right sorts of credentials, and that doesn't even include the costs of materials, which are increasing every day it seems, and the exorbitant labor costs for that crew that's properly certified." But as he went on to explain, that cost also clearly had a bright side: "The outcome is that you've created a better experience for your visitors," and that better experience would ultimately translate to "more than recouping your losses on the other side."

What was truly at the heart of comments like Ted's and Dylan's, then, was a belief that their organizations' patrons and customers would exercise their own *ease of justification* when talking about their restaurant or performance venue to others. Indeed, as Scott reported in the unexpectedly personal history he traced of the matched pair of gender-neutral restrooms in his urban restaurant, restroom-related enthusiasm was most powerful when coming from patrons instead of organizational insiders. "So, I went to Las Vegas a few years ago," he recalled with a smile, "and I can't remember which casino it was, but there was this one-sided glass that allowed you to, like, look out over the city as you were using the toilet. And it was just wild." For him, "seeing things as a customer" induced him to consider his own restaurant, including his then-gender-separated restrooms, "through that lens." His eyes then flashed with a burst of panic. "Not that I hadn't before," he quickly added, "but I had in a way that was more about the menu and our wait staff and things like that." His smile returned as he finished his thought: "And that's when I thought to myself, 'Hey, bathrooms don't have to be unsexy. They should be just as sexy and appealing as everything else.' You never know what'll get people talking." Likewise, when Lisa told me about her urban restaurant's rationale for replacing the "classic men's and women's room signs" on their single-user restrooms with ones that simply said "restroom," she emphasized that even the most seemingly idiosyncratic details—such as restroom signs—could be a surprisingly effective conversational catalyst. In her words:

> We expect that these changes, including the bathroom, will not only please
> our customers enough to convince them to come back again and again, but
> it'll also convince them to recommend us to their friends, to use our space
> for their work functions, to recommend us to their clients, to recommend

that colleagues in from out of town stop in for a drink—or better yet, dinner—while they're here. And every little thing we can do to ensure that press on top of providing one of the best dining experiences in [neighborhood] is money well spent.

And when I asked why, exactly, she thought a new sign would be noticed, she responded without a moment of hesitation—by turning the conversation back around to me: "You know the answer to that question better than anyone. Gender-neutral is the hot new thing, right?"

THE FOURTH ELEMENT OF GENDER'S INSTITUTIONAL ACCOMPLISHMENT: DISCURSIVE CIRCUITS

Thus, whether my most loquacious interview participants hailed from upscale art museums in one of America's largest cities, or from suburban shopping malls targeting middle-class families, they shared one fundamental quality in common: they viewed their restroom spaces as inextricable from their organizations' respective missions and, furthermore, inextricable from conveying those aims to visiting patrons. But as their skillful control of our interview dialogues further revealed, physical entities like ungendered restrooms cannot promote themselves. They also require the *ease of justification:* that is, a seamless ability to, in this case, discursively defend all manner of organizational realities aloud as agentic, intentional choices designed to reflect highly esteemed institutional values. And when I found myself on the receiving end of that masterful interactional labor, I felt firsthand just how potent that ease was. I may have requested each interview, I may have been the academic expert in the room, and I may have been asking the questions. But what happened in so many interview moments was a clear reversal of control, because my respondents recognized me as a person who might exercise my own *ease of justification* on their organizations' behalf. As they effortlessly took the helm of our conversations, their words and actions evinced an expectation that innovative, attention-grabbing restrooms could move their most urbane and affluent customers to share their favorable impressions with their urbane and affluent social networks. And in doing so, my respondents underscored how the ability to talk casually and convincingly about a topic as mundane as an ungendered restroom can be a surprisingly powerful signal of class privilege.

In "The Complexity of Intersectionality," Leslie McCall observes that feminist scholarship about intersecting forms of categorical inequality—especially scholarship focused on gender, race, and class—often undersells the potency of the third member of that trio. In reflecting on her own research trajectory, she writes, "I took the emphasis on differences among women as a call to examine structural inequalities among women, especially among different classes of women, since much less attention is devoted to class than to race in the new literature on intersectionality."[24] Such an absence was especially notable, she went on, because "a major new social issue was becoming the subject of intense research and political debate"[25] in the late 1990s and first decade of the twenty-first century: the large and growing increase in earnings inequality between affluent, highly educated Americans and their less-wealthy, less-educated counterparts. But that intellectual oversight was not just a problem for gender scholars—because, as Julie Bettie observes in the prelude to her book *Women without Class*, scholars studying class in that era were often just as inattentive to gender: "Among studies of the class structure, women may have been included in class taxonomies, but without any theorization of gender."[26] In other words, research on class inequalities may have considered the perspective of women, or perhaps even included sex as a variable, but it rarely featured a rigorous or sustained gender analysis. And despite the frequency with which both of those programmatic statements have been cited in the last decade—McCall with more than forty-five hundred citations and Bettie with over a thousand at the time of my writing—the practice of treating gender and class as separate analytic categories largely continues in academic sociology to this day.[27]

My findings in this chapter help correct that imbalance, as they show how beliefs about gender are inextricable from the cultural foundations of class stratification.[28] When my respondents talked with me about how their infrastructure reflected lofty aspirations like family-friendliness, the comfort of queer teens, or acceptance for a new age of gender neutrality, they did not speak of such ends as intrinsically worthwhile. Instead, they anchored those esteemed values to the expectations and preferences of their most valued—and most affluent—patrons, customers, and visitors.

At times, those rhetorical maneuvers made appeals to middle-class respectability, as was the case with Julia's remarks about the normalizing power of "family values," which are never as "apolitical" as she contended.[29] But at other times, my respondents were able to connect much more radical beliefs about gender to contemporary status culture. When Lisa so pointedly asked me, "Gender-neutral is the hot new thing, right?" her riposte to my interview probe was a comment, not a question, because gender-neutral fashion, gender-neutral parenting practices, and gender-neutral names are, indeed, on trend in the 2010s. Thus, by uncovering the subtle (and sometimes not-so-subtle) moral claims in my respondents' accounts, I find that support for ungendered restrooms has become a constitutive element of cosmopolitanism for the American middle and upper classes over the last three decades—one that parallels Bethany Bryson's observations about "multicultural capital": that is, an apparent increase in cultural tolerance that nonetheless functions as a mechanism of social exclusion.[30]

But an even more critical contribution to the sociological conversation about gender and class comes from my personal experience of being on the receiving end of such claims. Although my respondents could have offered perfunctory responses to my interview questions (and at times, they did), most of them actively and deftly maneuvered our conversations toward a gender-infused narrative meant to resonate with me—a fellow member of the highly educated, professional class who might sing their organizations' praises to my equally well-off friends and colleagues. And if I had any questions about their intentions in doing so, the details of our interview conversations certainly answered them. Over and over again, my participants asserted that restroom renovations might convince their patrons to speak highly of their organization. Those expectations were sometimes subtle, sneaking into phrases like "popular appeal" or "a lasting impression" within our dialogues; more often, however, they were overt, as my respondents openly discussed what they hoped "*our* customers" or "*our* patrons" would take away from their visits. Now, of course, economic pressures push organizations of all types to adapt in response to consumer preferences, and projecting a customer-centered image is an intuitive path to ensuring future popularity and success. But as Pierre Bourdieu reminds us in *Distinction*, cultural consumption is always cultural communication, and that communication always "fulfill[s] a social function of legitimating social differences."[31] And so, even though my respondents may have simply been fulfilling their professional responsibilities, their words nevertheless show that a "taste"[32] for ungendered restrooms is a signal of class privilege in the twenty-first century United States—one that marks them, their organizations, and their patrons as culturally superior.

And that power of words brings me to the fourth element of theorizing gender as an institutional accomplishment: *circuits* of discursive power. Power, of course, is familiar terrain for sociologists of gender, including the intersectional theorists I invoked above.[33] Yet what I mean here is not a diffused, general tendency for certain individuals or organizations to be seen as more valuable or competent than others—which, yes, does exist and does merit theorizing.[34] Instead, I use the term *circuit* to capture the dynamic, localized, and magnetic ways in which gender ideologies can function as moral and relational currents in specific conversational moments.[35] In this chapter, for instance, my respondents were a critical component of the flows of power I observed. Not only did their conversational prowess charge our conversations with popular ideas about families, gender neutrality, or even aesthetics as they energetically defended the value of ungendered restrooms, but it also allowed them to amplify or adapt those efforts whenever needed. Those interactional efforts thus helped transduce ideology into inequality—because when class-privileged people (like my respondents) voice the value or significance of certain gender-related beliefs (like the trendiness of gender neutrality) or organizational actions (like the construction of an ungendered restroom), they innervate those beliefs or actions with symbolic power. But circuits must always be complete to be operational, and it was only through the presence of other components—that is, visitors, customers, or an interested outsider like me—that such transduction could successfully occur. An electric metaphor, therefore, reminds us that power does not passively reside in individuals but arises actively in relationships, especially those between an organization and its patrons.

Thus, in a market with so many similar products, stores, goods, and experiences, even talk of toilets can become a shrewd technique for a cultural organization to set itself apart—or, better yet, to help its patrons set themselves apart. As Georg Simmel argues in his classic sociological essay

"Fashion," the adoption of new styles, forms, and aesthetic judgments all allow those who wish to distance themselves from the conformity of a social group to do so.[36] And at their core, the wide variety of claims my respondents made about their organizations' values did mark them, their organizations, and their customers as distinctive—in both the lay and Bourdieusian sense. But Simmel also notes that fashion's differentiating power comes in large part from its continually evolving character. As a result, ungendered restrooms may be the way of the future. Or they may not. Only time will tell which way the pendulum of fashion will swing next for the gendering of public restrooms, because the rising popularity of gender neutrality today is no guarantee that the gender binary will become passé as the twenty-first century continues to unfold tomorrow. But however regulatory structures, beliefs about gender, and architectural fads may shift in the future, the organizations with the cultural resources necessary to stay on top of those transformations—that is, those with the personnel willing and able to transmogrify organizational innovations as mundane as a new bathroom into agentic and value-driven claims about family-friendliness, progressive politics, and above all, being unmistakably au courant—will, without question, be the organizations best positioned to stay atop that ever-changing tide.

6 Transforming the Toilet

The open dormitory didn't solve any problems. In fact, it
created new problems.

Betsy Wade, "Open Dorms and Co-ed Bathrooms," *Wall Street
Journal*, October 1973

In the spring of 2002, a small change to housing policies at Haverford
College and Swarthmore College made a huge public splash: undergraduate students living on campus would henceforth be allowed to opt into
mixed-gender dorm rooms. Coeducational dormitories had been commonplace in many American colleges and universities since the late 1960s—
with a few other liberal arts colleges, like Wesleyan University, quietly
allowing for mixed-gender rooms and unisex bathrooms as early as the
mid-1990s. Yet coed rooms, which one writer for the *Pittsburgh Post-
Gazette* colorfully described as "the ultimate step in gender blending,"[1]
remained largely off-limits until the early years of the twenty-first century.
That is, until queer and transgender student activists at schools like
Haverford and Swarthmore inaugurated a new roommate revolution. For
them, the assumption that "the whole world is heterosexual"[2] was inappropriate and exclusionary in any setting. When written into college housing policy, it created an especially "awkward"[3] situation for students who
might be "uncomfortable about sharing living space with a roommate of
the same sex, because of either homophobia or sexual tension."[4]

Unsurprisingly, as gender-neutral housing gained more traction at
those colleges, gender and sexual minority students were quick to sing

its praises. Zachary Strassburger, a sophomore at Wesleyan, wistfully remarked that "the camaraderie of life in a college dorm" was one of the many things he looked forward to experiencing during his first year of college. Unfortunately, the school's housing policy mandated that first-year students had to be paired with roommates of the same legal sex. That arrangement, he explained, was neither sustainable for transgender students like him nor pleasant for their would-be roommates: "I know that I would be really uncomfortable, and I think the people I was living with would feel really weird about it." He reluctantly took the only offer the university's housing officials could provide at the time: a single room. But with the arrival of a new gender-blind floor in one of Wesleyan's dormitories—and a new mission statement in their Office of Residential Life professing support for "students whose gender identification and/or gender expression varies from the standard paradigm and for students who believe that their gender should not factor into the decision of whom to live with"[5]—future first-year transgender students would no longer have to choose between having a roommate and feeling safe and secure in their rooms.

Oddly enough, however, the most frequent occupants of new mixed-gender rooms were not students marginalized owing to their gender identity or their sexual orientation. As Haverford senior Jesse Littlewood saw it, "not making assumptions" about "sexuality or orientation" was certainly an important reason for the college to offer mixed-gender rooming options. But for straight, cisgender students like him, gender-neutral housing meant he could live with his two best friends—friends who simply happened to be women. In fact, while journalists joked that mixed-gender rooms might "[open] the door to school-sanctioned hanky-panky," the whole arrangement was surprisingly benign to all those involved. Littlewood's girlfriend, Laura Smoot, had absolutely no interest in using gender-neutral policies as a means of living with him. It was "good to have space," she reasoned, and she was "definitely not worried about him cheating." After all, "Ginger and Liz" were "extremely good friends" of hers, too, so any such worry would "be extremely silly." Even their parents were supportive. When the *Philadelphia Inquirer* asked the mother of one of Littlewood's roommates for her opinion on the situation, she replied simply, "I trust them. They are all good buddies."[6]

ppl respect the intentions behind it

Such nonchalance was especially notable in light of the cultural tenor surrounding inclusive housing—and its frequent companion, all-gender restrooms—at other colleges and universities throughout the United States. Elsewhere in the Northeast, the vice president of student affairs at Washington and Jefferson College openly denounced both spatial innovations. To him, "the idea of asking students to learn how to cohabit" was "frankly irresponsible," and he reckoned that "all sorts of pitfalls" would unfold if his liberal arts college ungendered any residential or restroom spaces.[7] In fact, even when undergraduate activists worked diligently with university staff to craft a gender-neutral pilot program that would be acceptable to queer students and concerned administrators alike—as they did at Tufts University, where would-be roommates had to "[promise] that they were not romantically involved"—gender-neutral housing proposals were often dashed at the last minute by a president or senior dean out of "concerns about encouraging sexual activity."[8] Such concerns were so pronounced that residential life staff at schools like the "ultra-liberal" University of California, Berkeley, were "surprised to hear about" any "Eastern schools permitting coed rooming." As their associate director for residence life noted to the press, "We have coed suites, coed bathrooms and also single sex [spaces]. But we haven't heard anything about mixed-gender rooms."[9] *even most liberal colleges are unsure*

But back at Wesleyan, college staff welcomed gender-neutral spaces with open arms, finding them neither as radical nor as revolutionary as their counterparts elsewhere seemed to believe they were. To them, whether the beneficiaries of ungendering efforts were first-year students or second-semester seniors, gender-neutral housing was not "much different from other living options"[10] that the university already offered, such as substance-free dormitories or other forms of affinity housing. Similarly, at Swarthmore, a strong "taboo against intimate relationships with roommates"[11]—one upheld and defended by students themselves—likely helped smooth the pathway to administrative acceptance for mixed-gender rooms. But for their director of residence life, gender-neutral housing really did seem to be an unremarkable next step in the natural evolution of their residential offerings. "We had coed by building. We had coed by hall. Now we have coed by room," she explained. "Lots of men and women are just friends, and why not live together?"[12] Even Haverford's director of

almost like a natural progression

student housing, who was not yet ready to extend gender-neutral options to their first-year students, intimated that the moral outrage proffered by her counterparts elsewhere was overblown. "We haven't done bed checks since the '60s," she said. "We're treating them as young adults."[13] *washington*

Because that one small policy change could kill two birds with one stone—by better meeting the residential needs of gender and sexual minority students and giving all students more choice and freedom in their living arrangements—insiders and outsiders alike expected support for gender-neutral spaces to soon spread like wildfire. As Swarthmore's residential life director reported, the "only problem" with gender-neutral rooms was "moving someone new in when someone leaves, which is a little more complicated in coed situations." But because students were so fond of mixed-gender spaces, she expected them to become popular on "most campuses" across the country within "three to five years."[14] Echoing that expectation, one writer for the *St. Louis Post-Dispatch* expressed his belief that coed dorm rooms might currently be too transgressive to be workable outside of "a handful of East Coast colleges," but it would "be only a matter of time before more traditional Midwestern schools" were certain to "follow suit."[15] And sure enough, at nearby Carnegie Mellon University, one housing director had already received "a couple of inquiries from students" about gender-blind housing, and he promised to give an official gender-neutral program serious consideration if that scattershot interest materialized into something more substantive: "We would entertain it if students brought us a proposal, much as what we would do with any other idea they might have."[16] *they're very open to it*

.   .   .   .   .

Well before the turn of the twenty-first century, when the prospect of gender-neutral housing was gaining notoriety in the popular press, many residential revolutions had already taken place in American higher education. As early as the 1960s, the absolute rule of *in loco parentis*—a judicial doctrine that allowed colleges and universities to function "in the place of a parent" to mold the moral character of their students—was steadily dissolving. In its stead, federal laws geared toward educational equity, like Title IX of the Education Amendments of 1972, took hold, as did many campus-level policies meant to facilitate more independence for under-graduate students. As a result, many universities that had long resisted coeducation abandoned the single-sex model, and women at all types of postsecondary institutions increasingly enrolled in majors and partici-pated in extracurricular activities that were once the sole province of men. Thus, over the course of the 1970s and 1980s, colleges and universities began to revamp numerous aspects of their physical environments to accommodate those transformations. From athletic facilities and student health centers to residential and restroom arrangements, spaces that were once incontrovertibly gendered became slowly, but surely, more mixed. By the closing years of the twentieth century, mixed-gender dorm rooms were, in many respects, exactly what Swarthmore's director of residence life observed in her comments to the press: simply the newest twist of that longer trajectory.[17]

At the same time, however, the emergence of gender-neutral housing did mark an important rupture from the past—because it was also inextri-cably intertwined with a revolutionary new social movement on college and university campuses: lesbian, gay, bisexual, transgender, and queer (LGBTQ) student activism.[18] Between the mid-1990s and early 2010s, many different institutional transformations arose in response to such efforts. Universities across the country hired student affairs staff to over-see LGBTQ-related activities and support services, created physical LGBTQ centers to house those staff and programs, added sexual orienta-tion and gender identity to their nondiscrimination policies, and insti-tuted training programs and workshops to educate interested faculty and staff on gender and sexuality issues. But the most publicly visible—and most hotly contested—among those changes were pressures to remove gender designations from campus spaces traditionally separated on the basis of gender: not just housing but restrooms as well.[19] And just as coed-ucational dormitories evolved from an unusual institutional experiment in the 1960s and 1970s to the dominant paradigm for undergraduate resi-dence life in the 1980s and 1990s, gender-inclusive residences and restrooms diffused throughout the first two decades of the twenty-first century in a similar fashion. First found at a small handful of liberal arts colleges known for progressive campus activism, they are now offered at over 150 institutions of higher education as of my data collection for this chapter in 2014—a total that has again grown larger since.[20]

This chapter seeks out the cultural underpinnings of that rising tide, using sixty-four interviews with university administrators, LGBTQ center directors, residential life staff, and facility directors to explain the emergence and rising popularity of gender-neutral campus spaces over the last twenty years.[21] Although mixed-gender dorm rooms and all-gender restrooms are distinctive institutional innovations, I package them together in this chapter because they have most often emerged as two halves of a common campus project—a project that most universities first approached with a high level of trepidation. At times, that caution was intimately connected to securing the safety and personal privacy of undergraduate students, especially women, most of whom were living on their own for the first time. But much more often, my respondents emphasized uncertainty about the consequences of such spatial transformations for their institution as a whole. A rare few colleges and universities, especially those well-known for espousing progressive politics, could trust that their public image would not suffer from allowing men and women to share residential and restroom spaces in unprecedented ways. Most, however, were hesitant to adopt novel configurations of gendered space without clear assurance that such organizational transformations would not tarnish the public reputation of their respective institutions.

Yet the same reputational forces responsible for that initial reluctance would, slowly but surely, become important catalysts of support for gender-inclusive housing and restrooms—within individual campuses and across the postsecondary landscape. As progressively minded administrators and staff sought to convince their more skeptical colleagues that ungendered spaces might be worthwhile, they reached out to their counterparts at other schools to determine how best to garner that support. That cross-campus contact often yielded an overwhelming potpourri of advice, but one approach to engendering change recurred in my respondents' conversations with more frequency than all others: they should make an argument that gender-neutral housing and all-gender restrooms could launch their college into a new echelon of publicly celebrated, LGBTQ-friendly institutions. That discursive strategy, which I refer to as *interactional isomorphism,* is an important means through which radical innovations once considered deviant or risky can become normalized. However, such interpersonal efforts can be a double-edged sword. As performance metrics to assess diversity have become ever more commonplace in higher education, rhetorical work to tether all-gender spaces to rankings and reputation has caused the most visible of spatial changes to be those most tirelessly pursued. For restrooms especially, then, moves toward greater inclusivity have often been more symbolic than substantive—and have done more to reinforce institutional inequalities than truly eradicate them.

"WHAT MAKES AN INSTITUTION ELITE IS AN UNWILLINGNESS TO CHANGE"

"Innovation is what America has always been about,"[22] observed then-president Barack Obama in his State of the Union address in 2012, and most of us living in the United States today are surrounded by evidence for that claim. Companies like Facebook thrive on a motto of "Move fast and break things,"[23] many of the most popular TED talks of all time celebrate the transformative power of creativity, and *Harvard Business Review* routinely extols the virtues of so-called disruptive innovation.[24] Institutions of higher education are no strangers to such claims, either. The Association of Governing Boards of Universities and Colleges promotes "a culture of innovation" as essential for developing "bold solutions to the challenges facing colleges and universities today."[25] Small public colleges and major private universities alike are developing innovation labs, creating academic tracks that allow undergraduate students to major or minor in innovation, and hosting innovation conferences for leaders from all manner of professional fields: technology, education, entrepreneurship, medicine, and beyond. In fact, in a world of mounting criticisms of higher education—"that graduation rates are too low, that levels of student engagement and learning outcomes are unacceptable, and that a college education does not provide good value for the money,"[26] as one *Chronicle of Higher Education* article argued in 2013—novelty and reinvention are not just lofty rhetorical ideals. For faculty, administrators, and students alike, they are an unavoidable necessity for a college or university to remain viable and, indeed, successful in the twenty-first century.

But when it came to early conversations about gender-inclusive housing and restrooms, many of my respondents found that not all kinds of institutional innovation are equally prized. Instead, would-be changes to residential and restroom spaces seemed to have a particularly fraught character. As I talked to one LGBTQ center director about the lead-up to their large, public university's gender-neutral housing debut, they mentioned that "many individuals who were otherwise very supportive and very proactive about creating an inclusive, LGBTQ-friendly culture in their departments or centers" recoiled at the idea of gender-neutral housing. That resistance, they added, was so profound that it "became an impassable line in the sand." When I asked what that metaphor meant, they explained that many of the administrators and staff who had pushed hardest "for language about sexual orientation and gender identity in [the university's] non-discrimination policy" were the first people to express "reservations" about a possible gender-neutral housing program. For those resisters, "the possibility that men and women might be able to share a dorm room was a step too far. Societal norms about gender and privacy was [sic] the line that couldn't be crossed." Other respondents, like another LGBTQ center director from a small, private college, went even further. That director, too, described concerns about restroom changes as being "very connected to gendered privacy" but also observed that any challenge to the gendered status quo—spatial or otherwise[27]—was likely to evoke similar forms of consternation: "If you ask me, the issue here is the intractability of the gender binary and all the cultural baggage that comes with it. I think that it's still very scary to a lot of people to think about challenging or contesting the binary in any way."

Much like Laurel Westbrook and Kristen Schilt find in their analysis of public conversation about transgender access to public restrooms,[28] that fear often revolved around the protection of female students. For one LGBTQ center director from a large private university, a campus-wide push to "ungender as many single-stall restrooms as possible" in their academic buildings was met with administrative dismay. "With our location being in such a high-traffic area, and with individuals from outside the

still stuck in the past

university community constantly moving around and through our build-ings," they explained, "one of the worries was that there would be targeting of our female students." The consequence was that "what started as trying to get a form to order new signs [for the restroom doors]" ultimately "escalated into a much bigger issue of campus security." But often, such a desire to protect individual women from harm paled in comparison to a desire to protect the entire college or university from being known as a place where young women might be harassed or assaulted. As one resi-dence life director from another, equally large and equally private univer-sity recalled, "Tensions about Title IX and sexual harassment were fresh on everyone's mind when we first started to figure out how to inaugurate gender-neutral housing and unisex bathrooms." That led the school to "put off an official policy for quite some time," because they had "witnessed some very public, very vitriolic backlash to gender-neutral programs hap-pen at other universities." And so, because they "didn't want the same to happen here at [university name]," they were "*very* cautious and *very* deliberate" (emphases theirs) about how they moved forward.

Such concerns with an institution's public image were, at times, so pro-nounced in my respondents' accounts that they transcended gender alto-gether. When I asked one residence life director to talk me through their school's timeline for adopting gender-neutral facilities, they explained that their large public university was quick to approve a "by-request model of individual accommodations" in housing, because "giving a trans-identified student priority for a single room was no different than some of the other accommodations we've been making for students for many years based on other grounds, like religious needs." But to expand that excep-tion-driven approach into a "formal policy that any student could take advantage of, whether or not they had a gender-based need" was consider-ably more difficult. "The biggest challenge was convincing our administra-tion," they explained, "which was not enthusiastic about the possibility of being one of the first institutions in the country to move away from the request-based model of inclusive housing." A similar apprehension about being a forerunner was echoed by another LGBTQ center director from a comparable institution. When I asked what the most salient obstacle to gender-inclusive facilities was for their campus, they replied, "The novelty, I think. You have to keep in mind that, back when housing first became an issue that our students were raising, there was no template. We were one of the first schools in the nation to try to make this happen for our students, and that made answering questions from all the different offices involved about what the program should look like and how it might affect us long-term really quite challenging."

In other words, my respondents found themselves confronting what Paul DiMaggio and Walter Powell refer to as the "legitimacy imperative"—that is, the requirement that an organization's actions be perceived as reasonable, desirable, and appropriate by other, similar organizations—a requirement that often reinforces tradition rather than facilitating change.[29] Because, as several of my respondents further observed, if their college or university were to hastily adopt untested innovations, the result might be irreparable damage to its public image. One administrator from a small private college put it this way: "Our reputation precedes us in a positive way, and any risk of damage to that is a serious concern. Prospective students, alumni donors, potential faculty hires all have an image of [college name] in mind: what kind of institution we are and what kind of institution we are not. If we lose that reputation, then we lose those resources, and if we lose those resources, we lose our place among the top liberal arts colleges in the United States." Another administrator from a similar college recalled that there was genuine sympathy among their colleagues for "the student movement to get gender-neutral housing in place." However, that sympathy was insufficient to override concern with preserving "the university's character." In their case, the college's board of trustees "was supportive in principle" but, unfortunately, "refused any possibility of moving forward that academic year." When I pushed for more details, that same administrator pivoted from the local nuances of the university's process to a bold proclamation: "Part of what makes an institution elite is an unwillingness to change. That reality means that the first answer to any sort of request for a new program—especially a controversial one—defaults to no."

In fact, while such reputational pressures were quickest to arise in conversation with respondents from flagship state universities and highly selective private colleges,[30] they were no less potent an influence for other types of institutions. When I asked one administrator from a large university in the Midwest to describe what, if anything, they remembered being difficult about progress toward a formal policy for gender-neutral housing,

I was told that some types of innovation are more challenging than others because of their partisan charge. "As a public, state-funded university," they explained, "we have to engage with the diverse system of values and priorities that come from the entire state of [state name]. That diversity is often a rich and wonderful resource for our students, faculty, and staff, but it also creates a situation in which we have to be very careful about when, how, and why we take on projects that might be controversial." Similar sentiments anchored the comments of an LGBTQ center director from an equally large southern school, who explained that even a progressive local context or campus culture could do little to urge along university programs or policies that seemed to be at odds with a broader political climate. "[City name] has a very liberal political orientation, and that goes for the university community just as much as it does our surrounding geography," they said. "But at the end of the day, [state name] is still a very conservative state, and our status as a public university in that broader context exerts a substantial influence on what we're able to provide."

And so, even for schools with some form of coeducational housing already in place from earlier decades or with many single-stall restrooms already available in multiple academic buildings, making an official commitment to produce ungendered spaces was a difficult, if not impossible, proposition. Whether they anchored their concerns in the unique plight of female students or in a generalized concern with gender trouble, the danger associated with inclusive spaces was a powerful dissuading force. Yet beneath that ideological veneer lurked a more intractable concern about the prophesized damage of gender-neutral housing and all-gender restrooms: the imagined harm that might befall a college's public reputation if it were to adopt too radical of an institutional innovation. In other words, gender-inclusive facilities represented a double deviance from institutional norms. Not only did they defy moral pressures to uphold traditional gender and sexual mores, but they also spurned organizational pressures to maintain consonance with the other universities most like one's own. Thus, as many of my respondents witnessed firsthand, radical innovations in higher education could be acceptable, even desirable, but only up to a point. If those innovations might challenge deeper cultural ideologies, especially those related to gendered privacy or sexual propriety, they were almost always ruled too precarious to pursue, at least until a more reliable set of templates had fallen into place.

"THE LOGICAL NEXT STEP, GIVEN OUR PROGRESSIVE REPUTATION"

As recent research at the intersection of cultural sociology and the sociology of organizations has shown, however, the very same reputational pressures that so often discourage radical innovations—like gender-inclusive facilities—can also serve as a potent catalyst of change. For many decades, social scientists have known that categories and classifications fundamentally shape the identities and behavior of all organizations, including colleges and universities. Over the last few years, work in that vein has shown that an organization's category memberships are so powerful that they can sometimes facilitate deviance from long-standing institutional or cultural norms. The catch, though, is that not all categories are equally effective at enabling radical innovation. Instead, empirical evidence suggests that high-status classifications have the most insulating power: not only do they protect organizations from the negative consequences that typically accrue when adopting illegitimate products or challenging long-standing moral values, but also, when organizations in high-status categories adopt transgressive products or practices, those products or practices automatically become more likely to be adopted by other organizations. As a result, what was once a radical transgression can quickly become a normative expectation, simply because the choices made in high-status organizations are assumed to be superior to other options. In other words, for organizations, one of the utmost privileges of membership in a privileged cultural category is being able to choose their own courses of action with the reassurance that outsiders will unquestioningly interpret such choices as valid.[31]

In keeping with such observations, a handful of participants in my interview sample offered a local history of gender-inclusive facilities that was remarkably free of resistance. For them, being in an especially "inclusive" or "student-centered" group of colleges and universities allowed inclusive housing and restrooms to flourish amid the challenges of uncertainty and the risks of violating gender and sexual mores. As one LGBTQ center director from a large public university explained, "When I started talking to my colleagues about getting gender-neutral restrooms identified in a central database and, from there, installed in buildings that didn't have them, I took for granted that people understood the value of inclusion. We really try to embody the idea that higher education is for the people, and so it was simply a matter of explaining that this was a small change we could make that, one, resonated with our values, and two, would ensure more people felt welcome on this campus." In fact, many of the same organizational categories emphasized in my conversations with respondents from initially hesitating colleges were the impetus behind a seamless adoption for such first-movers. For instance, where several of my respondents from private colleges and universities portrayed their institutions as hypersensitive to change, others found the opposite. In one such case, an LGBTQ center director from a small private college replied again and again to my interview questions that there was "really no resistance" to their requests to first introduce, and later expand, gender-inclusive housing offerings. When I expressed my surprise at that reality and asked if they, too, were struck by how responsive their institution was to those requests, I was met with a simple, potent response: "Not at all. It was the logical next step, given our progressive reputation. That we would support inclusive housing was almost a foregone conclusion."

The problem for administrators and staff elsewhere, then, was the lack of model institutions in the "right" organizational category, particularly in the earlier years of gender-neutral conversations. For colleges and universities that were themselves located in an elite institutional category, only a select group of organizational peers "counted as persuasive evidence," in the words of one LGBTQ center director from a midsized private college, "that their own institution should move ahead" with ungendered spaces:

> Every single person I initiated a dialogue with asked me what [Ivy League university], [another Ivy], and [another Ivy] had decided to do about gender-neutral housing and restrooms, and just about every single person who had a favorable response at first backed down considerably when my response was that none of the three had yet put an official policy on the books. It was exhausting to rehash that same response over and over again,

especially as it became more and more clear that successful launches at [large public flagship university] and [small liberal arts college] weren't the evidence necessary to convince the administration to move forward.

Meanwhile, for respondents in other parts of the country or in other types of universities, that same basic principle could also cut the opposite way. That is, even when high-status models—such as Ivy League schools, well-regarded private colleges in the region, or a state's flagship university—shifted in the direction of adopting inclusive facilities, they could seem too culturally and institutionally distinctive for others to be willing and able to emulate them. Another LGBTQ center director, this time from a large public university, recalled precisely such an obstacle in their retelling of their institution's progress toward gender-neutral residential offerings:

> When we were still in the realm of informal talks about making small changes to better support our trans students, our board of trustees was opposed to gender-neutral housing. They felt that it was one thing for an institution like [Ivy League university] in an especially liberal part of the country to start experimenting with new housing options for their LGBT students, or for small liberal arts colleges who pride themselves on unusually progressive practices, but there was a lot of anxiety about how things would play out if we piloted the same sort of program here.

To get the power of classification on their side, such respondents reported, subsequently required a torrent of interpersonal labor. Often, that labor unfolded across multiple offices on a single college or university campus as my respondents strove to convince a sufficient volume of supporters that gender-inclusive facilities were worth pursuing. One LGBTQ center director from a small, private college articulated such a perspective while recalling "countless hours spent on the phone" with colleagues across their campus: "Because we're such a small, close-knit campus, when a new issue or program is on the table, I have to make a *lot* of phone calls to a *lot* of offices, and I have to do a *lot* of explaining why that new proposal is so important. Convincing a critical mass of powerful supporters that a new project fits with our institutional mission is crucial if we want it to be a success" (emphases theirs). And while quantity of contact was indeed helpful, quality of contact was often the necessary magic bullet, because harnessing support from high-ranking or well-loved campus leaders often led to more efficient and thorough changes to residential and restroom policies. "Most people are open to a conversation anytime something new comes up, but . . ." another LGBTQ center director opined, before trailing off into a long silence. I prodded gently, "But?" "But this is [a major athletic conference] school. If I really want something to happen, my first stop is with my colleagues in athletics. That's the most powerful area of this campus. If I can get them on board, it's so much more likely that a conversation will translate into action."

Making the most of those intracampus efforts, moreover, required my respondents to draw on an intercampus resource: conversations with their counterparts at other colleges and universities in their peer networks. In one interview with an LGBTQ center director from a small, teaching-focused college, our discussion took a turn toward what they described as "the unique challenges of the liberal arts environment," foremost among which was "spending hours and days on the phone" whenever new changes to student affairs were on the table. But as that director worked to lay necessary interactional groundwork for administrative approval of gender-inclusive facilities, they found that they had a new set of phone calls ahead: "The first question I got from every office was: 'What's [liberal arts college] doing? What's [another LAC] doing? What's happening with our peer institutions out on the East Coast, like [another LAC] and [another LAC]?'" Worse yet, finding answers to those questions was rarely straightforward, because their outreach efforts often yielded varied, sometimes even contradictory, advice. "What I heard from [large public university] was to downplay the transgender side of things and to just focus on giving students more choices," noted one residence life director from an equally large, public university, "but at least three other colleagues in student affairs swore up and down that branding this specifically as LGBT affinity housing was the best way to start the ball rolling." That left them in the frustrating position of having to "separate the wheat from the chaff, so to speak."

Yet as varied as that advice might be, my respondents found one strategy above all others to be most reliable—and that one strategy was right in line with the predictions of organizational sociology: to speak as specifically as possible to vaunted institutional categories. For one LGBTQ center director, that reframing was crucial for motivating their administration to invest in a pilot program for inclusive housing: "I had been saying, 'We can be a leader on this,' 'We should be a leader on this,' for some time, but what finally resonated was changing the conversation to be: 'We're going to be behind [large public university] and [large private university] on this if we don't get moving.'" Moreover, such boundary-drawing strategies enabled respondents looking to expand their gender-neutral options beyond a pilot program to move closer to their ideal restroom and residential vision. "One of the tricky things for us was having to translate what had been effective in a private, liberal arts setting to something that would be as effective in a regional, comprehensive setting," reported another LGBTQ center director toward the end of our interview, "so while [liberal arts college] and [another LAC] had exactly the sort of program we were aiming for, we ended up basing our initial protocol after what had been developed at [large public university]." But "with each new semester," they added, "we started saying, 'What about making sure we get an inclusive restroom in the renovations to [academic building name]?' Or, 'Hey, why don't we also add a gender-neutral floor in [dormitory name]? That would make us stand out beyond what [another regional university] has.'"

In some ways, those interpersonal efforts exemplify *institutional isomorphism:* a term used by organizational sociologists to capture the tendency of organizations to change and evolve in tandem with one another, owing to a shared cultural environment with shared expectations about how organizations in that environment should act.[32] But in this particular case, the legitimacy of gender-inclusive facilities did not stem mechanically from the mere prevalence of such spaces among comparable colleges. In fact, legitimacy could *not* stem from mere prevalence because, in most cases, other universities with inclusive facilities were too rare or too different to serve as viable models. For my respondents, then, legitimacy could only come from the contagious spread of boundary-drawing strategies among networked organizational actors—that is, from the e-mails, phone calls, and in-person visits to other schools that allowed them to learn what sorts of rhetorical moves helped engender innovation elsewhere and thus might be effective on their own campuses.[33] In other words, garnering support for inclusive facilities required what I call *interactional isomorphism:* the active, embodied work of organizational actors to seek out,

mimic, extend, and manipulate the specific categorical distinctions that
had secured changes to protocols, policies, and procedures in other, similar organizations. And that active, embodied work had two consequences
for my interview respondents: not only did it help garner support for
innovations within their own colleges or universities, but it also allowed
innovation to diffuse across the wider institutional landscape.

"WHAT KIND OF 'TOP TEN' SCHOOL SETTLES FOR A BARE MINIMUM?"

But targeted interactional labor has not been the only factor leading to
increasing support for ungendered campus housing and restrooms over
the last decade. Substantive shifts in the broader cultural landscape, too,
have primed universities to be newly amenable to policies meant to support gender and sexual minority students—especially the rise of diversity
programming as politically and institutionally desirable. Starting in the
1980s, college and university administrators began adopting discourses
and developing programs to signal their compliance with laws related to
racial and gender equity; by the 1990s and early 2000s, those logics had
evolved into a marketing strategy for many universities, public and private
alike, to attract competitive applicants from as wide a range of demographic groups as possible. Today, as Mitchell Stevens and Josipa Roksa
observe, there is a "diversity imperative" in elite college admissions in the
United States—that is, an expectation "that academically excellent schools
also be racially heterogeneous."[34] Moreover, that imperative now encom-
passes many more aspects of diversity than race alone. In fact, even institutional recognition of transgender people—who, as historian Susan
Stryker observes, have traditionally been so troubling to "the categories on
which normative sexualities depend"[35] that they have been relegated to
the periphery of the gay and lesbian rights movement—now represents a
valuable opportunity for all manner of organizations to craft a public
image of inclusivity in the twenty-first century.[36]

Multiple respondents in my interview sample confirmed that such
changes had indeed accelerated over the last few years. They pronounced
diversity and inclusion to be "ends worth pursuing for their own sake,"

Abiding to law

"more and more central" to the university context "in the last twenty years," and "canopies which go far beyond race—there's gender, sexuality, cultural background, musical tastes, preferences in literature, personalities and cognitive style, and so on." Moreover, they attributed the increasing popularity of gender-inclusive facilities to that expanding embrace. In the words of one administrator from a small private college:

> Everyone—except maybe one or two people—is on board with diversity, which makes for a different conversation about social justice. There's simply much more willingness to give programs like gender-neutral housing the benefit of the doubt, especially when it comes to making our campus safer and more comfortable for our minority students, including our gender and sexual minority students. Inclusive housing, inclusive restrooms . . . these are changes that would have happened no matter what, because they *are* the right thing to do, but their compatibility with a campuswide push toward equity and inclusion made the path to actualization much smoother.

Beyond making the removal of gender designations from residential and restroom spaces more palatable, the growing premium placed on diversity and inclusion also made those changes more rapid. "We had a lot of buildings with single-stall restrooms, but they were paired: one male, one female," explained one facilities director from a large, public university, "and those were obvious candidates to be converted into gender-neutral, because they really just needed a sign change." The problem was that other facility updates constantly took priority: "You know the matrix of importance versus urgency, right? The gender-neutral thing was always important, but it was never urgent." That is, until the facilities director's equity and inclusion office wanted to create a digital directory of their university's all-gender restrooms. "Suddenly," that director went on, "this was an equity issue, and everything kicked into high gear. New signs were ordered, old signs were replaced, and everything was done by the end of the week."

But the diversity imperative was not the only recent transformation in higher education to which my respondents ascribed the increasing popularity of gender-neutral spaces. Another development—an unparalleled concern with educational rankings when assessing or amending institutional policies or procedures—was also afoot. "Everything in the last five years has become so data-driven," recalled one LGBTQ center director from a midsized private college, "so what began as a relatively narrow request from a small group of students evolved into a cog in the university's bureaucratic machine. Suddenly, this was something else we could quantify, use to self-assess and as a basis for meaningful comparison to other institutions." In fact, for many respondents, what Michael Sauder and Wendy Espeland refer to as the "discipline of rankings"[37] completely inverted the reputational risk once associated with inclusive facilities. No longer was it dangerous to consider an expansive adoption of gender-neutral housing and restrooms, it was dangerous to *not* do so. That sentiment was epitomized by the comments of another LGBTQ center director from a different private university. As they explained, *The Advocate,* a special-interest magazine targeting an LGBTQ-identified readership, "put out a list of the 'top ten trans-friendly colleges'" in the early 2010s, "and that was a watershed moment." I asked why that was, and they replied in detail: "Everyone saw that schools like [Ivy League university], [large public flagship university], [another Ivy], [another flagship], and even [large private university] were on that list, so there was a lot of asking, 'Why aren't we on that list? What would it take to get us there?'"

There was just one problem: new forms of external surveillance placed a premium on highly visible facility updates, and what was most visible was not always most beneficial to gender-diverse students, faculty, and staff. For one administrator from a large, public university, the capacious all-gender restroom in their student union epitomized that debacle. As they explained, "Getting something like all-gender restrooms incorporated in absolutely all parts of campus is a tough challenge with a campus of our size, at least if you're trying to do so quickly, so we decided to regroup and reprioritize." Consequently, that administrator undertook a campuswide inventory of restroom spaces, and their inventory yielded a short list of "high priority" buildings: those that had voluminous foot traffic, those centrally located on campus, or both—such as the student union. "On the one hand," they went on to say, "that was very obviously a good thing. Not as good or as thorough as collecting data on restroom need and restroom use, but certainly serviceable, in that it guided where our energy should go first." Unfortunately, things took a not-so-positive turn when it came time to translate that energy into action: "On the other hand, those data became a rationale to prioritize buildings that needed the most inclusive 'look,' regardless of what was financially sensible or optimal from a frequency-of-use standpoint." In other words, even the most objectively onerous restroom renovations could readily become university priorities if—but only if—they would provide the right kind of optics to students, visitors, and of course, external evaluators: "It's not a mistake that the first buildings we focused on were also ones in our official campus tour guide, nor that almost every entrance to the student union points the way to that biggest 'all-gender' bathroom."

Ironically, then, my respondents found that their careful interactional work to connect the necessity of gender-inclusive spaces to vaunted institutional categories could subsequently backfire.[38] One LGBTQ center director from a large, public university described precisely such a turn of events. "Our vision was to model our gender-neutral program after some of the most progressive housing policies in the nation, like the ones at [small liberal arts college] and [small liberal arts college]," they recalled, and the school's efforts to "copy those existing models as closely as possible at a larger scale" allowed it to achieve a notable reputational boost: "We ended up being ahead of a lot of other colleges with a profile like ours." That boost also paved the way for several other institutional changes, such as modifications to their student health insurance "to ensure trans health care was included." But as more students expressed interest in gender-neutral housing, it became harder and harder to keep up with that increasing demand. When I asked about the nature of that difficulty, I was met with some hemming and hawing about "housing shortages" and "unusually large admissions yields" before receiving a more candid answer. "Sometimes, I think that playing the 'public image' card shoehorned us some," they finally confessed, before segueing into a longer lament about the dark side of notoriety:

> Don't get me wrong. Being a first-mover is tough, and like we were talking about before, it was not at all a cakewalk to get the ball rolling on any of our gender-neutral policies. I just think there's a certain . . . sparkle, I suppose, to being one of the first to do something new, or to make a major improvement over what your peer institutions are doing. It gives you an ability to say, "Let's do this, let's get out there, let's be the leader." That same kind of

argument isn't nearly as effective the second or third or seventh time you use it, and it's also not ideal when you're trying to expand a functioning program, or make it better meet student needs. To make a case for small, incremental improvements is, in some respects, harder, because those tweaks don't have the same kind of quantifiable yield that you get from a dramatic initial change.

The power of classification thus turned out to be as much an unexpected curse as a fortuitous blessing—especially when it came to restrooms. "There's a logic to it," remarked an LGBTQ center director from a midsized private university. "If we're already recognized as one of the top institutions in the country for our work with LGBT students, why would we need to do more than we're already doing? But it's a sad logic, because . . ." They paused. "Well, for one, what kind of 'top ten' school settles for a bare minimum on any measure? For two . . ." They paused again. "The bar on trans issues is still so astoundingly low." And so, even at a school "well-known for queer- and trans-friendliness" like theirs, there was "little incentive" to add an all-gender restroom to older campus buildings: "The restroom situation is improving in some parts of campus, but we're still pushing to get our more centrally located buildings safe and accessible for our trans and gender-variant students and staff." In other words, as another LGBTQ center director observed, concern with rankings and reputation might catalyze change to university policies, but it did little to revolutionize infrastructure. "Our original goal was to get at least one inclusive restroom in every single building: residential, academic, libraries, athletic facilities, the whole lot," they said, "but as our students started to map out which buildings needed what, it became painfully obvious that making all of those changes at once was going to cost much more than we anticipated." The good news was that their institution was quick to craft "a policy in line with those at our peer institutions, mandating that all new construction would need to accommodate a gender-inclusive restroom" moving forward to prevent such problems from accruing in the future. The bad news was that "peer pressure" would do little to alter the gender separation permeating most of their existing campus restrooms: "Let's be honest: how often do you think we build new buildings from the ground up?"

THE FIFTH ELEMENT OF GENDER'S INSTITUTIONAL
ACCOMPLISHMENT: ORGANIZATIONAL NETWORKS

Thus, from the new value ascribed to diversity and inclusion to the rise of quantitative metrics for trans-friendliness, a confluence of institutional changes has allowed gender-inclusive facilities to move from the margins of higher education to the mainstream. And that remarkable diffusion of support for gender-diverse students, faculty, and staff over the last two decades has come as much from within American colleges and universities as from cultural changes beyond them, thanks to the work of people like my respondents and their exercise of *interactional isomorphism*— that is, the interpersonal labor of observing, borrowing, and building upon rhetorical strategies (especially boundary-drawing strategies) that have prompted change in other, similar settings in order to achieve parallel change in one's own organization. Unfortunately, however, support for gender-neutral housing and all-gender restrooms in principle has not always yielded substantive change in practice, especially when it comes to bathrooms. As support for gender and sexual minority students has evolved into a measurable dimension of campus climate that one college can use to evaluate itself against others, the specter of external surveillance has meant that those facility policies and changes that are most visible and most quantifiable have often been those most readily prioritized. In fact, even among those colleges and universities at the vanguard of spatial ungendering, the lack of an ongoing reputational incentive to further reduce the prevalence of gender separation in their residential and restroom spaces has often ground progress to a halt—thereby leaving gender in many dormitories and bathrooms no more undone than before.

In her aptly titled "Undoing Gender," Francine Deutsch takes the possibility that the gender system could be unraveled at any moment as her departure point, calling our attention to the revolutionary potential of social interactions to dismantle institutional inequalities. As she observes, the models of gender put forth by late-twentieth-century academic sociologists revolve around a radical observation: "gender is dynamic," not an immobile collection of norms and practices inculcated into us "by parents, teachers, and other authority figures" when we are children.[39] To overcome gendered inequalities, therefore, does not require us "to wait for another generation to be socialized differently."[40] Instead, social transformation is possible "within a much shorter time span," because "what is considered appropriate gendered behavior changes over time,"[41] and that incessant churn imbues all social interactions with the power to resist, challenge, or even upend the gender order. But just as central to Deutsch's reflection on the interaction order of gender is a call to action: all too often, she finds, sociologists of gender focus myopically on "documenting the persistence of inequality,"[42] and that undermines our ability to use our collective intellectual insights "as a theory of resistance."[43] Thus, she exhorts us to act differently: "By examining the effects of subversive action on its audience, we may be able to identify the conditions under which those actions change normative conceptions of gender, and how and when these new conceptions can take advantage of or even drive institutional change."[44] In other words, Deutsch reasons, if gender is always being done, then it could just as easily be undone—and we sociologists are uniquely positioned to illuminate where, when, and how that resistance can coalesce into a dismantling of the gender system.

And while Deutsch's focus is directed more toward individual behavior than organizational behavior, I nonetheless find her emphasis on the microsociological building blocks of macrosociological change quite useful for making sense of my findings in this chapter. The initial resistance to gender-inclusive facilities reported by many of my respondents was very much grounded in "conventional gender relations,"[45] in the form of paternalistic concerns about premarital cohabitation and the alleged vulnerability of young women's bodies. And while the grip of those traditional ideologies has been loosening since the fall of *in loco parentis* in the mid-twentieth century, they have relaxed even further in recent years, owing to the tireless, on-the-ground "subversive action"[46] undertaken by my respondents to argue in favor of residential and restroom ungendering. Such interactional efforts have also clearly concatenated into institutional changes—because *interactional isomorphism* truly has helped transform a once-untouchable form of organizational gender deviance into a normative element of the higher-education landscape. Or, as Deutsch rightfully predicts, "Gendered institutions can be changed, and the social interactions that support them can be undone."[47] In fact, there is now tremendous pressure for colleges and universities to "do more and do better," as one administrator put it, when it comes to their queer and transgender students, and that pressure has only increased with each passing year. All of those gains reflect unquestionably marked ruptures in the status quo of gender separation in dorms and bathrooms alike from a mere decade or two ago, and they very well may portend the rise of a much more sweeping gender revolution—not just within higher education, but in American society writ large.

But my interview data also reveal that undoing gender does not always mean undoing inequity. Even when administrators and staff work from the most noble of intentions to enact genuine change on their campuses— which, I firmly believe, my respondents have done—their conversations about inclusive facilities overwhelmingly revolve around the individualistic "reputation race"[48] endemic to twenty-first-century higher education. Thus, much like feminist theorist Sara Ahmed has observed in her research on diversity discourses in higher education, I find that well-meaning efforts to rethink various forms of social difference often do little to displace existing educational hierarchies.[49] Whether my respondents worked at some of the oldest and most elite colleges in the United States or smaller regional schools with much less national renown, increasing institutional support for gender-neutral housing and all-gender restrooms has often been predicated on self-interested expectations: of an enhanced reputation for LGBTQ-friendliness, an improved performance on diversity metrics, or a heightened ability to outpace one's institutional peers. As a result, interactional efforts to lessen the impact of the gender binary may have allowed support for the undoing of some gender distinctions in campus architecture to blossom, but they have also reinforced a sense that gender-inclusive spaces exist largely for reputational ends. Consequently, unless sociologists fully consider the context and content of face-to-face work to undo gender, we cannot possibly identify the conditions under which truly revolutionary change—gendered or otherwise—might be possible.

So, before I move into my final chapter and consider what truly revolutionary change to restrooms might require, context and content lead me to the fifth element of theorizing gender as an institutional accomplishment: the *networked* character of gendered organizations and the gendered individuals acting within them. In part, networks bring us full circle to this book's introduction, as the social connections linking the colleges and universities I study here are, in many respects, the epitome of the fundamental interdependence of organizations. In each and every corner of this chapter, that interdependence has foreclosed or facilitated gendered possibilities: because a refusal to challenge long-standing gender and sexual mores can be as much about reputation management as about moral panic; because the transference of boundary-drawing strategies from person to person (and from organization to organization) can enable the absorption of radical gender ideologies into the mundanity of everyday bureaucracy; and above all else, because the degree to which gendered infrastructure can bend, break, or evolve is often contingent on peer comparisons, prestige, and public image. But networks do more than provide context for doing or undoing gender. Networks also emerge in the content of social interactions—because individual workers, like my respondents, often invoke them as a justification for how their organizations ought to negotiate the gender order. Consequently, only through attention to networks at both levels do we see how interactional attempts to reduce gendered inequalities can, ultimately, reinforce other forms of social stratification—which is the result when gender-inclusive spaces allow a college or university to showcase its commitment to diversity and inclusion, accumulate the myriad rewards associated with such a reputation, and secure the promise of continued social status for the future.

Thus, while *The Advocate*'s article from 2012 about the most trans-friendly colleges and universities in the United States reported, "Not surprisingly, the top ten list favors large, public four-year colleges and universities in the Northeast and West Coast where there are more politically progressive and trans-visible areas,"[50] it is also not surprising that half of the institutions on the list also reside on *Forbes Magazine*'s list of the twenty-two richest colleges and universities in America.[51] Nor is it surprising that, when publications like *USA Today* and *Inside Higher Ed* celebrate the "changing climate" for gender diversity within higher education, they mention schools like my graduate alma mater, Princeton University, much more often than our smaller liberal arts counterparts doing exceptional, student-centered work.[52] Increasing administrative support for gender-inclusive housing and restrooms on college campuses may thus represent a profound shift toward a safer and more comfortable college experience for gender and sexual minority students—and a much-needed one at that, because such support does have a tangible impact on the health and happiness of transgender students, faculty, and staff.[53] Yet as Max Weber once wrote in his classic theory of social stratification, "Class, Status, Party," "the development of status is essentially a question of stratification resting upon usurpation."[54] And as long as accolades for queer- and trans-friendliness continue to be usurped by colleges and universities already at the top of educational status hierarchies—rightfully or not—the promise of institutional inclusion offered by gender-inclusive facilities will continue to be used as a means of reproducing much more tenacious patterns of social and cultural exclusion.

Conclusion

And what one has is a case of institutional reflexivity: toilet
segregation is presented as a natural consequence of the difference
between the sex-classes, when in fact it is rather a means of
honoring, if not producing, this difference.

Erving Goffman, "The Arrangement between the Sexes,"
Theory and Society, September 1977

On March 23, 2016, the North Carolina General Assembly convened a
special one-day session to debate and vote on House Bill 2, the Public
Facilities Privacy and Security Act. "HB2," or "the North Carolina bathroom bill" as it quickly became known in press coverage across the United
States, proposed two additions to North Carolina state law. First, it would
define biological sex as "the physical condition of being male or female"
specifically as "stated on a person's birth certificate." Second, it would limit
access to gender-segregated restrooms in educational, public, and work
spaces to users whose biological sex, as now stringently defined by the
other aspects of the bill, matched the designation on a given restroom
door.[1] The bill passed quickly through both houses of the state legislature
(with unanimous approval in the state senate, as Democrats walked out in
protest of the bill) before being signed into law that very same night by
Governor Pat McCrory. In his view, the need for "immediate"[2] action was
simple: a number of local policies had recently been approved across
North Carolina to prevent discrimination in public accommodations
related to sexual orientation and gender identity—most notably in the city
of Charlotte, where a new ordinance ensured that transgender residents
could access public restrooms congruent with their gender identity. That

"ordinance defied common sense," McCrory explained in a tweet accompanying his late-night approval of HB2, because it meant "allowing men to use women's bathroom/locker room for instance. That's why I signed a bipartisan bill to stop it."[3] *how mough?*

But just as quickly as HB2 had moved through the state legislature and into North Carolina law, political countermobilization erupted. The day after the governor's signature and tweet, protestors gathered at the North Carolina State Capitol to speak out against the bill's passage—and against the dubious means through which that passage, they said, had been accomplished. (One particularly cheeky citizen even had a porta-potty delivered to the capitol grounds, though the lack of an appropriate permit meant it had to remain on the bed of the delivery truck which brought it.) By the end of the week, national nonprofit organizations like the American Civil Liberties Union and Lambda Legal had filed a complaint with the United States District Court on behalf of a transgender University of North Carolina–Greensboro student, a transgender UNC–Chapel Hill employee, and a lesbian North Carolina Central University law professor. The suit charged HB2 with multiple violations of the Equal Protection Clause of the Fourteenth Amendment and the portions of Title IX pertaining to gender and educational equity. Plus, in the weeks to follow, backlash against HB2 moved lawmakers in nearby states considering their own restroom-related gender restrictions to reject such possibilities. This included Georgia's governor, Nathan Deal, who vetoed a religious freedom bill perceived to be "anti-LGBT" because it did not adequately "reflect the character of our state and the character of our people."[4] *influenced other nearby states b act differently*

Much of that national outrage against HB2 did indeed stem from the law's character, which the *Charlotte Observer*'s editorial board agreed was "inherently discriminatory." However, many civic officials within North Carolina's state borders worried about another side of HB2—the risk that it might hamper the state's economic prosperity. Attorney General Roy Cooper, for instance, characterized HB2 as "a national embarrassment" when he publicly announced that his office would not defend the governor or the measure in the forthcoming legal battles over its constitutionality. More importantly, he expected that embarrassment to cost the state of North Carolina—quite literally. "The threats to our economy will grow even darker the longer this law stays in effect," he explained, with the

initial costs of a "flood of litigation" quickly trailed by further fiscal consequences. Pointing to the losses Indiana had suffered in the wake of passing
a religious freedom law several months earlier, he observed that "business
left the state, or thought twice about bringing in new jobs, and millions of
dollars in revenue was lost." Consequently, he concluded, not only did
HB2 legalize discrimination against "the LGBT community" but it was
also poised to do harm to every single one of the "innocent people" of
North Carolina "who work hard every day and pay taxes."[5]

Sure enough, those prophesized losses did begin to add up. PayPal canceled their plans for an expansion of their offices in Charlotte, specifically
citing HB2 as the reason for their change of heart. Television studio
Lionsgate moved their production plans for a new comedy series from
Charlotte, noting that they would be "hard pressed" to pursue any future
work in North Carolina as long as "this regressive law remains on the
books." Artistic talents ranging from Bruce Springsteen to Cirque du Soleil
canceled scheduled performances in North Carolina, opting to absorb
their own loss of revenue in order to protest the new state law. And not to
be outdone, small businesses unable to relocate outside of state lines
found their own means of leaping into the political fray. Two owners of
local breweries, for instance, joined forces to craft a new beer—"Don't Be
Mean to People: A Golden Rule Saison"—as a fundraiser against HB2,
promising to donate all of the proceeds from the sales of the brew to
Equality North Carolina and Queer Oriented Radical Days of Summer, a
summer camp founded to empower queer and transgender youth from
southern states to take on future political activism. Meanwhile, entrepre-
neurs whose wares were featured on the state's official tourism websites
asked to sever ties with North Carolina's national advertising campaign,
as they believed that HB2 was "bad, and bad for business."[6]

The one upside of HB2, however, was an important exception built into
its official guidelines: nothing in any of its sections would prohibit local
boards of education or public agencies "from providing accommodations
such as single occupancy bathroom or changing facilities." As a result, gas
stations and grocery stores alike began advertising their unisex restrooms
in their storefront windows. The Raleigh Convention Center reached out
to event organizers unable to relocate their events, offering inventive solutions that would temporarily reconfigure some of their existing restrooms

led to many stores and stations to create gender neutral restrooms into gender-neutral options for conference-goers. Nearby hotels moved quickly to add a gender-neutral restroom to their lobby or another heavily trafficked public area for the benefit of their guests. Many restaurants and bars with single-user restroom spaces took gender-specific signs down altogether and replaced them with "all-gender" labels. Various programs and departments in some of North Carolina's institutions of higher education reached out to their students, faculty, and staff to share the locations of the nearest gender-inclusive restroom space, and several others, like Cape Fear Community College, added deadbolts to the main entrances of their existing, multiuser gender-neutral restrooms—suddenly allowing them to function as impromptu "single-user" restrooms in compliance with HB2's new requirements.

And the effects of that restroom revolution would come to be felt far beyond the North Carolina state line—as, not to be outdone, businesses in other southern states followed suit with their own push toward gender neutrality. Right after the passage of HB2, a Kroger grocery store in Athens, Georgia, gained national attention after a shopper posted a picture of a new sign on their unisex restroom to Facebook that went viral. "We have a UNISEX bathroom because sometimes gender specific toilets put others into uncomfortable situations," the sign read, "And since we have a lot of friends coming to see us, we want to provide a place for our friends who are: Dads with daughters, Moms with sons, Parents with disabled children, Those in the LGBTQ community, Adults with aging parents who may be mentally or physically disabled. THANK YOU for helping us provide a safe environment for EVERYONE!"[7] Ellwood Thompson's, a grocery store in Richmond, Virginia, also invoked HB2 as their rationale for relabeling their single-user restrooms as gender-neutral. As the store's marketing manager explained, Ellwood's had long been a haven for progressive-minded community members, including a number of trans-identified employees and customers. Switching all of their restrooms to gender-neutral so that those individuals could "feel comfortable" was thus an easy choice to make. "Ellwood's doesn't mind being a leader or an activist on this," he said. "If it draws negative attention, we don't mind it at all."[8]

.   .   .   .   .

In the nearly ten-year lifespan of this project—from chapter 6's embryonic form as a research proposal written in my first year of graduate school to this full-length book—public conversations about ungendered restrooms have undergone numerous and unprecedented shifts across the United States. The number of colleges and universities publicly reporting gender-neutral housing and restroom offerings for their undergraduate students more than quadrupled between 2009 and 2016 and, as chapter 6 recounts, also spread far beyond the realm of small liberal arts colleges into institutions of all types and in all geographic regions. Legal debates about restrooms for transgender employees have moved out of the judicial realm analyzed in chapter 3 and into local and state legislatures—often in ways that replace (rather than reinforce) biological criteria for access to gender-separated restrooms with identity-based criteria. And perhaps most strikingly of all, the very possibility of an "all-gender" or "gender-inclusive" restroom, one distinctive from a "family" or "unisex" restroom, has become markedly less rare in contemporary bureaucracies of all kinds—not just in queer spaces or radically progressive establishments, but also in restaurants, libraries, museums, and performance venues like those featured in chapters 4 and 5, as well as in many other civic and commercial spaces, including airports, convention centers, parks, and public schools throughout the country.

On the one hand, then, we might conclude from the precipitous speed of such transformations that gender is becoming less salient to individuals and institutions alike. In many respects, the emergent institutional logics analyzed in this book do lend themselves to such a conclusion, and even more so when considering that such change is still very much ongoing. In June 2014, for instance, a nationally representative *CBS News* poll revealed that 59 percent of Americans believed that transgender people should use the gender-specific public restroom corresponding to their gender assigned at birth, while only 26 percent believed that individuals should choose the gender-specific public restroom that makes them most comfortable; eight months later, in February 2015, a parallel, nationally representative poll carried out by Reuters/Ipsos found that the percentage of respondents in support of restricted restroom access had fallen to 39 percent and the percentage in support of restroom self-determination had climbed to 44 percent.[9] Plus, in more general terms, survey data collected over the last few years by my colleagues across the social sciences reveal unprecedented levels of favorable attitudes toward transgender people and a parallel decline in support for beliefs that men and women should fulfill distinctive social roles.[10] In short, the rigidity of gender separation in public restrooms and other public spaces—as well as the rigidity of the gender binary itself—appears to be loosening considerably as the twenty-first century continues to unfold.

Yet there has also been a stasis in the gender separation of public restrooms and the gender ideologies on which that separation is based. In a number of states and municipalities, including North Carolina, efforts to prohibit discrimination on the basis of gender identity—or to lessen the absolute gender separation of public restrooms—have been met with a legislative backlash intended to shore up the stringency of legal definitions of biological sex and of requirements for gender-segregated public toilets. Many institutions of higher education, including several flagship state universities, continue to rebuff the requests of student activists to reduce spatial gender segregation in undergraduate campus life in both residence halls and restrooms; others might profess a commitment to embracing gender diversity in their institutional mission statements, but their campus-specific design standards remain unaltered, causing renovations and new construction to proceed without making room for gender-inclusive bathrooms. Where individual organizations or neighborhoods have wanted to move toward a greater number of ungendered restrooms—in some cases, preferring not to build any gender-segregated restrooms at all—local building codes and state laws about women's "potty parity" often foil those aspirations. And even when organizations work around those myriad constraints and implement ungendered toileting spaces in their physical infrastructure, they most often add them as a third alternative to existing men's and women's spaces—thus leaving conventional, gender-separated arrangements largely undisrupted.

Consequently, we might conclude that such realities illustrate an extraordinarily robust cultural investment in gender as a binary system. Indeed, in recent public discourse about ungendered restrooms, the rise of alternatives to conventional, gender-segregated restroom spaces has only occasionally displaced binary ways of thinking. This is mirrored in many of the findings of my book. Courts of law, like those profiled in chapter 3, continue to assert that there is an unshakable foundation of embodied, emotional substance to the experience of being a man or a woman, even as those same courts have begun to selectively recognize transgender individuals as included in the law's penumbra of protection against sex discrimination. For many of the cultural, public, and commercial establishments discussed in chapters 4 and 5 that have opted to install new ungendered restrooms or rebrand existing ones with more up-to-date signage, their spoken justifications for such changes continue to rest on decidedly traditional rationales—with talk of "opposite sex" caretakers for individuals with disabilities or "mothers of small children" emerging as a common theme. Even colleges and universities interested in following in the footsteps of the institutions sampled as part of chapter 6's research continue to rehash anxieties about premarital cohabitation or female vulnerability on their respective campuses, despite the ample volume of evidence that such innovations can be implemented successfully without imperiling individual students or a university's reputation.

But ultimately, rather than concluding that something remarkable is happening to gender in this contemporary moment or that cultural beliefs about gender difference remain unassailable even in the face of complicating evidence, I conclude by circling back to where *Bathroom Battlegrounds* began—because my analysis of the institutional logics shaping American public restrooms over their nearly two-hundred-year history reveals that the cultural meaning and social consequences of gender have never been settled or final. That meaning and those consequences are, instead, perpetually negotiated by individuals and organizations alike, and public restrooms have long been a material and ideational prism through which that negotiation has been filtered. Gender, I thus contend on the basis of this book's cultural analysis, is an *institutional accomplishment*: a dynamic social undertaking through which individual social actors work actively to solve pressing organizational problems; draw from existing gender ideologies—or produce new ones—in order to creatively and effectively navigate those issues; respond to and reproduce the status hierarchies predominant in their local institutional field as a part of that navigation; concretize the results of all that cultural and interactional labor into organizational procedures, regulatory structures, and physical spaces (including, but certainly not limited to, restrooms); and grapple anew with the history of those concretized choices as new and pressing organizational problems emerge.

And so, this final chapter picks up where the first appearance of that definition left off: by delivering on the promise and the plan conveyed at the end of this book's first chapter. To do so, I briefly revisit the intellectual motivation for this project from that introduction, reveal how the individual "elements" of gender's institutional accomplishment from my empirical chapters interrelate with one another, and assemble those five separate insights into a cohesive theoretical précis. Then, after my final effort to cement the novelty of my contributions to academic sociology, I conclude by considering the implications of my findings beyond the ivory tower. There, in what may perhaps be the most important work of *Bathroom Battlegrounds*, I consider the cultural power of conversation in all its many forms and, moreover, the possibility that certain kinds of toilet-related talk might have surprisingly transformative social consequences.

TOWARD A RELATIONAL THEORY OF THE GENDERED ORGANIZATION

As a brief reminder from this book's introduction, the dominant understanding of gender in academic sociology today is that gender is a multifaceted and multilayered social institution. That leading paradigm typically revolves around two complementary arguments. One is that gender is an actively constructed social and cultural process, not a static pair of binary categories or a predetermined biological inevitability. The other is that gender's social construction unfolds in several realms concurrently: within our individual personalities, amid our interpersonal interactions with one another, and across the social institutions that contextualize and shape the world around us.[11] And those two intertwining principles have fueled a renaissance of middle-range sociological studies of gender in recent years—including this project's five empirical chapters—which seek to better understand when and how those principles play out in a range of cultural settings and around a range of social practices. Yet as I also observed toward the end of my book's introduction, such cornerstones of gender theory in sociology have been limited by a shared tendency to undertheorize the meso level of analysis—that is, of organizations. Consequently, one of the cross-cutting projects of *Bathroom Battlegrounds* has been to craft a generative dialogue between several of the most-cited institutional theories of gender and several of the most-cited institutional theories of culture and organizations from the last thirty-some years.

Over the last five chapters, those efforts have revealed five cultural pathways through which restrooms have come to be gendered, ungendered, or both: the *occupational osmosis* through which cultural beliefs hegemonic in a particular moment or particular context become absorbed into professional practices, the embodied work of *feeling gender* that connects the internal psychic experience of being a gendered body to the external social demands associated with gender category membership; the *legal consonance* that allows organizational actors to creatively invoke the law and engender changes to bureaucratic policy, procedure, and infrastructure; the *ease of justification* accessible to class- and status-privileged social actors as they deftly steer conversations about even the most taboo of topics toward their preferred narrative; and the *interactional isomorphism* that allows strategies for institutional innovation to diffuse through an individual organization as well as that organization's broader institutional field. But each of those five chapters has done much more than reveal a pathway through which ideologies, institutions, and inequalities collide. Each has also revealed one of five elements of gender's social construction, which, in my opinion, merit more attention from academic sociologists, and thus merit recapitulation, connection, and elaboration here.

To pick up where my last empirical chapter left off: the fifth of those elements is an unmistakably sociological one—an emphasis on the social *networks* that connect organizations and the individuals working within them. Despite their temporal distance from one another of over one hundred years, chapter 2 and chapter 6 converge here: they both illustrate how flows of shared culture and shared language among individual social actors allow transformations of the gender order to take hold. But as chapter 6 demonstrates even more clearly, those interpersonal networks are inextricable from organizational ones. The LGBTQ center directors, campus administrators, and student affairs staff with whom I spoke sought advice from their counterparts at other schools about the possibility of adding or expanding their gender-inclusive facility offerings, and they used the narratives shared by those counterparts as templates for action. More importantly, though, they recognized that the prevalence of such innovations at other, similar colleges and universities—that is, those in their closest organizational networks—was often the evidence required to convince other decision makers to act to approve facility changes.

But among this project's most recurrent findings is that class and status refract those networks. And that, of course, feeds into my fourth element: *circuits* of discursive power. One of the commonalities between chapter 5 and chapter 6 is my revelation that certain kinds of gender diversity have become an important form of moral currency for affluent Americans over the last three decades—whether their aim was the creation of more ungendered restrooms in buildings across their university campus or simply to convince an interested listener that even the most seemingly insignificant element of restroom design was a deliberate and meaningful aesthetic choice. But social class distinctions were on much fuller display in chapter 5. With an enormous shift in elite taste over the last few decades toward the appearance of cultural openness and tolerance, representatives from cultural organizations were, themselves, important conduits of cultural capital. As they imaginatively spun ungendered restrooms as a fashionable lark with troubling gender boundaries, they also marked their establishments as inimitably progressive, forward-thinking, modern, chic, and beyond.

The problem was that evidence for those moral commitments was not always quick or easy to actualize—which brings me to the third element of gender's institutional accomplishment: the material *inertia* of the past. Chapter 4 and chapter 5 intersect on this point, as respondents from cultural and municipal organizations alike pointed to specific, physical elements of their restroom infrastructure—signs, toilets, décor, and more—to illustrate how, exactly, their ungendered restrooms served as signals of their commitments to their patrons' most cherished values. But much to the chagrin of many of chapter 4's interviewees, that material character constrained as much as it enabled. Because buildings are physical things that require a sizable bundle of financial resources if they are to be dismantled or reconfigured, gender ideologies that had been built into public architecture many decades before were often determinative of spatial possibilities in the present day. Thus, for them, rethinking the gender order was surprisingly straightforward, while securing the resources necessary to transfer those ideals into infrastructure was what proved most onerous.

Yet even the most intractable buildings could, sometimes, be creatively reworked should a living, breathing, emoting organizational actor tap into the right argument for change. Living, breathing, and emoting thus bring us to the second element of gender's institutional accomplishment: the centrality of embodied *affect*. In fact, while chapter 3 and chapter 4 have profound differences—with the former documenting the transformation of legal frameworks about disability into a resource for restroom degendering, and the latter seeking a pattern in restroom-related sex discrimination rulings within the federal courts—they both reveal that the imagined needs and feelings of human bodies fundamentally shape the decision-making work of all manner of formal organizations. But affect was all the more apparent throughout chapter 3. Not only have federal cases about workplace restroom inequities increasingly embedded cultural tropes about inherent, binary gender difference and the heterosexualized nature of privacy into the law over the last six decades, but they have also increasingly implied and asserted how each of us ought to feel and experience our own gender in our own bodies.

That ever-deepening precedent, then, points the way to the first element of the institutional accomplishment of gender: *flux*—not to gender ideologies in and of themselves, which are certainly ever-changing as well, but to the many other institutional logics that shape gender's construction. For the judges tasked with the sex discrimination suits detailed in chapter 3, and the members of the emerging professional class who penned the articles published in architectural periodicals analyzed in chapter 2, their sole aim may have been to simply establish consonance with constitutional precedent or expert language elsewhere in their professional fields. But the oblique pathway through which gender was absorbed into that mundane bureaucratic work was nonetheless potent and long-lasting. Especially for the professional discourses in chapter 2, as builders and engineers moved away from celebrating the intrinsic virtues of new plumbing technology and toward an effusive valorizing of luxury, they cemented normative gender expectations into professional best practices that would come to shape restroom infrastructure up through the present day.

And that notion of gender as collateral damage leads to one final observation: that the beliefs about gender most ascendant in a particular time and space are inextricably tied to the many other ideological and institutional forces converging in that moment. In other words, the institutional accomplishment of gender is, above all, a *relational* process. By this I do not simply mean that gender has relational components, with the category "female" almost always constructed in reference to the category "male" and vice versa—which is also unquestionably true. Nor am I referring to the ways in which gender is constructed in relation to other embodied systems of cultural and social power, like race, class, and sexuality—as scholars writing from an intersectional vantage point have always rightfully averred. Certainly, there is ample evidence of those two understandings of relationality discussed in the last six chapters, and no theory of gender would be complete without acknowledging them. But what I mean to add here is an understanding that gender can never be theorized as a discrete, independent substance at all, because gender is always being redefined, renegotiated, and renewed—that is, *co-constructed*—in a dynamic and interdependent way with other social and cultural processes, and especially with processes that unfold in and through meso-level social groupings, like the myriad formal organizations I study in this book.

TOWARD A RELATIONAL SOCIOLOGY OF GENDER

Framing gender as an institutional accomplishment, then, does not just offer sociologists a new theory of the gendered organization. It also offers a starting point from which sociologists might take a truly relational approach to conceptualizing and studying *gender*—full stop. To illustrate that aspiration, a short series of visualizations might prove helpful. Many existing theories of gender imply that gender could be depicted with a permeable bull's-eye arrangement. Barbara Risman's social-structure model, for instance, argues that envisioning gender as a "multidimensional structural model" will allow sociologists "to seriously investigate the direction and strength of causal relationships between gendered

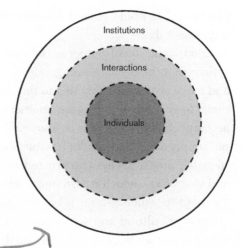

Figure 9. Visual model of gender as "an institution," with emphasis on the nestedness of each level of analysis.

phenomena" on each of three nested dimensions: individuals, interactions, and institutions.[12] We might illustrate that nestedness with a series of circles like those shown in figure 9.

But Risman also goes on to add that "the most important feature" of her model is "its dynamism," by which she means, "No one dimension determines the other. Change is fluid and reverberates throughout the structure dynamically."[13] We might, therefore, opt for a visualization that gives each level of analysis more equivalence, perhaps by explicitly visualizing possible intersections between those levels, as shown in figure 10. Such an image certainly gets us closer to foregrounding relationships, because we can now more clearly see each level's overlap with one or both of the other layers. Both visuals also suggest the omnipresence of change, as we can imagine how certain kinds of gender ideologies might flow through the pores in a particular level's perimeter, thereby allowing, for instance, new patterns of gendered interactions to concatenate into new gendered institutions.

Whether we opt for a bull's-eye or three-way Venn diagram, however, the problem is that such schemata implicitly treat all three layers of analysis as distinctive and separate even as they might explicitly exhort sociologists to see them as inextricably interconnected.[14] Moreover, such models lead us to treat the individuals, interactions, and institutions that comprise

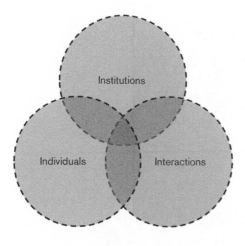

Figure 10. Visual model of gender as "an institution," with emphasis on the equivalent influence of each level of analysis.

the gender structure as discrete, preexisting entities, which limits our ability to theorize those individuals, interactions, and institutions as the complex cultural constructions that they truly are. Now, I want to be clear here: yes, there are relationships already evident in such diagrams; yes, the levels of analysis in both variations do overlap; and yes, the boundaries of each level of analysis are permeable. And, as I hope I made clear earlier in this chapter, I am certainly not the first sociologist to attempt to think relationally or processually about gender in recent decades. But if we were to model what Patricia Yancey Martin calls the "complexities and multi-facetedness"[15] of gender in a way that gives true primacy to relationality, I believe the result would look more like the illustration in figure 11. In that configuration, processes, not entities, form the model's explicitly visualized components; recurrent patterns and sequences of behavior arise as those processes intersect; individuals, interactions, and institutions become the imagined or implicit conduit connecting those processes; and no discrete boundaries are depicted at all, permeable or otherwise.

And with that image in mind, I can finally unpack my choice of the term *element* to describe the five processes outlined above and detailed across the five previous chapters. In part, I opt for the word *element* because of its first dictionary definition: it refers to any subcomponent of a more complex whole.[16] This makes it an apt linguistic choice for my relational approach to advancing gender theory in sociology, because, as I

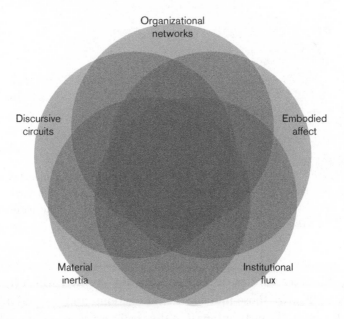

Figure 11. Visual model of gender as an institutional accomplishment.

outlined at much greater length in my introduction, one of my overarching goals for *Bathroom Battlegrounds* has been to rethink gendered organizations as fundamentally interrelated and interdependent. But in much larger part, I opt for the word *element* to evoke a molecular metaphor. Consider, for instance, hydrogen and oxygen. Under normal conditions, both exist as colorless and odorless diatomic gases. Each has its own unique physical properties and propensities to bind or react with other molecules, including one another. But when hydrogen and oxygen combine, two different molecules can result: water (the far more likely outcome under normal conditions) or hydrogen peroxide—each a colorless liquid at room temperature, but each with its own unique chemical properties that are not reducible to those of its component parts.[17] Following that logic, the elements of gender's institutional accomplishment have different properties and propensities of their own; moreover, those properties and propensities should—and do—change radically when one element is combined with another, with the same two elements potentially

chem metaphor works well here

yielding different sociological patterns, depending on the circumstances of their reaction.

To make those abstract claims a bit more tangible, one final return to the specifics of my restroom data might prove helpful. Take chapter 6 as an example. It epitomizes the flow of information and personnel highlighted in the organizational networks element: had many of the college and university staff I spoke with been unable to borrow strategies for change from their peers at comparable institutions, the adoption or expansion of gender-inclusive facilities would have proven slow, if not impossible, to enact. That same chapter also draws attention to the discursive circuits of power surrounding university staff and administrators, because they also had to choose the right words for the right audience when voicing their pleas for change. And, of course, institutional flux in relation to diversity and inclusion—a cultural change with influence far beyond higher education—has allowed certain discursive strategies within certain networks to succeed in new and transformative ways. That three-way processual intersection, then, is what allowed the pattern of action that I call interactional isomorphism to emerge. Or, for a different illustration of those same three processes, we could revisit chapter 2. Though professional periodicals do not provide direct evidence of the influence of either networks or circuits, we can intuit that both elements would have intersected with the flux that was impinging on early-twentieth-century professionals working to improve public plumbing. The result was a sociological outcome quite similar to institutional isomorphism: occupational osmosis.

But those two patterns also have important differences, just as water and hydrogen peroxide do. Certainly, both interactional isomorphism and occupational osmosis are pathways through which gender ideologies inform organizational work; both require the active involvement of human actors to engender that process of translation; both revolve around patterned invocations of cultural categories and classifications; both hold the power to produce beliefs about what gender is and what it means; both serve as a magnifying glass for other forms of cultural and social power. Occupational osmosis, however, leaves a formal, material record of organizational action in ways that interactional isomorphism might not; it also has a more resinous tenacity, owing to the legitimacy usually afforded to expert claims in the professions. This makes it more analogous to water from my earlier chemical comparison, because of the difficulty of splitting hydrogen back from oxygen once the two have combined into that highly stable molecule. Interactional isomorphism, on the other hand, is more pliable and more personal: it arises between individual social actors in face-to-face circumstances, elastically engaging whatever cultural or organizational categories are most relevant in a specific micro-sociological moment. But that flexibility comes at the cost of stability—in parallel to hydrogen peroxide, which is quick to decompose, even if there are no other molecules available for it to react with.

In fact, to emphasize the idea that my five elements often bond together and, when they do so, can produce several different patterns of social action—patterns with different characteristics from one another and from their constituent elements—I could double down on my molecular meta-phor even further and visualize my elements with fuzzy boundaries rather than crisp ones, as seen in figure 12. Such an adjustment better mimics recent images of intermolecular bonds captured in the natural sciences,[18] but it also offers a visual reminder that individuals, interactions, and insti-tutions are—like electrons surrounding an atom's nucleus—never fixed in place and always free to move in response to changes in the processes of which they are a part.[19] And so, the ultimate reason I frame gender as an institutional accomplishment—not just as an institution nor merely an accomplishment—is to reinforce that dynamism. As the preceding five chapters show over and over again, different cultural processes have exerted a stronger or weaker influence on the gendering of restrooms in different historical moments and within different organizational contexts, and it is that series of unique processual intersections that produce what gender is, what gender means, and what gender does in those moments and contexts.

But there is one more reason I opt for a molecular metaphor, and that reason takes us to process at a different register altogether—one pertain-ing to the process of producing sociological knowledge. While I have made every effort to assemble a robust foundation of qualitative evidence from which to build this new theoretical framework, the empirical underpin-nings of my work do have numerous limitations. At the most immediate level, my textual evidence from chapters 2 and 3 and my interview data

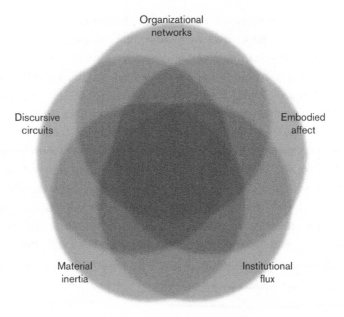

Figure 12. Visual model of gender as an institutional accomplishment, with emphasis on the permeability of each element.

from chapters 4 through 6 are far from representative of all restroom-related decisions made in the United States, both historically and contemporarily. I have also come nowhere near accounting for the entire world of public restrooms in the United States. Were I to ethnographically observe decision-making about restroom design in real time, or rifle through the correspondence of nineteenth-century urban architects as they debated how best to organize public plumbing, other patterns of individual and organizational action—and, by extension, other elements of gender's social construction—would probably reveal themselves. And zooming out even further still, decisions about whether and how to separate public restrooms by gender are, unquestionably, just one diminutive drop in a vast sea of gendered phenomena. But just as Niels Bohr's original theory of atomic structure quickly became surpassed by new quantum theories as more (and better!) experimental evidence became available, I genuinely intend for my new theoretical model for the sociology of gender to follow a similar path.

the sociology of gender is dynamic, ever-evolving, just like Bohr's o.g. theory of atomic structure

Thus, I end the academic portion of *Bathroom Battlegrounds* once and for all with a lofty hope: that my institutional accomplishment framework prompts new conversations and new research within the sociology of gender, conversations and research that are extended and refined over time as more (and better!) sociological evidence becomes available. In fact, whether my molecular metaphor gains traction or it quickly becomes eclipsed by a more generative paradigm, I simply have two goals here. First, for future research to give the meso-level elements of gender's social construction the attention they deserve, and second, for future theorists to grant unquestionable primacy to process and plasticity over stasis and solidity. Those two priorities, I believe, are the key to truly understanding how gender ideologies, gendered institutions, and gender-related inequalities are reinforced as well as transformed—and, by extension, to creating a more robust, more utile, and more transformative account of how gender shapes our social worlds.

BUT CAN WE BUILD BETTER BATHROOMS?

All that said, I could end *Bathroom Battlegrounds* on that programmatic and decidedly sociological note. And there would certainly be some merit in such a denouement. As is the case with many university press books written by and for social scientists, the primary goal for this book is to lay out a new understanding of my research topic (in this case, public restrooms) while also contributing to a broader intellectual project: understanding one facet of human behavior (in this case, the intertwining social forces of gender ideologies, categorical inequality, and institutional change). But as is often the case in sociological research on emergent social problems, that topic and those social forces cannot be neatly bound off as intellectual fodder alone. Rather, the gendering of public restrooms, the cultural construction of class distinctions, and processes of institutional change are all real-world entities, and they all carry with them real-world implications. In other words, relationality strikes again—this time, between the academic world and that beyond the ivory tower. And when one writes a book about bathrooms, boundaries, and human behavior, even the most academic of audiences tend to be much more interested in those real-world implications than in the nuances of social theory.

Those interests—from colleagues and nonacademics alike—typically take the form of questions. Often, and unsurprisingly, they revolve around gender. "Why do men leave the toilet seat up?" wonder the many women I've discussed my work with over the years who cohabit with us in domestic spheres. "Why is the line for the women's room always so much longer than ours?" ask men who have attended concerts or sporting events with such ubiquitous and puzzling queues. "Why are men's public restrooms always so disgusting?" inquire conversational partners of all genders who have confronted an odorous stall firsthand—or have fielded complaints about such odors from close friends or family members. While I empathize (particularly about that third question) and gently explain that my research focuses more on organizational behavior than such individual matters, the Erving Goffman quote prefacing this conclusion offers me a useful touchstone to field their queries: bathrooms, especially public ones, are nothing if not shrines to gender. Or, when those questions have a more practical bent—something like, "How does one plan, design, and construct a restroom to be as inclusive as possible?"—I defer to a different set of scholars who have thought more deeply and systematically about such matters than I. Sociologists Harvey Molotch and Laura Norén, for instance, sketch out a particularly promising possibility in the conclusion to their edited anthology about public restrooms, the aptly named *Toilet*,[20] with much more creativity and aplomb than I could ever hope to muster on the spot.

Sometimes, though, I get more interesting questions: questions about how to engender organizational change. Numerous undergraduate students—many of whom take my classes or attend my talks because they identify as feminists, as queer, as trans, as activists, or as all of the above—have pressed me over the years about the details of their college's administrative apparatus. "Will this work on *our* dean of undergraduate life?" I've been asked during more than one visit to a new campus to share my research where students are dissatisfied with their bathroom options. "Could this *really* be true at a school as genuinely inclusive as ours?" wonder others at places already well-known and well-regarded for their "trans-friendliness." Feminist parents usually want to know how to change the local small businesses in their area. If they've experienced frustration at the implications of finding a changing table in only one gender-separated bathroom (alas, always the women's room), I might hear, "How can I convince my local shopping mall or public library to put a changing table in the men's room, too?" Or, "What would it take to convince my local lawmakers to make family restrooms a requirement for more buildings in my area?" Unfortunately, though, interesting questions don't always have interesting answers, and they often cause me to inhabit the role of sociological killjoy. I report, woefully, that my data are descriptive rather than predictive, but that the legal and material complexities of restroom infrastructure probably mean that such changes are likely not as simple or as straightforward as they might imagine.

But a variation on that theme of change that I wish were asked much more often—and that I wish were asked in general, not just of me—is one captured in the title of architect Joel Sanders's and historian Susan Stryker's recent piece for *Metropolis* magazine: "Could the Restroom Become Public Space?"[21] That's because, as the six previous chapters bear out over and over again, change to the gender order *is* complicated, but it is also inevitable—and if you can muster enough persistence to get the right privileged or powerful people with the right cultural or financial resources on your side, you can also accelerate its pace. Finding the right legal appeal and the right emotional evidence *does* yield outcomes in the federal courts that offer retribution to workers maligned by their employer's bathroom policies or provisions. Finding the right bit of wordsmithing *can* convince a stranger that a restroom is a beautiful piece of postmodern architecture. Finding the right justification in a conversation with a dean or vice provost *will* land gender-inclusive restrooms on a college or university's strategic planning documents. Again, those local transformations are rarely simple, rarely agreed to upon first inquiry, and rarely quick to arrive, whether the obstacles to enacting them are moral, material, managerial, or all of the above. But the obstacle that has been so much more obstinate in the United States (and obstinate throughout our nation's history of indoor plumbing) is a consistent disinterest among the public and politicians alike for true public restrooms.

In my view, then, what we need most is not *more inclusive* public restrooms—where "more" is a quantitative modifier indicating that we need a greater number of bathrooms open to people of all genders, accessible to people with different bodies, and so forth. Instead, what we need are *more public* inclusive restrooms—where "more" is a qualitative modifier indicating that we need to collectively approach restrooms, particularly inclusive ones, as a public good.

To be clear, I am not saying that more inclusive restroom design and a greater number of ungendered restrooms are unworthy aims—far from it. There are still a worrisome number of public restrooms in the United States that are far from accessible to people with disabilities, both those that are truly public and those that are privately owned. Plus, given the issues faced by all manner of gender-diverse people (ranging from physiological ailments induced by having to "hold it" in a public space to the psychic toll of assessing if a gender-separate restroom might be safe), such increases are at once symbolically meaningful and socially necessary. Geographically, too, it is unquestionably true that not all places in the United States are as open to ungendered restrooms as the organizations I study in this book. The northeastern states in which I conducted many of my in-depth interviews are perhaps not the most progressive parts of the United States, but the local public libraries and restaurants within those suburbs serve more "blue" than "red" patrons by far. Similarly, because of my choice to study colleges and universities that have already ungendered their facilities in some capacity, one might get the sense that all students who locate themselves under the transgender umbrella, identify as nonbinary, or express their gender in unconventional ways are happy and healthy in higher education. But as the undergraduate students at Princeton with whom I have shared my work in progress over the years have so often reminded me, their ability to explore or express their gender on our "top ten trans-friendly college"[22] campus would never have been possible at the regional state college so many of their high school friends and acquaintances attend. That there is still much work to be done is, unfortunately, a profound understatement.

But with ample evidence at my disposal that American political institutions have made so many strides toward expanding restroom access and availability over the last few decades—ranging from the fall of exclusionary legislation like Jim Crow laws to the rise of inclusive efforts like the Americans with Disabilities Act—and that there are now more ungendered restrooms in a wider range of organizations than ever before, I nonetheless conclude that the private nature of so many public restrooms in the United States is a much more intractable problem. While European cities like London funnel financial and human resources into providing attended public restrooms (open during business hours in their most trafficked central corridors), standalone public restrooms (that operate around the clock), and even public urinals (located, logically, outside of popular pubs and bars), American cities like Seattle sink millions of dollars into self-cleaning toilets only to have those toilets become so filthy that they need to be closed—then sold on eBay for a scant twenty-five hundred dollars each. And while engineers in Tokyo compete to develop the world's most futuristic, automated toilet technology possible with the aim of disseminating that technology across East Asia, private financiers in New York create a tiny number of luxury public restrooms, and they do so solely with the aim of enhancing business prospects on Fifth Avenue. In other words, the provision of public restrooms in the United States has long been driven more by power, profit, and status than an increasing interest in providing public infrastructure to all Americans. And those failures have, in the words of sociologists Noah McClain and Ashley Mears, left consistent access to public restrooms in the contemporary United States only "free to those who can afford it."[23]

To overcome that cultural inertia, which appears to run deeper than gender mores and even the inherited material history of buildings themselves, will require a much more radical series of social and political transformations than mere adjustments to state plumbing codes or organizational policies alone could ever hope to engender. Indeed, as countless social scientists have demonstrated in over a hundred years' worth of research on inequality in the United States, our nation is a melting pot—but not one swirling with a heterogeneous array of cultures and ethnicities, as the image conventionally goes. Instead, our melting pot dangerously simmers individualism, the myth of meritocracy, and the facade that each of us is equally free and empowered to act. In other words, as Peggy McIntosh infamously observes in "White Privilege: Unpacking the Invisible Knapsack," the narratives at the heart of American culture disguise an insidious reality: "Keeping most people unaware that freedom of confident action is there for just a small number of people props up those in power, and serves to keep power in the hands of the same groups that have most of it already."[24] While McIntosh is reflecting on her racial privilege as a white woman, in a moment of allyship that might seem a world apart from the ungendered restrooms I study here, I invoke her observations as I finish out my book to suggest that her words and mine share a common set of aims: shining light on the taken-for-granted cultural assumptions that permeate so many aspects of our everyday lives and, more importantly, revealing how those assumptions reinforce hierarchies of social and cultural power.

Rather than ending on a pessimistic note, however, I want to conclude by saying that I find cause for a great deal of optimism in my qualitative data. That's because, as I suggest above with my quip that "change *is* complicated, but it is also inevitable," my data reveal that talk in and of itself—whether concretized in written documents or fleetingly shared aloud in conversation—*can* be a powerful catalyst of change. In fact, all the mechanisms through which gender has shaped the history and current realities of American public restrooms that I outline in the previous five chapters revolve around talk: occupational osmosis allowed bourgeois privacy beliefs to seep into written professional guidelines for twentieth-century architecture, feeling gender can only convince a federal court to find restroom-related discrimination in the workplace if effectively conveyed aloud, legal consonance transforms seemingly unrelated legislative mandates into a discursive weapon against an outdated building, the ease of justification enables certain organizational actors to persuade external audiences and their patrons of the value of their architectural choices, and interactional isomorphism is a powerful person-to-person conduit of strategies for engendering organizational change, even in the face of substantial opposition. And while we may not find the outcomes of all those organizational processes equally palatable or progressive, they all point to a common reality: only through collective communication do our culture and our institutions evolve.

So, if we talk more about gender, perhaps we can begin to dismantle ideological systems that not only make it dangerous for transgender people to pee in public but difficult for women to persist in scientific career fields and achieve equal airtime in politics. If we talk more about class and status, perhaps inclusive and accessible restrooms can become the norm rather than a moneymaking status signal, organizations might reinvest in the true needs of their patrons rather than a marketable oversimplification of their desires, and the tales we so often tell about success might reflect the truth of inherited privilege rather than perpetuating the mythology of pulling oneself up by one's bootstraps. And if we talk more about the public good, perhaps more access to more opportunity can take hold—whether that opportunity manifests as the dignity to relieve oneself in a clean and safe restroom on the street or as access to high-quality primary and secondary education regardless of the geographic circumstances of one's birth. In fact, by constructing this sociological history of the gender separation of American public restrooms and this cultural analysis of present-day efforts to enact gender-inclusive alternatives, my greatest hope is that perhaps *my* words can help dissolve many of those assumptions and hierarchies—or at least contribute to their weakening.

All in all, then, I hope that *Bathroom Battlegrounds* has revealed how public restrooms have never been nearly as marginal, taboo, or inconsequential as American culture socializes us to believe; how social theory offers an unparalleled tool kit for making sense of the omnipresent public debacles and private decisions that shape the details of public restrooms and the gender order they represent; and how public restrooms might, in turn, help my fellow academic sociologists generate more robust theories of gender ideologies, gendered institutions, and intersecting social inequalities. But above all else, I hope that engaging with this book prompts you, dear reader, to do more *talking* about bathrooms.

APPENDIX Data and Methodolo

Any man who remains in a public restroom for more than five
minutes is apt to be either a member of the vice squad or someone
on the make. As yet, he is not suspected of being a social scientist.

Laud Humphreys, "Serving as Watchqueen," *Tearoom Trade:
Impersonal Sex in Public Places*, 1970

Between March and August of 1967, Laud Humphreys, a doctoral candidate in
the Sociology Department at Washington University in St. Louis, undertook his
now-infamous dissertation research on the anonymous sexual encounters had by
men in public restrooms. Later published as the ethnographic book *Tearoom
Trade*, the project was decades ahead of its time in many respects: not only did it
approach the topic of same-gender sexual desire with dignity and generosity, but
Humphreys also took great care to emphasize that many men seeking tearoom
encounters did not see themselves as "gay" or "homosexual"—because, yes, they
may have pursued casual sex with other men, but they still identified as "straight."
The problem, however, was the questionable means through which Humphreys
found his research participants. Because he tracked down tearoom users through
their license plate numbers, then used public records to find their residential
addresses so that he could interview them about their sexual behaviors under the
guise of a community health survey, *Tearoom Trade* now serves as the example
par excellence in undergraduate research methods courses of how *not* to use
deception when conducting social scientific research.

As Earl Babbie points out in his reflections on Humphreys's unfortunate legacy, however, the project prompted outrage at a time when research ethics were,
as he puts it, "a rather low priority for many social scientists."[1] As a result, he
argues, the furor over *Tearoom Trade* was not truly about privacy violations—the
men were having sexual encounters in *public* restrooms, after all. Instead, that
furor almost certainly stemmed from the project's subject matter: "Laud

phreys didn't just study S-E-X but observed and discussed *homo*sexuality. nd it wasn't even the caring-and-committed-relationships-between-two-people-who-just-happen-to-be-of-the-same-sex homosexuality but tawdry encounters between strangers in public toilets. Only adding the sacrifice of Christian babies could have made this more inflammatory for the great majority of Americans in 1970."[2] Likewise, in their book *Laud Humphreys: Prophet of Homosexuality and Sociology*, John F. Galliher, Wayne Brekhus, and David P. Keys observe that Humphreys's work was doomed from the start because it was "triply marginalized": first, the study featured "devalued men"; second, it involved the recording of "otherwise intimate sexual behavior"; and third, that behavior was itself "a violation of legal statutes prohibiting sexual relations in public."[3]

Yet what such rehabilitations forget, I might suggest, is that the stigma associated with Humphreys's ethnographic study likely had as much to do with the project's location as with its content. Many of the reasons that public restrooms invoke polemical contestation in political spheres—their moral charge, their bridging of public and private, their connectedness to gender and the body, their multiple nexuses of legal regulation—also make them challenging topics for academic study. And I witnessed that challenge firsthand as I tried to launch this book (then my dissertation) at the midpoint of my doctoral studies. My original plan for this project was ethnomethodological: with all the ruckus surrounding "bathroom bills" in state politics in the early 2010s, I wanted to go "backstage,"[4] as Erving Goffman would put it, and understand the "interaction order"[5] of gender-segregated public restrooms that made the specter of ungendered toilets so threatening. I planned to ask people on the street to tell me stories about their restroom experiences, both most recent and most memorable, and I would use those accounts to explore how patterns of social interaction within one of the last consistently gender-separated spaces in the contemporary United States might illuminate the structure of the gender order writ large.[6] Over and over again, however, faculty members whose input I solicited on my research design urged me to choose a more "mainstream" topic or, at the very least, to use more "impressive" research methods. The project sounded intriguing, their logic generally went, but it was much too risky for a first book.

As foolhardy young graduate students are wont to do, I took half of that advice. (To any student readers in the audience: do not take that sentence as carte blanche for ignoring your own advisors. I wish I had taken some of that advice more seriously, but I digress; this is a methods chapter, not a memoir.) My compromise was to keep the topic but change the methods: I would pivot from seeking out on-the-spot restroom narratives to studying organizational decisions about restroom design and, in doing so, employ a more palatable combination of content analysis and in-depth interviewing. Still, my process of data collection was not without substantial challenges. Tracking down historical documents to analyze was tricky on two fronts. First, countless euphemisms have been used to refer to bathrooms over their multicentury lifespan, and second, few nineteenth- and twentieth-century professionals would deign to write about toilet matters at length. Worse yet, as I recounted in the course of my analytic work in chapter 5, obtaining interview respondents was often an exercise in frustration. My original plan was to seek a balanced sample of restroom decision makers—one-third would come from the field of higher education, one-third from municipal organizations like libraries and museums, and one-third from local cultural establishments like restaurants and nightclubs—but it quickly became obvious that such a framework would not neatly pan out in practice.

Respondents from colleges and universities were generally excited to speak with me, likely because of their familiarity with the academic research process and the increased profile of restroom-related issues on their campuses in the first decade of the twenty-first century. For other types of organizations, however, I quickly learned that I would need to frame my interest in terms broader than "bathrooms" if I hoped to obtain a space on a busy professional's calendar. And because that reconnoitered framing strategy still only worked a small percentage of the time, I started to open myself up to a broader spectrum of jobholders within the organizations I wished to study. My interview sample thus turned out to be more of a diverse hodgepodge than a well-balanced assemblage: I interviewed museum executives responsible for vetting all building-related decisions, library supervisors who participated in renovation planning but did not hold ultimate control of their space, owners of local restaurants, and managers at all echelons of an organization's internal staff structure. At times, I spoke with individuals charged specifically with making decisions about an organization's physical environment; at others, I talked with the people intimately involved in the push for gender-neutral bathrooms in particular. Sometimes, I even spoke to a person who did not fill any of those roles but was nonetheless quite knowledgeable about an organization's restroom history and could thus fill me in on the bureaucratic machinations that precipitated their current spaces.

But rather than viewing such diversity as a liability, I take my cues from grounded theory strategies for social scientific inquiry and suggest that such variation is an asset.[7] As Barney Glaser and Anselm Strauss write, "[D]ifferent people in different positions may offer as 'the facts' very different information about the same subject, and they vary that information considerably when talking to different people." And while "some sociologists" may see those "circumstances as presenting an un-bounding relativism of facts," they argue instead that "a proportioned view of the evidence" that "has taken into consideration more aspects of the substantive or formal area" is ultimately the key to producing more robust theories of the middle range.[8] Put more simply, by looking across multiple kinds of organizations, by speaking with individuals holding many kinds of professional positions, and by allowing my sampling procedures to shift and evolve as my understanding of my project shifted and evolved, I was able to capture a truly heterogeneous corpus of qualitative data. That heterogeneous corpus, in turn, has allowed me to build more robust explanations for the restroom-related organizational decisions I study in this book, because the repeated emergence of similar rhetorical themes across quite different interview events suggest the existence of an underlying sociological pattern worth isolating and theorizing.

My choice to take so much epistemological guidance from grounded theory also explains a notable absence in the overwhelming majority of this manuscript: the issue of race. Although I touch on racial distinctions in public restrooms at a small handful of relevant junctures—most notably the postwar-era portions of the first chapter's historical synthesis and the denouement of the second chapter's analysis of plumbing periodicals—the simple truth is that racial classifications did not appear as an explicit consideration particularly often in the documents I collected and the interviews I conducted. To be clear, that does *not* mean that race has been marginal to the history of gender-separated public restrooms and contemporary efforts to create ungendered alternatives; if anything, the opposite is true. The legal doctrine of "equal but separate"[9] justified state-sponsored racial segregation in restrooms throughout much of the twentieth-century—even outside of the American South—and the ebb and flow of true public restroom construction for many decades preceding and following were intimately intertwined with racial politics. Plus, my two core analytic interests in this book, gender and class, are always racialized, and ample research from critical race studies rightfully observes that the absence of explicit racial discourse more often signals the reproduction of racial oppression than its true eradication.[10] Unfortunately, however, taking a fully intersectional approach to my evidence—that is, one that considers race as thoroughly as it does gender and class—is beyond the scope of my data. Should readers be interested in learning more about such matters, I recommend the sources I cite in endnotes 31 and 32 of chapter 1, most of which speak to race-related restroom segregation at length.

All that said, however, I do not claim a "pure" grounded-theory approach to my work in this book. Doing so would require me to approach my evidence without any theoretical predictions or personal preconceptions in mind, which, I believe, is an impossible charge for a social scientist to enact. Instead, just as I weave together many different kinds of qualitative data in order to construct an evidentiary foundation for *Bathroom Battlegrounds,* I also weave together many different approaches to studying qualitative evidence from the social sciences in order to craft a methodological base for the book's analytic work. I refer to that methodological synthesis as a *cultural analysis of ideational space.*

The phrase *cultural analysis* refers to my treatment of public restrooms as cultural objects. Throughout this book, I focus the bulk of my analytic attention on the two major components of all cultural objects as Wendy Griswold defines them: "shared significance" (that is, the collective project of meaning-making within a given social setting) and "embodiment in form" (that is, the installation of that shared significance into the physicality of the object in question).[11] But I also explore the ways in which meaning is generated in situ and, in particular, through the invocation and creation of cultural classifications in the course of everyday decision-making work within a range of organizational settings. In terms of invocation, I look for moments in my textual and interview data in which preexisting cultural categories are mentioned (including organization-specific categories, like private colleges versus public universities, as well as wider-reaching classificatory arrays, such female and male). Then, in terms of creation, I also look for moments in which novel cultural groupings arise (such as when an interview respondent groups together their organization with other, similar organizations in an emergent fashion). In other words, I investigate what Andrew Abbott calls "boundaries of things," by looking for moments in which texts or individuals deductively speak to established categorical distinctions, as well as "things of boundaries," by looking for moments in which texts or individuals inductively generate new distinctions—both in the course of everyday meaning-making.[12]

The phrase *ideational space* refers to my efforts to foreground those conceptual processes without sacrificing attention to the inherent materiality of public restrooms. In other words, my analytic work in this book stems from two inter-related impulses. The first is to understand how various social actors, groups, and organizations have *ideated* bathrooms: what popular discourses have said about them in public; how legal and professional organizations have historically framed them as a site necessitating gender separation; and why cultural, educational, and municipal organizations believe the adoption of ungendered restroom spaces to be worth pursuing today. But I am just as interested in a second impulse, which is to take seriously the tangible components of bathroom *spaces:* the historical evolution of their physical locations, their current layout and fixtures, the design standards that have governed their dimensions and their placement in building infrastructure, their separation into multiple rooms or consolidation into a single space by particular formal organizations, and the influence of institutional context on each of these axes of difference. Put more simply, my goal is not only to document the various cultural categories that anchor organizational debates and decision-making about gender and public restrooms, but also, more importantly, to understand "how institutions *think*"[13] (emphasis mine) about physical restroom spaces—hence the epigraph from Mary Douglas preceding each of the book's two halves.

Many of the antecedents to such an approach derive from the sociological and anthropological literatures on ethnographic methods. From Diane Vaughn's approach to historical ethnography, I borrow an emphasis on analogic comparison, and I build much of my explanatory account by comparing "similar events or activities across different social settings" in an effort to craft "more refined and generalizable theoretical explanations."[14] Following from Susan Leigh Star's work on the ethnography of infrastructure, I supplement that comparative approach with an interrogation of the "invisible work" that unfolds behind the scenes of mundane organizational work to craft, implement, and maintain infrastructure.[15] Plus, my focus on materiality owes much to urban geographers who practice "spatial ethnography," because such a framework understands everyday physical spaces to be fluidly constructed and constantly altered in response to changing social conditions.[16] But rather than taking a case-study or single-site approach, my primary interest is in developing an account of meaning-making and boundary-drawing processes *across* organizations rather than *within* one. This is more like what anthropologist David Valentine calls an "ethnography of a category"—that is, a study of the "emergence and institutionalization of transgender as a category of collective identity and political activism," which necessarily requires a "move through many contexts, lives, and spaces."[17]

Because of the inherent difficulty of studying restrooms with ethnographic methods, however, my analytic approach relies largely on after-the-fact narratives of organizational decision-making processes—that is, textual and interview data that tell the stories of restroom-related debates and decisions that have already been made.[18] For my interview data in particular, this limits my ability to assess the veracity of my respondents' accounts—and thus to explore the telling disjunctures between what my participants say and what they do, as true ethnographic methods allow.[19] However, as Michèle Lamont and Ann Swidler observe in their recent defense of interview methods in cultural sociology,[20] in-depth interviewing is nonetheless well suited to realizing one of the central goals of this project: understanding how individuals make sense of and leverage cultural categories as they go about their everyday lives and, in this particular case, construct and deploy those categories in the decision-making work of the everyday institutional settings they inhabit.[21]

More importantly, by bringing historical methods and interview methods together in the same project, I also offer a new contribution to that ongoing conversation about qualitative methods in cultural sociology, because I find that there is something inherently *productive* about post hoc justificatory narratives: their utterance fundamentally affects future social action. In her book *Gender Trouble*, Judith Butler canonically characterizes gender as "the repeated stylization of the body, a set of repeated acts within a highly rigid regulatory frame that congeal over time to produce the appearance of substance, of a natural sort of being,"[22] and she further argues that gender's legitimacy comes from that iterative and citational enactment. A parallel reality is true of the justificatory narratives I study: they come to seem (and be) real only through repetition and recursion, but the appearance of substance that comes with that patterning confers a powerful sense of rightfulness and order on them. Moreover, I find that this legitimizing power becomes even stronger as such patterns shape the doing of everyday organizational work. In other words, post hoc justificatory narratives—

and the interpersonal flows of boundary work with which they are fundamentally entwined, whether written or spoken—are a crucial conduit through which the gender order is upheld or, sometimes, able to be transformed. In addition to the theoretical contributions *Bathroom Battlegrounds* makes, then, it also makes a methodological one: re-centering justification in its own right as a cultural process imbricated in the social construction of gender, the evolution of institutional logics, and above all, the reproduction of social inequality.

In terms of the specifics, then, my final data for this project include a diverse array of primary sources as well as in-depth interviews conducted with actors within formal organizations that had adopted one or more gender-neutral restrooms in the last fifteen years. Because each chapter relies on a different set of data, I conclude this appendix by discussing them each in turn.

In chapter 1, my historical narrative derives predominately from a synthesis of secondary sources from the academic fields of history, sociology, law, politics, and related fields. That synthesis is also informed by an original sample of 4,348 newspaper articles pertaining to public restrooms published between 1883 and 2011 in major North American newspapers. I retrieved that document sample in May 2015 through a series of parallel key term searches in ProQuest Historical Newspapers and ProQuest Newsstand, and I supplemented those results with 912 additional articles from a Google News alert I used to aggregate newspaper coverage related specifically to ungendered public restrooms from January 2012 up through the final revisions to this book in December 2018. Although I do not cite any of those newspaper data in the context of the first chapter's historical narrative, I do rely on them to open each subsequent chapter with a brief encapsulation of public discourse about restrooms in the time period roughly corresponding to that chapter's core content.

For chapter 2, my document sample consists of 186 articles published between 1872 and 1926 in architectural, engineering, planning, health, and medical periodicals in which plumbing, sanitation, and restrooms were central issues. I reviewed the Avery Index for Architectural Periodicals, Proquest Central, and JSTOR in December 2016 for periodicals associated with fields relevant to the project (such as those listed above). After creating a listing of 90 such periodicals, I enlisted the help of six undergraduate research assistants to review each issue of each periodical for articles addressing restroom-related matters, and I also searched each periodical digitally for key terms relevant to the project (e.g., *water closet, comfort station, lavatory, toilet,* and so forth). That combined search process yielded a database of 1,140 articles, which I reviewed for relevance to this project; that review led to the final sample of 186 articles that form the core of that chapter. Additionally, rather than focusing solely on public comfort stations (that is, the most common name for public toilet structures erected in the decades immediately before and after the turn of the twentieth century), I also include articles addressing a number of related fixtures and facilities in my archive: domestic bathrooms, civic sewer systems, and quasi-public toilets in privately owned businesses and public establishments. Although chapter 2 focuses primarily on the evolution of professional discourses within those fields responsible for designing and constructing true public toilets, articles about those other sanitary technologies provide useful comparative cases—because they reveal where architectural accounts of public plumbing overlap with other professional discourses and, more importantly, where they diverge.

For chapter 3, my document sample consists of 256 federal opinions written between 1967 and 2013 in response to legal disputes within which gender, restrooms, and work were central issues. I retrieved my initial document sample from Westlaw in January 2014 with a series of key term searches designed to return results for federal case law arbitrating litigation within which the core dispute pertained to gender and public restrooms. That initial sample consisted of 838 federal court opinions; then, after previewing each document to assess its relevance to this project and eliminating those that turned out to be irrelevant, I retained a sample of 388 opinions covering a wide range of legal disputes related to gender and public restrooms, including cases about age discrimination, cruel and unusual punishment, fair housing practices, freedom of speech, racial discrimination, educational equity, and even tax law. After more carefully reviewing that subsample, I opted to retain overturned decisions (because the language and assumptions of such documents nonetheless do important cultural work) but restricted my topical scope to cases in which the dispute over gender and restrooms was primarily an issue of gender discrimination or gender equity in the particular context of work environments—which yielded the final document sample of 256. That narrow focus allowed me to trace the evolution of one focused thread of legal precedent over time and to systematically explore differences between cases resolved in the plaintiff's favor (that is, by finding that actionable sex discrimination did, in fact, occur) versus those resolved in the defendant's favor (that is, by finding that charges of sex discrimination were without merit).

In chapters 4 and 5—which were originally meant to be one chapter, before my inductive process of data analysis led me to split them into two—I draw on 64 semistructured, in-person interviews conducted between September 2014 and August 2015 with representatives from cultural and municipal organizations in the northeastern United States. Organizations in my sample either publicly advertised the availability of a degendered restroom on their website or are identified as offering at least one unisex or gender-neutral restroom on REFUGE Restrooms, a website maintaining a database of publicly available unisex and accessible restroom spaces.[23] I also intentionally sampled organizations across geographic differences: some were located in urban settings (n = 33) such as Philadelphia and New York City; suburban settings (n = 25) across Pennsylvania, New York, and New Jersey; and rural settings (n = 6) in those same states.

Specifically, my sample for chapter 4 includes respondents from public libraries (n = 12), public parks and historic sites (n = 8), and transit centers (n = 4). That sample varies not only across organizational type and geographic location, but also across wealth: I interviewed respondents from organizations situated in counties and towns with per capita incomes running the gamut from a state's lowest decile to its highest. My choice to group together different organizational types from different geographic contexts thus built several comparative possibilities into my interview sample. Some of those comparative dimensions would reveal surprising similarities in restroom decision-making, such as those between historic sites with infrastructure remaining largely intact since the eighteenth century and libraries whose interiors had recently been taken down to the studs and built back up with entirely new materials. But other organizational differences, such as the economic context a public organization inherited by virtue of its geography, would come to shape the arrival of ungendered restrooms in ways that differed dramatically—even between organizations with virtually identical institutional identities located a mere handful of miles apart from one another.

My sample for chapter 5 varies similarly, with my respondents representing restaurants (n = 14), museums (n = 14), shopping malls (n = 6), and performance venues (n = 6) and their restrooms, all of which were given labels ranging from "all-gender" to "gender-neutral," "gender-inclusive," "unisex," and simply "restroom," with no additional modifier. That afforded me two built-in dimensions of comparison. On the organizational side, respondents in the four organizational categories included in my sample drew from different funding sources, professed divergent institutional missions and aims, offered quite different types of cultural products to their customers and patrons, and operated around distinctive bureaucratic structures—and thus could reasonably be expected to approach the question of ungendered restrooms with vastly different approaches. On the restroom side, surveying a wide range of restroom labels allowed me to compare the organizational logics motivating decision makers to label their restroom spaces in particular ways—and thus to analyze how and why the seemingly unimportant detail of restroom signage actually conveyed quite a bit of information about what a particular ungendered restroom represented to the organization in which it was enmeshed.

For chapter 6, I draw on 64 semistructured, long-distance interviews via Skype or telephone with respondents from colleges and universities across the United States with gender-neutral housing and restroom policies already in place. Between September 2013 and December 2014, I conducted those interviews with campus administrators responsible for oversight of undergraduate residence life, either directly or indirectly (n = 26), directors of LGBT centers (n = 22), directors of residence life (n = 9), and staff in facilities management (n = 7). I also intentionally sampled institutions across four dimensions of difference: whether their primary funding source was public (n = 36) or private (n = 28); whether their primary institutional mission was research (n = 38) or teaching (n = 26); whether their undergraduate enrollment size was under five thousand (n = 26), between five and fifteen thousand (n = 14), or above fifteen thousand (n = 24); and whether their location was in the Northeast (n = 22), Midwest (n = 16), West (n = 15), or South (n = 11). Because inclusive housing and inclusive restrooms often come to college campuses as inseparable halves of a common institutional project, I also collected interview data about gender-inclusive housing for that chapter. Beyond signaling my familiarity with gender-neutral issues to my respondents, that methodological choice also enabled a built-in comparative case: the ability to analyze when my respondents elided housing and restrooms into a single decision-making category and when they distinguished them—boundary processes with important implications for the chapter's argument.

Notes

INTRODUCTION

1. Kevin Liptak and Sunlen Serfaty, "White House Seeks Ban on Gay and Gender Identity Conversion Therapies," *CNN Wire*, April 8, 2015.

2. Valerie Jarrett, "Protecting LGBT Workers Means Protecting All Workers," *The Advocate*, April 8, 2015.

3. *An Act Relating to Human Rights; Prohibiting Unfair Discriminatory Practices on the Basis of Sexual Orientation*, Minnesota House File 585 (1993); see also Chapter 363A of the Minnesota Statutes.

4. *Restrooms and Other Gender Specific Facilities*, District of Columbia Municipal Regulations (2006), title 4, section 4–802.

5. Jarrett, "Protecting LGBT Workers."

6. Mitch Kellaway, "The White House's Executive Office Now Has Gender-Neutral Bathroom," *The Advocate*, April 8, 2015.

7. Mike Huckabee, "It's Time to Quit Watching the World Burn, It's Time to Get Involved," paper presented at the National Religious Broadcasters Convention, Nashville, TN, February 26, 2015.

8. *An Act to Amend Section 221.5 of the Education Code, Relating to Pupil Rights*, California Assembly Bill 1266 (2013).

9. Tim Donnelly, "Transgender Restroom Law Humiliates the 98%," *WMD*, August 15, 2013.

10. Steven Rothaus, "Proposed Law Would Limit Transgender Protections throughout Florida," *Miami Herald*, February 6, 2015.

11. *An Act Relating to Single-Sex Public Facilities; Providing Purpose and Legislative Findings*, Florida House Bill 583 (2015); the full text of the bill's preamble reads: "The purpose of this act is to secure privacy and safety for all individuals using single-sex public facilities. The Legislature finds that: (a) There is a longstanding history of restricting access to single-sex public facilities on the basis of sex. (b) There is an expectation of privacy in single-sex public facilities. (c) Users of single-sex public facilities reasonably expect not to be exposed to individuals of the other sex while using those facilities. (d) Single-sex public facilities are places of increased vulnerability and present the potential for crimes against individuals using those facilities, including, but not limited to, assault, battery, molestation, rape, voyeurism, and exhibitionism."

12. *An Act Relating to the Use of Public Locker Rooms, Shower Facilities, and Toilet Facilities; Creating a Criminal Offense*, Texas House Bill 1748 (2015).

13. Ruth Marcus, "Beyond the Bathroom Wars for Transgender Rights," *Washington Post*, April 10, 2015.

14. Alison Knezevich, "Transgender Bill Stirs Fear, Controversy in Baltimore County," *Baltimore Sun*, February 19, 2012; one of his cosponsors, Councilwoman Cathy Bevins, also expressed nearly identical sentiments about the "many concerned phone calls and emails from constituents" being directed to her office about the measure, saying, "I hate it that it's boiled down to being called 'the bathroom bill.'"

15. Chad Griffen and Mara Kiesling, "We Must Stop the Legislative War on Transgender People," *The Advocate*, April 24, 2015.

16. Mary Douglas, *Purity and Danger: An Analysis of Concepts of Pollution and Taboo* (New York: Routledge, 1966), 4. Douglas is also one among many twentieth-century social theorists to take up cleanliness as a central analytic object. In Sigmund Freud's infamous early twentieth-century work on psychosexual development, e.g., healthy personality development for children hinges on a positive experience in moving through the anal stage—during which they master control of their excretory functions. More importantly, he finds, learning to regard bodily excretions as "worthless, disgusting, horrible, and despicable" is an integral part of full and welcome participation in civilized social life, and "a person who is not clean—who does not hide his excreta—is offending other people; he is showing no consideration for them"; see Sigmund Freud, *Civilization and Its Discontents* (London: Hogarth Press, 1949). Similarly, according to Norbert Elias's history of the development of manners in Western societies, expectations of bodily cleanliness became increasingly strict through the Middle Ages and the sixteenth century. Over time, as a more hierarchical social order began to emerge, conformity with standards of appropriate conduct shifted from being imposed by external restraints to being produced by "the sociogenetic apparatus

of individual self-control": emotional responses on the part of individual social actors, who themselves learned to express "displeasure, distaste, disgust, fear, or shame" when exposed to bodily effluvia; see Norbert Elias, *The Civilizing Process*, trans. Edmund Jephcott (Oxford: Basil Blackwood, 1978), 369 and 108.

17. Patricia Cooper and Ruth Oldenziel, "Cherished Classifications: Bathrooms and the Construction of Gender/Race on the Pennsylvania Railroad during World War II," *Feminist Studies* 25, no. 1 (1999): 7–41.

18. Mitchell Duneier, "Race and Peeing on Sixth Avenue," in *Racing Research, Researching Race: Methodological Dilemmas in Critical Race Studies*, ed. France Winddance Twine and Jonathan W. Warren (New York: New York University Press, 2000), 216.

19. National Council on Disability, "The Impact of the Americans with Disabilities Act: Assessing the Progress toward Achieving the Goals of the ADA," July 26, 2007.

20. Jacques Lacan, *Ecrits: A Selection*, trans. Alan Sheridan (New York: W. W. Norton, 1977).

21. An important note on language—both for this introduction and the chapters that follow: as part of my effort to present gender as a fluid social process (rather than a static pair of binary categories), I strive to use gender-neutral language whenever possible throughout this book. This will often manifest in noun phrases like "gendered people" and "gendered bodies," as is the case in this particular paragraph, but it will also entail the frequent use of nonbinary pronouns: that is, singular *they* in lieu of the gendered *her or his* (or, worse, *his or her*). For readers who find this convention objectionable—or incorrectly believe it to be a needless progressive affectation—I recommend an excellent post written by Dennis Baron for the Oxford English Dictionary's blog in 2018 entitled "A Brief History of Singular 'They,'" accessible at public.oed.com/blog/a-brief-history-of-singular-they.

22. See Alice Kessler-Harris, *Out to Work: A History of Wage-Earning Women in the United States* (New York: Oxford University Press, 1982); Francine D. Blau, Mary C. Brinton, and David B. Grusky, eds., *The Declining Significance of Gender?* (New York: Russell Sage Foundation, 2006); Claudia Buchmann, Thomas A. DiPrete, and Anne McDaniel, "Gender Inequalities in Education," *Annual Review of Sociology* 34 (2008): 319–37; Thomas A. DiPrete and Claudia Buchmann, "Gender-Specific Trends in the Value of Education and the Emerging Gender Gap in College Completion," *Demography* 43, no. 1 (2006): 1–24; and Claudia Buchmann and Thomas A. DiPrete, "The Growing Female Advantage in College Completion: The Role of Family Background and Academic Achievement," *American Sociological Review* 71, no. 4 (2006): 515–41.

23. Barbara Miller Solomon, *In the Company of Educated Women: A History of Women and Higher Education in America* (New Haven, CT: Yale University Press, 1985); Mabel Newcomer, *A Century of Higher Education for American*

Women (Washington, DC: Zenger, 1959); Leslie Miller-Bernal and Susan L. Poulson, eds., *Going Coed: Women's Experiences in Formerly Men's Colleges and Universities, 1950–2000* (Nashville: Vanderbilt University Press, 2004); Andrea G. Radke-Moss, *Bright Epoch: Women and Coeducation in the American West* (Lincoln: University of Nebraska Press, 2008); Alexandra Kalev, "Cracking the Glass Cages? Restructuring and Ascriptive Inequality at Work," *American Journal of Sociology* 114, no. 6 (2009): 1591–1643; Matt L. Huffman, Philip N. Cohen, and Jessica Pearlman, "Engendering Change: Organizational Dynamics and Workplace Gender Desegregation, 1975–2005," *Administrative Science Quarterly* 55, no. 2 (2010): 255–77; Fidan Ana Kurtulus and Donald Tomaskovic-Devey, "Do Female Top Managers Help Women to Advance? A Panel Study Using EEO-1 Records," *Annals of the American Academy of Political and Social Science* 639, no. 1 (2012): 173–97.

24. See Cheryl Pellerin, "Carter Opens All Military Occupations, Positions to Women," *Department of Defense News*, December 3, 2015; and "Guide to Gender Integration and Analysis," United States Agency for International Development, March 31, 2010.

25. Maria Charles and David B. Grusky, *Occupational Ghettos: The Worldwide Segregation of Women and Men* (Stanford, CA: Stanford University Press, 2004); Nancy Folbre, *Who Pays for the Kids? Gender and the Structures of Constraint* (New York: Routledge, 1994); Jerry A. Jacobs, "Long-Term Trends in Occupational Segregation by Sex," *American Journal of Sociology* 95, no. 1 (1999): 160–73; Trond Petersen and Laurie A. Morgan, "Separate and Unequal: Occupation-Establishment Sex Segregation and the Gender Wage Gap," *American Journal of Sociology* 101, no. 2 (1995): 329–65; Jane Waldfogel, "The Effect of Children on Women's Wages," *American Sociological Review* 62, no. 2 (1997): 209–17; Michelle J. Budig and Paula England, "The Wage Penalty for Motherhood," *American Sociological Review* 66, no. 2 (2001): 204–25; Shelley J. Correll, Stephen Benard, and In Paik, "Getting a Job: Is There a Motherhood Penalty?" *American Journal of Sociology* 112, no. 5 (1996): 1297–1338; Paula England, Michelle Budig, and Nancy Folbre, "Wages of Virtue: The Relative Pay of Care Work," *Social Problems* 49, no. 4 (2002): 455–73; David S. Pedulla and Sarah Thébaud, "Can We Finish the Revolution? Gender, Work-Family Ideals, and Institutional Constraint," *American Sociological Review* 80, no. 1 (2015): 116–39.

26. Yu Xie and Kimberlee A. Shauman, *Women in Science: Career Processes and Outcomes* (Cambridge, MA: Harvard University Press, 2003); Maria Charles and Karen Bradley, "Indulging Our Gendered Selves? Sex Segregation by Field of Study in 44 Countries," *American Journal of Sociology* 114, no. 4 (2009); Elaine Howard Ecklund, Anne E. Lincoln, and Cassandra Tansey, "Gender Segregation in Elite Academic Science," *Gender and Society* 26, no. 5 (2012): 693–717; Erin Cech, Brian Rubineau, Susan Silbey, and Caroll Seron, "Professional Role

Confidence and Gendered Persistence in Engineering," *American Sociological Review* 76, no. 5 (2011): 641–66; Jennifer L. Glass, Sharon Sassler, Yael Levitte, and Katherine M. Michelmore, "What's So Special about STEM? A Comparison of Women's Retention in STEM and Professional Occupations," *Social Forces* 92, no. 2 (2013): 723–56; Joscha Legewie and Thomas A. DiPrete, "The High School Environment and the Gender Gap in Science and Engineering," *Sociology of Education* 87, no. 4 (2014): 259–80; Stephen L. Morgan, Dafna Gelbgiser, and Kim A. Weeden, "Feeding the Pipeline: Gender, Occupational Plans, and College Major Selection," *Social Science Research* 42, no. 4 (2013): 989–1005.

27. Amy Chozick, "Finally, an Explanation for Hillary Clinton's Long Bathroom Break," *New York Times*, December 20, 2015.

28. Gayle Rubin, "The Traffic in Women: Notes on the 'Political Economy' of Sex," in *Toward an Anthropology of Women*, ed. Rayna R. Reiter (New York: Monthly Review Press, 1975).

29. See Helena Z. Lopata and Barrie Thorne, "On the Term 'Sex Roles,'" *Signs* 3, no. 3 (1978): 718–21; Cynthia Fuchs Epstein, *Deceptive Distinctions: Sex, Gender, and the Social Order* (New Haven, CT: Yale University Press, 1988); Mirra Komarovsky, "The Concept of Social Role Revisited," *Gender and Society* 6, no. 2 (1992): 301–13; and Joan Acker, "From Sex Roles to Gendered Institutions," *Contemporary Sociology* 21, no. 5 (1992): 565–69.

30. Candace West and Don H. Zimmerman, "Doing Gender," *Gender and Society* 1, no. 2 (1987): 125–51.

31. A brief note on language: although many contemporary feminist scholars argue for the continued linguistic distinction between *sex* and *gender* (with the former representing various "biological" differences and the latter representing "cultural" or "social" differences), I consider that distinction theoretically and empirically problematic. "Sex" categories are as thoroughly socially constructed as categories of gender identity and expression; see Joan Fujimura, "Sex Genes: A Critical Sociomaterial Approach to the Politics and Molecular Genetics of Sex Determination," *Signs* 32, no. 1 (2006): 49–82; and Thomas Laqueur, *Making Sex: Body and Gender from the Greeks to Freud* (Cambridge, MA: Harvard University Press, 1992). Consequently, I use *gender* as an umbrella term throughout this book to emphasize the socially constructed character of both gendered bodies and gender identities, and I use *sex* only when directly echoing the language of my primary and secondary sources.

32. See Raewyn Connell, *Gender and Power: Society, the Person and Sexual Politics* (Stanford, CA: Stanford University Press, 1987); Judith M. Gerson and Kathy Peiss, "Boundaries, Negotiation, Consciousness: Reconceptualizing Gender Relations," *Social Problems* 32, no. 4 (1985): 317–31; Deniz Kandiyoti, "Bargaining with Patriarchy," *Gender and Society* 2, no. 3 (1985): 274–90; Suzanne J. Kessler and Wendy McKenna, *Gender: An Ethnomethodological Approach* (Chicago: University of Chicago Press, 1978); Mirra Komarovsky, "The Concept

of Social Role Revisited," *Gender and Society* 6, no. 2 (1992): 301–13; and Acker, "From Sex Roles to Gendered Institutions."

33. Patricia Yancey Martin, "Gender as Social Institution," *Social Forces* 82, no. 4 (2004): 1264; Barbara J. Risman, "Gender as a Social Structure: Theory Wrestling with Activism," *Gender and Society* 18, no. 4 (2004): 434; see also Judith Lorber, *Breaking the Bowls: Ungendering and Feminist Change* (New York: W. W. Norton, 2005); Francine M. Deutsch, "Undoing Gender," *Gender and Society* 21, no. 1 (2007): 106–27; Barbara J. Risman, "From Doing to Undoing: Gender as We Know It," *Gender and Society* 23, no. 1 (2009): 81–84; Paula England, "The Gender Revolution: Uneven and Stalled," *Gender and Society* 24, no. 2 (2010): 149–66; and Barbara J. Risman and Georgiann Davis, "From Sex Roles to Gender Structure," *Current Sociology* 61, no. 5–6 (2013): 733–55.

34. "Middle-range" is sociologist Robert K. Merton's term for any social theory that is more expansive than a summary of patterns observed in one's data but also more restrictive than an account of social organization or social change writ large; see Merton, "On Sociological Theories of the Middle Range," in *Social Theory and Social Structure* (New York: Free Press: 1968).

35. Two of the American Sociological Association's recent winners of the Sex and Gender Section's Distinguished Book Award epitomize this tendency. Georgiann Davis's *Contesting Intersex: The Dubious Diagnosis* (New York: New York University Press, 2015), e.g., offers a nuanced journey into the lives of intersex activists as they navigate the pathologizing efforts of medical institutions, but it also offers sociologists an account of how science and culture shape—and are shaped by—the gender binary. Similarly, Kimberly Kay Hoang's *Dealing in Desire: Asian Ascendancy, Western Decline, and the Hidden Currencies of Global Sex Work* (Oakland: University of California Press, 2015) offers a surprising ethnographic look into the everyday lives of Vietnamese sex workers while advancing a powerful argument about how gender and race both inform and structure foreign capital.

36. E.g., media messages are actively produced by certain kinds of formal organizations, and those messages and organizations must both be responsive to the local, state, and federal laws that govern them; see also Lauren B. Edelman and Mark C. Suchman, "The Legal Environments of Organizations," *Annual Review of Sociology* 23 (1997): 479–515.

37. For an overview of the institutionalist approach to organization theory, see W. Richard Scott, *Institutions and Organizations: Ideas and Interests* (Thousand Oaks, CA: Sage, 2008).

38. See Kieran Healy, "Fuck Nuance," *Sociological Theory* 35, no. 2 (2017): 118–27.

39. See Tey Meadow, *Trans Kids: Being Gendered in the Twenty-First Century* (Oakland: University of California Press, 2018); Gayle S. Rubin, "Thinking Sex: Notes for a Radical Theory of the Politics of Sexuality," in *Pleasure and*

Danger: Exploring Female Sexuality, ed. Carole Vance (New York: Routledge and Kegan Paul, 1984), 267–319; and Heather Love, "Doing Being Deviant: Deviance Studies, Description, and the Queer Ordinary," *Differences* 26, no. 1 (2015): 74–95.

40. Rosabeth Moss Kanter, *Men and Women of the Corporation* (New York: Basic Books, 1977).

41. Joan Acker, "Hierarchies, Jobs, Bodies: A Theory of Gendered Organizations," *Gender and Society* 4, no. 2 (1990): 139–58; see also Patricia Yancey Martin and David Collinson, "'Over the Pond and across the Water': Developing the Field of 'Gendered Organizations,'" *Gender, Work & Organization* 9, no. 3 (2002): 244–65.

42. For a review of such work, see Dana M. Britton, "The Epistemology of the Gendered Organization," *Gender and Society* 14, no. 3 (2000): 418–34; and Dana M. Britton and Laura Logan, "Gendered Organizations: Progress and Prospects," *Sociology Compass* 2, no. 1 (2008): 107–21.

43. For theoretical work in this vein, see Joan Acker, "Inequality Regimes Gender, Class, and Race in Organizations," *Gender and Society* 20, no. 4 (2006): 441–64; Jane Ward, "'Not All Differences Are Created Equal' Multiple Jeopardy in a Gendered Organization," *Gender and Society* 18, no. 1 (2004): 82–102; and Evangelina Holvino, "Intersections: The Simultaneity of Race, Gender and Class in Organization Studies," *Gender, Work & Organization* 17, no. 3 (2010): 248–77.

44. For recent empirical examples, see Kalev, "Cracking the Glass Cages?"; Huffman, Cohen, and Pearlman, "Engendering Change"; and Kurtulus and Tomaskovic-Devey, "Do Female Top Managers Help Women to Advance?"

45. For theoretical work in this vein, see Patricia Yancey Martin, "'Said and Done' Versus 'Saying and Doing' Gendering Practices, Practicing Gender at Work," *Gender and Society* 17, no. 3 (2003): 342–66; and Patricia Yancey Martin, "Practising Gender at Work: Further Thoughts on Reflexivity," *Gender, Work & Organization* 13, no. 3 (2006): 254–76.

46. Max Weber, "Bureaucracy," in *From Max Weber: Essays in Sociology,* edited and trans. H. H. Gerth and C. Wright Mills (Berkeley: University of California Press, 1948).

47. See also John W. Meyer and Brian Rowan, "Institutionalized Organizations: Formal Structure as Myth and Ceremony," *American Journal of Sociology* 83, no. 2 (1977): 340–63; John Dowling and Jeffrey Pfeffer, "Organizational Legitimacy: Social Values and Organizational Behavior," *Pacific Sociological Review* 18, no. 1 (1975): 122–36; Heather A. Haveman, "Follow the Leader: Mimetic Isomorphism and Entry into New Markets," *Administrative Science Quarterly* 38, no. 4 (1993): 593–627; David Strang and John W. Meyer, "Institutional Conditions for Diffusion," *Theory and Society* 22, no. 4 (1993): 487–511; Mark C. Suchman, "Managing Legitimacy: Strategic and Institutional Approaches," *Academy of Management Review* 20, no. 3 (1995): 571–610; and

230   NOTES TO PAGES 18-19

David L. Deephouse, "Does Isomorphism Legitimate?" *Academy of Management Journal* 39, no. 4 (1996): 1024–39.

48. Michael T. Hannan and John Freeman, "Structural Inertia and Organizational Change," *American Sociological Review* 49, no. 2 (1984): 149–64; Glenn R. Carroll, "Organizational Ecology," *Annual Review of Sociology* 10 (1984): 71–93; Michael T. Hannan, *Organizational Ecology* (Cambridge, MA: Harvard University Press, 1989); Howard Aldrich and Martin Ruef, eds., *Organizations Evolving* (London: Sage, 2006); Martin Ruef, "The Emergence of Organizational Forms: A Community Ecology Approach," *American Journal of Sociology* 106, no. 3 (2000): 658–714; John H. Freeman and Pino G. Audia, "Community Ecology and the Sociology of Organizations," *Annual Review of Sociology* 32 (2006): 145–69.

49. Paul J. DiMaggio and Walter W. Powell, "The Iron Cage Revisited: Institutional Isomorphism and Collective Rationality in Organizational Fields," *American Sociological Review* 48, no. 2 (1983): 147–60. See also Lynne G. Zucker, "Institutional Theories of Organization," *Annual Review of Sociology* 13 (1987): 443–64; Walter W. Powell and Paul DiMaggio, eds., *The New Institutionalism in Organizational Analysis* (Chicago: University of Chicago Press, 1991); W. Richard Scott, *Institutions and Organizations* (Thousand Oaks, CA: Sage, 1995); and Mary C. Brinton and Victor Nee, eds., *The New Institutionalism in Sociology* (New York: Russell Sage Foundation, 1998).

50. See also Michèle Lamont, Stefan Beljean, and Matthew Clair, "What Is Missing? Cultural Processes and Causal Pathways to Inequality," *Socio-Economic Review* 12, no. 3 (2014): 573–608.

51. Ezra Zuckerman, "The Categorical Imperative: Securities Analysts and the Illegitimacy Discount," *American Journal of Sociology* 104, no. 5 (1999): 1398–1438; Greta Hsu and Michael T. Hannan, "Identities, Genres, and Organizational Forms," *Organization Science* 16, no. 5 (2005): 474–90.

52. Chad Navis and Mary Ann Glynn, "How New Market Categories Emerge: Temporal Dynamics of Legitimacy, Identity, and Entrepreneurship in Satellite Radio, 1990–2005," *Administrative Science Quarterly* 55, no. 3 (2010): 439–71; Alexander K. Davis, "Toward Exclusion through Inclusion: Engendering Reputation with Gender-Inclusive Facilities at Colleges and Universities in the United States, 2001–2013," *Gender and Society* 32, no. 3 (2018): 321–47.

53. Martin Ruef and Kelly Patterson, "Credit and Classification: The Impact of Industry Boundaries in Nineteenth-Century America," *Administrative Science Quarterly* 54, no. 3 (2009): 486–520.

54. Greta Hsu, "Jacks of All Trades and Masters of None: Audiences' Reactions to Spanning Genres in Feature Film Production," *Administrative Science Quarterly* 51, no. 3 (2006): 420–50; Damon J. Phillips and Ezra W. Zuckerman, "Middle-Status Conformity: Theoretical Restatement and Empirical Demonstration in Two Markets," *American Journal of Sociology* 107, no. 2 (2001):

379–429; Cathryn Johnson, Timothy J. Dowd, and Cecilia L. Ridgeway, "Legitimacy as a Social Process," *Annual Review of Sociology* 32 (2006): 53–78; Michael Jensen, "Legitimizing Illegitimacy: How Creating Market Identity Legitimizes Illegitimate Products," in *Categories in Markets: Origins and Evolution,* ed. Michael Lounsbury (Bingley, UK: Emerald Group Publishing, 2010).

55. Tim Hallett and Marc J. Ventresca, "Inhabited Institutions: Social Interactions and Organizational Forms in Gouldner's *Patterns of Industrial Bureaucracy," Theory and Society* 35, no. 2 (2006): 215.

56. For an excellent review of the "inhabited institutions" approach, see Amy Binder, "For Love and Money: Organizations' Creative Responses to Multiple Environmental Logics," *Theory and Society* 36, no. 6 (2007): 547–71. On emotion and embodiment, see Roger Friedland, "Moving Institutional Logics Forward: Emotion and Meaningful Material Practice," *Organization Studies* 39, no. 4 (2018): 515–42; on rhetoric and conversation, see Roy Suddaby and Royston Greenwood, "Rhetorical Strategies of Legitimacy," *Administrative Science Quarterly* 50, no. 1 (2005): 35–67; on cognition and evaluation, see Mark C. Pachucki, "Classifying Quality: Cognition, Interaction, and Status Appraisal of Art Museums," *Poetics* 40, no. 1 (2012): 67–90, and Gino Cattani, Simone Ferriani, Giacomo Negro, and Fabrizio Perretti, "The Structure of Consensus: Network Ties, Legitimation, and Exit Rates of U.S. Feature Film Producer Organizations," *Administrative Science Quarterly* 53, no. 1 (2008): 145–82.

57. Dorothy E. Smith, *The Everyday World as Problematic: A Feminist Sociology* (Toronto: University of Toronto Press, 1987); Dorothy E. Smith, *Institutional Ethnography: A Sociology for People* (Lanham, MD: AltaMira Press, 2005).

58. R. W. Connell, *Gender and Power: Society, the Person and Sexual Politics* (Stanford, CA: Stanford University Press, 1987), 134; for more on categories and classification, see Epstein, *Deceptive Distinctions,* or, more recently, Asia Friedman, *Blind to Sameness: Sexpectations and the Social Construction of Male and Female Bodies* (Chicago: University of Chicago Press, 2013).

1. POLITICIZING THE POTTY

1. Betsy Wade, "Coed Dorms 'In' with Nary a Ripple," *New York Times,* January 11, 1971, 51.

2. Robert Reinhold, "Coeds to Share Harvard Housing; A Faculty Approves Plan for Radcliffe Exchange," *New York Times,* December 10, 1969, 38.

3. Ibid.

4. Wade, "Coed Dorms 'In' with Nary a Ripple."

5. Reinhold, "Coeds to Share Harvard Housing."

6. Wade, "Coed Dorms 'In' with Nary a Ripple."

7. Reinhold, "Coeds to Share Harvard Housing."

8. James Ring Adams, "Open Dorms and Co-Ed Bathrooms," *Wall Street Journal*, October 9, 1973, 26.

9. Wade, "Coed Dorms 'In' with Nary a Ripple."

10. Adams, "Open Dorms and Co-Ed Bathrooms."

11. "Co-ed Dorms: An Intimate Revolution on Campus," *Life*, November 20, 1970.

12. Brian Sullivan, "Flush Toilet Criticized as Wasteful," *Washington Post*, January 23, 1971, D3.

13. Michael Mok, "Blame the Outmoded U.S. Bathroom," *Life*, May 20, 1966, 84C–84D.

14. See, e.g., Günther Fink, Isabel Günther, and Kenneth Hill, "Slum Residence and Child Health in Developing Countries," *Demography* 51, no. 4 (2014): 1175–97; Colin McFarlane, Renu Desai, and Steve Graham, "Informal Urban Sanitation: Everyday Life, Poverty, and Comparison," *Annals of the Association of American Geographers* 104, no. 5 (2014): 989–1011; Brenda Chalfin, "Public Things, Excremental Politics, and the Infrastructure of Bare Life in Ghana's City of Tema," *American Ethnologist* 41, no. 1 (2014): 92–109.

15. See notes 16 through 20 below.

16. Barry Schwartz, "The Social Psychology of Privacy," *American Journal of Sociology* 73, no. 6 (1968): 741–52; Spencer E. Cahill, William Disler, Cynthia Lachowetz, Andrea Meaney, Robyn Tarallo, and Teena Willard, "Meanwhile Backstage Public Bathrooms and the Interaction Order," *Journal of Contemporary Ethnography* 14, no. 1 (1985): 33–58; Edward M. Bruner and Jane Paige Kelso, "The Voices and Words of Women and Men: Gender Differences in Graffiti: A Semiotic Perspective," *Women's Studies International Quarterly* 3, no. 2 (1980): 239–52; Arnold Arluke, Lanny Kutakoff, and Jack Levin, "Are the Times Changing? An Analysis of Gender Differences in Sexual Graffiti," *Sex Roles* 16, no. 1–2 (1987): 1–7; David Inglis, *A Sociological History of Excretory Experience, Defecatory Manners, and Toiletry Technologies* (Lewiston, NY: Edwin Mellen Press, 2001); Martin S. Weinberg and Colin J. Williams, "Fecal Matters: Habitus, Embodiments, and Deviance," *Social Problems* 52, no. 3 (2005): 315–36.

17. Richard L. Bushman and Claudia L. Bushman, "The Early History of Cleanliness in America," *Journal of American History* 74, no. 4 (1988): 1213–38; Marilyn T. Williams, *Washing "the Great Unwashed": Public Baths in Urban America, 1840–1920* (Columbus: Ohio State University Press, 1991); Daniel Eli Burnstein, *Next to Godliness: Confronting Dirt and Despair in Progressive Era New York City* (Urbana: University of Illinois Press, 2006); Kathleen M. Brown, *Foul Bodies: Cleanliness in Early America* (New Haven, CT: Yale University Press, 2009).

18. Joyce Appleby, "Recovering America's Historic Diversity: Beyond Exceptionalism," *Journal of American History* 79, no. 2 (1992): 419–31; Maureen Ogle, *All the Modern Conveniences: American Household Plumbing, 1840–1890* (Baltimore: Johns Hopkins University Press, 1996); Jamie Benidickson, *The*

Culture of Flushing: A Social and Legal History of Sewage (Vancouver: University of British Columbia Press, 2007); Brown, *Foul Bodies.*

19. Suellen M. Hoy, *Chasing Dirt: The American Pursuit of Cleanliness* (New York: Oxford University Press, 1995); Barbara Penner, *Bathroom* (London: Reaktion Books, 2013); Ogle, *All the Modern Conveniences;* Bushman and Bushman, "The Early History of Cleanliness in America."

20. As Williams observes on page 28 of in *Washing "the Great Unwashed"*: "In 1897 the Mayor's Committee on Public Baths and Comfort Stations in New York reported that 'New York and other American cities are far behind those of Europe, especially London, Birmingham, Glasgow, Paris and Berlin.'" See also Paul Starr, *The Social Transformation of American Medicine* (New York: Basic Books, 1982); John Duffy, *The Sanitarians: A History of American Public Health* (Urbana: University of Illinois Press, 1990); Nancy Tomes, *The Gospel of Germs: Men, Women, and the Microbe in American Life* (Cambridge, MA: Harvard University Press, 1998); Eran Ben-Joseph, *The Code of the City: Standards and the Hidden Language of Place Making* (Cambridge, MA: MIT Press, 2005); David Cutler and Grant Miller, "The Role of Public Health Improvements in Health Advances: The Twentieth-Century United States," *Demography* 42, no. 1 (2005): 1-22; Dell Upton, *Another City: Urban Life and Urban Spaces in the New American Republic* (New Haven, CT: Yale University Press, 2008); Martin V. Melosi, *The Sanitary City: Environmental Services in Urban America from Colonial Times to the Present* (Pittsburgh: University of Pittsburgh Press, 2008); Russ Lopez, *Building American Public Health: Urban Planning, Architecture, and the Quest for Better Health in the United States* (New York: Palgrave Macmillan, 2012); Adam Mack, *Sensing Chicago: Noisemakers, Strikebreakers, and Muckrakers* (Urbana: University of Illinois Press, 2015).

21. David Glassberg, "The Design of Reform: The Public Bath Movement in America," *American Studies* 20, no. 2 (1979): 5-21; Andrea Renner, "A Nation That Bathes Together: New York City's Progressive Era Public Baths," *Journal of the Society of Architectural Historians* 67, no. 4 (2008): 504-31; Peter C. Baldwin, "Public Privacy: Restrooms in American Cities, 1869-1932," *Journal of Social History* 48, no. 2 (2014): 264-88.

22. Alice Domurat Dreger, *Hermaphrodites and the Medical Invention of Sex* (Cambridge, MA: Harvard University Press, 1998), 11; see also Thomas Walter Laqueur, *Making Sex: Body and Gender from the Greeks to Freud* (Cambridge, MA: Harvard University Press, 1990); Joanne J. Meyerowitz, *How Sex Changed: A History of Transsexuality in the United States* (Cambridge, MA: Harvard University Press, 2002).

23. Hugh G. J. Aitken, *Scientific Management in Action: Taylorism at Watertown Arsenal, 1908-1915* (Princeton, NJ: Princeton University Press, 1960); Samuel Haber, *Efficiency and Uplift: Scientific Management in the Progressive Era, 1890-1920* (Chicago: University of Chicago Press, 1964); Theda Skocpol,

Protecting Soldiers and Mothers: The Political Origins of Social Policy in the United States (Cambridge, MA: Harvard University Press, 1992); Ulla Wikander, Alice Kessler-Harris, and Jane Lewis, eds., *Protecting Women: Labor Legislation in Europe, the United States, and Australia, 1880–1920* (Urbana: University of Illinois Press, 1995); Robert Kanigel, *The One Best Way: Frederick Winslow Taylor and the Enigma of Efficiency* (New York: Viking, 1997); Marc Linder and Ingrid Nygaard, *Void Where Prohibited: Rest Breaks and the Right to Urinate on Company Time* (Ithaca, NY: ILR Press, 1998); Julie Novkov, "Historicizing the Figure of the Child in Legal Discourse: The Battle over the Regulation of Child Labor," *American Journal of Legal History* 44, no. 4 (2000): 369–404; Susan J. Pearson, "'Age Ought to Be a Fact': The Campaign against Child Labor and the Rise of the Birth Certificate," *Journal of American History* 101, no. 4 (2015): 1144–65.

24. *An Act to Secure Proper Sanitary Provisions in Factories and Workshops,* Massachusetts Acts, chapter 103 § 2, March 24, 1887.

25. *An Act to Regulate the Employment of Women and Children in Manufacturing Establishments, and to Provide for the Appointment of Inspectors to Enforce the Same,* New York Acts, chapter 409 § 13, May 18, 1889.

26. Raymond Munts and David C. Rice, "Women Workers: Protection or Equality?" *Industrial and Labor Relations Review* 24, no. 1 (1970): 3–13; Carroll Smith-Rosenberg, *Disorderly Conduct: Visions of Gender in Victorian America* (New York: A. A. Knopf, 1985); Terry S. Kogan, "Sex-Separation in Public Restrooms: Law, Architecture, and Gender," *Michigan Journal of Gender and Law* 14, no. 1 (2007): 1–58; Penner, *Bathroom;* Williams, *Washing "the Great Unwashed."*

27. *Muller v. Oregon,* 208 U.S. 412 (1908).

28. American Public Health Association, *A Half Century of Public Health, Jubilee Historical Volume; in Commemoration of the Fiftieth Anniversary Celebration of Its Foundation, New York City, November, 14–18, 1921,* ed. Mazÿck P. Ravenel (New York: American Public Health Association, 1921); Holly J. McCammon, Karen E. Campbell, Ellen M. Granberg, and Christine Mowery, "How Movements Win: Gendered Opportunity Structures and U.S. Women's Suffrage Movements, 1866 to 1919," *American Sociological Review* 66, no. 1 (2001): 49–70; Smith-Rosenberg, *Disorderly Conduct;* Kogan, "Sex-Separation in Public Restrooms."

29. Alice Kessler-Harris, *Out to Work: A History of Wage-Earning Women in the United States* (New York: Oxford University Press, 1982); Kogan, "Sex-Separation in Public Restrooms."

30. Paula Baker, "The Domestication of Politics: Women and American Political Society, 1780–1920," *American Historical Review* 89, no. 3 (1984): 620–47; William H. Wilson, *The City Beautiful Movement* (Baltimore: Johns Hopkins University Press, 1989); Stanley K. Schultz, *Constructing Urban Culture:*

American Cities and City Planning, 1800–1920 (Philadelphia: Temple University Press, 1989); Michael McGerr, "Political Style and Women's Power, 1830–1930," *Journal of American History* 77, no. 3 (1990): 864–85; Anne Firor Scott, *Natural Allies: Women's Associations in American History* (Urbana: University of Illinois Press, 1991); Maureen A. Flanagan, *Seeing with Their Hearts: Chicago Women and the Vision of the Good City, 1871–1933* (Princeton, NJ: Princeton University Press, 2002); Holly J. McCammon, "'Out of the Parlors and into the Streets': The Changing Tactical Repertoire of the U.S. Women's Suffrage Movements," *Social Forces* 81, no. 3 (2003): 787–818; Maureen Flanagan, "Private Needs, Public Space: Public Toilets Provision in the Anglo-Atlantic Patriarchal City: London, Dublin, Toronto and Chicago," *Urban History* 41, no. 2 (2014): 265–90; Baldwin, "Public Privacy."

31. Kenneth T. Jackson, *Crabgrass Frontier: The Suburbanization of the United States* (New York: Oxford University Press, 1985); Cotten Seiler, *Republic of Drivers: A Cultural History of Automobility in America* (Chicago: University of Chicago Press, 2008); Sarah A. Seo, "Antinomies and the Automobile: A New Approach to Criminal Justice Histories," *Law and Social Inquiry* 38, no. 4 (2013): 1020–40.

32. Taunya Lovell Banks, "Toilets as a Feminist Issue: A True Story," *Berkeley Journal of Gender, Law and Justice* 6, no. 2 (1991): 263–89; Patricia Cooper and Ruth Oldenziel, "Cherished Classifications: Bathrooms and the Construction of Gender/Race on the Pennsylvania Railroad during World War II," *Feminist Studies* 25, no. 1 (1999): 7–41; Barbara Young Welke, *Recasting American Liberty: Gender, Race, Law, and the Railroad Revolution, 1865–1920* (Cambridge: Cambridge University Press, 2001); Kerry Segrave, *Vending Machines: An American Social History* (Jefferson, NC: McFarland and Company, 2002); Robin Dearmon Muhammad, "Separate and Unsanitary: African American Women Railroad Car Cleaners and the Women's Service Section, 1918–1920," *Journal of Women's History* 23, no. 2 (2011): 87–111; see also Kathryn H. Anthony and Meghan Dufresne, "Potty Parity in Perspective: Gender and Family Issues in Planning and Designing Public Restrooms," *Journal of Planning Literature* 21, no. 3 (2007): 267–94; Olga Gershenson and Barbara Penner, eds., *Ladies and Gents: Public Toilets and Gender* (Philadelphia: Temple University Press, 2009).

33. W. J. Curran, "The Constitutionality of Prohibiting the Operation of Pay Toilets," *American Journal of Public Health* 67, no. 12 (1977): 1205–6; Bruce Edsall Seely, *Building the American Highway System: Engineers as Policy Makers* (Philadelphia: Temple University Press, 1987); Ruth Rosen, *The World Split Open: How the Modern Women's Movement Changed America* (New York: Viking, 2000); Robert R. Weyeneth, "The Architecture of Racial Segregation: The Challenges of Preserving the Problematical Past," *Public Historian* 27, no. 4 (2005): 11–44; Christopher W. Wells, "Fueling the Boom: Gasoline Taxes, Invisibility, and the Growth of the American Highway Infrastructure, 1919–1956,"

Journal of American History 99, no. 1 (2012): 72–81; Mark H. Rose, *Interstate: Highway Politics and Policy since 1939* (Knoxville: University of Tennessee Press, 2012).

34. John D'Emilio, *Sexual Politics, Sexual Communities: The Making of a Homosexual Minority in the United States, 1940–1970* (Chicago: University of Chicago Press, 1983); Gayle Rubin, "Thinking Sex: Notes for a Radical Theory of the Politics of Sexuality," in *Pleasure and Danger: Exploring Female Sexuality*, ed. Carole S. Vance (New York: Routledge and Kegan Paul, 1984); George Chauncey, *Gay New York: Gender, Urban Culture, and the Makings of the Gay Male World, 1890–1940* (New York: Basic Books, 1994); Margot Canaday, "'Who Is a Homosexual?': The Consolidation of Sexual Identities in Mid-Twentieth-Century American Immigration Law," *Law and Social Inquiry* 28, no. 2 (2003): 351–86; Irus Braverman, "Governing with Clean Hands: Automated Public Toilets and Sanitary Surveillance," *Surveillance and Society* 8, no. 1 (2010): 1–27; Clara Greed, "The Role of the Toilet in Civic Life," in *Ladies and Gents: Public Toilets and Gender*, ed. Olga Gershenson and Barbara Penner (Philadelphia: Temple University Press, 2009); Baldwin, "Public Privacy."

35. Paul C. Glick, "A Demographer Looks at American Families," *Journal of Marriage and Family* 37, no. 1 (1975): 15–26; Leila J. Rupp, "The Women's Community in the National Woman's Party, 1945 to the 1960s," *Signs* 10, no. 4 (1985): 715–40; Willard L. Rodgers and Arland Thornton, "Changing Patterns of First Marriage in the United States," *Demography* 22, no. 2 (1985); Herbert Jacob, *Silent Revolution: The Transformation of Divorce Law in the United States* (Chicago: University of Chicago Press, 1988); Joanne J. Meyerowitz, ed., *Not June Cleaver: Women and Gender in Postwar America, 1945–1960* (Philadelphia: Temple University Press, 1994); Sarah A. Soule and Susan Olzak, "When Do Movements Matter? The Politics of Contingency and the Equal Rights Amendment," *American Sociological Review* 69, no. 4 (2004): 473–97; Linda Eisenmann, *Higher Education for Women in Postwar America, 1945–1965* (Baltimore: Johns Hopkins University Press, 2006); Sally Schwager, "Educating Women in America," *Signs* 12, no. 2 (1987): 333–72; Claudia Goldin, "The Quiet Revolution That Transformed Women's Employment, Education, and Family," *American Economic Review* 96, no. 2 (2006): 1–21; Babette Faehmel, *College Women in the Nuclear Age: Cultural Literacy and Female Identity, 1940–1960* (New Brunswick, NJ: Rutgers University Press, 2012).

36. For two other examples of such debates as they unfolded in legal journals, see "Sex Discrimination in Employment: An Attempt to Interpret Title VII of the Civil Rights Act of 1964," *Duke Law Journal* (1968): 671–723; and James C. Oldham, "Questions of Exclusion and Exception Under Title VII—'Sex Plus' and the BFOQ," *Hastings Law Journal* 55 (1971–1972): 55–94.

37. Pauli Murray and Mary O. Eastwood, "Jane Crow and the Law: Sex Discrimination and Title VII," *George Washington Law Review* 34, no. 2 (1965): 238.

38. Charles W. Whalen, *The Longest Debate: A Legislative History of the 1964 Civil Rights Act* (Washington, DC: Seven Locks Press, 1985); Cynthia Deitch, "Gender, Race, and Class Politics and the Inclusion of Women in Title VII of the 1964 Civil Rights Act," *Gender and Society* 7, no. 2 (1993): 183-203; Mary Anne Case, "Reflections on Constitutionalizing Women's Equality," *California Law Review* 90, no. 3 (2002): 765-90; Nicholas Pedriana and Robin Stryker, "The Strength of a Weak Agency: Enforcement of Title VII of the 1964 Civil Rights Act and the Expansion of State Capacity, 1965-1971," *American Journal of Sociology* 110, no. 3 (2004): 709-60; Nancy MacLean, *Freedom Is Not Enough: The Opening of the American Workplace* (New York: Russell Sage Foundation, 2006); Rosalind Rosenberg, *Divided Lives: American Women in the Twentieth Century* (New York: Macmillan, 2008); Frank Dobbin, *Inventing Equal Opportunity* (Princeton, NJ: Princeton University Press, 2009); Cary Franklin, "Inventing the 'Traditional Concept' of Sex Discrimination," *Harvard Law Review* 125, no. 6 (2012): 1307-80.

39. *Separate Toilet Rooms for Males and Females*, Arkansas Code, chapter 5 § 11-5-112.

40. Linder and Nygaard, *Void Where Prohibited*.

41. James C. Todd, "Title IX of the 1972 Education Amendments: Preventing Sex Discrimination in Public Schools," *Texas Law Review* 53 (1974): 103; Mary Anne Case, "Why Not Abolish the Laws of Urinary Segregation?" in *Toilet: Public Restrooms and the Politics of Sharing*, ed. Harvey Molotch and Laura Norén (New York: New York University Press, 2010).

42. On the history of transgender activism in the United States, see Katrina Roen, "'Either/Or' and 'Both/Neither': Discursive Tensions in Transgender Politics," *Signs* 27, no. 2 (2002): 501-22; David Valentine, *Imagining Transgender: An Ethnography of a Category* (Durham, NC: Duke University Press, 2007); on the challenges of gender-segregated restrooms faced by transgender, genderqueer, and gender nonconforming individuals, see Sally Munt and Cherry Smyth, eds., *Butch/Femme: Inside Lesbian Gender* (London: Cassell, 1998); Judith Halberstam, *Female Masculinity* (Durham, NC: Duke University Press, 1998); Kath Browne, "Genderism and the Bathroom Problem: (Re)materialising Sexed Sites, (Re)creating Sexed Bodies," *Gender, Place and Culture* 11, no. 3 (2004): 331-46; Brett Beemyn, Billy Curtis, Masen Davis, and Nancy Jean Tubbs, "Transgender Issues on College Campuses," *New Directions for Student Services* 111 (2005): 49-60; Sheila L. Cavanagh, *Queering Bathrooms: Gender, Sexuality, and the Hygienic Imagination* (Toronto: University of Toronto Press, 2010); Petra L. Doan, "The Tyranny of Gendered Spaces—Reflections from beyond the Gender Dichotomy," *Gender, Place and Culture* 17, no. 5 (2010): 635-54; Catherine Connell, "The Politics of the Stall: Transgender and Genderqueer Workers Negotiating 'the Bathroom Question,'" in *Embodied Resistance: Challenging the Norms, Breaking the Rules*, ed. Chris Bobel and Samantha Kwan (Nashville: Vanderbilt

University Press, 2011); Jody L. Herman, "Gendered Restrooms and Minority Stress: The Public Regulation of Gender and Its Impact on Transgender People's Lives," *Journal of Public Management and Social Policy* 19, no. 1 (2013): 65–80; Gayle Salamon, "Boys of the Lex: Transgenderism and Rhetorics of Materiality," *GLQ* 12, no. 4 (2006): 575–97.

43. As sociologist David Inglis observes in *A Sociological History of Excretory Experience,* toilet habits are very often used to assert the cultural and biological inferiority of subaltern groups and classes: as an example, he documents how that discrimination against British gypsy communities is frequently justified by the stereotype that they live in squalid conditions with filthy toilet facilities.

44. Charles Tilly, *Durable Inequality* (Berkeley: University of California Press, 1998); as Tilly puts it on page 7, "Durable inequality among categories arises because people who control access to value-producing resources solve pressing organizational problems by means of categorical distinctions."

2. PROFESSIONALIZING PLUMBING

1. "For but One Station," *Baltimore Sun,* April 12, 1907, 14.

2. "Comfort Station Wanted," *Baltimore Sun,* August 11, 1908, 8.

3. "Plea for Comfort Station," *Baltimore Sun,* June 8, 1909, 5.

4. "Comfort Station Wanted."

5. "Might Become Eyesore," *Baltimore Sun,* March 26, 1907, 12.

6. See Colin Campbell, "Beltway Traffic Earns Baltimore No. 19 on Most Congested City Ranking," *Baltimore Sun,* September 27, 2017.

7. "Many Object to Site," *Baltimore Sun,* March 18, 1907, 14.

8. "Comfort House Opposed," *Baltimore Sun,* February 14, 1907, 14.

9. "Plans for a Public Comfort Station," *New York Tribune,* February 16, 1897, 5; "New Public Comfort Station," *Baltimore Sun,* May 6, 1908, 9.

10. "Many Object to Site."

11. "For but One Station."

12. Peter C. Baldwin, "Public Privacy: Restrooms in American Cities, 1869–1932," *Journal of Social History* 48, no. 2 (2014): 266; Sam Bass Warner, *The Urban Wilderness: A History of the American City* (Berkeley: University of California Press, 1972); Regina Markell Morantz, "Making Women Modern: Middle Class Women and Health Reform in 19th Century America," *Journal of Social History* 10, no. 4 (1977): 490–507; Herbert G. Gutman, "Work, Culture, and Society in Industrializing America, 1815–1919," *American Historical Review* 78, no. 3 (1973): 531–88; Kenneth T. Jackson, *Crabgrass Frontier: The Suburbanization of the United States* (New York: Oxford University Press, 1987); Eric H. Monkkonen, *America Becomes Urban: The Development of U.S. Cities & Towns, 1780–1980* (Berkeley: University of California Press, 1988); Paul S. Boyer, *Urban*

Masses and Moral Order in America, 1820–1920 (Cambridge, MA: Harvard University Press, 1992); Thomas J. Misa, *A Nation of Steel: The Making of Modern America, 1865–1925* (Baltimore: Johns Hopkins University Press, 1998); Dell Upton, *Another City: Urban Life and Urban Spaces in the New American Republic* (New Haven, CT: Yale University Press, 2008); Stanley Plotkin, "History of Vaccination," *Proceedings of the National Academy of Sciences* 111, no. 34 (2014): 12283–87.

13. Maureen Ogle, *All the Modern Conveniences: American Household Plumbing, 1840–1890* (Baltimore: Johns Hopkins University Press, 1996); Nancy Tomes, *The Gospel of Germs: Men, Women, and the Microbe in American Life* (Cambridge, MA: Harvard University Press, 1998); Martin V. Melosi, *The Sanitary City: Environmental Services in Urban America from Colonial Times to the Present* (Pittsburgh: University of Pittsburgh Press, 2008).

14. Barbara Welter, "The Cult of True Womanhood: 1820–1860," *American Quarterly* 18, no. 2 (1966): 151–74.

15. Theda Skocpol, *Protecting Soldiers and Mothers* (Cambridge, MA: Harvard University Press, 2009); Linda K. Kerber, "Separate Spheres, Female Worlds, Woman's Place: The Rhetoric of Women's History," *Journal of American History* 75, no. 1 (1988): 9–39; Mary P. Ryan, *Women in Public: Between Banners and Ballots, 1825–1880* (Baltimore: Johns Hopkins University Press, 1990).

16. George J. Engelmann, "Causes Which Imperil the Health of the American Girl, and the Necessity of Female Hygiene," *Medical News*, December 6, 1890, 599.

17. R. T. Trall, "Department of Our Social Relations: Co-education of the Sexes," *Phrenological Journal and Science of Health*, January 1875, 32.

18. "Public Urinals," *Medical News*, March 15, 1902, 514.

19. Alcinous B. Jamison, "Rational Sanitation and Hygiene, with Special Reference to Personal Cleanliness," *Health*, July 1902, 657.

20. Cynthia Fuchs Epstein, *Deceptive Distinctions: Sex, Gender, and the Social Order* (New Haven, CT: Yale University Press, 1988).

21. Jamison, "Rational Sanitation and Hygiene," 657.

22. Harvey B. Bashore, "Outlines of Rural Hygiene," *Medical Record*, June 12, 1897, 837.

23. "Sanitary Engineering," *Scientific American Building Edition*, November 1, 1896, 74.

24. "The Sanitary Protective League," *Medical Record*, May 26, 1888, 587.

25. Stephen Smith, "The Necessity of International Sanitary Regulations Governing the Migration of Large Bodies of People in the Prevention of the Spread of Contagious and Epidemic Diseases," *Medical Record*, October 13, 1894, 449.

26. "State Sanitary Convention," *Pacific Medical Journal*, May 1, 1894, 265.

27. "Public Baths and Public-Comfort Stations for New York City," *Medical News*, November 7, 1896, 529.

28. Charles N. Dowd, "A Study of the Hygienic Condition of Our Streets," *Medical Record*, June 21, 1890, 700.

29. "Hygiene and State Medicine in the United States," *Medical Record*, April 14, 1900, 633.

30. "Railway Sanitation," *Medical Record*, November 18, 1905, 822.

31. Stanley Cohen, *Folk Devils and Moral Panics: The Creation of the Mods and Rockers* (London: Routledge, 2002 [1972]): 172; see also Erich Goode and Nachman Ben-Yehuda, "Moral Panics: Culture, Politics, and Social Construction," *Annual Review of Sociology* 20 (1994): 149–71.

32. Andrew Abbott, *The System of Professions: An Essay on the Division of Expert Labor* (Chicago: University of Chicago Press, 2014): 16; see also Elizabeth H. Gorman and Rebecca L. Sandefur, "'Golden Age,' Quiescence, and Revival: How the Sociology of Professions Became the Study of Knowledge-Based Work," *Work and Occupations* 38, no. 3 (2011): 275–302; William J. Goode, "Community within a Community: The Professions," *American Sociological Review* 22, no. 2 (1957): 194–200; Magali Sarfatti Larson, *The Rise of Professionalism: A Sociological Analysis* (Berkeley: University of California Press, 1979); Randall Collins, *The Credential Society: An Historical Sociology of Education and Stratification* (New York: Academic Press, 1979); Thomas L. Haskell, *The Authority of Experts: Studies in History and Theory* (Bloomington: Indiana University Press, 1984); Eliot Freidson, *Professionalism, the Third Logic: On the Practice of Knowledge* (Chicago: University of Chicago Press, 2001); Michèle Lamont and Virág Molnár, "The Study of Boundaries in the Social Sciences," *Annual Review of Sociology* 28 (2002): 167–95; and W. Richard Scott, "Lords of the Dance: Professionals as Institutional Agents," *Organization Studies* 29, no. 2 (2008): 219–38.

33. "Important Improvements in Water Closets," *The Technologist, or Industrial Monthly: a Practical Journal for Manufacturers, Mechanics, Builders, Inventors, Engineers, Architects*, February 1, 1875, 31.

34. John McCurdy, "Water-Closets and Privy Vaults," *The Sanitarian*, March 1, 1887, 224.

35. "Modern Plumbing," *National Builder*, March 1, 1908, 38.

36. "Sanitary House Decoration," *National Builder*, November 1, 1902, 22.

37. "The Plumber and the Doctor," *American Carpenter and Builder*, July 1, 1910, 67.

38. "A Bibliography of Baths and Bathing," *American Architect and Building News*, January 14, 1905, 14.

39. "Plumbing a Science," *National Builder*, August 1, 1898, 11.

40. "Plumbing as a Practical Science," *Builder*, April 20, 1903, 9.

41. For a detailed definition of this term, see Thomas S. Kuhn, *The Structure of Scientific Revolutions* (Chicago: University of Chicago Press, 1962).

42. William H. Allen, "Sanitation and Social Progress," *American Journal of Sociology* 8, no. 5 (1903): 633. Incidentally, the intertwining tensions Allen

raises—between viewing sociology as a science or as a more humanistic enterprise, and between viewing it as a wholly academic entity or an applied method of untangling real-world social problems—continue to animate the field today. The more things change, the more they stay the same, no?

43. "Some Common Facts about Plumbing," *Architectural Record*, July 1892, 108.

44. "Sanitary Problems," *National Builder*, October 1, 1915, 68.

45. "Some Suggestions in Bathrooms," *American Builder*, February 1, 1922, 102.

46. "Sanitation in Public Toilet Rooms," *Carpentry and Building*, September 1, 1906, 300.

47. Charles de Montesquieu, *The Spirit of the Laws*, trans. Anne M. Cohler, Basia Carolyn Miller, and Harold Samuel Stone (Cambridge: Cambridge University Press, 1989 [1749]), 338; Adam Smith, *Lectures on Justice, Police, Revenue and Arms*, ed. Edwin Cannan (Oxford: Clarendon Press, 1896 [1763]), 234; Karl Marx, *Capital*, vol. 1, *A Critique of Political Economy* (London: Penguin Books, 2004 [1867]); Thorstein Veblen, *The Theory of the Leisure Class* (New York: Oxford University Press, 2007 [1899]).

48. Marion Fourcade and Kieran Healy, "Moral Views of Market Society," *Annual Review of Sociology* 33 (2007): 299–300.

49. Klaus Weber, Kathryn L. Heinze, and Michaela DeSoucey, "Forage for Thought: Mobilizing Codes in the Movement for Grass-Fed Meat and Dairy Products," *Administrative Science Quarterly* 53, no. 3 (2008); Kieran Healy, *Last Best Gifts: Altruism and the Market for Human Blood and Organs* (Chicago: University of Chicago Press, 2010); Rene Almeling, *Sex Cells: The Medical Market for Eggs and Sperm* (Berkeley: University of California Press, 2011); Viviana A. Zelizer, "The Purchase of Intimacy," *Law and Social Inquiry* 25, no. 3 (2000): 817–48; see also Nancy Folbre and Julie A. Nelson, "For Love or Money—or Both?" *Journal of Economic Perspectives* 14, no. 4 (2000): 123–40; Brian Steensland, "Cultural Categories and the American Welfare State: The Case of Guaranteed Income Policy," *American Journal of Sociology* 111, no. 5 (2006): 1273–1326; Sarah Quinn, "The Transformation of Morals in Markets: Death, Benefits, and the Exchange of Life Insurance Policies," *American Journal of Sociology* 114, no. 3 (2008): 738–80; Mabel Berezin, "Exploring Emotions and the Economy: New Contributions from Sociological Theory," *Theory and Society* 38, no. 4 (2009): 335–46; Michel Anteby, "Markets, Morals, and Practices of Trade: Jurisdictional Disputes in the U.S. Commerce in Cadavers," *Administrative Science Quarterly* 55, no. 4 (2010): 606–38; Frederick F. Wherry, *The Culture of Markets* (New York: Polity Press, 2012); and Lyn Spillman, *Solidarity in Strategy: Making Business Meaningful in American Trade Associations* (Chicago: University of Chicago Press, 2012).

50. "Practical Sanitation," *Health*, October 1907, 625.

51. "Arguments for a Public Comfort Station," *Building Age*, December 1, 1910, 525.

52. Roy Suddaby and Royston Greenwood, "Rhetorical Strategies of Legitimacy," *Administrative Science Quarterly* 50, no. 1 (2005): 35–67.

53. Molly W. Berger, *Hotel Dreams: Luxury, Technology, and Urban Ambition in America, 1829–1929* (Baltimore: Johns Hopkins University Press, 2011); John Henry Hepp, *The Middle-Class City: Transforming Space and Time in Philadelphia, 1876–1926* (Philadelphia: University of Pennsylvania Press, 2003).

54. "A Public Comfort Station at Cobb's Hill, N.Y.," *Building Age*, March 1, 1911, 184.

55. "The Need for Building Public Convenience Stations," *American Architect*, June 16, 1920, 773.

56. "Public Comfort Station in Newark, N.J.," *Building Age*, May 1, 1910, 219.

57. "Seattle's New Public Comfort Station," Building Age, October 1, 1911, 529.

58. "Business and Public Buildings in Colors," *American Builder*, April 1, 1926, 250.

59. "Women and Architecture," *Scientific American Building Monthly*, July 1, 1903, 2.

60. "Sanitary Instruction for Women," *Scientific American Building Monthly*, August 1, 1902, 36.

61. "Women and Architecture." The article also asks many rhetorical questions about such matters: "Should she not, then, know something about it? Should she not have sufficient acquaintance with construction to detect poor work and indicate how failures may be remedied? Should she not know what progress is being made in mechanical appliances for the dwelling and how her own personal daily labor may be lightened? Should she not be familiar with the progress of sanitary science as applied to dwellings, and be prepared to discuss at least the simplest problems which are likely to come before her? Should she not know something of the science of heating and ventilation, and be familiar with the practical aspects of household equipment?"

62. T. A. Tefft, "The Economy of the Bathroom," *National Builder*, September 1, 1913, 73.

63. Karl William Zoeller, "Good Plumbing Increases the Value of the Building," *American Builder*, October 1, 1924, 108.

64. W. K. Glen, "Modern Plumbing," *American Builder*, January 1, 1925, 172.

65. "America Leads in Plumbing Improvements," *American Builder*, June 1, 1922, 83.

66. John F. McClarren, "Park Buildings for Various Purposes," *American Builder*, September 1, 1919, 78.

67. Terry S. Kogan, "Sex-Separation in Public Restrooms: Law, Architecture, and Gender," *Michigan Journal of Gender and Law* 14, no. 1 (2007): 5–6.

68. Joan Acker, "Hierarchies, Jobs, Bodies: A Theory of Gendered Organizations," *Gender and Society* 4, no. 2 (1990): 144.

69. Joan Acker, "Inequality Regimes: Gender, Class, and Race in Organizations," *Gender and Society* 20, no. 4 (2006): 441.

70. Baldwin, "Public Privacy."

71. International Conference of Building Officials, "Chapter 1: Title and Scope," *Uniform Building Code, 1927 Edition*, sec. 102.

72. Andrew Brown-May and Peg Fraser, "Gender, Respectability, and Public Convenience in Melbourne, Australia, 1859–1902," in *Ladies and Gents: Public Toilets and Gender,* ed. Olga Gershenson and Barbara Penner (Philadelphia: Temple University Press, 2009).

73. Malcolm A. Bouton, "Plumbing Codes in Public Health," *American Journal of Public Health* 46, no. 11 (1956): 1439.

74. Ibid., 1440.

75. "Plumbing a Science," *National Builder,* August 1, 1898, 11.

3. REGULATING RESTROOMS

1. "Women on the March," *Time,* September 7, 1970, 12.

2. Ethel L. Payne, "So This Is Washington," *Chicago Daily Defender,* May 23, 1970, 5.

3. Linda Charlton, "Women March Down Fifth in Equality Drive," *New York Times,* August 27, 1970.

4. Regarding confining the women's parade, see "Women on the March," 12; on the blaring horns, see Charlton, "Women March Down Fifth."

5. "Women on the March," 13.

6. Ibid., 12.

7. Ibid., 13.

8. "House Debates Amendment to End Sex Discrimination," *New York Times,* October 7, 1971, 43.

9. Marya Mannes, "Equal Rights Amendment Battle Is between Closed and Open Minds," *Baltimore Sun,* April 24, 1973, B6.

10. See, e.g., Birch Bayh, "The Need for the Equal Rights Amendment," *Notre Dame Lawyer* 48 (1972): 80–91.

11. "Equal Rights: Who Is Against It and Why," *New York Times,* September 13, 1970, E6.

12. Spencer Rich, "Senate Showdown Due on Rights for Women," *Washington Post,* March 21, 1972, A9.

13. Spencer Rich, "Women's Rights Survive Vote," *Washington Post,* March 22, 1972, A1.

14. "Equal Rights," E6.

15. "Mrs. Ervin Says the Senator Is Right," *Washington Post*, September 19, 1970, C2.

16. "So This Is Washington," 5.

17. "Equal Rights," E6.

18. "ERA Running into Trouble," *Atlanta Constitution*, February 9, 1973, 11A; "How Equal?" *Washington Post*, September 11, 1970, C3.

19. Ellen Goodman, "His and Hers . . . or Theirs?" *Boston Globe*, October 2, 1970, 13.

20. Paul G. Edwards, "Virginia Senate Defeats ERA," *Washington Post*, January 28, 1977, A1.

21. "Women Movement Optimistic about Ratification of ERA," *Hartford Courant*, November 18, 1974, 12.

22. Paul C. Glick, "A Demographer Looks at American Families," *Journal of Marriage and Family* 37, no. 1 (1975): 15–26; Alice Kessler-Harris, *Out to Work: A History of Wage-Earning Women in the United States* (New York: Oxford University Press, 1982); Leila J. Rupp, "The Women's Community in the National Woman's Party, 1945 to the 1960s," *Signs* 10, no. 4 (1985): 715–40; Willard L. Rodgers and Arland Thornton, "Changing Patterns of First Marriage in the United States," *Demography* 22, no. 2 (1985): 265–79; Herbert Jacob, *Silent Revolution: The Transformation of Divorce Law in the United States* (Chicago: University of Chicago Press, 1988); 265–79; Joanne J. Meyerowitz, ed., *Not June Cleaver: Women and Gender in Postwar America, 1945–1960* (Philadelphia: Temple University Press, 1994); Sarah A. Soule and Susan Olzak, "When Do Movements Matter? The Politics of Contingency and the Equal Rights Amendment," *American Sociological Review* 69, no. 4 (2004): 473–97; Linda Eisenmann, *Higher Education for Women in Postwar America, 1945–1965* (Baltimore: Johns Hopkins University Press, 2006); Pauli Murray and Mary O. Eastwood, "Jane Crow and the Law: Sex Discrimination and Title VII," *George Washington Law Review* 34 (1965): 232–56.

23. The number of restroom-related state laws increased again in the 2010s, as the transgender rights movement gained traction at the state and national levels in pursuing workplace discrimination protections—and as a backlash to that movement concomitantly succeeded in implementing newly stringent laws related to gender and restroom access. For more on these emergent issues, see Kristen Schilt and Laurel Westbrook, "Bathroom Battlegrounds and Penis Panics," *Contexts* 14, no. 3 (2015): 26–31.

24. Lawrence M. Friedman, *A History of American Law: Third Edition* (New York: Simon and Schuster, 2005); Thomas G. Hansford and James F. Spriggs, *The Politics of Precedent on the U.S. Supreme Court* (Princeton, NJ: Princeton University Press, 2006); William M. Landes and Richard A. Posner, "Legal Precedent: A Theoretical and Empirical Analysis," *Journal of Law and Economics* 19, no. 2 (1976): 249–307; Tracey E. George and Lee Epstein, "On the Nature of

Supreme Court Decision Making," *American Political Science Review* 86, no. 2 (1992): 323–37; James H. Fowler and Sangick Jeon, "The Authority of Supreme Court Precedent," *Social Networks* 30, no. 1 (2008): 16–30; Gregory A. Caldeira, "The Transmission of Legal Precedent: A Study of State Supreme Courts," *American Political Science Review* 79 (1985): 178–94; Yonatan Lupu and James H. Fowler, "Strategic Citations to Precedent on the U.S. Supreme Court," *Journal of Legal Studies* 42, no. 1 (2013): 151–86; Michael J. Gerhardt, *The Power of Precedent* (New York: Oxford University Press, 2011).

25. Ostapowicz v. Johnson Bronze Co., 369 F. Supp. 522 (1973), 536.

26. Rhoades v. Jim Dandy Co., not reported in F. Supp. (1978), 1.

27. Stapp v. Overnite Transportation Co., 995 F. Supp. 1207 (1998), 1211–12.

28. Wedow v. City of Kansas City, Mo., 442 F.3d 661 (2006), 667–68.

29. Spees v. James Marine, Inc., not reported in F. Supp. (2009), 5.

30. *Wedow*, 671–72.

31. Reed v. Shepard, 939 F.2d 484 (1991), 486.

32. Koschoff v. Runyon, not reported in F. Supp. (1999), 3.

33. *Koschoff*, 5.

34. Johnson v. Atlantic County, not reported in F. Supp. (2010), 4; Rodriguez v. Flow-Zone, LLC, not reported in F. Supp. (2011), 2; *Johnson*, 4.

35. *Reed*, 491–92.

36. *Koschoff*, 12.

37. Abigail C. Saguy, *What Is Sexual Harassment?: From Capitol Hill to the Sorbonne* (Berkeley: University of California Press, 2003), 2.

38. Catlett v. Missouri Highway and Transportation Commission, 589 F. Supp. 929 (1983), 928.

39. Mackey v. Shalala, 43 F. Supp. 559 (1999), 563.

40. *Mackey*, 565.

41. Gasperini v. Dominion Energy New England, Inc., not reported in F. Supp. (2012), 10.

42. See also Cecilia L. Ridgeway, "Interaction and the Conservation of Gender Inequality: Considering Employment," *American Sociological Review* 62, no. 2 (1997): 218–35; Cecilia L. Ridgeway and Lynn Smith-Lovin, "The Gender System and Interaction," *Annual Review of Sociology* 25 (1999): 191–216; and Cecilia L. Ridgeway and Shelley J. Correll, "Unpacking the Gender System: A Theoretical Perspective on Gender Beliefs and Social Relations," *Gender and Society* 18, no. 4 (2004): 510–31.

43. Max Weber, *The Protestant Ethic and the Spirit of Capitalism*, trans. Peter Baehr and Gordon C. Wells (New York: Penguin Books, 2002).

44. Catharine A. MacKinnon, *Toward a Feminist Theory of the State* (Cambridge, MA: Harvard University Press, 1989); Mary Joe Frug, *Postmodern Legal Feminism* (New York: Routledge, 1993); Lynne A. Haney, "Feminist State Theory: Applications to Jurisprudence, Criminology, and the Welfare State," *Annual Review*

of Sociology 26 (2000): 641–66; Yvonne Zylan, *States of Passion: Law, Identity, and the Social Construction of Desire* (New York: Oxford University Press, 2011).

45. EEOC v. M.D. Pneumatics, Inc., not reported in F. Supp. (1983), 6.

46. DeClue v. Central Illinois Light Co., 223 F.3d 434 (2000), 436.

47. *DeClue*, 437.

48. *DeClue*, 438.

49. Backus v. Baptist Medical Center, 510 F. Supp. 1191 (1981), 1193.

50. *Backus*, 1195.

51. Dothard v. Rawlinson, 433 U.S. 321 (1977), 346.

52. Women Prisoners of District of Columbia Department of Corrections v. District of Columbia, 877 F. Supp. 634 (1994), 665.

53. Forts v. Ward, 471 F. Supp. 1095 (1978), 1098.

54. *Forts*, 1099.

55. Margaret Mead, *Coming of Age in Samoa* (New York: William Morrow, 1928), as quoted in *Forts*.

56. *Forts*, 1098.

57. *Forts*, 1101.

58. Kastl v. Maricopa County Community College District, not reported in F. Supp. (2004), 1.

59. Etsitty v. Utah Transit Authority, not reported in F. Supp. (2005), 7.

60. Etsitty v. Utah Transit Authority, 502 F.3d 1215 (2007), 1224.

61. Gatena v. County of Orange, 80 F. Supp. 1331 (1999), 1333.

62. For more on this point, see Laurel Westbrook and Kristen Schilt, "Doing Gender, Determining Gender: Transgender People, Gender Panics, and the Maintenance of the Sex/Gender/Sexuality System," *Gender and Society* 28, no. 1 (2014): 32–57.

63. Tey Meadow, "'A Rose Is a Rose': On Producing Legal Gender Classifications," *Gender and Society* 24, no. 6 (2010): 814–37.

64. Jay Prosser, *Second Skins: The Body Narratives of Transsexuality* (New York: Columbia University Press, 1998). It also merits noting that Prosser takes great pains to distinguish "transsexual" experience from "transgender" experience, but I do not follow that convention here. Choosing language to describe all individuals who challenge or cross "socially constructed boundaries that contain imposed gender roles, norms, and expectations" (Megan Nanney and David L. Brunsma, "Moving beyond Cis-terhood: Determining Gender through Transgender Admittance Policies at U.S. Women's Colleges," *Gender and Society* 31, no. 2 [2017]: 165) is notoriously difficult for reasons too numerous to fully trace in the context of a footnote. However, because of shifting linguistic norms in transgender studies since the publication of *Second Skins*, I settle on the umbrella term *transgender* here—while also acknowledging that such a convention is necessarily imperfect, as not all people who trouble gender boundaries necessarily identify with such terminology.

65. Simone de Beauvoir, *The Second Sex*, trans. Constance Borde and Sheila Malovany-Chevallier (New York: Vintage Books, 2011 [1949]), 283; see, e.g., Michele Foucault, *Discipline and Punish: The Birth of the Prison* (New York: Vintage Books, 1995 [1975]); and Judith Butler, *Bodies That Matter: On the Discursive Limits of "Sex"* (New York: Routledge, 1993).

66. Jacques Lacan, "The Mirror-Phase as Formative of the Function of the I," *New Left Review* 51 (1968): 71–77; Kaja Silverman, *The Threshold of the Visible World* (New York: Psychology Press, 1996); Maurice Merleau-Ponty, *Phenomenology of Perception*, trans. Colin Smith (London: Routledge and Kegan Paul, 1962).

67. Gayle Salamon, *Assuming a Body: Transgender and Rhetorics of Materiality* (New York: Columbia University Press, 2010), 2.

68. Waldo v. Consumers Energy Co., not reported in F. Supp. (2011), 4.

69. *Waldo*, 5.

70. *Waldo*, 5.

71. Castro v. New York City Department of Sanitation, not reported in F. Supp. (2000), 5.

72. June Price Tangney, "Moral Affect: The Good, the Bad, and the Ugly," *Journal of Personality and Social Psychology* 61, no. 4 (1991): 599.

73. James v. National Railroad Passenger Corp., not reported in F. Supp. (2005), 1.

74. Kohler v. City of Wapakoneta, 381 F. Supp. 692 (2005), 697.

75. Cottrill v. MFA, Inc., 443 F.3d 629 (2006), 639.

76. Munday v. Waste Management of North America, Inc., 858 F. Supp. 1364 (1994), 1367.

77. Brown v. Snow, not reported in F. Supp. (2004), 11.

78. Ford-Fugate v. FedEx Freight, not reported in F. Supp. (2007), 5.

79. Schultze v. White, 127 Fed. Appx. 212 (2005), footnote 1.

80. Warner v. City of Terre Haute, Indiana, 30 F. Supp. 1107 (1998), 1116.

81. *Warner*, 1127.

82. Farmer v. Dixon Electrical Systems and Contracting, Inc., not reported in F. Supp. (2013), 3.

83. *Farmer*, 5.

84. Vroman v. A. Crivelli Buick Pontiac GMC, Inc., not reported in F. Supp. (2010), 2.

85. *Vroman*, 3.

86. Adams v. City of New York, 837 F. Supp. 108 (2011), 118, 126.

87. Candace West and Don H. Zimmerman, "Doing Gender," *Gender and Society* 1, no. 2 (1987): 126.

88. Ibid., 137.

89. Ibid., 136–37.

90. See, e.g., James F. Spriggs and Thomas G. Hansford, "The U.S. Supreme Court's Incorporation and Interpretation of Precedent," *Law and Society Review* 36, no. 1 (2002): 139–60.

91. West and Zimmerman, "Doing Gender," 142.

92. However, they, too, are certainly worthy of continued social-scientific inquiry because of their stratifying power; see note 93.

93. On affect in the social sciences, see Danilyn Rutherford, "Affect Theory and the Empirical," *Annual Review of Anthropology* 45 (2016): 285–300; on affect in queer studies, see Mel Y. Chen, *Animacies: Biopolitics, Racial Mattering, and Queer Affect* (Durham, NC: Duke University Press, 2012).

94. See, e.g., Randall Collins, "Situational Stratification: A Micro-Macro Theory of Inequality," *Sociological Theory* 18, no. 1 (2000): 17–43; James M. Jasper, "The Emotions of Protest: Affective and Reactive Emotions in and around Social Movements," *Sociological Forum* 13, no. 3 (1998): 397–424; Edward J. Lawler, "An Affect Theory of Social Exchange," *American Journal of Sociology* 107, no. 2 (2001): 321–52; Lauren A. Rivera, "Go with Your Gut: Emotion and Evaluation in Job Interviews," *American Journal of Sociology* 120, no. 5 (2015): 1339–89.

95. Arlie Russell Hochschild, "Emotion Work, Feeling Rules, and Social Structure," *American Journal of Sociology* 85, no. 3 (1979): 551–75.

96. See also Pierre Bourdieu, "The Force of Law: Toward a Sociology of the Juridical Field," *Hastings Law Journal* 38 (1986–87): 805–13.

4. WORKING AGAINST THE WASHROOM

1. Associated Press, "Woman Using Men's Room Makes Waves," *Chicago Tribune,* July 22, 1990; Lisa Belkin, "Flushed Out: Houstonians Defend Woman's Use of Men's Room at Crowded Concert," *Austin American Statesman,* July 21, 1990.

2. Associated Press, "Woman Using Men's Room Makes Waves."

3. Laura Tolley, "Police Refusing to Wash Hands of Men's Room Case," *Austin American Statesman,* July 26, 1990; Entering Restrooms of Opposite Sex, Houston Code of Ordinances, chapter 28 § 42.6, ordinance number 72–904; the full text of the statute reads, "It shall be unlawful for any person to knowingly and intentionally enter any public restroom designated for the exclusive use of the sex opposite to such person's sex without the permission of the owner, tenant, manager, lessee or other person in charge of the premises, in a manner calculated to cause a disturbance."

4. Paul Weingarten, "Men's Room Trip Opens Door to Women's Rights," *Chicago Tribune,* July 29, 1990.

5. Jon Hilkevitch, "When Scrambled Eggs Pass for Brains," *Chicago Tribune,* November 2, 1990.

6. "Woman Is Acquitted in Trial for Using the Men's Room," special to the *New York Times*, November 3, 1990.

7. Belkin, "Flushed out."

8. "Woman Is Acquitted"; Belkin, "Flushed out."

9. Weingarten, "Men's Room Trip."

10. Restroom Availability Where the Public Congregates, Texas Health and Safety Code §341.068.

11. Peggy Fikac and Suzanne Gamboa, "Richards Signs Law Requiring Additional Women's Restrooms," *Austin American Statesman*, June 16, 1993.

12. Elaine Ayala, "It's Been Debated in State Legislatures, City Halls, Architectural Circles and the Line to the Loo: Potty Parity," *Austin American Statesman*, August 7, 1990.

13. "Wrong Restroom the Right Move," *St. Petersburg Times*, November 3, 1990.

14. Edwart Gunts and Audrey Haar, "For Relief of Women, 'Female Urinal' Considered for New Stadium," *Baltimore Sun*, January 25, 1991.

15. Junda Woo, "'Potty Parity' Lets Women Wash Hands of Long Loo Lines," *Wall Street Journal*, February 24, 1994.

16. Ayala, "It's Been Debated."

17. Weingarten, "Men's Room Trip."

18. Ayala, "It's Been Debated."

19. Junda Woo, "Potty Parity."

20. Frank Dobbin, *Inventing Equal Opportunity* (Princeton, NJ: Princeton University Press, 2011), 18.

21. Lynn Hollen Lees, "Urban Public Space and Imagined Communities in the 1980s and 1990s," *Journal of Urban History* 20, no. 4 (1994): 463.

22. Erin Kelly and Frank Dobbin, "How Affirmative Action Became Diversity Management: Employer Response to Antidiscrimination Law, 1961 to 1996," *American Behavioral Scientist* 41, no. 7 (1998): 960–84; Lauren B. Edelman, Sally Riggs Fuller, and Iona Mara-Drita, "Diversity Rhetoric and the Managerialization of Law," *American Journal of Sociology* 106, no. 6 (2001): 1589–1641; Hazel V. Carby, "The Multicultural Wars," *Radical History Review* 1992, no. 54 (1992): 7–18; John W. Meyer, Patricia Bromley, and Francisco O. Ramirez, "Human Rights in Social Science Textbooks: Cross-National Analyses, 1970–2008," *Sociology of Education* 83, no. 2 (2010): 111–34; Rodney Benson, "American Journalism and the Politics of Diversity," *Media, Culture and Society* 27, no. 1 (2005): 5–20; Dolores Hayden, *The Power of Place: Urban Landscapes as Public History* (Cambridge, MA: MIT Press, 1997).

23. Americans with Disabilities Act of 1990 (ADA), 42 U.S.C. §§ 12101–12213 (2013).

24. For more on the history of the disability rights movement in the United States, see Jacqueline Vaughn, *Disabled Rights: American Disability Policy and*

the Fight for Equality (Washington, DC: Georgetown University Press, 2003); Tom Shakespeare, "The Social Model of Disability," in *The Disability Studies Reader*, ed. Lennard J. Davis, 4th ed. (New York: Routledge, 2013); and Douglas C. Baynton, "Disability and the Justification of Inequality in American History" in *The Disability Studies Reader*, ed. Lennard J. Davis, 4th ed. (New York: Routledge, 2013).

25. Erving Goffman, "The Arrangement between the Sexes," *Theory and Society* 4, no. 3 (1977): 315.

26. See Candace West and Don H. Zimmerman, "Doing Gender," *Gender and Society* 1, no. 2 (1987): 125–51. For empirical illustrations, see, e.g., Betsy Lucal, "What It Means to Be Gendered Me: Life on the Boundaries of a Dichotomous Gender System," *Gender and Society* 13, no. 6 (1999): 781–97; Stanley Lieberson, Susan Dumais, and Shyon Baumann, "The Instability of Androgynous Names: The Symbolic Maintenance of Gender Boundaries," *American Journal of Sociology* 105, no. 5 (2000): 1249–87; and Emily W. Kane, "'No Way My Boys Are Going to Be Like That!' Parents' Responses to Children's Gender Nonconformity," *Gender and Society* 20, no. 2 (2006): 149–76.

27. Laurel Westbrook and Kristen Schilt, "Doing Gender, Determining Gender: Transgender People, Gender Panics, and the Maintenance of the Sex/Gender/Sexuality System," *Gender and Society* 28, no. 1 (2014): 32–57. See also Lain A. B. Mathers, "Bathrooms, Boundaries, and Emotional Burdens: Cisgendering Interactions through the Interpretation of Transgender Experience," *Symbolic Interaction* 40, no. 3 (2017): 295–316; and Lisa F. Platt and Sarah R. B. Milam, "Public Discomfort with Gender Appearance-Inconsistent Bathroom Use: The Oppressive Bind of Bathroom Laws for Transgender Individuals," *Gender Issues* 35, no. 3 (2018): 181–201.

28. Geoffrey C. Bower and Susan Leigh Star, *Sorting Things Out: Classification and Its Consequences* (Cambridge, MA: MIT Press, 1999). See also Martha Lampland and Susan Leigh Star, eds., *Standards and Their Stories: How Quantifying, Classifying, and Formalizing Practices Shape Everyday Life* (Ithaca, NY: Cornell University Press, 2009); and Laurent Thévenot, "Postscript to the Special Issue: Governing Life by Standards: A View from Engagements," *Social Studies of Science* 39, no. 5 (2009): 793–813. Sociologists of culture also refer to this same basic principle with the term *affordances*—that is, the set of possible actions enabled and constrained by the inherent, physical properties of things. See James J. Gibson, *The Ecological Approach to Visual Perception* (New York: Psychology Press, 1986); Tia DeNora, *Music in Everyday Life* (Cambridge: Cambridge University Press, 2000); Terence E. McDonnell, "Cultural Objects as Objects: Materiality, Urban Space, and the Interpretation of AIDS Campaigns in Accra, Ghana," *American Journal of Sociology* 115, no. 6 (2010): 1800–1852; Wendy Griswold, Gemma Mangione, and Terence E. McDonnell, "Objects, Words, and Bodies in Space: Bringing Materiality into Cultural Analysis," *Qual-*

itative Sociology 36, no. 4 (2013): 343–64; and Fernando Domínguez Rubio, "Preserving the Unpreservable: Docile and Unruly Objects at MoMA," *Theory and Society* 43, no. 6 (2014): 617–45.

29. Quote from an interview with an architect in Rob Imrie and Emma Street, "Regulating Design: The Practices of Architecture, Governance and Control," *Urban Studies* 46, no. 12 (2009): 2507. See also Eran Ben-Joseph, *The Code of the City: Standards and the Hidden Language of Place Making* (Cambridge, MA: MIT Press, 2005); and Eran Ben-Joseph and Terry S. Szold, eds., *Regulating Place: Standards and the Shaping of Urban America* (New York: Routledge, 2005).

30. See, e.g., Harvey Luskin Molotch, *Where Stuff Comes from: How Toasters, Toilets, Cars, Computers, and Many Others Things Come to Be as They Are* (New York: Routledge, 2003).

31. Paul J. DiMaggio and Walter W. Powell, "The Iron Cage Revisited: Institutional Isomorphism and Collective Rationality in Organizational Fields," *American Sociological Review* 48, no. 2 (1983): 147–60. See also David Strang and Sarah A. Soule, "Diffusion in Organizations and Social Movements: From Hybrid Corn to Poison Pills," *Annual Review of Sociology* 24 (1998): 265–90.

32. As sociologists like Lauren Edelman argue, all manner of legal regulations are more ambiguous than cut-and-dried, and even the most seemingly self-evident portions of local or federal legislation are often replete with caveats and complications. Those caveats and complications consequently leave organizations with quite a bit of leeway in how, exactly, they achieve compliance with the various structures governing their specific institutional fields; see Lauren B. Edelman, "Legal Ambiguity and Symbolic Structures: Organizational Mediation of Civil Rights Law," *American Journal of Sociology* 97, no. 6 (1992): 1531–76. For the specifics of how that general tendency applies to the ADA in particular, see Jeb Barnes and Thomas F. Burke, "Making Way: Legal Mobilization, Organizational Response, and Wheelchair Access," *Law and Society Review* 46, no. 1 (2012): 167–98.

33. Toilet Rooms, 49 Code of Federal Regulations of the United States of America A4.22 (1993).

34. Susan S. Silbey, "The Sociological Citizen: Pragmatic and Relational Regulation in Law and Organizations," *Regulation and Governance* 5, no. 1 (2011): 1–13. For empirical illustrations of this basic point, see Kirsten Dellinger and Christine L. Williams, "The Locker Room and the Dorm Room: Workplace Norms and the Boundaries of Sexual Harassment in Magazine Editing," *Social Problems* 49, no. 2 (2002): 242–57; Ruthanne Huising and Susan S. Silbey, "Governing the Gap: Forging Safe Science through Relational Regulation," *Regulation and Governance* 5, no. 1 (2011): 14–42; Carol A. Heimer, "Resilience in the Middle: Contributions of Regulated Organizations to Regulatory Success," *The Annals of the American Academy of Political and Social Science* 649, no. 1 (2013):

139–56. Additionally, when it comes to antidiscrimination law, governing bodies regularly interpret statutory guidelines in light of their actual, on-the-ground use, giving "diversity" personnel and the administrative policies they enact a tremendous amount of influence over, e.g., how the federal courts officially define legal equality; see Frank Dobbin and Erin L. Kelly, "How to Stop Harassment: Professional Construction of Legal Compliance in Organizations," *American Journal of Sociology* 112, no. 4 (2007): 1203–43; Lauren Edelman, *Working Law: Courts, Corporations, and Symbolic Civil Rights* (Chicago: University of Chicago Press, 2016).

35. *Legal consonance* is a portmantologism, a play on two other phrases common in sociological parlance. *Legal consciousness* is a term from law-and-society scholarship meant to capture the many diverse ways in which law is experienced and understood by ordinary citizens, and *(cultural) resonance* is a term from social movement theory for discursive congruence between collective aims and broader societal values. For more on legal consciousness, see Patricia Ewick, *The Common Place of Law: Stories from Everyday Life* (Chicago: University of Chicago Press, 1998); Susan S. Silbey, "After Legal Consciousness," *Annual Review of Law and Social Science* 1 (2005): 323–68. For more on resonance, see David A. Snow, E. Burke Rochford Jr., Steven K. Worden, and Robert D. Benford, "Frame Alignment Processes, Micromobilization, and Movement Participation," *American Sociological Review* 51, no. 4 (1986): 464–81; and Robert D. Benford and David A. Snow, "Framing Processes and Social Movements: An Overview and Assessment," *Annual Review of Sociology* 26 (2000): 611–39.

36. Robert E. Park, Ernest W. Burgess, and Morris Janowitz, *The City: Suggestions for Investigation of Human Behavior in the Urban Environment* (Chicago: University of Chicago Press, 1925); William Julius Wilson, *The Truly Disadvantaged: The Inner City, the Underclass, and Public Policy* (Chicago: University of Chicago Press, 1987); Douglas S. Massey and Nancy A. Denton, *American Apartheid: Segregation and the Making of the Underclass* (Cambridge, MA: Harvard University Press, 1993); Tama Leventhal and Jeanne Brooks-Gunn, "Moving to Opportunity: An Experimental Study of Neighborhood Effects on Mental Health," *American Journal of Public Health* 93, no. 9 (2003): 1576–82; Sara Nephew Hassani, "Locating Digital Divides at Home, Work, and Everywhere Else," *Poetics* 34, no. 4–5 (2006): 250–72.

37. Kristin E. Smith and Rebecca Glauber, "Exploring the Spatial Wage Penalty for Women: Does It Matter Where You Live?" *Social Science Research* 42, no. 5 (2013): 1390–1401; Vincent J. Roscigno, Donald Tomaskovic-Devey, and Martha Crowley, "Education and the Inequalities of Place," *Social Forces* 84, no. 4 (2006): 2121–45; Daniel T. Lichter, Domenico Parisi, and Michael C. Taquino, "Toward a New Macro-Segregation? Decomposing Segregation within and between Metropolitan Cities and Suburbs," *American Sociological Review* 80, no. 4 (2015): 843–73.

38. Jesse C. Ribot and Nancy Lee Peluso, "A Theory of Access," *Rural Sociology* 68, no. 2 (2003): 156.

39. Linda M. Lobao, Gregory Hooks, Ann R. Tickamyer, eds., *The Sociology of Spatial Inequality* (Albany, NY: SUNY Press, 2007); Linda M. Lobao, "Continuity and Change in Place Stratification: Spatial Inequality and Middle-Range Territorial Units," *Rural Sociology* 69, no. 1 (2004): 1–30; David J. Peters, "American Income Inequality across Economic and Geographic Space, 1970–2010," *Social Science Research* 42, no. 6 (2013): 1490–1504.

40. Judith Lorber, "Shifting Paradigms and Challenging Categories," *Social Problems* 53, no. 4 (2006): 449.

41. Ibid., 449.

42. Ibid.

43. Ibid.

44. Ibid., 451.

45. Ibid., 449.

46. Ibid., 451.

47. Ibid., 452.

48. Denise E. Agosto, Kimberly L. Paone, and Gretchen S. Ipock, "The Female-Friendly Public Library: Gender Differences in Adolescents' Uses and Perceptions of U.S. Public Libraries," *Library Trends* 56, no. 2 (2007): 387–401; Nilay Yavuz and Eric W. Welch, "Addressing Fear of Crime in Public Space: Gender Differences in Reaction to Safety Measures in Train Transit," *Urban Studies* 47, no. 12 (2010): 2491–2515; see also Beatriz Colomina and Jennifer Bloomer, *Sexuality and Space* (Princeton, NJ: Princeton Architectural Press, 1992); Saskia Sassen, "Analytic Borderlands: Race, Gender and Representation in the New City," in *Re-Presenting the City* (London: Palgrave, 1996), 183–202; Iain Borden, Barbara Penner, and Jane Rendell, *Gender Space Architecture: An Interdisciplinary Introduction* (London: Routledge, 2002); Daphne Spain, "Gender and Urban Space," *Annual Review of Sociology* 40 (2014): 581–98.

49. Dean Spade, *Normal Life: Administrative Violence, Critical Trans Politics, and the Limits of Law* (Durham, NC: Duke University Press, 2015), 65.

50. Marc Galanter, "Why the 'Haves' Come Out Ahead: Speculations on the Limits of Legal Change," *Law and Society Review* 9, no. 1 (1974): 95–160.

5. LEVERAGING THE LOO

1. Richard L. Vernaci, "Porcelain Popularity," *Free Lance-Star*, March 29, 1991.

2. Beth Kaiman, "A Parent's Chore Made Easier," *Washington Post*, March 28, 1991.

3. Ibid.

4. Sharon Stangenes, "In Public Privies, It's His, Hers, Ours," *Chicago Tribune*, January 12, 1992.

5. Lyda Longa, "Family Friendly Malls Offer Diaper Tables and Other 'Signs of the Times,'" *Sun Sentinel*, December 21, 1992.

6. Kathleen Moloney, "Family Way," *Los Angeles Times*, April 12, 1992.

7. Longa, "Family Friendly Malls."

8. Moloney, "Family Way."

9. Michelle Hiskey, "The Ballpark," *Atlanta Journal-Constitution*, March 23, 1997.

10. Jim Thomas, "Unique: Soon-to-Rise St. Louis Dome Is 'State of Art,'" *St. Louis Post-Dispatch*, April 18, 1993.

11. Moloney, "Family Way."

12. Ned Zeman, "New at the Mall: One-Stop Pit Stop," *Newsweek*, December 15, 1991.

13. Lori Eickmann, "Upscale Family Restrooms Make the Mall an Easier Place to Go," *San Jose Mercury News*, March 28, 1995.

14. Richard A. Peterson and Roger M. Kern, "Changing Highbrow Taste: From Snob to Omnivore," *American Sociological Review* 61, no. 5 (1996): 900–907; Jordi López-Sintas and Tally Katz-Gerro, "From Exclusive to Inclusive Elitists and Further: Twenty Years of Omnivorousness and Cultural Diversity in Arts Participation in the USA," *Poetics* 33, no. 5–6 (2005): 299–319; Arthur S. Alderson, Azamat Junisbai, and Isaac Heacock, "Social Status and Cultural Consumption in the United States," *Poetics* 35, no. 2–3 (2007): 191–212; Sharon Zukin, "Consuming Authenticity," *Cultural Studies* 22, no. 5 (2008): 724–48; Sarah Cappeliez and Josée Johnston, "From Meat and Potatoes to 'Real-Deal' Rotis: Exploring Everyday Culinary Cosmopolitanism," *Poetics* 41, no. 5 (2013): 433–55; Josée Johnston, *Foodies: Democracy and Distinction in the Gourmet Foodscape* (New York: Routledge, 2014).

15. Sharon Zukin, Valerie Trujillo, Peter Frase, Danielle Jackson, Tim Recuber, and Abraham Walker, "New Retail Capital and Neighborhood Change: Boutiques and Gentrification in New York City," *City and Community* 8, no. 1 (2009): 47–64; Sharon Zukin, *Naked City: The Death and Life of Authentic Urban Places* (New York: Oxford University Press, 2010); Alison Pearlman, *Smart Casual: The Transformation of Gourmet Restaurant Style in America* (Chicago: University of Chicago Press, 2013); Timothy J. Dowd, Kathleen Liddle, Kim Lupo, and Anne Borden, "Organizing the Musical Canon: The Repertoires of Major U.S. Symphony Orchestras, 1842 to 1969," *Poetics* 30, no. 1–2 (2002): 35–61; Pierre-Antoine Kremp, "Innovation and Selection: Symphony Orchestras and the Construction of the Musical Canon in the United States (1879–1959)," *Social Forces* 88, no. 3 (2010): 1051–82.

16. Erving Goffman, *The Presentation of Self in Everyday Life* (London: Penguin, 1990 [1959]), 113.

17. Ibid., 121.

18. See Erving Goffman, *Relations in Public: Microstudies of the Public Order* (New York: Basic Books, 1971); Spencer E. Cahill, William Distler, Cynthia Lachowetz, Andrea Meaney, Robyn Tarallo, and Teena Willard, "Meanwhile Backstage: Public Bathrooms and the Interaction Order," *Journal of Contemporary Ethnography* 14, no. 1 (1985): 33–58; and Martin S. Weinberg and Colin J. Williams, "Fecal Matters: Habitus, Embodiments, and Deviance," *Social Problems* 52, no. 3 (2005): 315–36.

19. See Harvey Molotch and Laura Norén, eds., *Toilet: Public Restrooms and the Politics of Sharing* (New York: New York University Press, 2010).

20. Viviana A. Zelizer, "The Purchase of Intimacy," *Law and Social Inquiry* 25, no. 3 (2000): 817–48; Viviana A. Zelizer and Charles Tilly, "Relations and Categories," *Psychology of Learning and Motivation* 47 (2006): 1–31; Nina Bandelj, "Relational Work and Economic Sociology," *Politics and Society* 40, no. 2 (2012): 175–201.

21. Georg Simmel, *The Sociology of Georg Simmel*, trans. and ed. K. H. Wolff (Glencoe, IL: Free Press, 1950); John Urry, "The Sociology of Space and Place," in *The Blackwell Companion to Sociology*, ed. Judith R. Blau (Malden, MA: Blackwell Publishing, 2004): 1–15; Nicola Beisel, "Morals versus Art: Censorship, the Politics of Interpretation, and the Victorian Nude," *American Sociological Review* 58, no. 2 (1993): 145–62; Beth A. Eck, "Nudity and Framing: Classifying Art, Pornography, Information, and Ambiguity," *Sociological Forum* 16, no. 4 (2001): 603–32; David Grazian, *Blue Chicago: The Search for Authenticity in Urban Blues Clubs* (Chicago: University of Chicago Press, 2003); Kim M. Babon, "Composition, Coherence, and Attachment: The Critical Role of Context in Reception," *Poetics* 34, no. 3 (2006): 151–79; Josée Johnston and Shyon Baumann, "Democracy versus Distinction: A Study of Omnivorousness in Gourmet Food Writing," *American Journal of Sociology* 113, no. 1 (2007): 165–204; Andrew Cheyne and Amy Binder, "Cosmopolitan Preferences: The Constitutive Role of Place in American Elite Taste for Hip-Hop Music, 1991–2005," *Poetics* 38, no. 3 (2010): 336–64; Terence E. McDonnell, "Cultural Objects as Objects: Materiality, Urban Space, and the Interpretation of AIDS Campaigns in Accra, Ghana," *American Journal of Sociology* 115, no. 6 (2010): 1800–1852; Fernando Domínguez Rubio, "Preserving the Unpreservable: Docile and Unruly Objects at MoMA," *Theory and Society* 43, no. 6 (2014): 617–45; Jennifer A. Jordan, *Edible Memory: The Lure of Heirloom Tomatoes and Other Forgotten Foods* (Chicago: University of Chicago Press, 2015).

22. Viviana A. Rotman Zelizer, *The Social Meaning of Money* (New York: Basic Books, 1994).

23. Pierre Bourdieu, "Cultural Reproduction and Social Reproduction," in *Power and Ideology in Education*, ed. Jerome Karabel and A. H. Halsey (New York: Oxford University Press, 1977); Michèle Lamont and Annette Lareau,

"Cultural Capital: Allusions, Gaps and Glissandos in Recent Theoretical Developments," *Sociological Theory* 6, no. 2 (1988): 153–68; Randall Collins, "Situational Stratification: A Micro-Macro Theory of Inequality," *Sociological Theory* 18, no. 1 (2000): 17–43; Francie Ostrower, *Trustees of Culture: Power, Wealth, and Status on Elite Arts Boards* (Chicago: University of Chicago Press, 2002); Shamus Rahman Khan, *Privilege: The Making of an Adolescent Elite at St. Paul's School* (Princeton, NJ: Princeton University Press, 2011); Elizabeth A. Armstrong and Laura T. Hamilton, *Paying for the Party: How College Maintains Inequality* (Cambridge, MA: Harvard University Press, 2013); Lauren A. Rivera, *Pedigree: How Elite Students Get Elite Jobs* (Princeton, NJ: Princeton University Press, 2015); Annette Lareau, "Cultural Knowledge and Social Inequality," *American Sociological Review* 80, no. 1 (2015): 1–27.

24. Leslie McCall, "The Complexity of Intersectionality," *Signs: Journal of Women in Culture and Society* 30, no. 3 (2005): 1788.

25. Ibid.

26. Julie Bettie, *Women without Class: Girls, Race, and Identity* (Berkeley: University of California Press, 2003), 33.

27. With a few notable exceptions, see, e.g., Armstrong and Hamilton, *Paying for the Party*; Paula England, "Sometimes the Social Becomes Personal: Gender, Class, and Sexualities," *American Sociological Review* 81, no. 1 (2016): 4–28; Lauren A. Rivera and András Tilcsik, "Class Advantage, Commitment Penalty: The Gendered Effect of Social Class Signals in an Elite Labor Market," *American Sociological Review* 81, no. 6 (2016): 1097–1131.

28. See, e.g., Gayle Rubin, "The Traffic in Women: Notes on the 'Political Economy' of Sex," in *Toward an Anthropology of Women*, ed. Rayna R. Reiter (New York: Monthly Review Press, 1975); Heidi Hartmann, "Capitalism, Patriarchy, and Job Segregation by Sex," *Signs: Journal of Women in Culture and Society* 1, no. 3 (1976): 137–69; Heidi I. Hartmann, "The Family as the Locus of Gender, Class, and Political Struggle: The Example of Housework," *Signs: Journal of Women in Culture and Society* 6, no. 3 (1981): 366–94; Joan Acker, "Class, Gender, and the Relations of Distribution," *Signs: Journal of Women in Culture and Society* 13, no. 3 (1988): 473–97.

29. Indeed, as intersectional feminist theorists remind us, "family values" discourses have a profound political charge, because they tightly link cultural legitimacy to a very narrow vision of mainstream conformity—not just middle-class respectability but white and heterosexual respectability as well. Because such observations have been so frequently and thoroughly explicated in Black feminist thought and queer studies, a complete bibliography of respectability politics is far beyond the scope of what a single footnote can support. However, for the origins of the phrase *politics of respectability,* see Evelyn Brooks Higginbotham, *Righteous Discontent: The Women's Movement in the Black Baptist Church,*

1880–1920 (Cambridge, MA: Harvard University Press, 1994); for a detailed account of the political appeal of "family values" in the United States, see Patricia Hill Collins, "It's All in the Family: Intersections of Gender, Race, and Nation," *Hypatia* 13, no. 3 (1998): 62–82, and Judith Stacey, *In the Name of the Family: Rethinking Family Values in the Postmodern Age* (Boston: Beacon Press, 1996). And for an overview of how such strategies have been absorbed into the contemporary movement for queer and transgender rights, see Michael Warner, *The Trouble with Normal: Sex, Politics, and the Ethics of Queer Life* (New York: Free Press, 1999).

30. Bethany Bryson, *Making Multiculturalism: Boundaries and Meaning in U.S. English Departments* (Stanford, CA: Stanford University Press, 2005). For more on status culture, see Paul DiMaggio, "Cultural Capital and School Success: The Impact of Status Culture Participation on the Grades of U.S. High School Students," *American Sociological Review* 47, no. 2 (1982): 189–201; or Max Weber's original definition in Max Weber, *Economy and Society* (Berkeley: University of California Press, 1978 [1922]).

31. Pierre Bourdieu, *Distinction: A Social Critique of the Judgment of Taste,* trans. Richard Nice (Cambridge, MA: Harvard University Press, 1984), 7.

32. Ibid., 6.

33. Another common place to see power theorized in the contemporary sociology of gender is within work on femininities and masculinities; see, e.g., R. W. Connell, *Gender and Power: Society, the Person and Sexual Politics* (Stanford, CA: Stanford University Press, 1987). See also R. W. Connell, *Masculinities* (Cambridge: Polity Press, 1995); R. W. Connell and James W. Messerschmidt, "Hegemonic Masculinity Rethinking the Concept," *Gender and Society* 19, no. 6 (2005): 829–59; and Mimi Schippers, "Recovering the Feminine Other: Masculinity, Femininity, and Gender Hegemony," *Theory and Society* 36, no. 1 (2007): 85–102.

34. That presumption, in part, traces its intellectual lineage in sociology to Talcott Parsons's definition of power as a "generalized facility or resource." See "The Distribution of Power in American Society," *World Politics* 10, no. 1 (1957): 140.

35. This follows from Viviana Zelizer's definition of economic circuits, first developed in "Circuits in Economic Life," *Economic Sociology: The European Electronic Newsletter* 8, no. 1 (2006): 32; but it also reflects many of the observations about emotional energy and situational stratification that Randall Collins advances in *Interaction Ritual Chains* (Princeton, NJ: Princeton University Press, 2004).

36. Georg Simmel, "Fashion," *American Journal of Sociology* 62, no. 6 (1957): 541.

6. TRANSFORMING THE TOILET

1. Bill Schackner, "Boy, Girl, Boy, Girl: In Student Housing, Is the Coed Room the Wave of the Future?" *Pittsburgh Post-Gazette*, February 22, 2002, F2.

2. Lini S. Kadaba, "Mixed Doubles in Dorms," *Philadelphia Inquirer*, October 10, 2002, D1.

3. Ibid.

4. Tamar Lewin, "No Big Deal, but Some Dorm Rooms Have Gone Coed," *New York Times*, May 11, 2002, A13.

5. William Weir, "Gender Won't Count in New Dorm," *Hartford Courant*, May 18, 2003, A1.

6. Kadaba, "Mixed Doubles in Dorms."

7. Ibid.

8. Lewin, "No Big Deal, but Some Dorm Rooms Have Gone Coed."

9. Deborah Peterson, "Coed Dorm Rooms: The Next Step in Higher Education?" *St. Louis Post-Dispatch*, November 12, 2002, E1.

10. Weir, "Gender Won't Count in New Dorm."

11. Lewin, "No Big Deal, but Some Dorm Rooms Have Gone Coed."

12. Kadaba, "Mixed Doubles in Dorms."

13. Ibid.

14. Lewin, "No Big Deal, but Some Dorm Rooms Have Gone Coed."

15. Peterson, "Coed Dorm Rooms."

16. Schackner, "Boy, Girl, Boy, Girl."

17. Therese L. Baker and William Vélez, "Access to and Opportunity in Postsecondary Education in the United States: A Review," *Sociology of Education* 69 (1996): 82–101; Evan Schofer and John W. Meyer, "The Worldwide Expansion of Higher Education in the Twentieth Century," *American Sociological Review* 70, no. 6 (2005): 898–920; Claudia Buchmann and Thomas A. DiPrete, "The Growing Female Advantage in College Completion: The Role of Family Background and Academic Achievement," *American Sociological Review* 71, no. 4 (2006): 515–41; Yossi Shavit, Richard Arum, and Adam Gamoran, eds., *Stratification in Higher Education: A Comparative Study* (Stanford, CA: Stanford University Press, 2007); Maria Charles and Karen Bradley, "Indulging Our Gendered Selves? Sex Segregation by Field of Study in 44 Countries," *American Journal of Sociology* 114, no. 4 (2009): 924–76; Thomas J. Espenshade, *No Longer Separate, Not Yet Equal: Race and Class in Elite College Admission and Campus Life* (Princeton, NJ: Princeton University Press, 2009); David A. Hoekema, *Campus Rules and Moral Community: In Place of In Loco Parentis* (Lanham, MD: Rowman and Littlefield, 1994); William A. Kaplin, *The Law of Higher Education: Student Version* (San Francisco, CA: Jossey-Bass, 2014).

18. Identifying sufficiently inclusive language for such a diverse community of individuals is notoriously difficult; see also Megan Nanney and David L.

Brunsma, "Moving beyond Cis-Terhood: Determining Gender through Transgender Admittance Policies at U.S. Women's Colleges," *Gender and Society* 31, no. 2 (2017): 145–70. For that reason, I use the term *transgender* and the acronym *LGBTQ* for the sake of syntactical simplicity throughout this chapter, but I also acknowledge that such discursive conventions are necessarily imperfect, as not all people who fall under or near the umbrellas I am describing necessarily identify with such terminology.

19. See Brett Beemyn, Billy Curtis, Masen Davis, and Nancy Jean Tubbs, "Transgender Issues on College Campuses," *New Directions for Student Services* 111 (2005): 49–60; Brian J. Willoughby, Jason S. Carroll, William J. Marshall, and Caitlin Clark, "The Decline of In Loco Parentis and the Shift to Coed Housing on College Campuses," *Journal of Adolescent Research* 24, no. 1 (2009): 21–36.

20. According to the LGBTQ-centered nonprofit Campus Pride, the total number of colleges and universities publicly offering gender-neutral housing options had surpassed 250 by the time I completed revisions to this book in 2018; see www.campuspride.org/tpc/gender-inclusive-housing/.

21. Because several of my interview respondents in this chapter identify in some fashion as nonbinary and/or use gender-neutral pronouns (e.g., they/them/ theirs), and because using such pronouns only for those respondents could compromise their anonymity, I use gender-neutral pronouns for all respondents in this chapter. For a more substantive discussion of my reliance on singular *they* throughout the manuscript, see note 21 in the introduction.

22. "President Obama's State of the Union Address," *New York Times,* January 24, 2012, available at www.nytimes.com/2012/01/25/us/politics/state-of-the-union-2012-transcript.html.

23. Jonathan Taplin, *Move Fast and Break Things: How Facebook, Google, and Amazon Cornered Culture and Undermined Democracy* (New York: Little, Brown, and Company, 2017), iii.

24. Clayton M. Christensen, Michael E. Raynor, and Rory McDonald, "What Is Disruptive Innovation?" *Harvard Business Review,* December 1, 2015, https:// hbr.org/2015/12/what-is-disruptive-innovation.

25. "Innovation in Higher Education," Association of Governing Boards of Universities and Colleges, last updated October 31, 2017, www.agb.org /innovation.

26. Steven Mintz, "The Future Is Now: 15 Innovations to Watch For," *Chronicle of Higher Education,* July 22, 2013, www.chronicle.com/article/The-Future-Is-Now-15/140479.

27. Some participants went so far as to ground such observations in academic writing about such issues. One particularly memorable participant had an extended conversation with me about "classic sociological theories of gender, like 'Doing Gender,' performativity, Judith Butler, and all that." I didn't have the heart to inform them that Butler—for better or for worse—is not a sociologist.

28. Laurel Westbrook and Kristen Schilt, "Doing Gender, Determining Gender: Transgender People, Gender Panics, and the Maintenance of the Sex/Gender/Sexuality System," *Gender and Society* 28, no. 1 (2014): 32–57.

29. Paul J. DiMaggio and Walter W. Powell, "The Iron Cage Revisited: Institutional Isomorphism and Collective Rationality in Organizational Fields," *American Sociological Review* 48, no. 2 (1983): 147–60.

30. This pattern is consistent with the sociological literature on status signaling in higher education; see Nicholas A. Bowman and Michael N. Bastedo, "Getting on the Front Page: Organizational Reputation, Status Signals, and the Impact of U.S. News and World Report on Student Decisions," *Research in Higher Education* 50, no. 5 (2009): 415–36; Michael N. Bastedo and Nicholas A. Bowman, "College Rankings as an Interorganizational Dependency: Establishing the Foundation for Strategic and Institutional Accounts," *Research in Higher Education* 52, no. 1 (2010): 3–23.

31. David Strang and Sarah A. Soule, "Diffusion in Organizations and Social Movements: From Hybrid Corn to Poison Pills," *Annual Review of Sociology* 24 (1998): 265–90; Ezra W. Zuckerman, "The Categorical Imperative: Securities Analysts and the Illegitimacy Discount," *American Journal of Sociology* 104, no. 5 (1999): 1398–1438; Ezra W. Zuckerman, "Structural Incoherence and Stock Market Activity," *American Sociological Review* 69, no. 3 (2004): 405–32; Hayagreeva Rao, Philippe Monin, and Rodolphe Durand, "Border Crossing: Bricolage and the Erosion of Categorical Boundaries in French Gastronomy," *American Sociological Review* 70, no. 6 (2005): 968–91; Cathryn Johnson, Timothy J. Dowd, and Cecilia L. Ridgeway, "Legitimacy as a Social Process," *Annual Review of Sociology* 32 (2006): 53–78; Michael T. Hannan, László Pólos, and Glenn R. Carroll, *Logics of Organization Theory: Audiences, Codes, and Ecologies* (Princeton, NJ: Princeton University Press, 2007); Michael Jensen, "Legitimizing Illegitimacy: How Creating Market Identity Legitimizes Illegitimate Products," in *Categories in Markets: Origins and Evolution*, ed. Michael Lounsbury (Bingley, UK: Emerald Group Publishing, 2010); Damon J. Phillips, Catherine J. Turco, and Ezra W. Zuckerman, "Betrayal as Market Barrier: Identity-Based Limits to Diversification among High-Status Corporate Law Firms," *American Journal of Sociology* 118, no. 4 (2013): 1023–54; Amanda J. Sharkey, "Categories and Organizational Status: The Role of Industry Status in the Response to Organizational Deviance," *American Journal of Sociology* 119, no. 5 (2014): 1380–1433; Joel Podolny, *Status Signals: A Sociological Study of Market Competition* (Princeton, NJ: Princeton University Press, 2005).

32. Paul J. DiMaggio and Walter W. Powell, "The Iron Cage Revisited: Institutional Isomorphism and Collective Rationality in Organizational Fields," *American Sociological Review* 48, no. 2 (1983): 147–60; see also Lynne G. Zucker, "Institutional Theories of Organization," *Annual Review of Sociology* 13 (1987): 443–44; Walter W. Powell and Paul DiMaggio, eds., *The New Institutionalism*

in Organizational Analysis (Chicago: University of Chicago Press, 1991); W. Richard Scott, *Institutions and Organizations* (Thousand Oaks, CA: Sage, 1995); Mark C. Suchman, "Managing Legitimacy: Strategic and Institutional Approaches," *Academy of Management Review* 20, no. 3 (1995): 571–610; David L. Deephouse, "Does Isomorphism Legitimate?," *Academy of Management Journal* 39, no. 4 (1996): 1024–39; Mary C. Brinton and Victor Nee, eds., *The New Institutionalism in Sociology* (New York: Russell Sage Foundation, 1998).

33. In my previous research about public arguments for and against gender-inclusive facilities in student-run college newspapers, I refer to a variant of this process as "engendering reputation"—that is, the cultural work of (1) *constructing* discursive distinctions between institutions on the basis of their responsiveness to transgender issues; (2) *comparing* an institution's treatment of gender and sexual minority students (and performance on relevant external metrics) to the treatment by (and performance of) other institutions; (3) *evaluating* well-known, well-regarded, and well-ranked institutions more positively than those unknown, unregarded, and unranked; and (4) *leveraging* facility changes as a means through which an institution might improve its position within such status hierarchies. For more details, see Alexander K. Davis, "Toward Exclusion through Inclusion: Gender-Inclusive Facilities and Engendering Reputation at Colleges and Universities in the United States, 2001–2013," *Gender and Society* 32, no. 3 (2018): 321–47.

34. Mitchell L. Stevens and Josipa Roksa, "The Diversity Imperative in Elite Admissions," in *Diversity in American Higher Education: Toward a More Comprehensive Approach,* ed. Lisa M. Stulberg and Sharon Lawner Weinberg (New York: Routledge, 2011): 63.

35. Susan Stryker, "Transgender History, Homonormativity, and Disciplinarity," *Radical History Review* 2008, no. 100 (2008): 155.

36. Ellen C. Berrey, "Why Diversity Became Orthodox in Higher Education, and How It Changed the Meaning of Race on Campus," *Critical Sociology* 37, no. 5 (2011): 573–96, Daniel N. Lipson, "Embracing Diversity: The Institutionalization of Affirmative Action as Diversity Management at UC-Berkeley, UT-Austin, and UW-Madison," *Law and Social Inquiry* 32, no. 4 (2007): 985–1026; Jodi Melamed, "The Spirit of Neoliberalism: From Racial Liberalism to Neoliberal Multiculturalism," *Social Text* 24, no. 4 (Winter 2006): 1–24. Additionally, as intersectional work in queer studies has long recognized, part of what has led to shifts in institutional recognition has been the relegation of issues of race, disability, and above all, social class to the margins of the contemporary gay rights movement; see, e.g., Anna M. Agathangelou, M. Daniel Bassichis, and Tamara L. Spira, "Intimate Investments: Homonormativity, Global Lockdown, and the Seductions of Empire," *Radical History Review* 2008, no. 100 (2008): 120–43; Christina B. Hanhardt, *Safe Space: Gay Neighborhood History and the Politics of Violence* (Durham, NC: Duke University Press, 2013); Jasbir K. Puar, *Terrorist*

Assemblages: Homonationalism in Queer Times (Durham, NC: Duke University Press, 2007); David L. Eng, *The Feeling of Kinship: Queer Liberalism and the Racialization of Intimacy* (Durham, NC: Duke University Press, 2010); Elizabeth Jane Ward, *Respectably Queer: Diversity Culture in LGBT Activist Organizations* (Nashville: Vanderbilt University Press, 2008); David L. Eng, Judith Halberstam, and José Esteban Muñoz, eds., "What's Queer about Queer Studies Now," special issue, *Social Text* 23, nos. 3–4 (2005); Christina Crosby, Lisa Duggan, Roderick Ferguson, et al., "Queer Studies, Materialism, and Crisis: A Roundtable Discussion," *GLQ: A Journal of Lesbian and Gay Studies* 18, no. 1 (2012): 127–47.

37. Michael Sauder and Wendy Nelson Espeland, "The Discipline of Rankings: Tight Coupling and Organizational Change," *American Sociological Review* 74, no. 1 (2009): 63–82; see also Wendy Nelson Espeland and Michael Sauder, "Rankings and Reactivity: How Public Measures Recreate Social Worlds," *American Journal of Sociology* 113, no. 1 (2007): 1–40.

38. Robert Merton refers to outcomes such as this in more general terms as the "unintended consequences" of intentional action; see Robert K. Merton, "The Unanticipated Consequences of Purposive Social Action," *American Sociological Review* 1, no. 6 (1936): 894–904.

39. Francine Deutsch, "Undoing Gender," *Gender and Society* 21, no. 1 (2007): 107.

40. Deutsch, "Undoing Gender," 107.

41. Ibid.

42. Ibid., 114.

43. Ibid., 109.

44. Ibid., 120.

45. Ibid., 107.

46. Ibid., 120.

47. Ibid., 108.

48. Ellen Hazelkorn, *Rankings and the Reshaping of Higher Education: The Battle for World-Class Excellence* (New York: Palgrave Macmillan, 2015).

49. Sara Ahmed, *On Being Included: Racism and Diversity in Institutional Life* (Durham, NC: Duke University Press, 2012).

50. Genny Beemyn and Shane Windmeyer, "The Top 10 Trans-Friendly Colleges and Universities," *The Advocate*, August 15, 2012, www.advocate.com/politics/transgender/2012/08/15/top-10-trans-friendly-colleges-and-universities/.

51. In alphabetical order, the top ten list includes: Ithaca College, New York University, Princeton University, the University of California at Los Angeles, the University of California at Riverside, the University of Michigan, the University of Oregon, the University of Pennsylvania, and the University of Vermont. See Genny Beemyn and Shane Windmeyer, "The Top 10 Trans-Friendly Colleges and Universities," *The Advocate*, August 15, 2012; "22 Richest Schools in America,"

Forbes Magazine, July 30, 2014, www.forbes.com/sites/ccap/2014/07/30/22-richest-schools-in-america/.

52. Pat Eaton-Robb, "Yale's Gender Neutral Bathrooms Part of Changing Climate," *USA Today,* May 23, 2016, http://college.usatoday.com/2016/05/23/yales-gender-neutral-bathrooms-part-of-changing-climate/.

53. See, e.g., Brett Beemyn, "Serving the Needs of Transgender College Students," *Journal of Gay and Lesbian Issues in Education* 1, no. 1 (2003): 33–50; Brett Beemyn, Billy Curtis, Masen Davis, and Nancy Jean Tubbs, "Transgender Issues on College Campuses," *New Directions for Student Services* 2005, no. 111 (2005): 49–60; Tiana E. Krum, Kyle S. Davis, and M. Paz Galupo, "Gender-Inclusive Housing Preferences: A Survey of College-Aged Transgender Students," *Journal of LGBT Youth* 10, no. 1–2 (2013): 64–82; Kristie L. Seelman, "Recommendations of Transgender Students, Staff, and Faculty in the USA for Improving College Campuses," *Gender and Education* 26, no. 6 (2014): 618–35; Jonathan T. Pryor, "Out in the Classroom: Transgender Student Experiences at a Large Public University," *Journal of College Student Development* 56, no. 5 (2015): 440–55.

54. Max Weber, "Class, Status, Party," in *From Max Weber: Essays in Sociology,* ed. H. H. Gerth and C. Wright Mills (Berkeley: University of California Press, 2007 [1922]).

CONCLUSION

1. An Act to Provide for Single-Sex Multiple Occupancy Bathroom and Changing Facilities in Schools and Public Agencies and to Create Statewide Consistency in Regulation of Employment and Public Accommodations, General Assembly of North Carolina, House Bill DRH40005-TC-1B, Second Extra Session (March 23, 2016).

2. Steve Harrison, "Charlotte City Council Approves LGBT Protections in 7–4 Vote," *Charlotte Observer,* February 22, 2016.

3. Pat McCrory, Twitter post, March 23, 2016, 10:16 p.m., http://twitter.com/PatMcCroryNC/status/712825502772269056.

4. Lucy Westcott, "North Carolina Being Sued by ACLU Over Its Anti-LGBT Law," *Newsweek,* March 28, 2016.

5. Roy Cooper, "Comments on House Bill 2," North Carolina Department of Justice, March 29, 2016, available from www.ncdoj.gov; see also Anne Blythe, "NC Attorney General Refuses to Defend State from LGBT Legal Challenge," *Miami Herald,* March 29, 2016.

6. Andrea Wiegl, "Some Triangle Small-Business Owners Show Opposition to HB2 Legislation," *Raleigh (NC) News and Observer,* April 1, 2016.

7. Ryan Grenoble, "Georgia Kroger Has an Excellent Explanation for Its Unisex Bathroom," *Huffington Post,* March 28, 2016.

8. Brad Kutner, "Ellwood Thompson's Debuts Gender Neutral Restrooms after HB2 Fallout," *GayRVA*, April 12, 2016.

9. "Transgendered Students and School Bathrooms," CBS News Poll, June 8, 2014, available from www.cbsnews.com; Daniel Trotta, "Exclusive: Women, Young More Open on Transgender Issue in U.S.," Reuters, April 21, 2016, available from www.reuters.com.

10. See, e.g., Aaron T. Norton and Gregory M. Herek, "Heterosexuals' Attitudes toward Transgender People: Findings from a National Probability Sample of U.S. Adults," *Sex Roles* 68, no. 11 (2013): 738–53; David Broockman and Joshua Kalla, "Durably Reducing Transphobia: A Field Experiment on Door-to-Door Canvassing," *Science* 352, no. 6282 (2016): 220–24.

11. Patricia Yancey Martin, "Gender as a Social Institution," *Social Forces* 82, no. 4 (2004): 1249–73; Barbara J. Risman, "Gender as a Social Structure: Theory Wrestling with Activism," *Gender and Society* 18, no. 4 (2004): 429–50.

12. Risman, "Gender as a Social Structure," 434.

13. Ibid., 435.

14. See also Andrew Abbott, "Things of Boundaries," *Social Research* 62, no. 4 (1995): 857–82.

15. Martin, "Gender as a Social Institution," 1264.

16. The current edition of the *Oxford English Dictionary*, e.g., defines *element* as "component part of a complex whole." See *Oxford English Dictionary* online, Oxford University Press, www.oed.com/view/Entry/60353.

17. Since I can hear my former writing seminar students screaming about "common knowledge" in academic writing from here, I'll point out that one can find a nontechnical explanation of these chemical possibilities in "Why Does Combining Hydrogen and Oxygen Typically Produce Water Rather Than Hydrogen Peroxide?" available on the *Scientific American* website at www.scientificamerican.com/article/why-does-combining-hydrog/.

18. See, e.g., Jun Zhang, Pengcheng Chen, Bingkai Yuan, Wei Ji, Zhihai Cheng, and Xiaohui Qiu, "Real-Space Identification of Intermolecular Bonding with Atomic Force Microscopy," *Science* 342, no. 6158 (2013): 611–14.

19. This idea could also be translated into the language of Mustafa Emirbayer's, "Manifesto for a Relational Sociology": all of the elements of gender's institutional accomplishment are "preeminently dynamic in nature," working as "unfolding, ongoing processes rather than as static ties among inert substances." See Emirbayer, "Manifesto for a Relational Sociology," *American Journal of Sociology* 103, no. 2 (1997): 289.

20. Harvey Molotch and Laura Norén, *Toilet: Public Restrooms and the Politics of Sharing* (New York: New York University Press, 2010).

21. Joel Sanders and Susan Stryker, "Could the Restroom Become Public Space?" *Metropolis*, April 18, 2017, www.metropolismag.com/architecture/could-restroom-become-public-space/.

22. Genny Beemyn and Shane Windmeyer, "The Top 10 Trans-Friendly Colleges and Universities," *The Advocate,* August 15, 2012.

23. Noah McClain and Ashley Mears, "Free to Those Who Can Afford It: The Everyday Affordance of Privilege," *Poetics* 40, no. 2 (2012): 133–49.

24. Peggy McIntosh, "White Privilege: Unpacking the Invisible Knapsack," *Peace and Freedom Magazine,* July/August 1989, 10–12.

APPENDIX

1. Earl Babbie, "Laud Humphreys and Research Ethics," *International Journal of Sociology and Social Policy* 24, no. 3/4/5 (2004), 12.

2. Babbie, "Laud Humphreys and Research Ethics," 13.

3. John F. Galliher, Wayne H. Brekhus, and David P. Keys, *Laud Humphreys: Prophet of Homosexuality and Sociology* (Madison: University of Wisconsin Press, 2004), 6–7.

4. Erving Goffman, "On Face-Work," *Psychiatry* 18, no. 3 (1955): 213–31.

5. Spencer E. Cahill, William Distler, Cynthia Lachowetz, Andrea Meaney, Robyn Tarallo, and Teena Willard, "Meanwhile Backstage: Public Bathrooms and the Interaction Order," *Journal of Contemporary Ethnography* 14, no. 1 (1985): 33–58.

6. For the intellectual principles underlying such an approach as a general strategy for theory construction in sociology, see John Levi Martin, *Social Structures* (Princeton, NJ: Princeton University Press, 2009).

7. I thank Lynda Holmstrom for noting that this was an asset to my sample rather than a liability—and for a wonderful e-mail exchange following the 2014 Eastern Sociological Society Annual Meeting about my nascent work.

8. Barney G. Glaser and Anselm L. Strauss, *The Discovery of Grounded Theory: Strategies for Qualitative Research* (Chicago: Aldine Publishing Company, 2012 [1967]), 67–68.

9. Although the doctrine is more familiarly known as "separate but equal," the original laws in question—and the majority opinion in *Plessy* both use the phrase "equal but separate." See Plessy v. Ferguson, 163 U.S. 537 (1896), 547.

10. See, e.g., Joan Acker, *Class Questions: Feminist Answers* (Lanham, MD: Rowman and Littlefield Publishers, 2005); Kathy Davis, "Intersectionality as Buzzword: A Sociology of Science Perspective on What Makes a Feminist Theory Successful," *Feminist Theory* 9, no. 1 (2008): 67–85; Eduardo Bonilla-Silva, *Racism without Racists: Color-Blind Racism and the Persistence of Racial Inequality in the United States* (New York: Rowman and Littlefield, 2006).

11. Wendy Griswold "A Methodological Framework for the Sociology of Culture," *Sociological Methodology* 17, no. 1 (1987): 1–35.

12. Andrew Abbott, "Things of Boundaries," *Social Research* 62, no. 4 (1995): 857–82.

13. Mary Douglas, *How Institutions Think* (Syracuse, NY: Syracuse University Press, 1986).

14. Diane Vaughan, "Theorizing Disaster: Analogy, Historical Ethnography, and the Challenger Accident," *Ethnography* 5, no. 3 (2004): 315–47.

15. Susan Leigh Star, "The Ethnography of Infrastructure," *American Behavioral Scientist* 43, no. 3 (1999): 377–91.

16. See, e.g., Sharad Chari and Vinay Gidwani, "Introduction: Grounds for a Spatial Ethnography of Labor," *Ethnography* 6, no. 3 (2005): 267–81.

17. David Valentine, *Imagining Transgender: An Ethnography of a Category* (Durham, NC: Duke University Press, 2007), 28.

18. For more on narrative, see Charles Tilly, *Why?* (Princeton, NJ: Princeton University Press, 2006); Patricia Ewick and Susan Silbey, "Narrating Social Structure: Stories of Resistance to Legal Authority on JSTOR," *American Journal of Sociology* 108, no. 6 (2003): 1,328–72.

19. See Paul DiMaggio, "Culture and Cognition," *Annual Review of Sociology* 23 (1997): 263–87; Stephen Vaisey, "Motivation and Justification: A Dual-Process Model of Culture in Action," *American Journal of Sociology* 114, no. 6 (2009): 1,675–1,715; John Levi Martin, "Life's a Beach but You're an Ant and Other Unwelcome News for the Sociology of Culture," *Poetics* 38, no. 2 (2010): 229–44; Colin Jerolmack and Shamus Khan, "Talk Is Cheap: Ethnography and the Attitudinal Fallacy," *Sociological Methods and Research* 43, no. 2 (2014): 178–209.

20. Michèle Lamont and Ann Swidler, "Methodological Pluralism and the Possibilities and Limits of Interviewing," *Qualitative Sociology* 37, no. 2 (2014): 153–71.

21. See also Allison J. Pugh, "What Good Are Interviews for Thinking about Culture? Demystifying Interpretive Analysis," *American Journal of Cultural Sociology* 1, no. 1 (2013): 42–68.

22. Judith Butler, *Gender Trouble: Feminism and the Subversion of Identity* (London: Routledge, 1990), 33.

23. REFUGE Restrooms can be accessed at www.refugerestrooms.org.

Bibliography

Abbott, Andrew. *The System of Professions: An Essay on the Division of Expert Labor.* Chicago: University of Chicago Press, 2014.

———. "Things of Boundaries." *Social Research* 62, no. 4 (1995): 857–82.

Acker, Joan. "Class, Gender, and the Relations of Distribution." *Signs: Journal of Women in Culture and Society* 13, no. 3 (1988): 473–97.

———. *Class Questions: Feminist Answers.* Lanham, MD: Rowman and Littlefield Publishers, 2006.

———. "From Sex Roles to Gendered Institutions." *Contemporary Sociology* 21, no. 5 (1992): 565–69.

———. "Hierarchies, Jobs, Bodies: A Theory of Gendered Organizations." *Gender and Society* 4, no. 2 (1990): 139–58.

———. "Inequality Regimes: Gender, Class, and Race in Organizations." *Gender and Society* 20, no. 4 (2006): 441–64.

Agathangelou, Anna M., M. Daniel Bassichis, and Tamara L. Spira. "Intimate Investments: Homonormativity, Global Lockdown and the Seductions of Empire." *Radical History Review* 100 (2008): 120–45.

Agosto, Denise E., Kimberly L. Paone, and Gretchen S. Ipock. "The Female-Friendly Public Library: Gender Differences in Adolescents' Uses and Perceptions of U.S. Public Libraries." *Library Trends* 56, no. 2 (2007): 387–401.

Ahmed, Sara. *On Being Included: Racism and Diversity in Institutional Life.* Durham, NC: Duke University Press, 2012.

Aitken, Hugh G. J. *Scientific Management in Action: Taylorism at Watertown Arsenal, 1908–1915*. Princeton, NJ: Princeton University Press, 1960.

Alderson, Arthur S., Azamat Junisbai, and Isaac Heacock. "Social Status and Cultural Consumption in the United States." In "Social Status and Cultural Consumption in Seven Countries," edited by Tak Wing Chan and John H. Goldthorpe. Special issue, *Poetics* 35, nos. 2–3 (2007): 191–212.

Aldrich, Howard, and Martin Ruef. *Organizations Evolving*. 2nd ed. Thousand Oaks, CA: Sage Publications, 2006.

Allen, William H. "Sanitation and Social Progress." *American Journal of Sociology* 8, no. 5 (1903): 631–43.

Almeling, Rene. *Sex Cells: The Medical Market for Eggs and Sperm*. Berkeley: University of California Press, 2011.

American Public Health Association. *A Half Century of Public Health, Jubilee Historical Volume; in Commemoration of the Fiftieth Anniversary Celebration of Its Foundation, New York City, November 14–18, 1921*. Edited by Mazÿck P. Ravenel. New York: American Public Health Association, 1921.

Anteby, Michel. "Markets, Morals, and Practices of Trade: Jurisdictional Disputes in the U.S. Commerce in Cadavers." *Administrative Science Quarterly* 55, no. 4 (2010): 606–38.

Anthony, Kathryn H., and Meghan Dufresne. "Potty Parity in Perspective: Gender and Family Issues in Planning and Designing Public Restrooms." *Journal of Planning Literature* 21, no. 3 (2007): 267–94.

Appleby, Joyce. "Recovering America's Historic Diversity: Beyond Exceptionalism." *Journal of American History* 79, no. 2 (1992): 419–31.

Arluke, Arnold, Lanny Kutakoff, and Jack Levin. "Are the Times Changing? An Analysis of Gender Differences in Sexual Graffiti." *Sex Roles* 16, no. 1–2 (1987): 1–7.

Armstrong, Elizabeth A. *Paying for the Party: How College Maintains Inequality*. Cambridge, MA: Harvard University Press, 2013.

Babbie, Earl. "Laud Humphreys and Research Ethics." *International Journal of Sociology and Social Policy* 24, no. 3–5 (2004): 12–19.

Babon, Kim M. "Composition, Coherence, and Attachment: The Critical Role of Context in Reception." *Poetics* 34, no. 3 (2006): 151–79.

Baker, Paula. "The Domestication of Politics: Women and American Political Society, 1780–1920." *American Historical Review* 89, no. 3 (1984): 620–47.

Baker, Therese L., and William Vélez. "Access to and Opportunity in Postsecondary Education in the United States: A Review." *Sociology of Education* 69 (1996): 82–101.

Baldwin, Peter C. "Public Privacy: Restrooms in American Cities, 1869–1932." *Journal of Social History* 48, no. 2 (2014): 264–88.

Bandelj, Nina. "Relational Work and Economic Sociology." *Politics and Society* 40, no. 2 (2012): 175–201.

Banks, Taunya Lovell. "Toilets as a Feminist Issue: A True Story." *Berkeley Journal of Gender, Law and Justice* 6, no. 2 (1990–1991): 263–89.

Barnes, Jeb, and Thomas F. Burke. "Making Way: Legal Mobilization, Organizational Response, and Wheelchair Access." *Law and Society Review* 46, no. 1 (2012): 167–98.

Bastedo, Michael N., and Nicholas A. Bowman. "College Rankings as an Interorganizational Dependency: Establishing the Foundation for Strategic and Institutional Accounts." *Research in Higher Education* 52, no. 1 (2011): 3–23.

Bayh, Birch. "The Need for the Equal Rights Amendment." *Notre Dame Lawyer* 48 (1972): 80–91.

Baynton, Douglas C. "Disability and the Justification of Inequality in American History." In *The Disability Studies Reader*, edited by Lennard J. Davis. New York: Routledge, 2013.

Beauvoir, Simone de. *The Second Sex*. Translated by Constance Borde and Sheila Malovany-Chevallier. New York: Vintage Books, 2011 [1949].

Beemyn, Brett. "Serving the Needs of Transgender College Students." *Journal of Gay and Lesbian Issues in Education* 1, no. 1 (2003): 33–50.

Beemyn, Brett, Billy Curtis, Masen Davis, and Nancy Jean Tubbs. "Transgender Issues on College Campuses." *New Directions for Student Services*, no. 111 (2005): 49–60.

Beisel, Nicola. "Morals versus Art: Censorship, the Politics of Interpretation, and the Victorian Nude." *American Sociological Review* 58, no. 2 (1993): 145–62.

Ben-Joseph, Eran. *The Code of the City: Standards and the Hidden Language of Place Making*. Cambridge, MA: MIT Press, 2005.

Ben-Joseph, Eran, and Terry S. Szold, eds. *Regulating Place: Standards and the Shaping of Urban America*. New York: Routledge, 2005.

Benford, Robert D., and David A. Snow. "Framing Processes and Social Movements: An Overview and Assessment." *Annual Review of Sociology* 26 (2000): 611–39.

Benidickson, Jamie. *The Culture of Flushing: A Social and Legal History of Sewage*. Vancouver: University of British Columbia Press, 2007.

Benson, Rodney. "American Journalism and the Politics of Diversity." *Media, Culture and Society* 27, no. 1 (2005): 5–20.

Berezin, Mabel. "Exploring Emotions and the Economy: New Contributions from Sociological Theory." *Theory and Society* 38, no. 4 (2009): 335–46.

Berger, Molly W. *Hotel Dreams: Luxury, Technology, and Urban Ambition in America, 1829–1929*. Baltimore: Johns Hopkins University Press, 2011.

Bettie, Julie. *Women without Class: Girls, Race, and Identity*. Berkeley: University of California Press, 2003.

Binder, Amy. "For Love and Money: Organizations' Creative Responses to Multiple Environmental Logics." *Theory and Society* 36, no. 6 (2007): 547–71.

Blau, Francine D., Mary C. Brinton, and David B. Grusky, eds. *The Declining Significance of Gender?* New York: Russell Sage Foundation, 2006.

Bonilla-Silva, Eduardo. *Racism without Racists: Color-Blind Racism and the Persistence of Racial Inequality in the United States.* 2nd ed. New York: Rowman and Littlefield, 2006.

Borden, Iain, Barbara Penner, and Jane Rendell. *Gender Space Architecture: An Interdisciplinary Introduction.* London: Routledge, 2002.

Bourdieu, Pierre. "Cultural Reproduction and Social Reproduction." In *Power and Ideology in Education,* edited by J. Karabel and A. H. Halsey, 487–511. New York: Oxford University Press, 1977.

———. *Distinction: A Social Critique of the Judgment of Taste.* Translated by Richard Nice. Cambridge, MA: Harvard University Press, 1984.

———. "The Force of Law: Toward a Sociology of the Juridical Field." *Hastings Law Journal* 38 (1986–87): 805–13.

Bouton, Malcolm A. "Plumbing Codes in Public Health." *American Journal of Public Health* (1956): 1439–43.

Bowker, Geoffrey C., and Susan Leigh Star. *Sorting Things Out: Classification and Its Consequences.* Cambridge, MA: MIT Press, 1999.

Bowman, Nicholas A., and Michael N. Bastedo. "Getting on the Front Page: Organizational Reputation, Status Signals, and the Impact of *U.S. News and World Report* on Student Decisions." *Research in Higher Education* 50, no. 5 (2009): 415–36.

Boyer, Paul S. *Urban Masses and Moral Order in America, 1820–1920.* Cambridge, MA: Harvard University Press, 1992.

Braverman, Irus. "Governing with Clean Hands: Automated Public Toilets and Sanitary Surveillance." *Surveillance and Society* 8, no. 1 (2010): 1–27.

Brinton, Mary C., and Victor Nee. *The New Institutionalism in Sociology.* New York: Russell Sage Foundation, 1998.

Britton, Dana M. "The Epistemology of the Gendered Organization." *Gender and Society* 14, no. 3 (2000): 418–34.

Britton, Dana M., and Laura Logan. "Gendered Organizations: Progress and Prospects." *Sociology Compass* 2, no. 1 (2008): 107–21.

Broockman, David, and Joshua Kalla. "Durably Reducing Transphobia: A Field Experiment on Door-to-Door Canvassing." *Science* 352, no. 6282 (2016): 220–24.

Brown, Kathleen M. *Foul Bodies: Cleanliness in Early America.* New Haven, CT: Yale University Press, 2009.

Brown-May, Andrew, and Peg Fraser. "Gender, Respectability, and Public Convenience in Melbourne, Australia, 1859–1902." In *Ladies and Gents:*

Public Toilets and Gender, edited by Olga Gershenson and Barbara Penner, 75–89. Philadelphia: Temple University Press, 2009.

Browne, Kath. "Genderism and the Bathroom Problem: (Re)materialising Sexed Sites, (Re)creating Sexed Bodies." *Gender, Place and Culture* 11, no. 3 (2004): 331–46.

Bruner, Edward M., and Jane Paige Kelso. "Gender Differences in Graffiti: A Semiotic Perspective." *Women's Studies International Quarterly* 3, no. 2 (1980): 239–52.

Bryson, Bethany. *Making Multiculturalism: Boundaries and Meaning in U.S. English Departments.* Stanford, CA: Stanford University Press, 2005.

Buchmann, Claudia, and Thomas A. DiPrete. "The Growing Female Advantage in College Completion: The Role of Family Background and Academic Achievement." *American Sociological Review* 71, no. 4 (2006): 515–41.

Buchmann, Claudia, Thomas A. DiPrete, and Anne McDaniel. "Gender Inequalities in Education." *Annual Review of Sociology* 34 (2008): 319–37.

Budig, Michelle J., and Paula England. "The Wage Penalty for Motherhood." *American Sociological Review* 66, no. 2 (2001): 204–25.

Burnstein, Daniel Eli. *Next to Godliness: Confronting Dirt and Despair in Progressive Era New York City.* Urbana: University of Illinois Press, 2006.

Bushman, Richard L., and Claudia L. Bushman. "The Early History of Cleanliness in America." *Journal of American History* 74, no. 4 (1988): 1213–38.

Butler, Judith. *Bodies That Matter: On the Discursive Limits of "Sex."* New York: Routledge, 1993.

———. *Gender Trouble: Feminism and the Subversion of Identity.* New York: Routledge, 1990.

Cahill, Spencer E., William Distler, Cynthia Lachowetz, Andrea Meaney, Robyn Tarallo, and Teena Willard. "Meanwhile Backstage: Public Bathrooms and the Interaction Order." *Journal of Contemporary Ethnography* 14, no. 1 (1985): 33–58.

Caldeira, Gregory A. "The Transmission of Legal Precedent: A Study of State Supreme Courts." *American Political Science Review* 79, no. 1 (1985): 178–94.

Canaday, Margot. "'Who Is a Homosexual?': The Consolidation of Sexual Identities in Mid-Twentieth-Century American Immigration Law." *Law and Social Inquiry* 28, no. 2 (2003): 351–86.

Cappeliez, Sarah, and Josée Johnston. "From Meat and Potatoes to 'Real-Deal' Rotis: Exploring Everyday Culinary Cosmopolitanism." *Poetics* 41, no. 5 (2013): 433–55.

Carby, Hazel V. "The Multicultural Wars." *Radical History Review* 1992, no. 54 (1992): 7–18.

Carroll, Glenn R. "Organizational Ecology." *Annual Review of Sociology* 10 (1984): 71–93.

Case, Mary Anne. "Reflections on Constitutionalizing Women's Equality." *California Law Review* 90, no. 3 (2002): 765–90.

———. "Why Not Abolish the Laws of Urinary Segregation?" In *Toilet: Public Restrooms and the Politics of Sharing,* edited by Harvey Molotch and Laura Norén, 211–25. New York: New York University Press, 2010.

Cattani, Gino, Simone Ferriani, Giacomo Negro, and Fabrizio Perretti. "The Structure of Consensus: Network Ties, Legitimation, and Exit Rates of U.S. Feature Film Producer Organizations." *Administrative Science Quarterly* 53, no. 1 (2008): 145–82.

Cavanagh, Sheila L. *Queering Bathrooms: Gender, Sexuality, and the Hygienic Imagination.* Toronto: University of Toronto Press, 2010.

Cech, Erin, Brian Rubineau, Susan Silbey, and Caroll Seron. "Professional Role Confidence and Gendered Persistence in Engineering." *American Sociological Review* 76, no. 5 (2011): 641–66.

Chalfin, Brenda. "Public Things, Excremental Politics, and the Infrastructure of Bare Life in Ghana's City of Tema." *American Ethnologist* 41, no. 1 (2014): 92–109.

Chari, Sharad, and Vinay Gidwani. "Introduction: Grounds for a Spatial Ethnography of Labor." *Ethnography* 6, no. 3 (2005): 267–81.

Charles, Maria. *Occupational Ghettos: The Worldwide Segregation of Women and Men.* Stanford, CA: Stanford University Press, 2004.

Charles, Maria, and Karen Bradley. "Indulging Our Gendered Selves? Sex Segregation by Field of Study in 44 Countries." *American Journal of Sociology* 114, no. 4 (2009): 924–76.

Chauncey, George. *Gay New York Gender, Urban Culture, and the Makings of the Gay Male World, 1890–1940.* New York: Basic Books, 1994.

Chen, Mel Y. *Animacies: Biopolitics, Racial Mattering, and Queer Affect.* Durham, NC: Duke University Press, 2012.

Cheyne, Andrew, and Amy Binder. "Cosmopolitan Preferences: The Constitutive Role of Place in American Elite Taste for Hip-Hop Music, 1991–2005." *Poetics* 38, no. 3 (2010): 336–64.

Cohen, Stanley. *Folk Devils and Moral Panics: The Creation of the Mods and Rockers.* New York: Psychology Press, 2002 [1972].

Collins, Patricia Hill. "It's All in the Family: Intersections of Gender, Race, and Nation." *Hypatia* 13, no. 3 (1998): 62–82.

Collins, Randall. *The Credential Society: An Historical Sociology of Education and Stratification.* New York: Academic Press, 1979.

———. *Interaction Ritual Chains.* Princeton, NJ: Princeton University Press, 2004.

———. "Situational Stratification: A Micro-Macro Theory of Inequality." *Sociological Theory* 18, no. 1 (2000): 17–43.

Colomina, Beatriz, and Jennifer Bloomer. *Sexuality and Space*. Princeton, NY: Princeton Architectural Press, 1992.

Connell, Catherine. "The Politics of the Stall: Transgender and Genderqueer Workers Negotiating 'the Bathroom Question.'" In *Embodied Resistance: Challenging the Norms, Breaking the Rules*, edited by Chris Bobel and Samantha Kwan, 175–85. Nashville: Vanderbilt University Press, 2011.

Connell, R. W. *Gender and Power: Society, the Person and Sexual Politics*. Stanford, CA: Stanford University Press, 1987.

———. *Masculinities*. Cambridge, UK: Polity Press, 1995.

Connell, R. W., and James W. Messerschmidt. "Hegemonic Masculinity: Rethinking the Concept." *Gender and Society* 19, no. 6 (2005): 829–59.

Cooper, Patricia, and Ruth Oldenziel. "Cherished Classifications: Bathrooms and the Construction of Gender/Race on the Pennsylvania Railroad during World War II." *Feminist Studies* 25, no. 1 (1999): 7–41.

Correll, Shelley, J. S. Benard, and In Paik. "Getting a Job: Is There a Motherhood Penalty?" *American Journal of Sociology* 112, no. 5 (2007): 1297–1339.

Crosby, Christina, Lisa Duggan, Roderick Ferguson, Kevin Floyd, Miranda Joseph, Heather Love, Robert McRuer, et al. "Queer Studies, Materialism, and Crisis: A Roundtable Discussion." *GLQ: A Journal of Lesbian and Gay Studies* 18, no. 1 (2012): 127–47.

Curran, W. J. "The Constitutionality of Prohibiting the Operation of Pay Toilets." *American Journal of Public Health* 67, no. 12 (1977): 1205–6.

Cutler, David, and Grant Miller. "The Role of Public Health Improvements in Health Advances: The Twentieth-Century United States." *Demography* 42, no. 1 (2005): 1–22.

Davis, Alexander K. "Toward Exclusion through Inclusion: Engendering Reputation with Gender-Inclusive Facilities at Colleges and Universities in the United States, 2001–2013." *Gender and Society* 32, no. 3 (2018): 321–47.

Davis, Georgiann. *Contesting Intersex: The Dubious Diagnosis*. New York: New York University Press, 2015.

Davis, Kathy. "Intersectionality as Buzzword: A Sociology of Science Perspective on What Makes a Feminist Theory Successful." *Feminist Theory* 9, no. 1 (2008): 67–85.

Deephouse, David L. "Does Isomorphism Legitimate?" *Academy of Management Journal* 39, no. 4 (1996): 1024–39.

Deitch, Cynthia. "Gender, Race, and Class Politics and the Inclusion of Women in Title VII of the 1964 Civil Rights Act." *Gender and Society* 7, no. 2 (1993): 183–203.

Dellinger, Kirsten, and Christine L. Williams. "The Locker Room and the Dorm Room: Workplace Norms and the Boundaries of Sexual Harassment in Magazine Editing." *Social Problems* 49, no. 2 (2002): 242–57.

D'Emilio, John. *Sexual Politics, Sexual Communities: The Making of a Homosexual Minority in the United States, 1940–1970*. Chicago: University of Chicago Press, 1983.

DeNora, Tia. *Music in Everyday Life*. Cambridge: Cambridge University Press, 2000.

Deutsch, Francine M. "Undoing Gender." *Gender and Society* 21, no. 1 (2007): 106–27.

DiMaggio, Paul. "Cultural Capital and School Success: The Impact of Status Culture Participation on the Grades of U.S. High School Students." *American Sociological Review* 47, no. 2 (1982): 189–201.

———. "Culture and Cognition." *Annual Review of Sociology* 23 (1997): 263–87.

DiMaggio, Paul J., and Walter W. Powell. "The Iron Cage Revisited: Institutional Isomorphism and Collective Rationality in Organizational Fields." *American Sociological Review* 48, no. 2 (1983): 147–60.

DiPrete, Thomas A., and Claudia Buchmann. "Gender-Specific Trends in the Value of Education and the Emerging Gender Gap in College Completion." *Demography* 43, no. 1 (2006): 1–24.

Doan, Petra L. "The Tyranny of Gendered Spaces—Reflections from beyond the Gender Dichotomy." *Gender, Place and Culture* 17, no. 5 (2010): 635–54.

Dobbin, Frank. *Inventing Equal Opportunity*. Princeton, NJ: Princeton University Press, 2009.

Dobbin, Frank, and Erin L. Kelly. "How to Stop Harassment: Professional Construction of Legal Compliance in Organizations." *American Journal of Sociology* 112, no. 4 (2007): 1203–43.

Douglas, Mary. *How Institutions Think*. Syracuse, NY: Syracuse University Press, 1986.

———. *Purity and Danger: An Analysis of the Concepts of Pollution and Taboo*. New York: Routledge, 1966.

Dowd, Timothy J., Kathleen Liddle, Kim Lupo, and Anne Borden. "Organizing the Musical Canon: The Repertoires of Major U.S. Symphony Orchestras, 1842 to 1969." *Poetics* 30, no. 1 (2002): 35–61.

Dowling, John, and Jeffrey Pfeffer. "Organizational Legitimacy: Social Values and Organizational Behavior." *Pacific Sociological Review* 18, no. 1 (1975): 122–36.

Dreger, Alice Domurat. *Hermaphrodites and the Medical Invention of Sex*. Cambridge, MA: Harvard University Press, 1998.

Duffy, John. *The Sanitarians: A History of American Public Health*. Urbana: University of Illinois Press, 1990.

Duneier, Mitchell. "Race and Peeing on Sixth Avenue." In *Racing Research, Researching Race: Methodological Dilemmas in Critical Race Studies*, edited by France Winddance Twine and Jonathan W. Warren. New York: New York University Press, 2000.

Eck, Beth A. "Nudity and Framing: Classifying Art, Pornography, Information, and Ambiguity." *Sociological Forum* 16, no. 4 (2001): 603–32.

Ecklund, Elaine Howard, Anne E. Lincoln, and Cassandra Tansey. "Gender Segregation in Elite Academic Science." *Gender and Society* 26, no. 5 (2012): 693–717.

Edelman, Lauren B. "Legal Ambiguity and Symbolic Structures: Organizational Mediation of Civil Rights Law." *American Journal of Sociology* 97, no. 6 (1992): 1531–76.

———. *Working Law: Courts, Corporations, and Symbolic Civil Rights.* Chicago: University of Chicago Press, 2016.

Edelman, Lauren B., Sally Riggs Fuller, and Iona Mara-Drita. "Diversity Rhetoric and the Managerialization of Law." *American Journal of Sociology* 106, no. 6 (2001): 1589–1641.

Edelman, Lauren B., and Mark C. Suchman. "The Legal Environments of Organizations." *Annual Review of Sociology* 23 (1997): 479–515.

Eisenmann, Linda. *Higher Education for Women in Postwar America, 1945–1965.* Baltimore: Johns Hopkins University Press, 2006.

Elias, Norbert. *The Civilizing Process: Sociogenetic and Psychogenetic Investigations.* Translated by Edmund Jephcott. Oxford: Blackwell Publishers, 1978.

Ellen C. Berrey. "Why Diversity Became Orthodox in Higher Education, and How It Changed the Meaning of Race on Campus." *Critical Sociology* 37, no. 5 (2011): 573–96.

Emirbayer, Mustafa. "Manifesto for a Relational Sociology." *American Journal of Sociology* 103, no. 2 (1997): 281–317.

Eng, David L. *The Feeling of Kinship: Queer Liberalism and the Racialization of Intimacy.* Durham, NC: Duke University Press, 2010.

Eng, David L., Judith Halberstam, and José Esteban Muñoz, eds. "What's Queer about Queer Studies Now?" Special issue, *Social Text* 23, nos. 3–4 (2005).

England, Paula. "Sometimes the Social Becomes Personal: Gender, Class, and Sexualities." *American Sociological Review* 81, no. 1 (2016): 4–28.

———. "The Gender Revolution Uneven and Stalled." *Gender and Society* 24, no. 2 (2010): 149–66.

England, Paula, Michelle Budig, and Nancy Folbre. "Wages of Virtue: The Relative Pay of Care Work." *Social Problems* 49, no. 4 (2002): 455–73.

Epstein, Cynthia Fuchs. *Deceptive Distinctions: Sex, Gender, and the Social Order.* New Haven, CT: Yale University Press, 1988.

Espeland, Wendy Nelson, and Michael Sauder. "Rankings and Reactivity: How Public Measures Recreate Social Worlds." *American Journal of Sociology* 113, no. 1 (2007): 1–40.

Espenshade, Thomas J. *No Longer Separate, Not Yet Equal: Race and Class in Elite College Admission and Campus Life.* Princeton, NJ: Princeton University Press, 2009.

Ewick, Patricia. *The Common Place of Law: Stories from Everyday Life*. Chicago: University of Chicago Press, 1998.

Ewick, Patricia, and Susan Silbey. "Narrating Social Structure: Stories of Resistance to Legal Authority." *American Journal of Sociology* 108, no. 6 (2003): 1328–72.

Faehmel, Babette. *College Women in the Nuclear Age: Cultural Literacy and Female Identity, 1940–1960*. New Brunswick, NJ: Rutgers University Press, 2012.

Fink, Günther, Isabel Günther, and Kenneth Hill. "Slum Residence and Child Health in Developing Countries." *Demography* 51, no. 4 (2014): 1175–97.

Flanagan, Maureen. "Private Needs, Public Space: Public Toilets Provision in the Anglo-Atlantic Patriarchal City: London, Dublin, Toronto and Chicago." *Urban History* 41, no. 2 (2014): 265–90.

Flanagan, Maureen A. *Seeing with Their Hearts: Chicago Women and the Vision of the Good City, 1871–1933*. Princeton, NJ: Princeton University Press, 2002.

Folbre, Nancy. *Who Pays for the Kids? Gender and the Structures of Constraint*. New York: Routledge, 1994.

Folbre, Nancy, and Julie A. Nelson. "For Love or Money—or Both?" *Journal of Economic Perspectives* 14, no. 4 (2000): 123–40.

Foucault, Michele. *Discipline and Punish: The Birth of the Prison*. New York: Vintage Books, 1995 [1975].

Fourcade, Marion, and Kieran Healy. "Moral Views of Market Society." *Annual Review of Sociology* 33 (2007): 285–311.

Fowler, James H., and Sangick Jeon. "The Authority of Supreme Court Precedent." *Social Networks* 30, no. 1 (2008): 16–30.

Franklin, Cary. "Inventing the 'Traditional Concept' of Sex Discrimination." *Harvard Law Review* 125, no. 6 (2012): 1307–80.

Freeman, John H., and Pino G. Audia. "Community Ecology and the Sociology of Organizations." *Annual Review of Sociology* 32 (2006): 145–69.

Freidson, Eliot. *Professionalism, the Third Logic: On the Practice of Knowledge*. Chicago: University of Chicago Press, 2001.

Freud, Sigmund. *Civilization and Its Discontents*. New York: W. W. Norton, 1989.

Friedland, Roger. "Moving Institutional Logics Forward: Emotion and Meaningful Material Practice." *Organization Studies* 39, no. 4 (2018): 515–42.

Friedman, Asia. *Blind to Sameness: Sexpectations and the Social Construction of Male and Female Bodies*. Chicago: University of Chicago Press, 2013.

Friedman, Lawrence M. *A History of American Law*. 3rd ed. New York: Simon and Schuster, 2005.

Frug, Mary Joe. *Postmodern Legal Feminism*. New York: Routledge, 1993.

Fujimura, Joan H. "Sex Genes: A Critical Sociomaterial Approach to the Politics and Molecular Genetics of Sex Determination." *Signs* 32, no. 1 (2006): 49–82.

Galanter, Marc. "Why the 'Haves' Come Out Ahead: Speculations on the Limits of Legal Change." *Law and Society Review* 9, no. 1 (1974): 95–160.

Galliher, John F., Wayne Brekhus, and David P. Keys. *Laud Humphreys: Prophet of Homosexuality and Sociology.* Madison: University of Wisconsin Press, 2004.

George, Tracey E., and Lee Epstein. "On the Nature of Supreme Court Decision Making." *American Political Science Review* 86, no. 2 (1992): 323–37.

Gerhardt, Michael J. *The Power of Precedent.* New York: Oxford University Press, 2011.

Gershenson, Olga, and Barbara Penner, eds. *Ladies and Gents.* Philadelphia: Temple University Press, 2009.

Gerson, Judith M., and Kathy Peiss. "Boundaries, Negotiation, Consciousness: Reconceptualizing Gender Relations." *Social Problems* 32, no. 4 (1985): 317–31.

Gibson, James J. *The Ecological Approach to Visual Perception.* New York: Psychology Press, 1986.

Glaser, Barney G., and Anselm L. Strauss. *The Discovery of Grounded Theory: Strategies for Qualitative Research.* Chicago: Aldine, 1967.

Glass, Jennifer L., Sharon Sassler, Yael Levitte, and Katherine M. Michelmore. "What's So Special about STEM? A Comparison of Women's Retention in STEM and Professional Occupations." *Social Forces* 92, no. 2 (2013): 723–56.

Glassberg, David. "The Design of Reform: The Public Bath Movement in America." *American Studies* 20, no. 2 (1979): 5–21.

Glick, Paul C. "A Demographer Looks at American Families." *Journal of Marriage and Family* 37, no. 1 (1975): 15–26.

Goffman, Erving. "On Face-Work." *Psychiatry* 18, no. 3 (1955): 213–31.

———. *Relations in Public: Microstudies of the Public Order.* New York: Basic Books, 1971.

———. "The Arrangement between the Sexes." *Theory and Society* 4, no. 3 (1977): 301–31.

———. *The Presentation of Self in Everyday Life.* New York: Doubleday, 1959.

Goldin, Claudia. "The Quiet Revolution That Transformed Women's Employment, Education, and Family." *American Economic Review* 96, no. 2 (2006): 1–21.

Goode, Erich, and Nachman Ben-Yehuda. "Moral Panics: Culture, Politics, and Social Construction." *Annual Review of Sociology* 20 (1994): 149–71.

Goode, William J. "Community within a Community: The Professions." *American Sociological Review* 22, no. 2 (1957): 194–200.

Gorman, Elizabeth H., and Rebecca L. Sandefur. "'Golden Age,' Quiescence, and Revival: How the Sociology of Professions Became the Study of Knowledge-Based Work." *Work and Occupations* 38, no. 3 (2011): 275–302.

Grazian, David. *Blue Chicago: The Search for Authenticity in Urban Blues Clubs.* Chicago: University of Chicago Press, 2003.

Greed, Clara. "The Role of the Toilet in Civic Life." In *Ladies and Gents: Public Toilets and Gender,* edited by Olga Gershenson and Barbara Penner, 35–47. Philadelphia: Temple University Press, 2009.

Griswold, Wendy. "A Methodological Framework for the Sociology of Culture." *Sociological Methodology* 17 (1987): 1–35.

Griswold, Wendy, Gemma Mangione, and Terence E. McDonnell. "Objects, Words, and Bodies in Space: Bringing Materiality into Cultural Analysis." *Qualitative Sociology* 36, no. 4 (2013): 343–64.

Gutman, Herbert G. "Work, Culture, and Society in Industrializing America, 1815–1919." *The American Historical Review* 78, no. 3 (1973): 531–88.

Haber, Samuel. *Efficiency and Uplift: Scientific Management in the Progressive Era, 1890–1920.* Chicago: University of Chicago Press, 1964.

Halberstam, Judith. *Female Masculinity.* Durham, NC: Duke University Press, 1998.

Hallett, Tim, and Marc J. Ventresca. "Inhabited Institutions: Social Interactions and Organizational Forms in Gouldner's *Patterns of Industrial Bureaucracy.*" *Theory and Society* 35, no. 2 (2006).

Haney, Lynne A. "Feminist State Theory: Applications to Jurisprudence, Criminology, and the Welfare State." *Annual Review of Sociology* 26 (2000): 641–66.

Hanhardt, Christina B. *Safe Space: Gay Neighborhood History and the Politics of Violence.* Durham, NC: Duke University Press, 2013.

Hannan, Michael T., László Pólos and Glenn R. Carroll. *Logics of Organization Theory: Audiences, Codes, and Ecologies.* Princeton, NJ: Princeton University Press, 2007.

———. *Organizational Ecology.* Cambridge, MA: Harvard University Press, 1989.

Hannan, Michael T., and John Freeman. "Structural Inertia and Organizational Change." *American Sociological Review* 49, no. 2 (1984): 149–64.

Hansford, Thomas G., and James F. Spriggs. *The Politics of Precedent on the U.S. Supreme Court.* Princeton, NJ: Princeton University Press, 2006.

Hartmann, Heidi. "Capitalism, Patriarchy, and Job Segregation by Sex." *Signs: Journal of Women in Culture and Society* 1, no. 3 (1976): 137–69.

Hartmann, Heidi I. "The Family as the Locus of Gender, Class, and Political Struggle: The Example of Housework." *Signs: Journal of Women in Culture and Society* 6, no. 3 (1981): 366–94.

Haskell, Thomas L. *The Authority of Experts: Studies in History and Theory.* Bloomington: Indiana University Press, 1984.

Hassani, Sara Nephew. "Locating Digital Divides at Home, Work, and Everywhere Else." In "The Digital Divide in the Twenty-First Century," edited by Keith Roe. Special issue, *Poetics* 34, nos. 4–5 (2006): 250–72.

Haveman, Heather A. "Follow the Leader: Mimetic Isomorphism and Entry into New Markets." *Administrative Science Quarterly* 38, no. 4 (1993): 593–627.

Hayden, Dolores. *The Power of Place: Urban Landscapes as Public History.* Cambridge, MA: MIT Press, 1997.

Hazelkorn, Ellen. *Rankings and the Reshaping of Higher Education: The Battle for World-Class Excellence.* 2nd ed. New York: Palgrave Macmillan, 2015.

Healy, Kieran. "Fuck Nuance." *Sociological Theory* 35, no. 2 (2017): 118–27.

———. *Last Best Gifts: Altruism and the Market for Human Blood and Organs.* Chicago: University of Chicago Press, 2006.

Heimer, Carol A. "Resilience in the Middle: Contributions of Regulated Organizations to Regulatory Success." *Annals of the American Academy of Political and Social Science* 649, no. 1 (2013): 139–56.

Hepp, John Henry. *The Middle-Class City: Transforming Space and Time in Philadelphia, 1876–1926.* Philadelphia: University of Pennsylvania Press, 2003.

Herman, Jody L. "Gendered Restrooms and Minority Stress: The Public Regulation of Gender and Its Impact on Transgender People's Lives." *Journal of Public Management and Social Policy* 19, no. 1 (2013): 65–80.

Higginbotham, Evelyn Brooks. *Righteous Discontent: The Women's Movement in the Black Baptist Church, 1880–1920.* Cambridge, MA: Harvard University Press, 1994.

Hoang, Kimberly Kay. *Dealing in Desire: Asian Ascendancy, Western Decline, and the Hidden Currencies of Global Sex Work.* Oakland: University of California Press, 2015.

Hochschild, Arlie Russell. "Emotion Work, Feeling Rules, and Social Structure." *American Journal of Sociology* 85, no. 3 (1979): 551–75.

Hoekema, David A. *Campus Rules and Moral Community: In Place of In Loco Parentis.* Lanham: Rowman and Littlefield, 1994.

Holvino, Evangelina. "Intersections: The Simultaneity of Race, Gender and Class in Organization Studies." *Gender, Work and Organization* 17, no. 3 (2010): 248–77.

Hoy, Suellen M. *Chasing Dirt: The American Pursuit of Cleanliness.* New York: Oxford University Press, 1995.

Hsu, Greta. "Jacks of All Trades and Masters of None: Audiences' Reactions to Spanning Genres in Feature Film Production." *Administrative Science Quarterly* 51, no. 3 (2006): 420–50.

Hsu, Greta, and Michael T. Hannan. "Identities, Genres, and Organizational Forms." *Organization Science* 16, no. 5 (2005): 474–90.

Huffman, Matt L., Philip N. Cohen, and Jessica Pearlman. "Engendering Change: Organizational Dynamics and Workplace Gender Desegregation, 1975–2005." *Administrative Science Quarterly* 55, no. 2 (2010): 255–77.

Huising, Ruthanne, and Susan S. Silbey. "Governing the Gap: Forging Safe Science through Relational Regulation." *Regulation and Governance* 5, no. 1 (2011): 14–42.

Imrie, Rob, and Emma Street. "Regulating Design: The Practices of Architecture, Governance and Control." *Urban Studies* 46, no. 12 (2009): 2507–18.

Inglis, David. *A Sociological History of Excretory Experience: Defecatory Manners and Toiletry Technologies.* Lewiston, NY: Edwin Mellen Press, 2001.

Jackson, Kenneth T. *Crabgrass Frontier: The Suburbanization of the United States.* New York: Oxford University Press, 1987.

Jacob, Herbert. *Silent Revolution: The Transformation of Divorce Law in the United States.* Chicago: University of Chicago Press, 1988.

Jacobs, Jerry A. "Long-Term Trends in Occupational Segregation by Sex." *American Journal of Sociology* 95, no. 1 (1989): 160–73.

Jasper, James M. "The Emotions of Protest: Affective and Reactive Emotions in and around Social Movements." *Sociological Forum* 13, no. 3 (1998): 397–424.

Jensen, Michael. "Legitimizing Illegitimacy: How Creating Market Identity Legitimizes Illegitimate Products." In *Categories in Markets: Origins and Evolution,* edited by Greta Hsu, Giacomo Negro, and Ozgecan Kocak, 39–80. Bingley, UK: Emerald Group Publishing, 2010.

Jerolmack, Colin, and Shamus Khan. "Talk Is Cheap: Ethnography and the Attitudinal Fallacy." *Sociological Methods and Research* 43, no. 2 (2014): 178–209.

Johnson, Cathryn, Timothy J. Dowd, and Cecilia L. Ridgeway. "Legitimacy as a Social Process." *Annual Review of Sociology* 32 (2006): 53–78.

Johnston, Josée. *Foodies: Democracy and Distinction in the Gourmet Foodscape.* New York: Routledge, 2014.

Johnston, Josée, and Shyon Baumann. "Democracy versus Distinction: A Study of Omnivorousness in Gourmet Food Writing." *American Journal of Sociology* 113, no. 1 (2007): 165–204.

Jordan, Jennifer A. *Edible Memory: The Lure of Heirloom Tomatoes and Other Forgotten Foods.* Chicago: University of Chicago Press, 2015.

Kalev, Alexandra. "Cracking the Glass Cages? Restructuring and Ascriptive Inequality at Work." *American Journal of Sociology* 114, no. 6 (2009): 1591–1643.

Kandiyoti, Deniz. "Bargaining with Patriarchy." In "Special Issue to Honor Jessie Bernard," edited by Judith Lorber, *Gender and Society* 2, no. 3 (1988): 274–90.

Kane, Emily W. "'No Way My Boys Are Going to Be Like That!' Parents' Responses to Children's Gender Nonconformity." *Gender and Society* 20, no. 2 (2006): 149–76.

Kanigel, Robert. *The One Best Way: Frederick Winslow Taylor and the Enigma of Efficiency.* New York: Viking, 1997.

Kanter, Rosabeth Moss. *Men and Women of the Corporation.* New York: Basic Books, 1977.

Kaplin, William A. *The Law of Higher Education.* San Francisco: Jossey-Bass, 2014.

Kelly, Erin, and Frank Dobbin. "How Affirmative Action Became Diversity Management: Employer Response to Antidiscrimination Law, 1961 to 1996." *American Behavioral Scientist* 41, no. 7 (1998): 960–84.

Kerber, Linda K. "Separate Spheres, Female Worlds, Woman's Place: The Rhetoric of Women's History." *Journal of American History* 75, no. 1 (1988): 9–39.

Kessler, Suzanne J., and Wendy McKenna. *Gender: An Ethnomethodological Approach.* Chicago: University of Chicago Press, 1978.

Kessler-Harris, Alice. *Out to Work: A History of Wage-Earning Women in the United States.* New York: Oxford University Press, 1982.

Khan, Shamus Rahman. *Privilege: The Making of an Adolescent Elite at St. Paul's School.* Princeton, NJ: Princeton University Press, 2011.

Kogan, Terry S. "Sex-Separation in Public Restrooms: Law, Architecture, and Gender." *Michigan Journal of Gender and Law* 14, no. 1 (2007): 1–57.

Komarovsky, Mirra. "The Concept of Social Role Revisited." *Gender and Society* 6, no. 2 (1992): 301–13.

Kremp, Pierre-Antoine. "Innovation and Selection: Symphony Orchestras and the Construction of the Musical Canon in the United States (1879–1959)." *Social Forces* 88, no. 3 (2010): 1051–82.

Krum, Tiana E., Kyle S. Davis, and M. Paz Galupo. "Gender-Inclusive Housing Preferences: A Survey of College-Aged Transgender Students." *Journal of LGBT Youth* 10, no. 1–2 (2013): 64–82.

Kuhn, Thomas S. *The Structure of Scientific Revolutions.* Chicago: University of Chicago Press, 1962.

Kurtulus, Fidan Ana, and Donald Tomaskovic-Devey. "Do Female Top Managers Help Women to Advance? A Panel Study Using EEO-1 Records." *The Annals of the American Academy of Political and Social Science* 639, no. 1 (2012): 173–97.

Lacan, Jacques. *Écrits: A Selection.* Translated by Alan Sheridan. New York: W. W. Norton and Company, 1977.

———. "The Mirror-Phase as Formative of the Function of the I." *New Left Review,* no. 51 (1968): 71–77.

Lamont, Michèle, Stefan Beljean, and Matthew Clair. "What Is Missing? Cultural Processes and Causal Pathways to Inequality." *Socio-Economic Review* 12, no. 3 (2014): 573–608.

Lamont, Michèle, and Annette Lareau. "Cultural Capital: Allusions, Gaps and Glissandos in Recent Theoretical Developments." *Sociological Theory* 6, no. 2 (1988): 153–68.

Lamont, Michèle, and Virág Molnár. "The Study of Boundaries in the Social Sciences." *Annual Review of Sociology* 28 (2002): 167–95.

Lamont, Michèle, and Ann Swidler. "Methodological Pluralism and the Possibilities and Limits of Interviewing." *Qualitative Sociology* 37, no. 2 (2014): 153–71.

Lampland, Martha, and Susan Leigh Star, eds. *Standards and Their Stories: How Quantifying, Classifying, and Formalizing Practices Shape Everyday Life.* Ithaca, NY: Cornell University Press, 2009.

Landes, William M., and Richard A. Posner. "Legal Precedent: A Theoretical and Empirical Analysis." *Journal of Law and Economics* 19, no. 2 (1976): 249–307.

Laqueur, Thomas. *Making Sex: Body and Gender from the Greeks to Freud.* Cambridge, MA: Harvard University Press, 1990.

Lareau, Annette. "Cultural Knowledge and Social Inequality." *American Sociological Review* 80, no. 1 (2015): 1–27.

Larson, Magali Sarfatti. *The Rise of Professionalism: A Sociological Analysis.* Berkeley: University of California Press, 1979.

Lawler, Edward J. "An Affect Theory of Social Exchange." *American Journal of Sociology* 107, no. 2 (2001): 321–52.

Lees, Lynn Hollen. "Urban Public Space and Imagined Communities in the 1980s and 1990s." *Journal of Urban History* 20, no. 4 (1994): 443–65.

Legewie, Joscha, and Thomas A. DiPrete. "The High School Environment and the Gender Gap in Science and Engineering." *Sociology of Education* 87, no. 4 (2014): 259–80.

Leventhal, Tama, and Jeanne Brooks-Gunn. "Moving to Opportunity: An Experimental Study of Neighborhood Effects on Mental Health." *American Journal of Public Health* 93, no. 9 (2003): 1576–82.

Lichter, Daniel T., Domenico Parisi, and Michael C. Taquino. "Toward a New Macro-Segregation? Decomposing Segregation within and between Metropolitan Cities and Suburbs." *American Sociological Review* 80, no. 4 (2015): 843–73.

Lieberson, Stanley, Susan Dumais, and Shyon Baumann. "The Instability of Androgynous Names: The Symbolic Maintenance of Gender Boundaries." *American Journal of Sociology* 105, no. 5 (2000): 1249–87.

Linder, Marc, and Ingrid Nygaard. *Void Where Prohibited: Rest Breaks and the Right to Urinate on Company Time.* Ithaca, NY: ILR Press, 1998.

Lipson, Daniel N. "Embracing Diversity: The Institutionalization of Affirmative Action as Diversity Management at UC-Berkeley, UT-Austin, and UW-Madison." *Law and Social Inquiry* 32, no. 4 (2007): 985–1026.

Lobao, Linda M. "Continuity and Change in Place Stratification: Spatial Inequality and Middle-Range Territorial Units." *Rural Sociology* 69, no. 1 (2004): 1–30.

Lobao, Linda M., Gregory Hooks, and Ann R. Tickamyer, eds. *The Sociology of Spatial Inequality.* Albany, NY: SUNY Press, 2007.

Lopata, Helena Z., and Barrie Thorne. "On the Term 'Sex Roles.'" *Signs* 3, no. 3 (1978): 718–21.

Lopez, Russ. *Building American Public Health: Urban Planning, Architecture, and the Quest for Better Health in the United States.* New York: Palgrave Macmillan, 2012.

López-Sintas, Jordi, and Tally Katz-Gerro. "From Exclusive to Inclusive Elitists and Further: Twenty Years of Omnivorousness and Cultural Diversity in Arts Participation in the USA." In "Comparative Research on Cultural Production and Consumption," edited by Susanne Janssen and Richard A. Peterson. Special issue, *Poetics* 33, nos. 5–6 (2005): 299–319.

Lorber, Judith. *Breaking the Bowls: Degendering and Feminist Change.* New York: W. W. Norton, 2005.

———. "Shifting Paradigms and Challenging Categories." *Social Problems* 53, no. 4 (2006): 448–53.

Love, Heather. "Doing Being Deviant: Deviance Studies, Description, and the Queer Ordinary." *Differences* 26, no. 1 (2015): 74–95.

Lucal, Betsy. "What It Means to Be Gendered Me: Life on the Boundaries of a Dichotomous Gender System." *Gender and Society* 13, no. 6 (1999): 781–97.

Lupu, Yonatan, and James H. Fowler. "Strategic Citations to Precedent on the U.S. Supreme Court." *Journal of Legal Studies* 42, no. 1 (2013): 151–86.

Mack, Adam. *Sensing Chicago: Noisemakers, Strikebreakers, and Muckrakers.* Urbana: University of Illinois Press, 2015.

MacKinnon, Catharine A. *Toward a Feminist Theory of the State.* Cambridge, MA: Harvard University Press, 1989.

MacLean, Nancy. *Freedom Is Not Enough: The Opening of the American Workplace.* New York: Russell Sage Foundation, 2006.

Martin, John Levi. "Life's a Beach but You're an Ant, and Other Unwelcome News for the Sociology of Culture." *Poetics* 38, no. 2 (2010): 229–44.

———. *Social Structures.* Princeton, NJ: Princeton University Press, 2009.

Martin, Patricia Yancey. "Gender as Social Institution." *Social Forces* 82, no. 4 (2004): 1249–73.

———. "Practising Gender at Work: Further Thoughts on Reflexivity." *Gender, Work and Organization* 13, no. 3 (2006): 254–76.

———. "'Said and Done' Versus 'Saying and Doing' Gendering Practices, Practicing Gender at Work." *Gender and Society* 17, no. 3 (2003): 342–66.

Martin, Patricia Yancey, and David Collinson. "'Over the Pond and across the Water': Developing the Field of 'Gendered Organizations.'" *Gender, Work and Organization* 9, no. 3 (2002): 244–65.

Marx, Karl. *Capital*. Vol. 1, *A Critique of Political Economy*. London: Penguin Books, 2004 [1867].

Massey, Douglas S., and Nancy A. Denton. *American Apartheid: Segregation and the Making of the Underclass*. Cambridge, MA: Harvard University Press, 1993.

Mathers, Lain A. B. "Bathrooms, Boundaries, and Emotional Burdens: Cisgendering Interactions through the Interpretation of Transgender Experience." *Symbolic Interaction* 40, no. 3 (2017): 295–316.

McCall, Leslie. "The Complexity of Intersectionality." *Signs* 30, no. 3 (2005): 1771–1800.

McCammon, Holly J. "Out of the Parlors and into the Streets': The Changing Tactical Repertoire of the U.S. Women's Suffrage Movements." *Social Forces* 81, no. 3 (2003): 787–818.

McCammon, Holly J., Karen E. Campbell, Ellen M. Granberg, and Christine Mowery. "How Movements Win: Gendered Opportunity Structures and U.S. Women's Suffrage Movements, 1866 to 1919." *American Sociological Review* 66, no. 1 (2001): 49–70.

McClain, Noah, and Ashley Mears. "Free to Those Who Can Afford It: The Everyday Affordance of Privilege." In "Cultures of Circulation," edited by Melissa Aronczyk and Ailsa Craig. Special issue, *Poetics* 40, no. 2 (2012): 133–49.

McDonnell, Terence E. "Cultural Objects as Objects: Materiality, Urban Space, and the Interpretation of AIDS Campaigns in Accra, Ghana." *American Journal of Sociology* 115, no. 6 (2010): 1800–1852.

McFarlane, Colin, Renu Desai, and Steve Graham. "Informal Urban Sanitation: Everyday Life, Poverty, and Comparison." *Annals of the Association of American Geographers* 104, no. 5 (2014): 989–1011.

McGerr, Michael. "Political Style and Women's Power, 1830–1930." *Journal of American History* 77, no. 3 (1990): 864–85.

McIntosh, Peggy. "White Privilege: Unpacking the Invisible Knapsack." *Peace and Freedom Magazine*, July/August 1989, 10–12.

Meadow, Tey. "'A Rose Is a Rose': On Producing Legal Gender Classifications." *Gender and Society* 24, no. 6 (2010): 814–37.

———. *Trans Kids: Being Gendered in the Twenty-First Century*. Oakland: University of California Press, 2018.

Melamed, Jodi. "The Spirit of Neoliberalism: From Racial Liberalism to Neoliberal Multiculturalism." *Social Text* 24, no. 4 (2006): 1–24.

Melosi, Martin V. *The Sanitary City: Environmental Services in Urban America from Colonial Times to the Present.* Pittsburgh: University of Pittsburgh Press, 2008.

Merleau-Ponty, Maurice. *Phenomenology of Perception.* Translated by Colin Smith. London: Routledge and Kegan Paul, 1962.

Merton, Robert. "On Sociological Theories of the Middle Range." In *Social Theory and Social Structure.* New York: Free Press, 1949.

———. "The Unanticipated Consequences of Purposive Social Action." *American Sociological Review* 1, no. 6 (1936): 894–904.

Meyer, John W., Patricia Bromley, and Francisco O. Ramirez. "Human Rights in Social Science Textbooks: Cross-National Analyses, 1970–2008." *Sociology of Education* 83, no. 2 (2010): 111–34.

Meyer, John W., and Brian Rowan. "Institutionalized Organizations: Formal Structure as Myth and Ceremony." *American Journal of Sociology* 83, no. 2 (1977): 340–63.

Meyerowitz, Joanne J. *How Sex Changed: A History of Transsexuality in the United States.* Cambridge, MA: Harvard University Press, 2002.

———. *Not June Cleaver: Women and Gender in Postwar America, 1945–1960.* Philadelphia: Temple University Press, 1994.

Miller-Bernal, Leslie, and Susan L. Poulson. *Going Coed: Women's Experiences in Formerly Men's Colleges and Universities, 1950–2000.* Nashville: Vanderbilt University Press, 2004.

Misa, Thomas J. *A Nation of Steel: The Making of Modern America, 1865–1925.* Baltimore: Johns Hopkins University Press, 1998.

Molotch, Harvey Luskin. *Where Stuff Comes From: How Toasters, Toilets, Cars, Computers, and Many Others Things Come to Be as They Are.* New York: Routledge, 2003.

Molotch, Harvey Luskin, and Laura Norén. *Toilet: Public Restrooms and the Politics of Sharing.* New York: New York University Press, 2010.

Monkkonen, Eric H. *America Becomes Urban: The Development of U.S. Cities and Towns, 1780–1980.* Berkeley: University of California Press, 1988.

Montesquieu, Charles de. *The Spirit of the Laws.* Translated by Anne M. Cohler, Basia Carolyn Miller, and Harold Samuel Stone. Cambridge: Cambridge University Press, 1989 [1749].

Morantz, Regina Markell. "Making Women Modern: Middle Class Women and Health Reform in 19th Century America." *Journal of Social History* 10, no. 4 (1977): 490–507.

Morgan, Stephen L., Dafna Gelbgiser, and Kim A. Weeden. "Feeding the Pipeline: Gender, Occupational Plans, and College Major Selection." *Social Science Research* 42, no. 4 (2013): 989–1005.

Muhammad, Robin Dearmon. "Separate and Unsanitary: African American Women Railroad Car Cleaners and the Women's Service Section, 1918–1920." *Journal of Women's History* 23, no. 2 (2011): 87–111.

Munt, Sally, and Cherry Smyth, eds. *Butch/Femme: Inside Lesbian Gender.* London: Cassell, 1998.

Munts, Raymond, and David C. Rice. "Women Workers: Protection or Equality?" *Industrial and Labor Relations Review* 24, no. 1 (1970): 3–13.

Murray, Pauli, and Mary O. Eastwood. "Jane Crow and the Law: Sex Discrimination and Title VII." *George Washington Law Review* 34, no. 2 (1965–66): 232–56.

Nanney, Megan, and David L. Brunsma. "Moving beyond Cis-terhood: Determining Gender through Transgender Admittance Policies at U.S. Women's Colleges." *Gender and Society* 31, no. 2 (2017): 145–70.

Navis, Chad, and Mary Ann Glynn. "How New Market Categories Emerge: Temporal Dynamics of Legitimacy, Identity, and Entrepreneurship in Satellite Radio, 1990–2005." *Administrative Science Quarterly* 55, no. 3 (2010): 439–71.

Newcomer, Mabel. *A Century of Higher Education for American Women.* Washington, DC: Zenger, 1959.

Norton, Aaron T., and Gregory M. Herek. "Heterosexuals' Attitudes toward Transgender People: Findings from a National Probability Sample of U.S. Adults." *Sex Roles* 68, nos. 11–12 (2013): 738–53.

Novkov, Julie. "Historicizing the Figure of the Child in Legal Discourse: The Battle over the Regulation of Child Labor." *American Journal of Legal History* 44, no. 4 (2000): 369–404.

Ogle, Maureen. *All the Modern Conveniences: American Household Plumbing, 1840–1890.* Baltimore: Johns Hopkins University Press, 1996.

Oldham, James C. "Questions of Exclusion and Exception under Title VII—'Sex Plus' and the BFOQ." *Hastings Law Journal* 55 (1971–72): 55–94.

Ostrower, Francie. *Trustees of Culture: Power, Wealth, and Status on Elite Arts Boards.* Chicago: University of Chicago Press, 2002.

Pachucki, Mark C. "Classifying Quality: Cognition, Interaction, and Status Appraisal of Art Museums." *Poetics* 40, no. 1 (2012): 67–90.

Park, Robert E., Ernest W. Burgess, and Morris Janowitz. *The City: Suggestions for Investigation of Human Behavior in the Urban Environment.* Chicago: University of Chicago Press, 1925.

Parsons, Talcott. "The Distribution of Power in American Society." *World Politics* 10, no. 1 (1957): 123–43.

Pearlman, Alison. *Smart Casual: The Transformation of Gourmet Restaurant Style in America.* Chicago: University of Chicago Press, 2013.

Pearson, Susan J. "'Age Ought to Be a Fact': The Campaign against Child Labor and the Rise of the Birth Certificate." *Journal of American History* 101, no. 4 (2015): 1144–65.

Pedriana, Nicholas, and Robin Stryker. "The Strength of a Weak Agency: Enforcement of Title VII of the 1964 Civil Rights Act and the Expansion of State Capacity, 1965–1971." *American Journal of Sociology* 110, no. 3 (2004): 709–60.

Pedulla, David S., and Sarah Thébaud. "Can We Finish the Revolution? Gender, Work-Family Ideals, and Institutional Constraint." *American Sociological Review* 80, no. 1 (2015): 116–39.

Penner, Barbara. *Bathroom.* London: Reaktion Books, 2013.

Peters, David J. "American Income Inequality across Economic and Geographic Space, 1970–2010." *Social Science Research* 42, no. 6 (2013): 1490–1504.

Petersen, Trond, and Laurie A. Morgan. "Separate and Unequal: Occupation-Establishment Sex Segregation and the Gender Wage Gap." *American Journal of Sociology* 101, no. 2 (1995): 329–65.

Peterson, Richard A., and Roger M. Kern. "Changing Highbrow Taste: From Snob to Omnivore." *American Sociological Review* 61, no. 5 (1996): 900–907.

Phillips, Damon J., Catherine J. Turco, and Ezra W. Zuckerman. "Betrayal as Market Barrier: Identity-Based Limits to Diversification among High-Status Corporate Law Firms." *American Journal of Sociology* 118, no. 4 (2013): 1023–54.

Phillips, Damon J., and Ezra W. Zuckerman. "Middle-Status Conformity: Theoretical Restatement and Empirical Demonstration in Two Markets." *American Journal of Sociology* 107, no. 2 (2001): 379–429.

Platt, Lisa F., and Sarah R. B. Milam. "Public Discomfort with Gender Appearance-Inconsistent Bathroom Use: The Oppressive Bind of Bathroom Laws for Transgender Individuals." *Gender Issues* 35, no. 3 (2018): 181–201.

Plotkin, Stanley. "History of Vaccination." *Proceedings of the National Academy of Sciences* 111, no. 34 (2014): 12283–87.

Podolny, Joel. *Status Signals: A Sociological Study of Market Competition.* Princeton, NJ: Princeton University Press, 2005.

Powell, Walter W., and Paul J. DiMaggio, eds. *The New Institutionalism in Organizational Analysis.* Chicago: University of Chicago Press, 1991.

Prosser, Jay. *Second Skins: The Body Narratives of Transsexuality.* New York: Columbia University Press, 1998.

Pryor, Jonathan T. "Out in the Classroom: Transgender Student Experiences at a Large Public University." *Journal of College Student Development* 56, no. 5 (2015): 440–55.

Puar, Jasbir K. *Terrorist Assemblages: Homonationalism in Queer Times.* Durham, NC: Duke University Press, 2007.

Pugh, Allison J. "What Good Are Interviews for Thinking about Culture? Demystifying Interpretive Analysis." *American Journal of Cultural Sociology* 1, no. 1 (2013): 42–68.

Quinn, Sarah. "The Transformation of Morals in Markets: Death, Benefits, and the Exchange of Life Insurance Policies." *American Journal of Sociology* 114, no. 3 (2008): 738–80.

Radke-Moss, Andrea G. *Bright Epoch: Women and Coeducation in the American West.* Lincoln: University of Nebraska Press, 2008.

Rao, Hayagreeva, Philippe Monin, and Rodolphe Durand. "Border Crossing: Bricolage and the Erosion of Categorical Boundaries in French Gastronomy." *American Sociological Review* 70, no. 6 (2005): 968.

Renner, Andrea. "A Nation That Bathes Together: New York City's Progressive-Era Public Baths." *Journal of the Society of Architectural Historians* 67, no. 4 (2008): 504–31.

Ribot, Jesse C., and Nancy Lee Peluso. "A Theory of Access." *Rural Sociology* 68, no. 2 (2003): 153–81.

Ridgeway, Cecilia L. "Interaction and the Conservation of Gender Inequality: Considering Employment." *American Sociological Review* 62, no. 2 (1997): 218–35.

Ridgeway, Cecilia L., and Shelley J. Correll. "Unpacking the Gender System: A Theoretical Perspective on Gender Beliefs and Social Relations." *Gender and Society* 18, no. 4 (2004): 510–31.

Ridgeway, Cecilia L., and Lynn Smith-Lovin. "The Gender System and Interaction." *Annual Review of Sociology* 25 (1999): 191–216.

Risman, Barbara J. "From Doing to Undoing: Gender as We Know It." *Gender and Society* 23, no. 1 (2009): 81–84.

———. "Gender as a Social Structure: Theory Wrestling with Activism." *Gender and Society* 18, no. 4 (2004): 429–50.

Risman, Barbara J., and Georgiann Davis. "From Sex Roles to Gender Structure." *Current Sociology* 61, no. 5–6 (2013): 733–55.

Rivera, Lauren A. "Go with Your Gut: Emotion and Evaluation in Job Interviews." *American Journal of Sociology* 120, no. 5 (2015): 1339–89.

———. *Pedigree: How Elite Students Get Elite Jobs.* Princeton, NJ: Princeton University Press, 2015.

Rivera, Lauren A., and András Tilcsik. "Class Advantage, Commitment Penalty: The Gendered Effect of Social Class Signals in an Elite Labor Market." *American Sociological Review* 81, no. 6 (2016): 1097–1131.

Rodgers, Willard L., and Arland Thornton. "Changing Patterns of First Marriage in the United States." *Demography* 22, no. 2 (1985): 265–79.

Roen, Katrina. "'Either/Or' and 'Both/Neither': Discursive Tensions in Transgender Politics." *Signs* 27, no. 2 (2002): 501–22.

Roscigno, Vincent J., Donald Tomaskovic-Devey, and Martha Crowley. "Education and the Inequalities of Place." *Social Forces* 84, no. 4 (2006): 2121–45.

Rose, Mark H. *Interstate: Highway Politics and Policy since 1939*. Knoxville: University of Tennessee Press, 2012.

Rosen, Ruth. *The World Split Open: How the Modern Women's Movement Changed America*. New York: Viking, 2000.

Rosenberg, Rosalind. *Divided Lives: American Women in the Twentieth Century*. New York: Macmillan, 2008.

Rubin, Gayle. "The Traffic in Women: Notes on the 'Political Economy' of Sex." In *Toward an Anthropology of Women*, edited by Rayna R. Reiter. New York: Monthly Review Press, 1975.

———. "Thinking Sex: Notes for a Radical Theory of the Politics of Sexuality." In *Pleasure and Danger: Exploring Female Sexuality*, edited by Carole S. Vance, 267–319. New York: Routledge and Kegan Paul, 1984.

Rubio, Fernando Domínguez. "Preserving the Unpreservable: Docile and Unruly Objects at MoMA." *Theory and Society* 43, no. 6 (2014): 617–45.

Ruef, Martin. "The Emergence of Organizational Forms: A Community Ecology Approach." *American Journal of Sociology* 106, no. 3 (2000): 658–714.

Ruef, Martin, and Kelly Patterson. "Credit and Classification: The Impact of Industry Boundaries in Nineteenth-Century America." *Administrative Science Quarterly* 54, no. 3 (2009): 486–520.

Rupp, Leila J. "The Women's Community in the National Woman's Party, 1945 to the 1960s." *Signs* 10, no. 4 (1985): 715–40.

Rutherford, Danilyn. "Affect Theory and the Empirical." *Annual Review of Anthropology* 45 (2016): 285–300.

Ryan, Mary P. *Women in Public: Between Banners and Ballots, 1825–1880*. Baltimore: Johns Hopkins University Press, 1990.

Saguy, Abigail C. *What Is Sexual Harassment?: From Capitol Hill to the Sorbonne*. Berkeley: University of California Press, 2003.

Salamon, Gayle. *Assuming a Body: Transgender and Rhetorics of Materiality*. New York: Columbia University Press, 2010.

———. "Boys of the Lex: Transgenderism and Rhetorics of Materiality." *GLQ* 12, no. 4 (2006): 575–97.

Sassen, Saskia. "Analytic Borderlands: Race, Gender and Representation in the New City." In *Re-Presenting the City*, 183–202. London: Palgrave, 1996.

Sauder, Michael, and Wendy Nelson Espeland. "The Discipline of Rankings: Tight Coupling and Organizational Change." *American Sociological Review* 74, no. 1 (2009): 63–82.

Schilt, Kristen, and Laurel Westbrook. "Bathroom Battlegrounds and Penis Panics." *Contexts* 14, no. 3 (2015): 26–31.

Schippers, Mimi. "Recovering the Feminine Other: Masculinity, Femininity, and Gender Hegemony." *Theory and Society* 36, no. 1 (2007): 85–102.

Schofer, Evan, and John W. Meyer. "The Worldwide Expansion of Higher Education in the Twentieth Century." *American Sociological Review* 70, no. 6 (2005): 898–920.

Schultz, Stanley K. *Constructing Urban Culture: American Cities and City Planning, 1800–1920.* Philadelphia: Temple University Press, 1989.

Schwager, Sally. "Educating Women in America." *Signs* 12, no. 2 (1987): 333–72.

Schwartz, Barry. "The Social Psychology of Privacy." *American Journal of Sociology* 73, no. 6 (1968): 741–52.

Scott, Anne Firor. *Natural Allies: Women's Associations in American History.* Urbana: University of Illinois Press, 1991.

Scott, W. Richard. *Institutions and Organizations: Ideas and Interests.* Thousand Oaks, CA: Sage, 1995.

———. "Lords of the Dance: Professionals as Institutional Agents." *Organization Studies* 29, no. 2 (2008): 219–38.

Seelman, Kristie L. "Recommendations of Transgender Students, Staff, and Faculty in the USA for Improving College Campuses." *Gender and Education* 26, no. 6 (2014): 618–35.

Seely, Bruce Edsall. *Building the American Highway System: Engineers as Policy Makers.* Philadelphia: Temple University Press, 1987.

Segrave, Kerry. *Vending Machines: An American Social History.* Jefferson, NC: McFarland, 2002.

Seiler, Cotton. *Republic of Drivers: A Cultural History of Automobility in America.* Chicago: University of Chicago Press, 2008.

Seo, Sarah A. "Antinomies and the Automobile: A New Approach to Criminal Justice Histories." *Law and Social Inquiry* 38, no. 4 (2013): 1019–40.

"Sex Discrimination in Employment: An Attempt to Interpret Title VII of the Civil Rights Act of 1964." *Duke Law Journal* (1968): 671–723.

Shakespeare, Tom. "The Social Model of Disability." In *The Disability Studies Reader*, 4th ed., edited by Lennard J. Davis, 214–21. New York: Routledge, 2013.

Sharkey, Amanda J. "Categories and Organizational Status: The Role of Industry Status in the Response to Organizational Deviance." *American Journal of Sociology* 119, no. 5 (2014): 1380–1433.

Shavit, Yossi, Richard Arum, Adam Gamoran, and Gila Menachem. *Stratification in Higher Education: A Comparative Study.* Stanford, CA: Stanford University Press, 2007.

Silbey, Susan S. "After Legal Consciousness." *Annual Review of Law and Social Science* 1 (2005): 323–68.

———. "The Sociological Citizen: Pragmatic and Relational Regulation in Law and Organizations." *Regulation and Governance* 5, no. 1 (2011): 1–13.

Silverman, Kaja. *The Threshold of the Visible World.* New York: Psychology Press, 1996.

Simmel, Georg. "Fashion." *American Journal of Sociology* 62, no. 6 (1957): 541.

———. *The Sociology of Georg Simmel.* Translated and edited by Kurt H. Wolff. Glencoe, IL: Free Press, 1950.

Skocpol, Theda. *Protecting Soldiers and Mothers: The Political Origins of Social Policy in the United States.* Cambridge, MA: Harvard University Press, 1992.

Smith, Adam. *Lectures on Justice, Police, Revenue and Arms.* Edited by Edwin Cannan. Oxford: Clarendon Press, 1896 [1763].

Smith, Dorothy. *The Everyday World as Problematic: A Feminist Sociology.* Boston, MA: Northeastern University Press, 1987.

Smith, Dorothy E. *Institutional Ethnography: A Sociology for People.* Lanham, MD: AltaMira Press, 2005.

Smith, Kristin E., and Rebecca Glauber. "Exploring the Spatial Wage Penalty for Women: Does It Matter Where You Live?" *Social Science Research* 42, no. 5 (2013): 1390–1401.

Smith-Rosenberg, Carroll. *Disorderly Conduct: Visions of Gender in Victorian America.* New York: A.A. Knopf, 1985.

Snow, David A., E. Burke Rochford Jr., Steven K. Worden, and Robert D. Benford. "Frame Alignment Processes, Micromobilization, and Movement Participation." *American Sociological Review* 51, no. 4 (1986): 464–81.

Solomon, Barbara Miller. *In the Company of Educated Women: A History of Women and Higher Education in America.* New Haven, CT: Yale University Press, 1985.

Soule, Sarah A., and Susan Olzak. "When Do Movements Matter? The Politics of Contingency and the Equal Rights Amendment." *American Sociological Review* 69, no. 4 (2004): 473–97.

Spade, Dean. *Normal Life: Administrative Violence, Critical Trans Politics, and the Limits of Law.* Durham, NC: Duke University Press, 2015.

Spain, Daphne. "Gender and Urban Space." *Annual Review of Sociology* 40 (2014): 581–98.

Spillman, Lyn. *Solidarity in Strategy: Making Business Meaningful in American Trade Associations.* Chicago: University of Chicago Press, 2012.

Spriggs, James F., and Thomas G. Hansford. "The U.S. Supreme Court's Incorporation and Interpretation of Precedent." *Law and Society Review* 36, no. 1 (2002): 139–60.

Stacey, Judith. *In the Name of the Family: Rethinking Family Values in the Postmodern Age.* Beacon Press, 1996.

Star, Susan Leigh. "The Ethnography of Infrastructure." *American Behavioral Scientist* 43, no. 3 (1999): 377–91.

Starr, Paul. *The Social Transformation of American Medicine.* New York: Basic Books, 1982.

Steensland, Brian. "Cultural Categories and the American Welfare State: The Case of Guaranteed Income Policy." *American Journal of Sociology* 111, no. 5 (2006): 1273–1326.

Stevens, Mitchell L., and Josipa Roksa. "The Diversity Imperative in Elite Admissions." In *Diversity in American Higher Education: Toward a More Comprehensive Approach*, edited by L. M. Stulberg and S. L. Weinberg, 63–73. New York: Routledge, 2011.

Strang, David, and John W. Meyer. "Institutional Conditions for Diffusion." *Theory and Society* 22, no. 4 (1993): 487–511.

Strang, David, and Sarah A. Soule. "Diffusion in Organizations and Social Movements: From Hybrid Corn to Poison Pills." *Annual Review of Sociology* 24 (1998): 265–90.

Stryker, Susan. "Transgender History, Homonormativity, and Disciplinarity." *Radical History Review* 2008, no. 100 (2008): 145–57.

Suchman, Mark C. "Managing Legitimacy: Strategic and Institutional Approaches." *Academy of Management Review* 20, no. 3 (1995): 571–610.

Suddaby, Roy, and Royston Greenwood. "Rhetorical Strategies of Legitimacy." *Administrative Science Quarterly* 50, no. 1 (2005): 35–67.

Tangney, June Price. "Moral Affect: The Good, the Bad, and the Ugly." *Journal of Personality and Social Psychology* 61, no. 4 (1991): 598–607.

Taplin, Jonathan. *Move Fast and Break Things: How Facebook, Google, and Amazon Cornered Culture and Undermined Democracy*. New York: Little, Brown, 2017.

Thévenot, Laurent. "Postscript to the Special Issue: Governing Life by Standards: A View from Engagements." *Social Studies of Science* 39, no. 5 (2009): 793–813.

Tilly, Charles. *Durable Inequality*. Berkeley: University of California Press, 1998.

———. *Why?* Princeton, NJ: Princeton University Press, 2006.

Todd, James C. "Title IX of the 1972 Education Amendments: Preventing Sex Discrimination in Public Schools." *Texas Law Review* 53 (1974): 103–26.

Tomes, Nancy. *The Gospel of Germs: Men, Women, and the Microbe in American Life*. Cambridge, MA: Harvard University Press, 1998.

Upton, Dell. *Another City: Urban Life and Urban Spaces in the New American Republic*. Yale University Press, 2008.

Urry, John. "The Sociology of Space and Place." In *The Blackwell Companion to Sociology*, edited by Judith R. Blau, 3–15. Malden, MA: Blackwell Publishing, 2001.

Vaisey, Stephen. "Motivation and Justification: A Dual-Process Model of Culture in Action." *American Journal of Sociology* 114, no. 6 (2009): 1675–1715.

Valentine, David. *Imagining Transgender: An Ethnography of a Category*. Durham, NC: Duke University Press, 2007.

Vaughan, Diane. "Theorizing Disaster Analogy, Historical Ethnography, and the Challenger Accident." *Ethnography* 5, no. 3 (2004): 315–47.

Vaughn, Jacqueline. *Disabled Rights: American Disability Policy and the Fight for Equality.* Washington, DC: Georgetown University Press, 2003.

Veblen, Thorsten. *The Theory of the Leisure Class: An Economic Theory of Institutions.* New York: Oxford University Press, 2007 [1899].

Waldfogel, Jane. "The Effect of Children on Women's Wages." *American Sociological Review* 62, no. 2 (1997): 209–17.

Ward, Elizabeth Jane. *Respectably Queer: Diversity Culture in LGBT Activist Organizations.* Nashville: Vanderbilt University Press, 2008.

Ward, Jane. "'Not All Differences Are Created Equal' Multiple Jeopardy in a Gendered Organization." *Gender and Society* 18, no. 1 (2004): 82–102.

Warner, Michael. *The Trouble with Normal: Sex, Politics, and the Ethics of Queer Life.* New York: The Free Press, 1999.

Warner, Sam Bass. *The Urban Wilderness: A History of the American City.* Berkeley: University of California Press, 1972.

Weber, Klaus, Kathryn L. Heinze, and Michaela DeSoucey. "Forage for Thought: Mobilizing Codes in the Movement for Grass-Fed Meat and Dairy Products." *Administrative Science Quarterly* 53, no. 3 (2008): 529–67.

Weber, Max. "Bureaucracy." In *From Max Weber: Essays in Sociology,* edited by H. H. Gerth and C. Wright Mills, 196–244. Berkeley: University of California Press, 1946.

———. "Class, Status, Party." In *From Max Weber: Essays in Sociology,* edited by H. H. Gerth and C. Wright Mills, 180–95. Berkeley: University of California Press, 1946.

———. *Economy and Society.* Berkeley: University of California Press, 1978 [1922].

———. *The Protestant Ethic and the Spirit of Capitalism.* Translated by Peter Baehr and Gordon C. Wells. New York: Penguin Books, 2002.

Weinberg, Martin S., and Colin J. Williams. "Fecal Matters: Habitus, Embodiments, and Deviance." *Social Problems* 52, no. 3 (2005): 315–36.

Welke, Barbara Young. *Recasting American Liberty: Gender, Race, Law, and the Railroad Revolution, 1865–1920.* Cambridge: Cambridge University Press, 2001.

Wells, Christopher W. "Fueling the Boom: Gasoline Taxes, Invisibility, and the Growth of the American Highway Infrastructure, 1919–1956." *Journal of American History* 99, no. 1 (2012): 72–81.

Welter, Barbara. "The Cult of True Womanhood: 1820–1860." *American Quarterly* 18, no. 2 (1966): 151–74.

West, Candace, and Don H. Zimmerman. "Doing Gender." *Gender and Society* 1, no. 2 (1987): 125–51.

Westbrook, Laurel, and Kristen Schilt. "Doing Gender, Determining Gender: Transgender People, Gender Panics, and the Maintenance of the Sex/Gender/Sexuality System." *Gender and Society* 28, no. 1 (2014): 32–57.

Weyeneth, Robert R. "The Architecture of Racial Segregation: The Challenges of Preserving the Problematical Past." *Public Historian* 27, no. 4 (2005): 11–44.

Whalen, Charles W. *The Longest Debate: A Legislative History of the 1964 Civil Rights Act.* Washington, DC: Seven Locks Press, 1985.

Wherry, Frederick F. *The Culture of Markets.* Cambridge, UK: Polity Press, 2012.

Wikander, Ulla, Alice Kessler-Harris, and Jane Lewis, eds. *Protecting Women: Labor Legislation in Europe, the United States, and Australia, 1880–1920.* Urbana: University of Illinois Press, 1995.

Williams, Marilyn T. *Washing "the Great Unwashed": Public Baths in Urban America, 1840–1920.* Columbus: Ohio State University Press, 1991.

Willoughby, Brian J., Jason S. Carroll, William J. Marshall, and Caitlin Clark. "The Decline of In Loco Parentis and the Shift to Coed Housing on College Campuses." *Journal of Adolescent Research* 24, no. 1 (2009): 21–36.

Wilson, William H. *The City Beautiful Movement.* Baltimore, MD: Johns Hopkins University Press, 1989.

Wilson, William Julius. *The Truly Disadvantaged: The Inner City, the Underclass, and Public Policy.* Chicago: University of Chicago Press, 1987.

Xie, Yu, and Kimberlee A. Shauman. *Women in Science: Career Processes and Outcomes.* Cambridge, MA: Harvard University Press, 2003.

Yavuz, Nilay, and Eric W. Welch. "Addressing Fear of Crime in Public Space: Gender Differences in Reaction to Safety Measures in Train Transit." *Urban Studies* 47, no. 12 (2010): 2491–2515.

Zelizer, Viviana A. "The Purchase of Intimacy." *Law and Social Inquiry* 25, no. 3 (2000): 817–48.

Zelizer, Viviana A., and Charles Tilly. "Relations and Categories." In *The Psychology of Learning and Motivation,* edited by Arthur Markman and Brian Ross, 59:1–31. Waltham, MA: Academic Press, 2006.

Zelizer, Viviana A. Rotman. "Circuits in Economic Life." *Economic Sociology: The European Electronic Newsletter* 8, no. 1 (2006): 30–35.

———. *The Social Meaning of Money.* New York: Basic Books, 1994.

Zhang, Jun, Pengcheng Chen, Bingkai Yuan, Wei Ji, Zhihai Cheng, and Xiaohui Qiu. "Real-Space Identification of Intermolecular Bonding with Atomic Force Microscopy." *Science* 342, no. 6158 (2013): 611–14.

Zucker, Lynne G. "Institutional Theories of Organization." *Annual Review of Sociology* 13 (1987): 443–64.

Zuckerman, Ezra W. "The Categorical Imperative: Securities Analysts and the Illegitimacy Discount." *American Journal of Sociology* 104, no. 5 (1999): 1398–1438.

———. "Structural Incoherence and Stock Market Activity." *American Sociological Review* 69, no. 3 (2004): 405–32.

Zukin, Sharon. "Consuming Authenticity." *Cultural Studies* 22, no. 5 (2008): 724–48.

———. *Naked City: The Death and Life of Authentic Urban Places.* New York: Oxford University Press, 2010.

Zukin, Sharon, Valerie Trujillo, Peter Frase, Danielle Jackson, Tim Recuber, and Abraham Walker. "New Retail Capital and Neighborhood Change: Boutiques and Gentrification in New York City." *City and Community* 8, no. 1 (2009): 47–64.

Zylan, Yvonne. *States of Passion: Law, Identity, and the Social Construction of Desire.* New York: Oxford University Press, 2011).

Index

Page numbers in bold reference figures

Founded in 1893,
UNIVERSITY OF CALIFORNIA PRESS
publishes bold, progressive books and journals
on topics in the arts, humanities, social sciences,
and natural sciences—with a focus on social
justice issues—that inspire thought and action
among readers worldwide.

The UC PRESS FOUNDATION
raises funds to uphold the press's vital role
as an independent, nonprofit publisher, and
receives philanthropic support from a wide
range of individuals and institutions—and from
committed readers like you. To learn more, visit
ucpress.edu/supportus.

Made in United States
North Haven, CT
26 August 2023

40749607R00193